The
All England
Law Reports
Annual Review
1987

ENGLAND: Butterworth & Co (Publishers) Ltd
                88 Kingsway, **London** WC2B 6AB and
                61A North Castle Street, **Edinburgh** EH2 3LJ

AUSTRALIA: Butterworths Pty Ltd, **Sydney, Melbourne,
                Brisbane, Adelaide, Perth, Canberra** and **Hobart**

CANADA: Butterworths. A division of Reed Inc, **Toronto** and **Vancouver**

NEW ZEALAND: Butterworths of New Zealand Ltd, **Wellington** and **Auckland**

SINGAPORE: Butterworth & Co (Asia) Pte Ltd, **Singapore**

USA: Butterworth Legal Publishers, **St Paul**, Minnesota;
                Seattle, Washington; **Boston**, Massachusetts; and
                Austin, Texas
                D & S Publishers, **Clearwater**, Florida

©
BUTTERWORTH & CO (PUBLISHERS) LTD
1988

General Editor
JANE ALLEN, JP, MA

ISBN 0 406 86306 7

Printed in Great Britain by Thomson Litho Ltd, East Kilbride, Scotland

THE
ALL ENGLAND
LAW REPORTS
ANNUAL REVIEW
1987

London
BUTTERWORTHS
1988

Contributors

Administrative Law
Keith Davies, JP, MA, LLM
Barrister, Professor of Law,
University of Reading

Arbitration
J E Adams, LLB, FCIArb
Solicitor, Professor of Law,
Queen Mary College,
University of London

Commercial Law
N E Palmer, BCL, MA
Barrister, Professor of Law,
University of Essex

Company Law
D D Prentice, MA, LLB, JD
Barrister, Fellow of Pembroke College,
Oxford

Conflict of Laws
J G Collier, MA, LLB
Barrister, Fellow of Trinity Hall,
Cambridge

Consumer Law and *Solicitors*
Brian Harvey, MA, LLM
Solicitor, Professor of Property Law,
University of Birmingham

Contract
Michael P Furmston, TD, BCL, MA, LLM
Barrister, Professor of Law,
University of Bristol

Contempt of Court
C J Miller, BA, LLM
Barrister, Professor of Law,
University of Warwick

*Criminal Law, Criminal Procedure
and Sentencing*
G J Bennett, MA
Barrister, Lecturer in Law,
University of Leeds and
Brian Hogan, LLB
Barrister, Professor of Common Law,
University of Leeds

Employment Law
Ian Smith, MA, LLB
Barrister, Dean of the School of Law,
University of East Anglia

Evidence and *Practice and Procedure*
Adrian A S Zuckerman, LLM, MA
Fellow of University College, Oxford

Extradition
Ian M Yeats, BCL, MA
Barrister, Lecturer in Law,
Queen Mary College,
University of London

Family Law
S Cretney, DCL, FBA
Solicitor, Professor of Law,
University of Bristol

Land Law and *Trusts*
P J Clarke, BCL, MA
Barrister, Fellow of Jesus College,
Oxford

Landlord and Tenant
Philip H Pettit, MA
Barrister, Professor of Equity,
University of Buckingham

Medical Law
Andrew Grubb, MA
Barrister, Fellow of Fitzwilliam
College, Cambridge

Public International Law
C J Greenwood, MA, LLB
Barrister, Fellow of Magdelene
College, Cambridge

Shipping
Robert P Grime, BA, BCL
Professor of Law,
University of Southampton

Sport and the Law
Edward Grayson, MA
Barrister

Statute Law
F. Bennion, MA
Barrister, Research Associate of Oxford
Centre for Socio-Legal Studies

Succession
C H Sherrin, LLM, PHD
Barrister, Senior Lecturer in Law,
University of Bristol

Taxation
John Tiley, MA, BCL
Barrister, Fellow of Queen's College,
Cambridge

Tort
B A Hepple, MA, LLB
Barrister, Professor of English Law,
University College,
University of London

Town and Country Planning
Paul B Fairest, MA, LLM
Professor of Law,
University of Hull

Publishers' Note

This is the sixth All England Law Report Annual Review and as in previous years it is designed as a companion to the All England Law Reports. A number of academic lawyers have been invited to contribute articles evaluating the decisions of the courts relevant to their particular speciality and reported in that series in 1987. Not all of the cases, of course, fall neatly into one or other of the categories of conventional legal classification. The authors have tried to avoid duplication in their discussion of cases and there are a number of cross-references to be found in the articles. Some cases, however, are examined in more than one article because different aspects are of importance in different contexts.

What is new in the 1987 Review? An area of the law which has gained increasing prominence is that concerned with medical matters. This year a new article on Medical Law is contributed by Andrew Grubb. The complexities of the International Tin Council debacle are explained by Christopher Greenwood in the article on Public Internationl Law. Another new article, on Sport and the Law, comes from Edward Grayson whose book *Sport and the Law* was published by Butterworths early this year.

Cases from the 1987 All England Law Reports, Simon's Tax Cases and Butterworths Company Law Cases and Butterworths Trading Law Cases are printed in bold type in the Table of Cases. A bold page number indicates where discussion of the case is to be found.

This volume should be cited as All ER Rev 1987.

BUTTERWORTH LAW PUBLISHERS LTD

Contents

Table of Cases

A

B

C

D

H

Q

R

Abbreviations

BCLC	Butterworths Company Law Cases
BTLC	Butterworths Trading Law Cases
BTR	British Tax Review
CAA	Capital Allowances Act
CGT	Capital Gains Tax
CLJ	Cambridge Law Journal
CLR	Commonwealth Law Reports
Conv	The Conveyancer
Cr App R	Criminal Appeal Reports
Cr LR	Criminal Law Review
DLR	Dominion Law Reports
DLT	Development Land Tax
ECR	European Court Reports
EG	Estate Gazette
FA	Finance Act
Fam Law	Family Law
FLR	Family Law Reports
FSR	Fleet Street Reports
ICR	Industrial Cases Reports
IHTA	Inheritance Tax Act 1984
ILR	International Law Reports
Imm AR	Immigration Appeals Reports
IRLR	Industrial Relations Law Reports
JP	Justice of the Peace Reports
LGR	Local Government Review
LPA	Law of Property Act 1925
LQR	Law Quarterly Review
LRA	Land Registration Act 1925
LS	Legal Studies
LSG	Law Society Gazette
MLR	Modern Law Review
NLJ	New Law Journal
NLJR	New Law Journal Law Reports
Ox Jo LS	Oxford Journal of Legal Studies
P & CR	Property and Compensation Reports
RTR	Road Traffic Reports
SC	Session Cases
SJ	Solicitors' Journal
STC	Simon's Tax Cases
TA	Income and Corporation Taxes Act 1970
TC	Tax Cases
TMA	Taxes Management Act 1970

Administrative Law

KEITH DAVIES, MA, LLM
Barrister, Professor of Law, University of Reading

Public law supervision of self-regulatory body

Public law and private law—the great dichotomy has received further attention from the courts in the cases reported during 1987. The most fascinating of these was the decision of the Court of Appeal in *R v Panel on Take-overs and Mergers, ex parte Datafin plc (Norton Opax plc intervening)* [1987] 1 All ER 564. Sir John Donaldson MR was in sparkling form, as befits a judge deciding a case with a title almost worthy of Beachcomber. All three Lords Justices of Appeal had penetrating things to say about the issues of law involved and various legal fundamentals came under review.

The Master of the Rolls began with a flourish and continued in the same vein (ibid at 566):

> 'The Panel on Take-overs and Mergers is a truly remarkable body. Perched on the 20th floor of the Stock Exchange building of the City of London, both literally and metaphorically it oversees and regulates a very important part of the United Kingdom financial market. Yet it performs this function without visible means of legal support.'

Is 'this remarkable body' above the law? It 'is an unincorporated association without legal personality. . . . It has no statutory, prerogative or common law powers and it is not in contractual relationship with the financial market or with those who deal in that market'. Its individual members (numbering 'about 12') are the only relevant legal persons, since it has in itself no corporate personality; but its existence as an institution is an indisputable fact and an institution does not have to be a legal person.

Sir John Donaldson MR quickly came to the central element in the case (ibid at 567):

> 'The Panel is a self-regulating body . . . lacking any authority *de jure* it exercises immense power *de facto* by devising, promulgating, amending and interpreting the City Code on Take-overs and Mergers, by waiving or modifying the application of the code in particular circumstances, by investigating and reporting on alleged breaches of the code, and by the application or threat of sanctions. These sanctions are no less effective because they are applied indirectly and lack a legally enforceable base.'

The code itself speaks of referring cases 'to the Department of Trade and Industry, the Stock Exchange or other appropriate body'. This 'self-regulation' by the Panel means the regulation of others as well as of itself but does not preclude a decision to hand some matters over to a statutory body and the Stock Exchange is a statutory body just as the DTI is. For instance, 'listing of securities is a statutory function performed by the Stock Exchange in pursuance of the Stock Exchange (Listing) Regulations 1984 SI 1984/716, enacted in implementation of EEC Directives'.

The Master of the Rolls added (ibid at 568):

'I am content to assume for the purposes of this appeal that self-regulation is preferable in the public interest. But that said, what is to happen if the Panel goes off the rails? Suppose, perish the thought, that it were to use its powers in a way which was manifestly unfair. What then? . . . [it] would lose the support of public opinion in the financial markets. . . . Further or alternatively, Parliament could and would intervene. Maybe, but how long would that take and who in the meantime could or would come to the assistance of those who were being oppressed by such conduct?'

This is the age-old riddle of the far-fetched possibility. Practical people may say, why legislate for such an eventuality? Legalistic minds reply that it is precisely the odd cases which require legislation. In similar vein practical people counsel reliance on a 'gentleman's agreement'; legalistic minds retort that ninety-and-nine just persons will keep to it but the hundredth person, who is a sinner, will not.

The sin alleged in the instant case was not breach of the City Code on Take-overs and Mergers, which the Panel itself exists to deal with, but ultra vires conduct by the Panel, which is what Sir John Donaldson MR meant by speaking of the Panel 'going off the rails'. The applicants were companies which had made bids for shares in a company in process of being taken over. They were pipped at the post by certain other companies whose bid was slightly higher; and the applicants could not outbid them in turn because of the Panel's decision that to do so would be a breach of the Code. The nub of the matter was that the applicant companies were held to be acting in concert, quaintly referred to as 'concert parties' in City jargon, so that, under the Code, they could not bid higher in the circumstances of the case. They alleged that the rival bidders were also a 'concert party'. This was denied; and the Panel, adjudicating, upheld the denial. To attack that decision might be sour grapes caused by the rival companies' victory, or again it might genuinely stem from a belief that the decision was wrong.

Three possibilities arise: first, the applicant companies might legally have the right to appeal against the decision of the Panel which went against them, secondly they might have no such right, but might have the option of questioning the legality of the Panel's own conduct, and finally they might have no recourse at all to the courts for the Panel's decision.

The case in the Court of Appeal was brought by way of an application for judicial review. Leave to proceed was refused by Hodgson J in the Queen's Bench Division. Appeal against the refusal was heard later the same day by the Court of Appeal which allowed the appeal for leave and then heard and decided the substantive application. The significance of all this is that the applicants conceded (or appeared to have conceded) that they stood no chance with the first possibility above. The contest in essence lay simply between the second possibility, asserted by the applicants, and the third possibility, asserted by the Panel. Even so, as Sir John commented (ibid at 580):

'There was some failure on the part of the applicants to appreciate, or at least to act in recognition of the fact, that an application for judicial review is not an appeal. The panel and not the court is the body charged with the duty of evaluating the evidence and finding the facts. The role of the court is wholly different.'

This point has been made so many times that further repetition should now be unnecessary; but it will clearly have to be repeated many times yet. An aggrieved lay person will admittedly see little difference in substance between appealing successfully against a decision and upsetting it by judicial review. Yet lawyers are well aware that: (i) an appeal lies between the original parties, though before a different tribunal; whereas judicial review raises an independant issue between the aggrieved party and the first tribunal, (ii) an appeal can be either a public law or a private law matter; whereas judicial review lies solely in public law irrespective of whether the proceedings before the first tribunal are public or private,(iii) an appeal is concerned with the merits of the decision appealed against; whereas judicial review is concerned with the question whether the first tribunal functioned in a manner which was ultra vires or intra vires, and (iv) an appellant is entitled to redress as of right if the appeal succeeds; whereas judicial review is discretionary and can still be withheld by the court in the light of all the circumstances (for proper and not arbitrary reasons) if ultra vires conduct is proved, and even if it is granted this may well be irrespective of the merits, if any, of the applicant's case. This might, at any rate in theory, and depending on circumstances, be dealt with again on its merits and still fail.

Emphasising once again the true significance of judicial review, and drawing on the terminology enunciated by the late Lord Diplock in *Council of Civil Service Unions v Minister for the Civil Service* [1984] 3 All ER 935 at 950–951, Sir John Donaldson MR distinguished sharply between the Panel and the court ([1987] 1 All ER 564 at 580):

> · 'The role of the court is wholly different. It is, in an appropriate case, to review the decision of the panel and to consider whether there has been "illegality", ie whether the panel has misdirected itself in law, "irrationality", ie whether the panel's decision is so outrageous in its defiance of logic or of accepted moral standards that no sensible person who had applied his mind to the question to be decided could have arrived at it, or "procedural impropriety", ie a departure by the panel from any procedural rules governing its conduct or a failure to observe the basic rules of natural justice, which is probably better described as "fundamental unfairness" since justice in nature is conspicuous by its absence.'

This disposes of the applicants' choice between the first and second possibilities. But the nub of the case advanced by the respondent Panel, 'the only issue which may matter in the longer term' was the choice between the second and third possibilities, ie between the proposition that the Panel is not exempt from judicial review and the proposition that it is.

> 'Counsel for the panel waxed eloquent on the disastrous consequences of the court having and exercising jurisdiction to review the decisions of the panel, and his submissions deserved, and have received, very serious consideration.'

The question of general principle here is fundamental. It arose in *Czarnikow v Roth Schmidt & Co* [1922] All ER Rep 45, in which an earlier 'self-regulatory body', the Refined Sugar Association, purported to exclude sugar traders from recourse to the courts. The Court of Appeal dealt briskly with this idea (ibid at 50, per Scrutten LJ). 'In my view to allow English citizens to agree to exclude this safeguard for the administration of the law is contrary to public policy. There must be no Alsatia in England where the

Kings's writ does not run.' 'Alsatia' was a medieval area of sanctuary in London, where criminals could take refuge from the law. A similar issue had been similarly dealt with in *Chester v Bateson* [1920] 1 KB 829. In fairness it may be said that the attempts to exclude the courts in these cases were probably made with appeals on merits in mind, not judicial review; but they were being contested on the basis that *all* recourse, including judicial review, was excluded, and it was this that the courts objected to.

The *Czarnikow* case appears to have involved not public but private law, ie contract. Yet this may not be a realistic distinction if the 'self-regulatory' function of the Refined Sugar Association was at all comparable with that of the Panel on Take-overs and Mergers. Presumably neither body could convincingly be treated as a private club; and there must be limits, even in the most modest private contract, to the possibility of ousting the jurisdiction of the courts. Public policy is relevant (sometimes) to the law of contract. In fact, in a very real sense, private law must ultimately defer to public law—the courts are public, and so is the constitutional status of all citizens. (In some quarters the word 'public' is regarded with disdain; but the English legal system has not yet been privatised.) The distinction in English law between public and private law has itself been criticised, as Lloyd LJ in the instant case pointed out; though the critics might come in time to regret this. And the authority of the House of Lords, in and since the decision in *O'Reilly v Mackman* [1982] 3 All ER 1124, sustains the distinction.

All three judges in the instant case were firm about public law. To quote Lloyd LJ ([1987] 1 All ER 564 at 583): 'It may be said that to refer to "public law" in this context is to beg the question. But I do not think it does. The essential distinction . . . is between a domestic or private tribunal on the one hand and a body of persons who are under some public duty on the other.' Nicholls LJ said (ibid at 587):

> 'given the leading and continuing role played by the Bank of England in the affairs of the panel, the statutory source of the powers and duties of the Council of the Stock Exchange, the wide-ranging nature and importance of the matters covered by the code, and the public law consequences of non-compliance, the panel is performing a public duty. . . . '

Sir John Donaldson MR stressed the contrast with private law, and showed how the latter is not relevant here (ibid at 577):

> 'Given that it is really unthinkable that . . . the panel should go on its way cocooned from the attention of the courts, in defence of the citizenry we sought to investigate whether it could conveniently be controlled by established forms of private law, eg torts such as actionable combinations in restraint of trade, and, to this end, pressed counsel for the applicants to draft a writ. Suffice to say that the result was wholly unconvincing. . . . '

To quote Lloyd LJ again (ibid at 582): 'It is clearly better, as a matter of policy, that legal proceedings [here] should be in the realm of public law rather than private law, not only because they are quicker but also because the requirement of leave under Order 53 will exclude claims which are clearly unmeritorious.'

Having resoundingly disposed of the Panel's central argument of law the Court of Appeal then gave judgment in its favour, by finding that the substance of the applicant companies' complaint did not disclose any ultra vires activity by the Panel. Its decision had disposed of the complaint fairly and squarely on the merits as it was empowered to do. The Panel had denied the court's jurisdiction, was made to accept it, and was then told that the court, duly exercising its jurisdiction, upheld the Panel. This was a satisfactory outcome if the principle of self-regulation in the City is accepted.

Sir John Donaldson MR pointed out that (ibid at 578):

> 'all who are concerned with take-over bids should have well in mind a very special feature of public law decisions, such as those of the panel, namely that however wrong they may be, however lacking in jurisdiction they may be, they subsist and remain fully effective unless and until they are set aside by a court of competent jurisdiction. Further more, the court has an ultimate discretion whether to set them aside and may refuse to do so in the public interest, notwithstanding that it holds and declares the decision to have been made ultra vires. . . . '

Thus the need for speedy and expert financial decisions in matters of great technical complexity will not be prejudiced.

> 'In that context the panel and those affected should treat its decisions as valid and binding, unless and until they are set aside. Above all they should ignore any application for leave to apply of which they become aware, since to do otherwise would enable such applications to be used as a mere ploy in take-over battles which would be a serious abuse of the process of the court and could not be adequately penalised by awards of costs.'

Even when a remedy is to be granted, the probability is that a declaration should be chosen rather than certiorari to quash. The law is thus established for future cases without blighting the speedy effectiveness of the Panel's self-regulatory processes. The Master of the Rolls' view was strongly expressed in favour of a 'hands off' approach by the courts (ibid at 579):

> 'The only circumstances in which I would anticipate (sic) the use of the remedies of certiorari and mandamus would be in the event, which I hope is unthinkable, of the panel acting in breach of the rules of natural justice, in other words unfairly . . . there is little scope for complaint that the panel has promulgated rules which are ultra vires, provided only that they do not clearly violate the principle proclaimed by the panel of being based on the concept of doing equity between one shareholder and another.'

But public law still stands where it did, and the Panel on Take-overs and Mergers, however peculiar, is subject to its dominion.

Damages in relation to judicial review

The fundamental distinction between public and private law was again thrown into sharp relief by the judgment of McNeill J in *R v Secretary of State for the Home Dept ex p Dew* [1987] 2 All ER 1049. The applicant had been arrested for a serious criminal offence and received a bullet-wound in his arm. He was remanded in custody, tried convicted and sentenced to 18 years' imprisonment. McNeill J said (ibid at 1051):

'the foundation of his application for judicial review is that the Secretary of State and the prison authorities failed to provide for him, or delayed in providing for him, proper medical treatment for his injured arm. The injuries were undoubtedly serious. As a matter of history, the appropriate treatment has now been provided, but it had not been provided at the date when leave to move for judicial review was given. Counsel for the respondents says quite simply that a claim so founded is a claim in private law and is not a matter of public law: the matter should have been, and could still be, pursued by writ and an action. He makes no concessions as to liability in such an action. It is, he contends, an abuse of process to bring such a claim under the guise of judicial review, which is a public law remedy.'

We see here the distinction between public law and private law, which Lord Diplock placed in the limelight in *O'Reilly v Mackman* [1982] 3 All ER 1124, strongly taking root. The judge accepted the respondents' argument; and on the rock of that distinction the applicant's case foundered. It was the converse of *O'Reilly v Mackman*. In that case the aggrieved prisoner had brought a private law action by writ (and originating summons) and failed because it should have been a public law action by way of judicial review; this time the aggrieved prisoner brought a public law action by way of judicial review and failed because it should have been a private law action by writ. Both decisions, however, were held not to preclude alternative proceedings being brought to remedy the alleged wrongdoing.

Section 31 of the Supreme Court Act 1981, as is well known, gives statutory expression to the revised (1977) version of Order 53 of the Rules of the Supreme Court and these are the source of authority for judicial review. Section 31(4) says:

'On any application for judicial review the High Court may award damages to the applicant if—(a) he has joined with his application a claim for damages arising from any matter to which the application relates; and (b) the court is satisfied that, if the claim had been made in an action begun by the applicant at the time of making his application, he would have been awarded damages. . . . '

The applicant's case was that the respondents had wronged him in regard to the delay in arranging necessary medical treatment for his injured arm, that the wrong lay in public law because they were acting in a public capacity, that judicial review was therefore the correct proceeding, that damages were the appropriate remedy, and that s 31(4) authorised the award of such damages.

The answer to this is clear and conclusive (despite some lack of clarity in previous judgments) namely that s 31(4) is purely ancillary to judicial review and only applies when an arguable case for judicial review has been made at the outset. RSC Ord 53, r 9(5), provides that where the relief sought in judicial review is a declaration or an injunction or damages, the court has discretion to order that proceedings should not be discontinued but should proceed *as if begun by writ*, if it thinks that the relief thus sought 'should not be granted on an application for judicial review'. This last phrase is decidedly ambiguous and it is not surprising that in the instant case the applicant sought to argue that it is capable of being applied to any claim against a public authority for damages (or injunction or declaration) with the further conclusion that plaintiffs can invariably start proceedings against a public authority in judicial review and switch effortlessly from public to private law proceedings under r 9(5) whenever necessary.

But that further conclusion has only to be stated to be seen to be wrong. If Parliament had intended judicial review to be the all-purpose proceeding against public authorities it would have legislated expressly to that effect. McNeill J said that ([1987] 2 All ER 1049 at 1061): 'judicial review and the remedies available under its umbrella must be founded on infringement of a public law right... [and] there is no general right in an individual to damages for an infringement of a public law right.' The counterpart to this is to recognise that if a public authority (eg a prison authority) has a duty of care, that 'might conveniently be described as public but it is not a duty which gives other than private law rights to persons injured' in the event of a breach of that duty. Breach of trust, breach of contract, commission of a tort—these are all private law matters, irrespective of whether the defendant is a public authority. In the instant case 'the applicant's right, assuming he had any right, was in private law from the beginning. It certainly can only be a private right now: at best a claim for damages in tort' because the applicant's injured arm had been given proper medical treatment before the issue of judicial review was tried.

In *Davy v Spelthorne BC* [1983] 3 All ER 278 at 286–7, Lord Wilberforce said: 'Since no prerogative... order in relation to the present claim could be sought, since consequently no declaration or injunction could be asked for, no right to judicial review exists... and no consequential claim for damages can be made....' In *R v East Berkshire Health Authority ex p Walsh* [1984] 3 All ER 425 at 442, Purchase LJ said that:

> 'it must first be established that there is an arguable case for a remedy under Order 53.... Section 31 of the Supreme Court Act 1981, although recognising the wider remedies available under Order 53, is no statutory justification for extending the area of jurisdiction beyond that of a supervisory function which is to be directed in relation to remedies sought against public or similar authorities whose actions under their statutory or other powers call for the court's intervention.'

McNeill J himself summed up by saying ([1987] 2 All ER 1049 at 1066):

> 'the terms of section 31... make it clear... that relief by way of injunction or declaration is only available in cases where relief by way of prerogative writ would have been available... section 31(4) appears to treat damages as a claim derivative from, and ancillary to, such relief and that alone... Rule 9(5) limits the power, to order proceedings to continue as if begun by writ, only to cases where the relief sought is a declaration, an injunction, or damages, such relief being by the same reason derivative or ancillary, that is to say all in the field of public law only.'

Public law jurisdiction is 'supervisory'; private law jurisdiction is not.

Reasonableness, fairness and 'legitimate expectation'

Within this framework of public law, various well-known principles have come under further scrutiny during 1987. These include reasonableness, fairness, and 'legitimate expectation'.

Reasonableness in the objective or 'Wednesbury' sense of the word—the positive side of 'irrationality' in Lord Diplock's terminology—was considered in *West Glamorgan CC v Rafferty* [1987] 1 All ER 1005. The appellant authority were held by the Court of Appeal to have acted unreasonably in deciding to evict gipsies from land which the authority wished to redevelop, without giving proper consideration to fulfilling the statutory function imposed on the authority by s 6 of the Caravan Sites Act 1968 to 'provide adequate accommodation for gipsies residing in or resorting to their area.' The proceedings had begun by originating summons for an order for possession of the disputed land, which ordinarily must have succeeded on a clear cause of action in trespass, ie in private law, if that trespass could properly have been considered in isolation. But since it could not be considered in isolation for the reasons stated, the council's resolution to seek possession was contestable in *public* law, and certiorari was granted to quash the resolution. A declaration also granted at first instance that the council must not seek possession until they had made reasonable alternative provision for the gipsies was set aside as excessive, though the first instance decision to set the possession order aside was upheld. The Court of Appeal, it should be noted, was dealing with two appeals together, from the private law action by the council for a possession order and from the public law action by way of judicial review; both were in the High Court. The proceedings in public law predominated over those in private law.

Fairness was considered in *Lloyd v McMahon* [1987] 1 All ER 1118, both by the Court of Appeal and by the House of Lords, in relation to local authority audit. The authority was Liverpool City Council. The action stemmed from the district auditor's issue of a certificate stating that a number of appellant councillors should become personally liable to make good a loss of £106,103 caused by their wilful default in not setting a rate at the due time. The auditor notified the councillors of his intention to issue the certificate and invited them first to make written representations, which they did. He decided that the certificate should be made. They appealed unsuccessfully on the ground that he ought to have afforded them an oral hearing as well.

Lord Templeman observed that one of the arguments for the appellant councillors was based on 'legitimate expectation' ([1987] 1 All ER 1118 at 1170).

> 'Counsel for the appellants, . . . submits that a legitimate expectation of being invited to an oral hearing is an objective fundamental right which, if not afforded, results in a breach of law or breach of natural justice which invalidates any decision based on written material. This extravagant language does not tempt me to elevate a catchphrase into a principle.'

Since 'legitimate expectation' is an aspect of the same basic concept as 'sufficient interest' or 'locus standi', Lord Templeman's caustic reaction is not surprising.

The expression came up again in *R v Secretary of State for the Home Dept ex p Ruddock* [1987] 2 All ER 518. Members of CND sought judicial review by way of declarations that a decision of the Home Secretary to sign a warrant for 'phone-tapping' was ultra vires. It was argued that the judge (Taylor J) must decline jurisdiction for reasons of national security; but he held that he had jurisdiction to consider the evidence and could not see that considering the application would be harmful to national security. It was also argued that 'legitimate expectation' was inapplicable; but the judge held that there was a 'legitimate expectation' that a minister would comply with his own published guidelines, which apparently he had not done in this case. However, the evidence did not establish that the Home Secretary had deliberately flouted the guidelines, or that no reasonable person in his position could have decided that the guidelines precluded the issue of the warrant in this case.

Thus it can be seen that the courts continue to balance precariously between the needs of the executive and the rights of the subject. They are holding fast to the distinction between public and private law, and this should help them to retain their equilibrium.

'Fettering' discretion

Authorities must not 'fetter' the exercise of their policy discretion incompatibly with the due exercise of their functions. This principle was raised in an unexpected context in *R v Waltam Forest London Borough Council, ex p Baxter* [1987] 3 All ER 671, namely in relation to a decision taken not by a public body but by some of its members—half a dozen councillors of the majority party in a local council. They voted in a party meeting against a proposed rate increase, but fell into line with the rest of the majority party when it came to voting in the council meeting.

A local ratepayers' group sought judicial review; but the Divisional Court and the Court of Appeal refused it. Although individual councillors have a duty to arrive at their own decision and not to abdicate responsibility by blindly following a party line—ie not to 'fetter' their discretion improperly—the mere fact of deciding to vote with their party group is no proof of much abdication or 'fettering'. Sir John Donaldson MR, quoting Glidewell LJ, said:

> '... if we were to quash the council's decision on the grounds that the majority group operated a whipping system ... we should be casting doubt on the legality of procedures adopted by political groups of local councillors throughout the country. We should also, by implication, be criticising the system operating in Parliament itself ([1987] 3 All ER 671 at 674).'

As the Master of the Rolls would say: 'Perish the thought.'

Arbitration

J E ADAMS LLB FCI Arb
Director of Training, Titmuss Sainer & Webb, Emeritus Professor of Law, Queen Mary College, University of London

There are only three arbitration decisions in the All England Reports for 1987 and each, not insignificantly, dealt with a non-domestic arbitration agreement. One of them (the *DST* case) signals a marked change in the attitude of English courts towards international commercial arbitration. The launching of a consultation process on the possible adoption in the UK of all or part of the UNICITRAL Model Law demonstrates the significance of this aspect of international commerce. A recent Hong Kong report, incidentally, favours adoption there of the Model Law; there are similar proposals in Australia, and New Zealand is also considering the issue. A continuing trend to unification is thus apparent.

Rights of joinder so as to seek stay

The original parties to the litigation in *Etri Fans Ltd v NMB (UK) Ltd* [1987] 2 All ER 763 were Etri, a 'sister company' of the French Etri SA, which designed, manufactured and marketed axial fans, and NMB (UK) the English subsidiary of the Japanese companies, Minebea Co Ltd and Kondo Co Ltd. The latter made fans allegedly later imported by NMB, but claimed by Etri to infringe the copyright of the French company (of which copyright the plaintiff was an assignee); Kondo held licences to manufacture fans and to sell fans (but not in the UK) granted by the French company. The Etri SA–Kondo agreement contained an arbitration clause, providing for ICC arbitration in the country of the defending party.

   NMB had no hope of obtaining a stay, because of the steps it had taken in the litigation, which went well beyond those permitted under s 1 of the Arbitration Act 1975. That particular bar would not have applied to the two parent companies, who applied to be joined in the extant litigation so as to be able to claim a stay. The Vice-Chancellor declined to allow joinder, and was upheld by the Court of Appeal (Fox and Woolf LJJ).

   As Woolf LJ, who delivered the only judgment, pointed out (ibid at 766b), if the applicants could meet the requirements of s 1 the court had to grant a stay; otherwise the court had a discretion under its residual jurisdiction. (There seems no doubt that a 'not' is missing in the relevant sentence in the printed report.) So first the statutory provisions fell to be scrutinised. The court assumed, on the facts summarised above, that Etri claimed through or under a party to the arbitration agreement (ie the French company), that it had commenced proceedings against NMB, which also claimed through or under a party to the agreement (ie Kondo) and that the proceedings were over a matter within the scope of the arbitration agreement. The appellants argued that they thus met all the requirements allowing an application to stay; Etri contended that only the party sued (or a claimant under or through it) qualified. Otherwise, it urged, parties to the litigation might find it stayed by the intervention of a party not welcome in the litigation. The latter arguments prevailed, both as a matter of the grammatical construction of the section (see 767a and b) and as leading to the more sensible result. A party wishing to abide by the agreement to arbitrate, if not sued, can merely proceed to do so; a co-defendant not party to the arbitration agreement (nor deriving status from a party) should not be able to force the other litigating parties into arbitration. This ruling, that only the party sued, and its 'satellites', have rights under s 1 was conclusive on the statutory jurisdiction.

As to the inherent jurisdiction, which was held to exist as part of the wider powers to curb abuse of the process of the court, counsel for the appellants had to concede that the circumstances for its exercise would be rare, given the full statutory coverage. The present facts fell squarely within the ambit of the statute, and Woolf LJ robustly denied any chance of exercise of the residual power in favour of a stay, even if the appellants were to be joined in the action (see pp 767–768). That absence of any prospect of obtaining a stay justified the refusal of joinder. The Vice-Chancellor had refused joinder on weighing the merits, on the basis that, once joined, the appellants would necessarily have to be entitled to a stay under s 1 of the 1975 Act, but, by the contrary analysis of the Court of Appeal of that section, that issue of discretion did not arise. The Vice-Chancellor's reasons for refusing joinder, however, coincided with the appellate court's reasons for refusing exercise of the inherent jurisdiction to grant stay.

What lay behind this somewhat arid squabble was real enough; the appellants wished to be respondents to an arbitration in Japan, not claimants in an arbitration in France, even if it meant, temporarily, becoming litigants in England! Their defeat seems to give no grounds for dismay, and the analysis of s 1 is welcome, if unremarkable.

Extrinsic evidence, further reasons and leave to appeal

The power given by s 1(5) of the Arbitration Act 1979 to order an arbitrator to give further reasons for his award was considered at some length by the Court of Appeal in *Universal Petroleum Co Ltd (in liq) v Handels–und Transport gesellschaft mbH* [1987] 2 All ER 737. The arbitrator had found that the contractual description of a cargo was merely 'unleaded gasoline', that the contractual terms were in a particular telex, and that the sellers (Universal) had not made an improper tender and so had dismissed the buyers' claim for damages. The buyers sought leave to appeal on the issue whether there was evidence to support the primary findings and applied, under s 1(5), for remission of the award for a statement of further reasons for the findings. The judge (Webster J) made the latter order in the light of material adduced before him which threw doubt on the findings, although they seemed consistent on the face of the award. With his leave, the sellers appealed.

As Kerr LJ indicated, the main issue was whether an award not susceptible of appeal under the 'Nema-Antaios guidelines' could be rendered appealable by insisting that the arbitrator state reasons for his factual findings, so laying them open to attack. As the learned Lord Justice concluded (ibid at 743f) the Schedule of Reasons which resulted from the judge's order 'reads like a cross-examination of the arbitrator for the purposes of a rehash in court of the arguments advanced in the arbitration'. A more obvious defiance of the statutory policy of greater finality in awards might be hard to find. However, the Court of Appeal ruled, with apt citations from Mustill and Boyd, that the judge had been wrong in principle to allow the buyers to lay before him the material which pointed the need for clarification of the grounds for the factual finding. The 1979 Act, in terms, limits appeals to points of law *'arising out of an award'*, and not out of an arbitration (at 746d). The Court of Appeal approach followed that of an earlier decision *(Athens Cape Naviera SA v Deutsche Dampfschiffartsgesellschaft 'Hansa' AG, The Barenbels* [1984] 1 Lloyds Rep 528) which had held a judge wrong to admit affidavit evidence to bolster an application for leave to appeal, Kerr LJ having, understandably, equated such evidence and statements from advocates (at 742j). So on three bases—policy, interpretation and precedent—the appeal succeeded.

Moreover, the judgment gives guidance to arbitrators and arbitrands. The latter, or their advocates, should ask specifically for reasons for the primary findings of fact to be included in the award, whereever there is likely to be difficulty on that score; arbitrators should endeavour to deal, with reasons, with all issues raised which may go to 'appealability', particularly having regard to the statutory requirement for leave that 'the determination of the question of law concerned could substantially affect the rights of one or more of the parties'. Clearly this judgment is one more to be digested to form an entry in the (mythical) Manual of Preferred Conduct in Arbitrations (post-1979 Act edition—desirably in loose-leaf format). This is emphasised by the treatment by the court of some further issues subsidiary to the main issue, (which was conclusive of the appeal). The s 1(5) jurisdiction is to be sparingly exercised, awards should deal with all important issues even if several lead to the same result, consideration of an application for further reasons must be considered against the likelihood of the eventual grant of leave to appeal, the sub-section may not be used to overcome the *Barenbels* obstacle but, exceptionally, extrinsic matters may be raised in seeking to uphold the award. (These guide-lines appear at [1987] 2 All ER 737 at 750). The judgment concludes with some strong criticisms of the events in the particular case, which the learned Lord Justice stated and hoped was most exceptional at and deplorable.

Awards based on 'lex mercatoria'

The third case, *Deutsche Schachtbau-und Tiefbohrgesellschaft gmbH v Ras A. Khaimah National Oil Co* [1987] 2 All ER 769 is one of the most significant decisions in a move towards acceptance of the concept of internationa' arbitration, yet, paradoxically, it is a poor advertisement for that process. When disputes arose under an oil exploration agreement, the plaintif' ('DST') went to arbitration in Geneva, but the defendant ('Raknoc') sued ir the court of R'as Al Khaimah. DST obtained an award for 4.6 millior dollars in its favour, Raknoc obtained a judgment setting aside the agreement and damages of 1.4 million dollars and 110 million Dirham (about 29 million dollars in 1979). Neither party took any part in the other's proceedings, and each party rested on its laurels for some six years, for want of finding a means of enforcement. Then in 1986 DST heard that Shell International Petroleum was buying oil from Raknoc. It sought and obtained leave to enforce the award (with interest then totalling 3.7 million dollars) and a Mareva injuction relating to Raknoc's assets and, in particular, any sums due from Shell. Raknoc obtained leave to issue and serve a writ in Germany for enforcement of its judgment, as a basis for a counter-claim in DST's proceedings. Various interlocutory proceedings ensued, and the matter came before the Court of Appeal. Shell, in the meantime, was commercially embarrassed by the restraint on it and was allowed to intervene in the appeal to argue for discharge of the injunction.

The first issue was whether the award was to be enforced. It was a Convention award, so enforcement could only be refused on one of the grounds set out in s 5 of the 1975 Act, which reproduces Article V of the 1958 New York Convention. Raknoc's counsel raised five points. First came an issue on the proper law of the agreement to arbitrate, which was to be found in one short provision in the underlying contract specifying an ICC arbitration in Geneva, conducted in English. Raknoc argued for the law of R'as Al Khaimah, DST for that of Switzerland. The former was claimed to be the proper law of the contract. Unsurprisingly, by reference to English authority and the relevant ICC rules, the agreement to arbitrate was found to be independent of the principal contract and to be, obviously, governed by Swiss law. That provided also the answer to the second issue, namely the effect of the R'as Al Khaimah judgment ruling the contract invalid; that was irrelevant to the validity of the award. Moreover, the setting aside of the initial leave to issue a writ for enforcement (one of the intervening steps below) was upheld, in the light of s 32 of the Civil Jurisdiction and Judgments Act 1982, so, as the Master of the Rolls put it, that judgment 'disappears from the scene'.

Next, the defendant attacked the award as dealing with matters outside the scope of the submission, a ground of attack under s 5(2)(d)(reproducing Article V(1)(c) of the Convention). DST had claimed on behalf of itself and others, apparently members of a consortium. Raknoc identified one member as not being party to any arbitration agreement, and the award mentioned another company similarly placed. No steps to attack the award in Switzerland on the basis of the alleged irregularities had been mounted, and the plea of excess of jurisdiction failed.

We come now to the nub of the decision. Under ICC Rules, Art 13(3), if the parties have not chosen the law to be applied to the merits the arbitrator(s) must choose that law. Here the three arbitrators had settled on 'internationally accepted principles of law governing contractual relations'. They explained, and justified that choice, in a statement which is set out at [1987] 2 All ER at 776h–777a. Raknoc's counsel argued that it was contrary to English public policy to enforce an award based on such a non-national set of general and possibly vague, principles. If such a flouting of public policy could be shown, s 5(2) of the 1975 Act (reproducing Art V(2)(b) of the Convention) would allow refusal of enforcement. So the well-known debate over the acceptability of 'lex mercatoria' awards has come to court in England.

The Master of the Rolls dealt first with two cases on awards made 'ex aequo et bono'. He cited at length (at 777e–778a) Megaw J's rejection of such an extra-legal criterion in *Orion Cia Espanola de Seguros v Belfort Maatschappij Voor Algemene Verzekgrigeen* [1962] 2 Lloyds Rep 257 and the somewhat guarded acceptance of such a provision, by giving it a rather limited scope, by Lord Denning MR in *Eagle Star Insurance Co Ltd v Yuval Insurance Co Ltd* [1978] 1 Lloyd's Rep 357 (the citation is at [1987] 2 All ER at 778). Nothing more is said about those two cases, but it seems a fair inference that the approach of the latter is endorsed. Turning to the issue in the instant case, the Master of the Rolls posed, and answered, three questions arising from an award based on general principles. One asks if the parties intended to create legally enforceable rights and obligations; here they clearly did (at 779a and f). Next one determines if their formulation of that intent fails for uncertainty, a question to be answered in the light of the court's reluctance to allow a contract so to fail (at 779c and d). Again, that test was passed (at 779f and g). Finally, would it be against public policy for the state to become involved in enforcement? (at 779e). Again, proceeding cautiously, the answer was 'No'. This answer is clearly welcome, especially in the context of ICC arbitrations where many panels will include arbitrators wholly inclined to apply the general principles of international commercial law.

The final ground, namely that summary enforcement should be denied and DST left to sue on the award, was swiftly disposed of (at 779j). Accordingly the appeal against leave to enforce failed, and the stay was removed.

The second limb of the decision, over the Mareva injuction, falls outside this writer's remit, but he will briefly summarise it. Strictly speaking, the restraint imposed was not a Mareva injunction, as DST was a judgment creditor, albeit under suspension till resolution of the appeal, backed up by the stay (at 780e–j). The trading debt, of some 4.8 million dollars in possible amount, was an asset within the jurisdiction, even though payable in New York. Despite that, enforcement, eg by garnishment, would be here (at 782d–f) and the discretionary remedy had been rightly granted (at 783f–j). Shell, against whom judgment had been obtained in the R'as Al Khaimah court, was later given leave to appeal to the House of Lords. However, that seems unlikely, on the face of it, to upset the rulings on the vital 'lex mercatoria' point.

Commercial Law

NE PALMER, BCL, MA
Barrister, Professor of Law, University of Essex

Banking

Deposit taking and commodity broking

We gave a brief account of the facts of *SCF Finance Co Ltd v Masri (No 2)* [1986] 1 All ER 40 last year in our discussion of the first instance decision of Leggatt J (see All ER Rev 1986, p 31). That decision has now been upheld by the Court of Appeal ([1987] 1 All ER 175). The court agreed with Leggatt J that, even if the plaintiff commodity brokers had accepted deposits from the defendant contrary to s 1(1) of the Banking Act 1979, the defendant's contractual liability to them should not be affected. Such a result was clearly dictated by s 1(8) of the Act, whereby a contravention of s 1 was stated not to impair the rights of either a depositor or a depositee under the general law of contract; and was consistent with the approach to statutory illegality advocated by Devlin J in his classic judgment in *St John Shipping Corp v Joseph Rank Ltd* [1956] 3 All ER 683. Even without the presence of s 1(8), the statute was one which the court would have been very reluctant to regard as affecting the contractual position. But the Court of Appeal declined to consider what the position would have been had one or both of the parties *knowingly* concluded a transaction contrary to s 1(1) of the 1979 Act.

The Court of Appeal discovered two further, anterior grounds for concluding that the plaintiffs' action should succeed. First, the moneys paid by the defendant did not qualify as 'deposits' in the sense of the word employed by s 1(4) of the Act, but fell instead within the definition of 'money . . . paid by way of security for payment for the provision of property or services . . . to be provided by the person by whom . . . the money is accepted' contained in s 1(6)(b), thereby attracting the exemption from characterisation as a deposit recognised by s 1(4)(b). Those (admittedly unusual) futures contracts which resulted in actual delivery of a physical commodity counted as a provision of 'property' for this purpose, whereas those which did not, counted as a provision of 'services'. The conclusion that the plaintiffs had not accepted deposits from the defendant was seen as consistent with the judicial policy of avoiding the construction of an ambiguous statute as one imposing criminal liability; but the court held that s 1(6)(b) was, in fact, 'capable of only one sensible meaning in relation to the facts of this case'.

Secondly, the court held that the moneys accepted by the plaintiffs, even if qualifying as 'deposits' in the statutory sense, had not been accepted by the plaintiffs in the course of 'carrying on . . . a deposit-taking business' within s 1(1) of the Act. Even if the deposited moneys were lent by the plaintiffs to others or used by them to finance other business activities, the plaintiffs' activities would still have been exempted from consitituting a deposit-taking business by virtue of s 1(3). The court discerned two possible bases for such exemption: first, that the plaintiffs did not, within the meaning of s 1(3)(a), hold themselves out 'to accept deposits on a day to day basis', and secondly, that the occasions upon which the plaintiffs accepted deposits from clients were to be regarded as 'particular occasions' within s 1(3)(b).

Undue influence

See *Goldsworthy v Brickell* [1987] 1 All ER 863, CA, discussed p 311, post.

Bankruptcy

In *Re Tucker (a bankrupt)* [1987] 2 All ER 23, the question arose as to the power of the bankruptcy court to authorise service out of the jurisdiction of a summons, under what was s 25 of the Bankruptcy Act 1914, on a stranger to the bankruptcy resident out of the jurisdiction. The provisions of s 25 are now contained in similar terms in ss 366 and 367 of the Insolvency Act 1986.

The debtor appeared to control the assets and to be the beneficial owner of a number of interrelated companies situated in the Channel Islands. The debtor's brother (the applicant) also appeared to be connected with a number of these Channel Island companies, and the trustee in bankruptcy considered that the applicant would be in a position to answer important questions relating to the bankruptcy. He therefore applied ex parte to the bankruptcy registrar for the issue of a summons under s 25 of the Bankruptcy Act 1914 requiring the applicant to produce documents relating to these companies and to attend the court for examination. The applicant, although a citizen of the United Kingdom, had not been resident in the jurisdiction since 1972 and was in fact resident in Belgium.

Upon application from the trustee in bankruptcy, the bankruptcy registrar issued a summons under s 25 requiring the applicant to produce various documents and to attend the court for examination. An order was also made authorising service of the summons outside the jurisdiction of the court. Section 25(1) of the 1914 Act (which remains in force only for current bankruptcies, and has now been replaced by s 366(1)(c) of the Insolvency Act 1986) allows the court to summon before it 'any person whom the court may deem capable of giving information respecting the debtor, his dealings or property'. The applicant did not challenge the trustee in bankruptcy's contention that he was a person 'capable of giving [such] information'. However, he did dispute the power of the court to order service abroad of a s 25 summons obliging a stranger to the bankruptcy to present himself, on pain of arrest, for examination before an English court.

Scott J examined various authorities and concluded that s 25(1) enables the court to summon before it British subjects even if resident outside the jurisdiction. The applicant was therefore clearly a person in respect of whom a s 25 summons could be issued. However, he refused to accept the trustee's submission that s 25(6) of the 1914 Act (s 367(c) of the 1986 Act) should be given a wide meaning so as to allow the examination of the applicant in Belgium. Following Wright J in *Re Drucker (No 2) ex p Basden* [1902] 2 KB 237, he held that the words 'or in any other place out of England' should be limited to places within the jurisdiction of the British Crown, in order that the court may compel persons to attend for examination.

Rule 86 of the Bankruptcy Rules 1952 (as amended) specifically provides for service out of the jurisdiction. It was agreed that before the amendment of the Bankruptcy Rules in 1962, an order for service out of the jurisdiction could not have been made unless the person to be served was the debtor. The applicant claimed that if the effect of the 1962 amendment was to authorise service of a s 25 summons on a stranger to the bankruptcy, this represented an extension of the jurisdiction of the court and, as such, was ultra vires since s 132(1) of the 1914 Act permitted the making of such general rules only where they did not extend the jurisdiction of the court. It was necessary to determine the precise meaning of the term 'jurisdiction'. Scott J considered statements made by Pickford LJ in *Guaranty Trust Co of New York v Hannay & Co* [1915] 2 KB 536 and by Diplock LJ in *Garthwaite v Garthwaite* [1964] 2 All ER 233, to the effect that 'jurisdiction' may be regarded in either a strict or a wide sense. In the strict sense the term relates to the limits placed on the power of the court to hear and determine certain issues, and in the wide sense it refers to the way in which the court may exercise the power to hear and determine issues which fall within its 'jurisdiction'. Scott J, following an unreported judgment of Sir Nicolas Browne-Wilkinson V-C (*Jogia's Trustee v D Pennellier & Co Ltd* (1986) 136 NLJ 776), held that the jurisdiction referred to in s 132(1) is jurisdiction in the strict sense, and the 1962 amendment effected a change in procedure rather than a change in jurisdiction. The court already had jurisdiction over the applicant by virtue of s 25. The 1962 amendment did not create that jurisdiction, it merely permitted service out of the jurisdiction of the summons.

Bills of exchange

In *Claydon v Bradley* [1987] 1 All ER 522, the plaintiffs agreed to lend £10,000 to a company. After £7,600 had been advanced, the company became insolvent. The plaintiffs now sought to recover this sum from the defendant, who was the major shareholder. They based their claim upon a document (headed by the company's name) which the defendant had signed when the money was advanced. This document acknowledged receipt of the sum of £10,000, recorded the interest payable, and described the advance 'as a loan to be paid back in full by 1 July 1983'. The plaintiffs maintained that this constituted a promissory note within s 83(1) of the Bills of Exchange Act 1882, thereby rendering the defendant personally liable for repayment under s 26(1) of the same Act.

The Court of Appeal rejected this characterisation of the document on two grounds. First, far from containing an unconditional promise of payment as required by s 83(1), the instrument was expressed to be payable on a contingency. That contingency arose from the words 'by 1 July', which indicated that the payer could choose to discharge the debt at a date earlier than that stipulated. Both Dillon and Neill LJJ found the present case indistinguishable from *Williamson v Rider* [1962] 2 All ER 268, where the instrument had promised that the debt would be paid 'on or before December 31' and a majority of the Court of Appeal had held that the promise was not unconditional. Their Lordships acknowledged that Canadian and Irish authority had since preferred the dissenting judgment of

Ormrod LJ in *Williamson v Rider*, which had maintained that the words in question imposed an obligation to pay on the stated date, with an option on the payer's part to discharge the debt at an earlier date; the mere fact that the payee was obliged to accept such optional earlier repayment did not, in Ormrod LJ's view, mean that the obligation to pay was itself contingent or conditional. Reference was also made by Dillon LJ in *Claydon* to the argument of Professor AH Hudson in (1962) 25 MLR 134, that no time of payment under a promissory note is conditional unless it is a time 'which may or may not arrive'. But, in the event, the court found itself bound by the majority view in *Williamson v Rider*.

Secondly, the Court of Appeal held that the document signed by the defendant failed as a promissory note because, assuming it to fall outside s 26(1), it amounted to no more than a receipt on behalf of the company, coupled with a statement of the terms on which the advance was to be repaid. Such a document could not have been intended to be negotiable, and the fact that the amount stated to be payable exceeded the amount actually advanced by £2,400 reinforced this conclusion. In so deciding, Dillon and Neill LJJ followed the analysis given in relation to the definition of promissory note in the Indian Negotiable Instruments Act 1881 and the Indian Stamp Act 1899 by the Privy Council in *Akbar Khan v Attar Singh* [1936] 2 All ER 545 (see ibid at 550, per Lord Atkin). Following that analysis, there was nothing in the wording of the document to indicate any undertaking of personal liability by the defendant herself. The mere fact that her own address was set out below the name of the company, rather than the address of the registered office, was immaterial in this regard because both addresses seemed 'to have been used indiscriminately'.

Carriers

In *Indian Oil Corp Ltd v Greenstone Shipping SA* [1987] 3 All ER 893, shipowners had intermixed an incoming cargo of Russian crude oil with a lesser quantity of Iranian crude, which had been left on the vessel from a previous voyage. The two parcels were of broadly equivalent quality and neither was substantially impaired by the intermixture. The indorsees of the bill of lading relating to the Russian crude ('the receivers') objected to the quantity of oil delivered to them at the port of discharge on two grounds. First, they complained that the amount delivered to them fell short of that which had been loaded by some 4,000 barrels. Secondly, they argued that the wrongful nature of the intermixture entitled them to the whole composite fund of pumpable oil in the vessel, and not merely to an amount equivalent to the quantity originally shipped.

The first claim was partially upheld by the arbitrators, who allowed it subject to a 'tolerance' of 0.55% from the bill of lading figure, thereby reducing the amount awarded by some 2,800 barrels. This aspect of the award was confirmed by Staughton J, who could discover no ground for holding the tolerance figure misconceived.

More interesting is his analysis of the second claim. Staughton J assumed for this purpose that the intermixture had occurred without the consent of the receivers, or of any prior owner, or of any agent of either of those parties. He was, however, reluctant to conclude that the shipowners performed the intermixture deliberately and 'for some commercial motive'. The worst that Staughton J was prepared to concede against the shipowners was that there was 'a hint, but no more' of wrongdoing on their part.

In the event, the question of consent or misconduct proved virtually immaterial. Staughton J dismissed the second claim by reference to a general principle which, while incorporating the wrongful nature of the intermixture, seems effectively indistinguishable from the rule to be applied where the intermixture is unattended by fault. He expressed the principle as follows (ibid at 907–8):

> '. . . where B wrongfully mixes the goods of A with goods of his own, which are substantially of the same nature and quality, and they cannot in practice be separated, the mixture is held in common and A is entitled to receive out of it a quantity equal to that of his goods which went into the mixture, any doubt as to that quantity being resolved in favour of A. He is also entitled to claim damages from B in respect of any loss he may have suffered, in respect of quality or otherwise, by reason of the admixture.'

Applying this principle, Staughton J held that the receivers were not entitled to claim that the intermixture caused the property in the entire corpus of intermixed oil to pass to them. Staughton J left open, however, the question whether a different rule might apply where the commodities of each owner are of substantially divergent quality.

Staughton J's discovery of a tenancy in common followed a long and interesting survey of the authorities. Some of these had favoured a more 'punitive' rule, whereby the party performing the intermixture would be deprived of his property in his own contribution (and debarred from asserting any proportional title in its physical successor) if he had acted wrongfully. The authorities were not entirely consistent on this point, because some suggested that the wrongful party's deprivation of ownership was limited to cases where he had intermixed the goods in order to disable the other proprietor from identifying his own, whereas others indicated that such a result might extend to any case where the other proprietor had simply not consented to the exercise. No doubt these inconsistencies could be attributed to the fact that each case turned largely on its own facts; on the other hand, the decisions were virtually unanimous in favour of some form of joint ownership when the intermixture was accidental. Staughton J, who regarded none of the traditional authorities as binding on him, painted an engaging picture of the society which had given birth to the old, punitive rule. It was a world of agricultural commodities, where corn and hay 'were to be found in heaps'; where civil cases were tried by juries on the evidence of illiterate witnesses; and where methods of measuring the quantities or qualities of commodities were crude. A rule devised in such conditions would be inappropriate for modern technological circumstances, where the machinery for gradation of volume and quality is much more accurate. Such matters rendered it far simpler to assess individual proprietary contributions in cases like the present, and argued strongly for a displacement of the old rule.

It did not follow that an innocent proprietor could never gain ownership of the whole of the amalgamated corpus. Staughton J recognised the importance, in this context, of a principle which had been accepted into

English law at least from *Armory v Delamirie* (1722) 1 Stra 505. According to this principle, whenever a wrongdoer 'has destroyed or impaired the evidence by which the innocent party could show how much he had lost, the wrongdoer must suffer from the resulting uncertainty' ([1987] 3 All ER 893 at 906). If, therefore, there were a complete absence of proof as to the quantity of the innocent party's goods which had been contributed to the mixture, 'the whole should belong to him'. But in cases where it was known that the amount contributed by the innocent party fell short of the overall quantum, both the demands of justice and the rule of the worst presumption against the wrongdoer would be satisfied by awarding him ownership of the largest proportion of the whole that would have been consistent with the evidence. Indeed, the availability of such a principle constituted a further reason for rejecting the punitive rule whereby total ownership would be conferred upon the innocent party.

A few final points may be worth making. First, it might have been useful for the Court of Appeal to have considered the *Armory* principle in *Associated Dairies Ltd v Securicor (Mobile) Ltd* (1985) *The Times*, 27 June, had the respondents; liability there been found to fall short of the overall quantum of the consignment. Secondly, the obvious suitability of Staughton J's reasoning to cases of commercial commodities like oil should not encourage later tribunals to generalise unduly from it; for there may be many other situations where a conclusion in favour of a single ownership remains preferable. An interesting peripheral example may be that of computer software, to which a licensee may frequently make both authorised and unauthorised amendments. In so far as it is legitimate to treat such a commodity as 'goods' at all, it may be thought that the functions and patterns of interests involved in the licensing of software argue strongly for an exclusive property in the original supplier-licensor, and merely for some *non*-proprietary restitutionary right (if any) in the amender-licensee.

Insurance

Duty of disclosure on part of insurers

Banque Keyser Ullmann SA v Skandia (UK) Insurance Co Ltd [1987] 2 All ER 923 raises many important points; only the briefest account can be given here. The plaintiff banks made loans to companies controlled by one Ballestero ('B'). The loans were secured by certain pledges of gemstones (which later proved to be worth far less than their accredited value) and by a series of credit insurances. These insurances were issued by Hodge and Skandia, although there was also a 'following' market. Hodge and Skandia were the successive employers of a senior underwriter named Dungate ('D'), around whose professional behaviour the instant proceedings revolved. The banks were parties to the contracts of insurance, either as assignees of the borrowing companies or as co-insureds. In concluding these transactions, the banks acted through a firm of brokers named Notcutts. These brokers were, in accordance with ordinary principles, deemed to act as the agents of the insured parties and not of the insurers.

Notcutts employed a manager called Lee ('L'). L knew that the loans would not be made by the banks until credit insurance for each loan was in place. He fraudulently issued false cover-notes relating to the first loan in January 1980, thereby leading the group of lender banks (who were led by Keysers) to believe that their security was in place, and inducing them to advance the funds. In June 1980 D became fortuitously aware of this deception, but did nothing to inform either L's superiors, or his own employers, or the banks. D knew that the banks would refuse to make further advances if the truth were revealed to them, and that his firm would accordingly lose the relevant commissions on later credit insurances; he therefore, in his own words, 'condoned' L's dishonesty. The banks proceeded to make further loans to B-controlled companies and D continued to issue insurances in respect of these loans: originally as an officer of Hodge and latterly, after his change of employment, as an officer of Skandia. In total, four subsequent loans were made, producing an aggregate exposure on the banks' part (counting the January 1980 loan) of some 80 million Swiss francs.

In due course, B disappeared with the money. The banks accepted that they were unable to recover on the policies of insurance because those policies excepted fraud. By a settlement with Notcutts (the employers of L) the banks accepted a payment of £10.5 million, representing the limit of Notcutts' own insurance. They now sought to recover the residual loss from their insurers. The banks alleged both a 'reciprocal' duty of utmost good faith on the insurers' part, which obliged the insurers to disclose the truth about L's deception, and a common law duty of care to similar effect. Subject to certain incidental qualifications, Steyn J upheld the claim on both grounds.

As regards the duty of utmost good faith, Steyn J held that an obligation on the part of an underwriter to disclose a deception committed by a broker Cainst his principal was supported both by professional opinion within the underwriting market and by substantial authority. As long ago as 1766, Lord Mansfield CJ had accepted that the insured's obligation to disclose material facts was complemented by an obligation upon the insurer to reveal those matters within his private knowledge which were calculated to influence the decision of the insured in concluding the insurance: *Carter v Boehm* [1558–1774] All ER Rep 183. Such an obligation arose, essentially, whenever good faith and fair dealing demanded disclosure; and it existed not as an implied term of the insurance contract, nor as a collateral contract, but as a separate and independent rule of law. It followed from the latter observation that the 'following' market were not caught by the duty of disclosure, because they had never employed D and could not be vicariously liable for him; their liability could arise only by virtue of an implied contractual term, and the duty of disclosure was not of that character. But Hodge and Skandia *were* under such a duty on the special facts of the case. Admittedly, the period of liability should be confined to those intervals during which D was actually employed by each insurer, but knowledge acquired while D was in the service of Hodge could nevertheless be material to a breach of duty of non-disclosure on the part of Skandia, his succeeding employers. The fact that D not only knew of L's fraud, but also knew that the banks had no means of discovering it, and chose to enter into further insurances with the banks knowing that these too were subject to the concealed risk of further fraud and resultant invalidity, pointed compellingly in favour of a duty in this case. As Steyn J remarked, if good faith and fair dealing were to have any meaning in such a context, they must have required D to place the banks in possession of the facts.

Steyn J went on to hold that (notwithstanding a dictum of Scrutton J in *Glasgow Assurance Corp Ltd v William Symondson & Co* (1911) 104 LT 254, 258) this duty could be actionable in damages, and that the remedial consequences of a breach were not restricted to the repayment of the premiums. In contradistinction to the remedy of avoidance of the policy, the criterion in this context was whether the insured could prove that the non-disclosure induced him personally to enter into the contract; the impact of the omission upon a notional assured was irrelevant here.

Steyn J also held that the obligation of disclosure could be rationalised as a duty of care in tort. He conceded that the two-tier approach advocated by Lord Wilberforce in *Anns v Merton London Borough Council* [1977] 2 All ER 492 at 498–99, did not afford a universal or mechanical formula for the establishment of duties of care in tort, and that something more than a mere foresight on D's part as to the *possibility* of financial damage to the banks would be necessary to establish tortious liability in this case; such losses would need to have been foreseeable as an obvious and manifest risk, rather than merely as a possible one. But once this requirement was satisfied, the mere fact that the liability asserted might be characterised as a liability for an omission, or as a liability for the independent wrongful act of a third party, did not compel its rejection. There was no absolute principle that a defendant could not be liable in tort for the independent wrongs of a third party, and the wrongs alleged here were not, having regard to the parties' prior relationship, accurately classified as mere omissions. Steyn J accepted that it was still necessary, for the purposes of the law of tort, to differentiate between malfeasance and non-feasance, however difficult the drawing of that conceptual line might prove in practice. His refusal to characterise this case as one of pure omission may, perhaps, be seen as recognising an example of an obligation of positive conduct which can arise from a defendant's undertaking of responsibility for the task in question: see *Christchurch Drainage Board v Brown* (1987) *The Times*, 26 October but cf the insurance case of *The Zephyr* [1985] 2 Lloyd's Rep 529.

Nor, in Steyn J's opinion, was an action in tort decisively prohibited by Lord Scarman's contention in *Tai Hing Cotton Mill Ltd v Liu Chong Hing Bank Ltd* [1985] 2 All ER 947 at 957 (see All ER Rev 1985, p 28) that the terms of a commercial contract should be seen as exclusively definitive of the parties' obligations, thereby ousting any further, extraneous duties in tort. Although generally disposed to accept this argument as correct, Steyn J pointed out that Lord Scarman's words were tentatively expressed, and must be regarded as subject to at least one exception in the case of a negligent misstatement which induces a contract: *Esso Petroleum Co Ltd v Mardon* [1976] 2 All ER 5. The instant case represented a further legitimate exception.

Steyn J went on to to hold that it was just and reasonable to impose liability in this case, and that the second of Lord Wilberforce's criteria of negligence liability in *Anns* was accordingly satisfied. None of the 'negative' reasons advanced by the insurers against the discovery of a duty of care was wholly convincing, and a suggestion that liability in this case would open the flood-gates to excessive claims was actually described by the judge as 'alarmist'. More significantly, there were strong positive reasons in favour of sustaining the duty. Among these were the manifest demands of justice and fair dealing, and the increasing necessity to eradicate commercial fraud.

The remainder of Steyn J's judgment was relatively straightforward. He held that other asserted grounds of liability on the part of the insurers failed; that the insurers had been in breach of their duties of utmost good faith and of care in failing to disclose L's fraud; that these breaches caused the banks' losses (with the exception of the January 1980 loan, which had already been made when the fraud was discovered by D); that the resultant financial damage was not too remote to be recoverable; and that there had been no significant breach of their reciprocal obligations, sufficient to preclude recovery, on the part of the banks. Each of these questions was interestingly argued, and their treatment would reward a closer analysis than the present confines can afford.

Finally, Steyn J considered the matter of contributory negligence. He accepted, of course, that the claim in negligence was capable in principle of being defeated or diminished by proof that the banks had failed to take reasonable care for the protection of their own interests. But the burden of proof was upon the insurers, and on the present facts it could not be said that the majority of the banks had contravened accepted canons of ordinary prudence in failing to investigate B's affairs more rigorously. The solitary exception was the Chemical Bank, whose damages were reduced by 50%.

But the claim for breach of the duty of utmost good faith was, conceptually, quite another matter. Liability under this category was wholly independent of fault or of negligence and did not, in Steyn J's view, qualify as a liability in tort for the purposes of the Law Reform (Contributory Negligence) Act 1945. It followed that the apportionment provisions of the Act would have been inapplicable as a matter of principle, irrespective of whether the banks had failed to demonstrate ordinary prudence in their affairs.

Illegality of attendant transaction

We shall dwell only briefly upon *Euro-Diam Ltd v Bathhurst* [1987] 2 All ER 113, because the decision of Staughton J has now been upheld by the Court of Appeal: (1987) *The Independent*, 16 December. The case provides an interesting supplement to *Thackwell v Barclays Bank plc* [1986] 1 All ER 676 (see All ER Rev 1986, pp 28–31) and will be analysed in depth in next year's Review.

Suppliers of diamonds sent them abroad to West Germany under a transaction of sale and return. The accompanying invoice understated the value of the diamonds by some US$91,000, the object of this understatement being to enable the customer to avoid paying German customs duty. After the theft of the diamonds in Germany, the insurers refused to pay out on the suppliers' policy. They argued, first, that the suppliers were in breach of the term implied by s 41 of the Marine Insurance Act 1906, that the insured 'adventure' would be carried out in as lawful a manner as the suppliers could dictate, and secondly that the attendant illegality of the supply transaction sufficiently infected the insurance contract as to render it unenforceable at common law.

Staughton J rejected both defences. He held the Marine Insurance Act immaterial in this context because the references in s 41 to the insuring of an 'adventure' had no application to a non-marine insurance contract relating to goods alone; and he doubted whether, in any event, the requirement imposed by s 41 that the adventure be pursued in a 'lawful manner' extends to the compliance with foreign laws. On the position at common law, Staughton J held (following, inter alia, the decision of Browne J in *Pye Ltd v BG Transport Service Ltd* [1966] 2 Lloyd's Rep 300) that the illegal transaction was not sufficiently closely related to the contract of insurance as to justify treating the insurance itself as illegal or unenforceable. The appropriate test was two-fold: first, does the plaintiff have to found his claim upon an illegal contract, or to plead such illegality in order to support his claim; and, secondly, is the plaintiff seeking recourse to the court in order to recover the proceeds of a crime, or assets so closely connected with an illegal activity as to render it offensive to the conscience of the court to award the claim? The first limb of this dual test was characterised by Staughton J as the *Bowmaker* principle (after *Bowmakers Ltd v Barnett Instruments Ltd* [1944] 2 All ER 579 at 582–83, per du Parcq LJ), and the second as the *Beresford* principle (after *Beresford v Royal Insurance Co Ltd* [1938] 2 All ER 602 at 607, per Lord Atkin); both were adopted and amplified by Hutchison J in the *Thackwell* case. If the answer in either case were affirmative, the claim should be denied; but if, as in the present proceedings, the claim neither involved the necessary invocation of an illegal transaction nor possessed so close an association with illegal activity as to render it obnoxious to the court, it should succeed.

The decision of Staughton J also contains some useful observations about the proper approach of the court to allegations that a claim is tainted by an illegality imposed by some foreign system of law.

Monopolies and mergers

During the year, two applications for judicial review were brought in respect of decisions by the Monopolies and Mergers Commission. The first arose in *R v Monopolies and Mergers Commission, ex p Elders IXL Ltd* [1987] 1 All ER 451. This Australian company sought to take over Allied-Lyons plc ('Allied') in October 1985, the bid being referred to the Monopolies and Mergers Commission on 5 December 1985. A central issue in the reference was the financing of the bid which was claimed to involve very substantial borrowings by Elders. Elders objected to disclosure of its detailed financing plans to Allied, but the Commission felt itself unable to carry out its statutory function fairly without giving Allied's senior management an opportunity of commenting on them. In reaching its decision, the Commission was influenced by the fact that it was the senior management of Allied, with their special knowledge of the company's business, who would be most able to make pertinent comments on the financial proposals made and their likely effect on the Allied business. The Commission felt that natural justice required that Allied should have this opportunity of comment on what was clearly a central issue.

Elders therefore made application for judicial review of this procedural decision and, since the reference was still pending, its application was heard on an expedited basis. Mann J found little difficulty however, in rejecting the application. From evidence given in camera on the details of the financing plan, he concluded that the Commission had been correct in its conclusion that it could not act fairly without revealing the essential details to Allied. He found that any detriment to Elders as a result of this disclosure could not be an overriding consideration, particularly in view of the fact that any disclosure to Allied would be in the terms of s 133 of the Fair Trading Act 'for the purpose of facilitating the performance of the Commission's functions . . .'. The criterion of the existence of such a purpose was subjective, not objective, and in this context Mann J referred to dicta by Lord Diplock in *Sweet v Parsley* [1969] 1 All ER 347 at 363–4. Underlying the judgment however, was the broader principle that while the rules of natural justice clearly apply to the Commission it must nevertheless, as a body carrying out an inquisitorial function, have a wide discretion as to the manner in which this is performed. If a merger is to be referred to the Commission for assessment of its likely effects on the public interest, the bidder's plans (including the financial details) are essential elements in the issues being investigated. Only in the most unusual circumstances could a bidder expect them to be kept a secret, at least from the target company's senior management.

A few weeks later, in *R v Monopolies and Mergers Commission, ex p Matthew Brown plc* [1987] 1 All ER 463 another application for judicial review was presented, in this case the challenge being not merely against a procedural decision in the course of the enquiry but against the actual report itself. The report had concluded that a proposed takeover of Matthew Brown plc by Scottish and Newcastle Breweries plc was not against the public interest and the bid itself had subsequently narrowly failed (it ultimately succeeded in late 1987).

The point of the challenge by Matthew Brown to the Commission's decision was that some of the evidence given by Scottish and Newcastle as to the exact concentration of licensed premises in North and West Cumbria had not been passed on to them and that therefore they had been prejudiced. Again on the facts, Macpherson J was able without difficulty to dimiss the claim. He found that it was clear that Matthew Brown had an ample opportunity of being heard on this particular issue, and that the maps and other documents whose non-production was complained about merely set out (in a slightly different form) evidence that was already thoroughly familiar to, and had been discussed by, all parties, and was publicly available. What is perhaps more important in this judgment is the review of the necessary elements in any decision-making process of inquisitorial bodies such as the Commission. In a central passage Macpherson J stated (ibid at 469),

> 'The Commission establishes, within the framework of the Fair Trading Act 1973, its own procedure and its own approach to each individual reference. Of course, it must heed all representations made either way. It has a discretion which is broad, which should not be prescribed or inflexible. The concept of fairness is itself flexible and should not be subject to the Court laying down rules or steps which have to be followed. The question in each case is whether

the Commission has adopted a procedure so unfair that no reasonable commission or group would have adopted it, so that it can be said to have acted with manifest unfairness. Provided each party has its mind brought to bear upon the relevant issues it is not in my judgment for the Court to lay down rules as to how each group should act in any particular inquiry.'

These two cases illustrate that, while the High Court will be ready to intervene in any case of manifest unfairness to a party involved in a reference to the Commission, the Commission remains master of its own proceedings and timetable. In view of the dismissal of both applications, the court did not have to rule on the difficult question (also touched upon in *Hoffman-La Roche & Co v Secretary of State for Trade and Industry* [1975] AC 295; [1974] 2 All ER 1128) of the nature of the remedy available to a successful applicant for judicial review in such circumstances. The ultimate remedy would appear to be the quashing of the relevant report or reference. This might, however, prove a victory of doubtful value for a dissatisfied party which might then be forced to undergo the delay and expense of a fresh reference, an outcome which the High Court might seek to avoid in all save the most extreme cases of procedural unfairness.

Sale of goods

Nemo dat quod non habet

In *National Employers' Mutual General Insurance Association Ltd v Jones* [1987] 3 All ER 385, the Court of Appeal considered the effect of s 9 of the Factors Act 1889, and s 25(1) of the Sale of Goods Act 1979, upon a series of purported sales, originating in a transaction between some thieves and the first in a chain of innocent purchasers. It was obvious that the thieves gained no title, and that ss 9 and 25(1) did not apply to the purported sale between the thieves and the first innocent purchaser, because the thieves had not 'bought or agreed to buy' the goods. By a majority, the court held that ss 9 and 25(1) were also incapable of creating a good title in favour of the subsequent acquirers, because none of the succeeding dispositions qualified as a sale, or as an agreement to sell, within the meaning of the subsection. However many later transactions occurred, and however innocent the purported purchasers, the owner's title prevailed.

The sequence of events upon which this conclusion was based was as follows. The plaintiff insurers were asserting, by subrogation, the title to a car which had originally belonged to a Miss Hopkin. The car had been stolen from Miss Hopkin and sold by the thieves to Lacey, who sold it to Thomas, who sold it to Autochoice, who sold it to Mid-Glamorgan Motors, who sold it to the defendant Jones. All of these parties appear to have acted in good faith. In his defence, Jones pleaded ss 9 and 25, contending that Mid-Glamorgan were buyers in possession with the consent of their own sellers Autochoice, and that Mid-Glamorgan could therefore pass as good a title to Jones as if they had been mercantile agents in possession of the car with the consent of the true owner (Miss Hopkin) and as if s 2(1) of the Factors Act 1889 had accordingly applied to the Mid-Glamorgan-Jones sale. May and Croom-Johnson LJJ rejected this argument, holding that Mid-Glamorgan had not 'bought or agreed to buy' the goods for the purposes of ss 9 and 25.

In so deciding, the court discarded several rival versions of the impact of ss 9 and 25(1) on post-theft dispositions. Under the most dramatic version, all of the transactions (including that whereby the thieves disposed of the goods) were to be regarded as involving the supposed purchaser in buying (or agreeing to buy) the goods. Once that supposed purchaser got possession, he could create a good title in a subsequent supposed purchaser, because he was deemed to dispose of the goods 'as a merchantile agent in possession of the goods with the consent of the owner.' This analysis would not, admittedly, enable the purchaser from the thieves to assert a new title, but it would enable him to create one in his own purchaser; and so on, down the line. We shall return shortly to the reasons why this version of ss 9 and 25(1) was found wanting.

The court also rejected certain analyses of ss 9 and 25(1) which had sought to sustain the owner's interest. For example, it had been suggested that the word 'owner' at the end of the subsection should be construed as 'original seller' whenever these two parties were different. It would follow from this that the innocent purchaser whose title was in question could assert no better title against the true owner than that original seller himself. Of course, the 'original seller' in this context would be the party with whose consent the innocent purchaser's own immediate vendor had got possession prior to the purported sale to the innocent purchaser himself; in other words, he would be the seller at one remove from the innocent purchaser whose title was directly in question. Professor Goode (following Professor Battersby and Mr Preston in (1975) 38 MLR 77) had sought to bridge the divide between the two expressions by rephrasing the word 'owner' as 'relevant owner', meaning 'the owner of the title which is the subject of the transaction'. Such a construction would enable only a possessory title to pass to the innocent purchaser when that was the total of the original seller's own entitlement, leaving the true owner's title unaffected.

If either of these versions were the correct interpretation of ss 9 and 25(1), however, it would be hard to explain why the subsection also contains a literal reference to 'the original seller'. It is unlikely that Sir Mackenzie Chalmers would have used two different phrases to connote the same party within a single subsection. Nor is it easy to understand why ss 9 and 25(1) would be necessary to produce the transfer of a mere possessory title from original seller to immediate seller to innocent purchaser, when such title can be transmitted by delivery alone (which ss 9 and 25(1) requires in order to operate). Nor, it seems, can such an analysis be given substance by adopting the view that a possession gained by theft or other unlawful dispossession is incapable of being enforced against third parties (see *Thackwell v Barclay's Bank plc* [1986] 1 All ER 676 at 689, per Hutchison J, but cf our discussion in All ER Rev 1986, p 25), and therefore that at common law a possession defensible against third parties would have been incapable of transmission by delivery alone. If a possessory title of this type cannot be improved, and rendered capable of vindication against third parties, by delivery alone, it is hard to see how s 25(1) reinforces it at all.

Both May and Croom-Johnson LJJ found the proposed glosses upon the word 'owner' artificial, and preferred to attach to the word its ordinary meaning. But they found the contrary version of ss 9 and 25(1) (which would have enabled the owner's title to be eclipsed by the second purported sale) no more convincing, agreeing with Atiyah that it seemed '. . . so contrary to everything one knows about the law that it cannot be right'. In their view, the answer lay in a proper construction of the words 'bought or agreed to buy', 'seller', and 'sale'. The coherence of that answer is, with respect, open to question.

According to May LJ, 'the essence of sale is the transfer of the ownership or general property in goods from a seller to a buyer for a price', and the words 'seller' and 'buyer' are to be construed accordingly. It follows that ss 9 and 25(1) can take effect only when there is 'a transaction in which the general property . . . has been acquired or it has been agreed should be acquired'. A purported sale by a thief does not qualify for this purpose because he has no general property capable of being transmitted; accordingly, the thief's purported purchaser has not, in the statutory sense, bought or agreed to buy the goods at all. When, moreover, the thief's purported purchaser himself purports to sell the goods, that transaction fails equally to qualify as a sale, and the immediate parties fail equally to qualify as seller and buyer, for the purposes of ss 9 and 25(1). Although May LJ does not specifically explain the latter conclusion, it is presumably founded on the fact that the intermediate purchaser-vendor again has no general property capable of being transmitted.

The general position governing successive dispositions by non-owners was therefore summarised by May LJ as follows ([1987] 3 All ER at 396):

> 'If the original transferor is a thief from the true owner, then he has never acquired property in the goods and no purported "sale" by him or by anyone to whom he may have purported to "sell" the goods can attract the consequences of s 9 of the 1889 Act or s 25 of the 1979 Act . . . there is only scope for s 25 to operate at all where the general property in the goods passed at some stage, at least temporarily, to a transferee from [*the original owner*].'

The reference to a purely temporary passing of property appears to have been inserted by May LJ to account for cases where the dishonest party acquired his possession from the true owner under a transaction voidable for fraud. Such a disposition could, in May LJ's view, qualify as a sale and attract ss 9 and 25(1), thereby protecting subsequent innocent purchasers, even (presumably) although the vitiated sale had since been avoided.

A similar approach was taken by Croom-Johnson LJ. In his view, ss 9 and 25(1) require a 'valid' or 'effective' transaction between the innocent purchaser's own immediate vendor and the party (sometimes called the original seller) who has purportedly sold, or agreed to sell, the goods to the immediate vendor. To be valid or effective, the transaction must be 'capable of transferring the true title'. The references to buying and selling in ss 9 and 25(1) therefore presuppose 'a valid transaction by or on behalf of the true owner at some stage'.

Croom-Johnson LJ conceded that the original seller might make a valid or effective sale even though he was not the owner of the goods at the time, because he may have been acting as an agent with the owner's authority. Croom-Johnson LJ might also have mentioned the type of sale discussed by Mustill J in *The Elafi* [1982] 1 All ER 208 at 215, where a seller undertakes to bring about the transmission of some third party's property to the buyer, without channelling the property through himself and without forfeiting his own position as a principal in the transaction. Such a disposition seems to offer a more convincing example of any possible difference of identity between original seller and owner than a sale by an agent, because in the latter case the seller is arguably the owner on whose behalf the goods are sold. It is unfortunate that Croom-Johnson LJ did not expressly allow such contracts a place within the operation of ss 9 and 25(1), and difficult to see how they could be brought within May LJ's definition of the necessary transaction at all.

The foregoing represents one example of a lack of exact correspondence between the majority judgments. Another example can be found in their Lordships' treatment of voidable sales. When May LJ spoke of such contracts, it was in the apparent context of the original seller's acquisition of title: he could be a seller to the immediate vendor if he had once gained property, even though he had subsequently been divested of that property by avoidance. In Croom-Johnson LJ's judgment, however, the purported buyer under the transaction between the original seller and the immediate vendor is regarded as having bought or agreed to buy the goods even though *that transaction itself* may be voidable:

> 'Buying and selling . . . means the transfer of title, of ownership. Agreeing to buy or sell means a binding agreement to the same effect. On this interpretation, the section requires an effective transaction, even though it may later be avoided by one of the parties on sufficient grounds ([1987] 3 All ER at 398).'

Both arguments may well be tenable; but the divergence contributes to a suspicion that the majority position was insufficiently co-ordinated and developed.

A more serious criticism of the majority analysis, however, is that it imposes an unacceptably rigid definition upon the words 'bought or agreed to buy', 'seller' and 'sale'. Why should these expressions not equally apply to a purported disposal of full proprietary rights by someone who has never had, and never stands any chance of getting, the property in the goods? The absence of property from the purported seller would not inhibit the purported buyer from exercising a remedy under s 12(1) of the 1979 Act, whereby in 'a contract of sale' there is an implied condition 'on the part of the seller' that 'he has the right to sell the goods'; indeed, this represents the very situation in which s 12(1) was designed to be invoked. A Court of Appeal which found it unpalatable to construe two different phrases within a single subsection (ie, 'original seller' and 'owner') as referring to the same person might also have found it unpalatable to attach two different meanings to the same phrase (ie 'seller' or 'sale') within the perimeter of a single statute. The point is incisively made by the dissenting judge, Sir Denys Buckley ([1987] 3 All ER 385 at 403–404):

> 'When a thief contracts to sell stolen property, the fact that he cannot transmit a good title in that property to the purchaser does not . . . mean that he has not contracted to sell it. He has contracted to sell it, and can be made liable in damages if and when the purchaser suffers damage by reason of the thief's breach of contract by selling without a good title.'

The force of these remarks can be judged by examining *Butterworth v Kingsway Motors Ltd* [1954] 2 All ER 694. At first sight, that decision might be thought to support the majority in *Jones*. There was an initially unlawful sale, followed by a chain of further dispositions to innocent purchasers, the last of whom succeeded in an action against his immediate predecessor for breach of the implied condition as to title. Nobody appears to have thought of arguing ss 9 or 25 in favour of the transmission of title to the second and subsequent purchasers. But the fact that the ultimate purchaser succeeded in an action under s 12 shows that, for the purposes of that section at least, the disposition to him was regarded as a contract of sale.

Certainly it is difficult to accept the suggestion in May LJ's judgment that the disposition by the alleged buyer in possession cannot qualify as a 'sale' within ss 9 and 25(1) unless the buyer in possession has, or is capable of acquiring, the property in the goods. The absence of property from the intermediate vendor constitutes the very reason for the existence of these provisions as exceptions to the rule nemo dat. If a purported *sale* in such circumstances is ineffective for the purposes of ss 9 and 25(1), the same is presumably true of a purported *pledge*; the transaction cannot truly constitute a pledge for the purposes of ss 9 and 25(1) unless the supposed pledgor actually enjoys the estate which he purports to confer by way of pledge, or is capable of acquiring it by virtue of some preceding transaction to which the proprietor of that interest is a party. But even if this reasoning were correct, it is not easy to see why the transaction between the intermediate disponor and the ultimate acquirer might not qualify as a 'disposition' within ss 9 and 25(1), whether it succeeds as a valid and effective sale or pledge, or not. (Cf the definition of the word 'disposition', as used in s 24 of the 1979 Act, given by Megaw LJ in *Worcester Works Finance Ltd v Cooden Engineering Co Ltd* [1971] 3 All ER 708 at 714, and cited with approval by Lloyd LJ in *Shaw v Commissioner of Police of the Metropolis* [1987] 3 All ER 405 at 410.) If the contrary were true, however, and the transaction between the intermediate disponor and the ultimate acquirer *were*, for example, identifiable as a 'sale', it might then seem irrational to attach a more exacting meaning to the words 'bought or agreed to buy' at the beginning of ss 9 and 25(1) than to the word 'sale' in the middle of it. It could, admittedly, be said in response that the word 'sale', as defined in s 2(4) of the Act, requires nothing less than an actual transfer of property between seller and buyer, whereas an agreement to sell (which is what the opening words to ss 9 and 25(1) partially contemplate) requires no such actual transmission. But a literal adherence to this distinction would entail the result that a sale, for the purposes of s 25(1), could be made only by a party who had the property to pass in the first place. In short, ss 9 and 25(1) would be capable of invocation only by those innocent purchasers who did not need it, because their immediate vendors already had title.

Reservations may also be expressed about certain remarks by Moore J in *Brandon v Leckie* (1972) 29 DLR (3d) 633, which was one of two Commonwealth authorities relied upon by the majority in *Jones* (see also *Elwin v O'Regan and Maxwell* [1971] NZLR 1124). Although the principal basis of his decision appears to have been that the intermediate disponor was not someone who had bought or agreed to buy the goods, Moore J also appears to suggest at one point that s 25(1) – or s 27(2) of the equivalent Albertan statute – applies only between a buyer and seller, and 'does not remove any right accruing in the true owner'. This observation may mean simply that the supposed buyer receives the supposed seller's possessory title, in which event s 25(1) is at worst platitudinous. But it may also mean that the innocent purchaser in a case like *Brandon* or *Jones*, while remaining exposed to an action for conversion by the true owner, is deemed as between himself and his immediate vendor to have gained the property in the goods and can therefore have no remedy against him under s 12(1) of the Act. A conclusion which contrives to give the ultimate acquirer the worst of both worlds in this manner has little to commend it, not least because it seems to deny the very function of ss 9 and 25(1) as an exception to the nemo dat rule.

In the final analysis, it seems impossible to disagree with Sir Denys Buckley's minority conclusion that the literal wording and common sense interpretation of ss 9 and 25(1) point ineluctably in favour of the ultimate innocent purchaser. Moreover, Sir Denys Buckley believed that such a result, enabling the title of the original owner to be occluded from the moment of the second innocent purchase in a series of post-theft dispositions, was justifiable on policy grounds ([1987] 3 All ER 385 at 403):

> 'The section as I would construe it confers no protection on a purchaser from a thief. Such a purchaser might by diligent inquiry have been able to discover that his vendor was a thief. The section, so construed, would, however, enable that purchaser to confer on an innocent purchaser from him an unassailable title. The latter purchaser would be unlikely to be aware of any circumstance that would put him on inquiry whether his vendor's vendor had stolen the goods. In such a case it would not, in my view, be at all irrational that the legislature should consider that it would be right to let the loss resulting from the theft rest where it falls on the original owner, who would, as was pointed out in argument, very probably be insured, rather than on the innocent purchaser.'

Having thus concluded, however, Sir Denys Buckley was at pains to remark that the operation of the section

> 'is not to strike from the hand of the original true owner of the goods his title of ownership, but to place in the hand of him who has acquired those goods from the notional mercantile agent an impregnable shield which makes it impossible thenceforth for the original true owner to assert his original title against him who has the goods (ibid at 405).'

Jones' case was consulted, but found to be of no assistance, by Lloyd LJ in *Shaw v Commissioner of Police of the Metropolis* [1987] 3 All ER 405. A rogue was allowed into possession of a Porsche car by a proposed vendor, whom the rogue had persuaded to sign a document stating that the rogue had bought the car and that the proposed vendor had no further responsibility for it. This document was, in fact, at variance with the actual agreement between the parties: the rogue had claimed to have a purchaser for the car, and its entrustment to him was solely for the purpose of enabling him to conclude a sale on the proposed vendor's behalf. The Court of Appeal refused to disturb Master Grant's finding that there was no supplementary agreement between the proposed vendor and the rogue, whereby the latter would buy the car on his own behalf if unable to sell it on behalf of the proposed vendor.

The rogue took the car and entered into an agreement to sell it to a bona fide purchaser (the plaintiffs). He did not purport to transfer the property in the car outright, but merely agreed that property should pass when he was paid. Unfortunately for the rogue, the innocent purchaser's bank refused to pay him cash on the strength of the innocent purchaser's draft. He thereupon disappeared. The amount of the draft was never deducted from the innocent purchaser's account, and the car eventually found its way into the hands of the police, who now instituted interpleader proceedings to determine the location of title as between the original owner ('the claimant') and the innocent purchaser ('the plaintiffs').

The rogue was not a mercantile agent, so that there was no prospect of the plaintiffs' asserting a good title under s 2(1) of the Factors Act 1889. Nor, in the Court of Appeal's view, could the plaintiffs rely on s 25(1) of the Sale of Goods Act 1979. The rogue had not 'bought or agreed to buy' the car from the claimant, but had merely contracted to act as agent for its sale to a third party. The court also held, disagreeing on this point with Master Grant, that neither the car registration document nor various other documents handed to the rogue (viz, the notification of sale or transfer slip and the 'certificate' mentioned above) were documents of title for the purposes of s 25(1). Lloyd LJ cited on this point *Joblin v Watkins & Roseveare (Motors) Ltd* [1949] 1 All ER 47, *Pearson v Rose & Young Ltd* [1950] 2 All ER 1027 at 1033, per Denning LJ, and *Central Newbury Car Auctions Ltd v Unity Finance Ltd* [1956] 3 All ER 905, 914 per Hodson LJ; he might also have mentioned *Beverley Acceptances Ltd v Oakley* [1982] RTR 417 at 432–33, 437 per Donaldson and Slade LJJ, although cf Lord Denning MR at 424–25 (a decision on the Factors Act 1889).

These conclusions reduced the plaintiffs to a defence based on s 21 of the 1979 Act, which embodies the notion of estoppel. Section 21 states that 'where goods are sold by a person who is not their owner', the basic principle of nemo dat quod non habet applies unless 'the owner . . . is by his conduct precluded from denying the seller's authority to sell'. The Court of Appeal conceded that the documentation given to the rogue by the claimant, coupled with the possession of the car itself, was sufficient in principle to amount to a representation that the rogue had become the owner of the car; in this respect, the plaintiffs' position could be likened to that of the innocent purchasers in *Henderson & Co v Williams* [1895] 1 QB 521 and *Eastern Distributors Ltd v Goldring* [1957] 2 All ER 525. But the operation of the statutory estoppel was, in the court's opinion, conditional upon the prefatory phrase 'where goods are sold . . .'. Unless the intermediate party had actually sold the goods to the innocent purchaser, s 21 could have no application in that innocent purchaser's favour. In this case, the transaction between the rogue and the plaintiffs did not constitute a 'sale' as defined by s 2(4) of the 1979 Act, but merely an 'agreement to sell' as defined by s 2(5).

In reaching this conclusion, Lloyd drew support from two considerations. The first was the observation by Megaw LJ in *Worcester Works Finance Ltd v Cooden Engineering Co Ltd* [1971] 3 All ER 708 at 714, that the phrase 'sale, pledge or other disposition' in ss 24 and 25 of the 1979 Act must involve some transfer of an interest in property, in the technical sense of the word 'property', as contrasted with mere possession. If the expression 'disposition' were to be thus limited, so, in his Lordship's view, should the word 'sold' in s 21. Since an agreement to sell involves no transfer of property, the present transaction failed to qualify for the purposes of s 21. In a sense, therefore, this was not a case of nemo dat at all.

Secondly, Lloyd LJ remarked that a victory for the plaintiffs under s 21 would enable them to keep a chattel for which, in the event, they had not paid. Although the claimant had been unusually credulous, it would have affronted the court's sense of justice if the plaintiffs were entitled to deprive him of the property in his car for nothing. Whereas this observation is true on the particular facts of *Shaw*, however, it does not necessarily follow that the innocent purchaser's acquisition of title under s 21 will always be contemporaneous with his payment for the goods. The sale between him and the intermediate vendor may stipulate some further deferral of the passing of property beyond the time of payment itself, or it may provide for the passing of property in advance of payment.

Re St Mary's, Barton-on-Humber [1987] 2 All ER 861 involved the disposal of certain church artefacts (the property of the parish) by the churchwardens, without a faculty. The churchwardens disposed of the artefacts (a royal coat of arms and an iron-bound parish chest) in the evident belief that they were of little value; in fact, after several changes of ownership and a substantial degree of restoration, the coat of arms was valued at a minimum of £9,000 as against an original sale price of £50 (the chest, regrettably, remained untraced). In denying the availability of any form of 'retrospective' faculty, Chancellor His Honour Judge Goodman also refused, on the particular facts, to grant a confirmatory faculty legalising for the future what had been done in the past. The decision is of passing interest to commercial lawyers because of Chancellor His Honour Judge Goodman's stern warning to antique dealers and other prospective purchasers of church property, 'who must be taken to know of the existence of the faculty jurisdiction', against purchasing such artefacts without satisfactory evidence that those purporting to sell the property had the proper authority for doing so: (ibid at 876). The Chancellor also believed that it would not be proper for the parish to be deprived of the coat of arms merely because, having been illegally sold, it had then been gratuitously restored by another person. The result was that Asprey's, who were the ultimate purchasers of the coat of arms and who had been found to have acted imprudently in failing to make the appropriate inquiries, were compelled to surrender it to the parish. It would be interesting to speculate about the rights of the purchaser against the churchwardens in such a situation (cf the remarks by Mustill J in *The Elafi* [1982] 1 All ER 208 at 215).

Reasonable fitness for purpose

The decision of the deputy judge in *Wormell v RHM Agriculture (East) Ltd* [1986] 1 All ER 769, (see All ER Rev 1986, pp 47–48), has been reversed by the Court of Appeal: [1987] 3 All ER 75. It will be recalled that the claim of the plaintiff farmer had succeeded on the ground that the instructions displayed upon the defendants' weedkiller were misleading, thereby rendering the product itself not reasonably fit for its purpose. The deputy judge had accepted the plaintiff's assertion that a warning exhibited on the container, cautioning the user against applying the weedkiller beyond a certain stage of crop-growth, could reasonably have been construed as adverting only to the risk of crop-damage in the event of an application outside the recommended period, and not as indicating that the weedkiller would be less effective in performing its intended function outside that period. In reversing this decision, the Court of Appeal did not deny that, as a matter of principle, instructions supplied with goods should count as part of the goods themselves for the purpose of evaluating merchantability or reasonable fitness. Rather, the Court of Appeal grounded its reversal upon the proper interpretation to be drawn from the present instructions. In the court's opinion, the references therein to crop growth stages and competitive growing, coupled with the unqualified statement that spraying after the stated growth stages was 'not recommended', defeated any argument that the misadventure against which the instructions were seeking to warn the user could reasonably have been construed as exuberant crop damage alone, rather than any reduced potency in the weedkiller as such. Nor, in the view of Nicholls LJ, did a later, explicit warning in the instructions about crop-damage specifically justify any reasonable inference that it was against that peril alone that the whole of the instructions was designed to warn the user. Although their message might have been more clearly expressed, the instructions clearly put the plaintiff upon notice not to use the weedkiller at the time when he used it; and that created a very strong inference that no responsibility whatever was being undertaken for the efficacy of the product beyond that period (ibid at 82), per Nicholls J:

> 'The instructions, or recommendations, put the user on notice not to use the product at that time. . . . [*They*] . . . are entitled to treat that as the clear starting point . . . . The starting point is that unsatisfactory results following from, and caused by, the use of a product otherwise than in accordance with manufacturers' recommendations are not, without more, results which should surprise the user, or results of which he can reasonably complain.'

Such reasoning seems, with respect, to be unexceptionable, and might be supported by reference to *Heil v Hedges* [1951] 1 TLR 512 (the case of the under-done pork chop).

Reasonable fitness for purpose, merchantable quality and defective containers

In *Aswan Engineering Establishment Co v Lupdine Ltd* [1987] 1 All ER 135, Aswan were a construction company which had purchased a large quantity of 'Lupguard' waterproofing compound from the first defendants, Lupdine. The compound was supplied to Aswan in heavy duty plastic pails, which Lupdine had previously acquired from the manufacturers, Thurgar Bolle ('TB'). Property in both the pails and the Lupguard passed from Lupdine to Aswan under the contract of sale.

Aswan were carrying on business in Kuwait, and the pails and their contents were duly shipped there by Aswan. On their arrival, they were left, still within their maritime containers, upon the quayside in full sunshine. The pails, which had been stacked 5 or 6 high inside the shipping containers, eventually collapsed in the heat and the Lupguard was effectively lost. Aswan successfully sued Lupdine for breach of contract, and no appeal was brought against that aspect of Neil J's decision. The present appeal concerned two related claims, both involving the pail manufacturers, TB. First, Lupdine appealed against the trial judge's decision that TB were not in breach of either s 14(2) or s 14(3) of the Sale of

Goods Act 1979 in supplying the plastic pails to Lupdine. Secondly, Aswan appealed against the trial judge's decision that TB were not liable to Aswan in negligence for the loss of the Lupguard.

The contract claim

(i) Merchantable quality

The principal question for the Court of Appeal was whether, as Lupdine had contended, s 14(6) of the Sale of Goods Act 1979—which defines 'merchantable quality' for the purpose of the term as to merchantability implied by s 14(2)—had changed the law. There seemed to be little doubt that under the old statutory obligation (s 14(2) of the Sale of Goods Act 1893) a seller could satisfy the implied term as to merchantable quality by showing that the goods which he had supplied were reasonably capable of being used for any one or more of the purposes for which goods of the type contracted-for would commonly be used: see, eg, Lord Wright's speech in *Canada Atlantic Grain Export Co v Eilers* (1929) 35 Ll L Rep 206 at 213. Conversely, goods were unmerchantable if they were 'of no use for any purpose for which such goods would normally be used': see, again, Lord Wright in *Cammell Laird & Co Ltd v Manganese Bronze & Brass Co Ltd* [1934] AC 402 at 430. It is true that a rival line of authority had sought to place equal emphasis not merely upon the common purpose for which the contractual goods would be bought, but upon the price at which the instant goods had been sold (a good example being the judgment of Dixon J in *Grant v Australian Knitting Mills* (1933) 50 CLR 387 at 418). Such authorities maintained that the essential question was whether a reasonable buyer, knowing of the defects in the relevant goods, would have purchased them without substantial abatement of price. But in many respects these two criteria could be regarded as different formulations of the same fundamental question; and in *Henry Kendall & Sons Ltd v William Lillico & Sons Ltd* [1969] 2 AC 31 at 37, Lord Reid adopted a combination of the two approaches as representing the most acceptable modern statement of the common law standard of merchantable quality. The result, according to Lloyd LJ in the *Aswan* case, was that goods would be held to satisfy this standard at common law even though they did not fulfil every purpose within a range of purposes for which goods were normally bought under that description. It was, in the Lord Justice's words ([1987] 1 All ER 135 at 145):
'... sufficient that they were suitable for one or more such purpose without abatement of price since, if they were, they were commercially saleable under that description'.

TB maintained that the position was effectively unchanged under s 14(6) of the 1979 Act, which endeavoured for the first time to give a statutory definition of merchantable quality. They pointed, inter alia, to the opinion of Lord Denning MR in *The Hansa Nord* [1976] QB 44 at 62, who evidently believed that the statutory definition was equally appropriate for contracts made before the parent statute came into force. It followed, in TB's contention, that since their plastic pails were suitable for *some* (indeed many) of the normal purposes for which they might be acquired, the mere fact that they were not universally suitable for exportation to Kuwait when stacked and treated in the manner involved in this case did not render them unmerchantable within the statutory meaning. Adequacy for exportation to most countries and in most normal conditions was, in their view, sufficient to meet the statutory standard.

Lupdine's counter-argument fastened on the particular wording of s 14(6), which required the goods to be 'as fit for the purpose *or purposes for which goods of that kind are commonly bought* as it is reasonable to expect having regard to any description applied to them, the price (if relevant) and all the other relevant circumstances' (emphasis added). In Lupdine's contention, the reference to 'purposes' now demanded that the goods should satisfy *every* normal function to which the goods might be put (including, on the present facts, export stacked 5 or 6 pails high in containers to Kuwait) before the goods could be properly characterised as merchantable.

The Court of Appeal rejected this wider construction, thereby preferring the view of the editor of Benjamin on *Sale* (2nd ed, 1981) para 801 and of Professor Atiyah in his *Sale of Goods* (7th ed, 1985) p 133 to those of Professor Goode in his *Commercial Law* (1982) p 261. The court drew support, inter alia, from certain words in s 14(3) of the 1979 Act, which deals with the implied condition as to fitness for purposes. Section 14(3) states that, once the appropriate conditions for the obligation have been met, the goods must be reasonably fit for their purpose 'whether or not that is a purpose for which such goods are commonly supplied'. Lloyd LJ held that ([1987] 1 All ER 135 at 147), far from assisting Lupdine, this provision actually militated against their argument; because it meant that, if s 14(2) *also* imposed an obligation that the goods be fit for *all* purposes, 'the distinction between the two subsections would be largely obliterated'. For this and other reasons, he held (and his fellow members of the Court of Appeal agreed) that the plastic pails were of merchantable quality here despite their failure to withstand the particular conditions to which they were subjected in Kuwait. In short, s 14(6) of the 1979 Act had not 'revolutionised the law' in the manner advanced by Lupdine. Lloyd LJ went on to observe that, even if Lupdine's version of the interpretation of s 14(6) had been the correct one, these pails would still have satisfied the demands of merchantable quality of the instant facts.

(ii) *Reasonable fitness for purpose*

This second aspect of Lupdine's claim was more readily resolved in TB's favour. Lloyd LJ held that Lupdine had placed no reliance upon TB's skill and judgment in supplying pails suitable for use in Kuwait and that the implied obligation contained in s 14(3) of the 1979 Act was accordingly inapplicable. In so concluding, he upheld the factual findings of the trial judge, with which, in Lloyd LJ's view, an appellate court should interfere only when a 'strong case' in favour of such intervention could be made out. No such case had been established here. The Lord Justice proceeded to remark that, even had the implied condition as to fitness been properly held to exist in the present circumstances, TB would not have been in breach of their obligations under s 14(3). The reason was (as Lord Wilberforce observed in *Ashington Piggeries Ltd v Christopher Hill Ltd* [1972] AC 441 at

97) that, the more broadly a buyer's purpose is defined for the purposes of that subsection, the less intensive or exacting is his responsibility. As Lloyd J expressed the position ([1987] 1 All ER at 149):

'If making known that the pails were wanted for export is a particular purpose within s 14(3), . . . then the purpose could hardly be wider. On the facts, these pails fell within that range. Indeed, so wide is the purpose cited that it could be said that the pails needed to be little, if anything, more than merchantable.'

The negligence claim

Aswan claimed that the loss of their Lupguard was occasioned by the negligence of TB in supplying the pails, when it was predictable that they would be put to use in high-temperature conditions and would therefore collapse, causing injury to their contents. Being aware of the difficulties of establishing a satisfactory cause of action in negligence when the injury consists of purely economic loss, Aswan sought to argue that the basis of their claim was damage to, or the destruction of, independent property belonging to them, such property consisting of the Lupguard contained in the pails. Lloyd LJ seemed willing to accept that the Lupguard might be regarded as a sufficiently distinct item of property from the pails themselves to enable Aswan to circumvent the apparent rule that no action in negligence lies against a manufacturer purely for the wasted cost to a consumer of the manufacturer's production of a defective product; Nicholls LJ was considerably more doubtful on this point. But both were agreed that, irrespective of the validity of the argument that this should be approached as a case of tortious damage to property rather than on of economic loss, the action in negligence should fail because it was not reasonably foreseeable to TB that the relevant misfortune would occur. As Lloyd LJ said (ibid at 153):

'. . . the Lupguard suffered damage because the pails were stacked six high and left for many days in temperatures of 70°C. Was that damage of the type that was reasonably foreseeable? In my opinion the answer is a categoric No.'

Furthermore, TB were entitled to assume that there would be 'some further discussion' between Lupdine and themselves before the pails were put to some special use. But no such discussion, or testing of their suitability, occurred before the pails were put to use on the Kuwait journey. This factor sufficed, as an alternative defence to TB, to bring the case within the exception from the ordinary principle of negligence liability, which Lord Atkin recognised in *Donoghue v Stevenson* [1932] AC 562 at 599, to cater for the event that the defendant would contemplate that the goods would be subjected to some intermediate examination before being put to the relevant use, and that such examination would reveal the defects in question.

Two final points

Two final points merit a brief mention. First, Lloyd LJ refused to accept that the trial judge had erred in requiring some element of reliance by Aswan upon TB's due exercise of proper care in manufacturing and supplying the pails. The basis for this objection had been that, since the instant case was to be approached as one of property damage rather than as one of economic loss, there had been no justification for imposing the reliance ingredient as Lord Roskill had done in *Junior Books Ltd v Veitchi Company Ltd* [1983] AC 520: this was, instead, a simple instance of basic negligence liability under the mainstream principle of *Donoghue v Stevenson*. But in Lloyd LJ's view it was entirely appropriate for the trial judge to regard Aswan's lack of reliance as material in determining TB's tortious obligations to them. The decision may, perhaps, have profited from a more rigorous analysis on this point.

Secondly, both Lloyd and Nicholls LJJ acknowledged, with variant degrees of certainty, the role of TB's contractual undertakings towards Lupdine in delineating their potential tortious obligations towards Aswan. Counsel for TB had argued that a finding of non-liability on TB's part towards Lupdine under the implied condition as to merchantable quality should be equally definitive and exclusive of TB's liability in negligence towards Aswan: in short, that 'remedies in contract and in tort must be harmonised' in a situation of this nature. Although Lloyd LJ's judgment falls some way short of unequivocal endorsement of this principle, that of Nicholls LJ moves somewhat closer to recognising the inter-reactive nature of contractual assumptions, and correlative tortious renunciations, of responsibility in 'series' transactions like that of manufacturer–retailer–consumer or employer–contractor–sub-contractor. Admittedly, aspects of his judgment seem to regard the absence of any applicable term as to merchantability in relation to the relevant defect as illustrating merely the non-foreseeability, in a tortious context, of the use and of the injury which occurred. But at other points it is, perhaps, just possible to read Nicholls LJ's judgment as favouring the recruitment of TB's *contractual* non-assumption of responsibility as an indicator of those tortious obligations which were (irrespective of the foreseeability of Aswan's damage) simply not being consensually assumed, or voluntarily undertaken, by TB. If this tentative interpretation of Nicholls LJ's judgment is supportable, the Lord Justice's approach seems to represent a beneficial doctrinal advance.

For discussion of two further important decisions in this area, *Bernstein v Pamson Motors (Golders Green) Ltd* [1987] 2 All ER 220 and *Rogers v Parish (Scarborough) Ltd* [1987] 2 All ER 232, see the title Consumer Law, pages 58–61, post.

Company Law

DD PRENTICE, MA, LLB, JD
Barrister, Fellow of Pembroke College, Oxford

Corporate capital

Re Scandinavian Bank Group plc [1987] 2 All ER 70, [1987] BCLC 220 is a case of considerable practical importance. A company applied for a reduction of capital and also for court approval of the restructuring of its capital so that it would be denominated in four currencies only one of which was sterling. The court endorsed the proposed restructuring reasoning that while a company's capital had to be stated in monetary terms this did not have to be sterling (or for that matter legal tender). Coupled with this, s 2(5)(a) of the Companies Act 1985 requiring the memorandum to state the 'amount of the share capital', did not require the capital to be stated in one single sum but it could be stated in terms of different amounts. Although not free from difficulty (see (1987) 104 LQR 168), the decision is of significant commercial importance; it will make the United Kingdom an attractive jurisdiction for foreign banks to incorporate subsidiaries as they will be able to denominate the subsidiary's share capital in the currency of the parent company and also more easily match liabilities with assets. One small point. If a company is a plc, it will have at least to have an allotted share capital of £50,000 as this is specifically required by ss 117(2) and 118(1) of the 1985 Act (see also s 370(6) which also prescribes a sterling figure).

Minority shareholder oppression

There has been the usual spate of cases under s 459 of the Companies Act 1985 which, as interpreted by the courts, is evolving as an effective remedy for minority shareholder oppression. The following are some of the points dealt with in the cases:

(i) Where a shareholder claims that a company's articles are subject to expectations and constraints limiting the exercise of the strict rights in the articles, the onus is on the shareholder to prove this. The initial presumption is that the articles 'adequately and exhaustively' state the basis on which the affairs of the company are to be conducted *(Re Posgate & Denby (Agencies) Ltd* [1987] BCLC 8). This is a useful reminder that the starting point for the analysis of the rights of a shareholder are the articles and that the burden is on the shareholder to prove that there are arrangements between the parties which constrain or qualify the terms of the articles (see *Tay Bok Choon v Tahansan Sdn Bhd* [1987] BCLC 472 where this burden was satisfied). In the case of a plc it will be virtually impossible for a shareholder to show that the articles are subject to any such constraints as with respect to such a company '[O]utside investors were entitled to assume that the whole of the constitution was contained in the articles, read, of course, together with the Companies Acts' *(Re Blue Arrow plc* [1987] BCLC 585 at 590).

(ii) Scott J held that the court lacks jurisdiction to make an interim award in anticipation of ultimately making an order under s 461 for the purchase of the petitioner's shares *(Re a company (No 004175 of 1986)* [1987] BCLC 574). This is in line with the general principle that the court only has jurisdiction to make an order under s 461 once there has been a finding of unfair prejudice under s 459 *(Re Bird Precision Bellows Ltd* [1985] BCLC 493). However, under s 37 of the Supreme Court Act 1981 the court has jurisdiction to appoint a receiver with respect to a company's affairs, and it will exercise this power to appoint a receiver to preserve the assets and manage the affairs of a quasi-partnership type of company in circumstances where it would make a similar appointment in the case of a partnership. The basic principle is that the court will make such an order so as to preserve the status quo until the petition under s 459 has been heard by the court *(Re a company (No 00596 of 1986)* [1987] BCLC 133).

(iii) A point of some practical importance was decided in *Re a company (No 007281 of 1986)* [1987] BCLC 593. In that case Vinelott J dismissed an application by a shareholder (3i) to have a petition presented against it struck out on the grounds that it was not involved in any dispute with the petitioner. In dismissing 3i's application, Vinelott J reasoned that an action for relief under s 459 was akin to an administration order as it could affect the rights of all the shareholders and therefore all shareholders should normally be joined. He recognized that in some situations it would be proper to dispense with this requirement to join all shareholders, although in the case of a company with the structure of a partnership this will seldom be the case.

(iv) *Re a company (No 00596 of 1986)* [1987] BCLC 133 is an important reminder that the alleged unfairly prejudicial conduct must relate to the manner in which the affairs of the company have been conducted. In that case a shareholder (without informing the other shareholders in the company) paid off a debt which the company owed to its bank and was accordingly subrogated to the bank's security. A petition was presented under s 459 alleging that this was unfairly prejudicial. Harman J dismissed the petition on the grounds that the discharging of the debt, and the acquisition of the bank's security, did not relate to the manner in which the affairs of the company were being conducted and therefore fell outside the terms of s 459. Of course, were the shareholder to use her position as a creditor to obtain subsequently an unfair advantage as a member, the matter would be different.

(v) Hoffman J has held that the exclusion of a member of a company from its affairs, and the payment to him of compensation for his shares under a standard pre-emption provision (which in the present case was triggered off when the member ceased to be an employee of the company), did not constitute unfair prejudice *(Re a company (No 004377 of 1986)* [1987] BCLC 94; see also Millett J in *Re a company No 003843 of 1986* [1987] BCLC 562 on a somewhat related point). He reasoned that on the facts of the case it was reasonably clear what was to happen when the members of the company were unable to co-operate and therefore the ouster of the petitioner from the affairs of the company on the payment of compensation was not unfairly prejudicial. There is dictum in the case that could be read as holding that a member ousted from a company and paid fair compensation under a standard pre-emption provision, would have no basis for an action under s 459. This would be an unfortunate development as it would almost constitute a charter for the majority to oust the minority. This would be particularly unfair, as the valuation of shares under s 461 will be different from that under a standard pre-emption provision; the latter method of valuation will make some discount for the fact that it is a minority holding that is being valued while the former normally will not. It is submitted that the presence of a pre-emption provision in a company's articles should have no bearing on the question of whether or not there has been unfair prejudice to the interests of the petitioner.

Receivers

The right of a security holder to appoint an administrative receiver to enforce his charge is one of the most significant aspects of his security. The extent to which this right is legally circumscribed, or the law restricts the manner in which a receiver can carry out his duties, directly affects the quality of a security holder's protection. There have been a number of recent cases in which the court has had to deal with a challenge to the right of a debenture holder to appoint a receiver, or with respect to the manner in which a receiver has carried out his duties. In *Lathia v Dronsfield Bros Ltd* [1987] BCLC 321, the plaintiff brought an action for damages against receivers and managers alleging that they had induced the company to breach a contract with the plaintiff for the supply of goods. The court held that, as the defendants had by the terms of their appointment been made the agents of the company, they would only be liable for damages for inducing a breach of contract if they had failed to act in good faith or outside the scope of their authority. As they had done neither, there was no basis on which they could be liable to the plaintiff. To apply the tort of inducing a breach of contract to the acts of a receiver would subvert the system of security (it would stand the normal priorities on their head) and therefore the outcome in *Lathia* is virtually inevitable. The reasoning in the case, however, is less than convincing and arguably a more appropriate way to deal with this issue is either through the doctrine of justification, or by showing that no damages could be attributed to the acts of the receiver in that the third party would have suffered the loss anyhow because of the company's financial difficulties.

It must be a not uncommon occurrence that after a receiver is appointed the chargee will discover information not known to him at the time the appointment is made. One of the questions before the court in *Byblos Bank SAL v Al-Khudhairy* [1987] BCLC 232 was whether the chargee could make use of this information to justify the appointment of a receiver which may have been otherwise improper. The court held that he could. From a practical point of view it is difficult to see what other result the court could have reached: had the court held that subsequently acquired information could not be used to validate retrospectively the receiver's appointment, the chargee would have had simply to make a fresh appointment and it is difficult to appreciate what would be achieved by this. The validity of a receiver's appointment has to be distinguished from the improper exercise by the debenture of his rights, for example, the negligent exercise of the power to appoint a receiver. As the law now stands there is no liability with respect to the latter, but there is the possibility that the law could develop in this direction.

Charges

It is simply not possible to do justice to the decision of Millett J in *Re Charge Card Services Ltd (No 2)* [1987] BCLC 17 in the space available. In the dispute as to whether it is legally possible for a customer of a bank to create a charge over a credit balance in its bank account in favour of the bank, Millett J held that it is not. As a matter of principle, Millett J held that it is not possible to assign, or make available to the debtor bank, the chose in action in the debt as this would involve the debtor in suing itself if it sought to enforce the charge. Where a bank is entitled to appropriate the account in satisfaction of its claim, the bank's obligations are to that extent simply released. The purported charge over the balance thus operates as a matter of substance by way of set off. This is probably not the last word on the issue of charges over credit balances and it would still be prudent to submit them for registration irrespective of the attitude of the registrar of companies; it must always be kept in mind that all that is required by s 395 of the Companies Act 1985 is that the particulars of the charge be delivered to the registrar. (See also *Mace Builders (Glasgow) Ltd v Lunn* [1987] BCLC 55 (CA) upholding the first instance judgment, and *Evans v Clayhope Properties Ltd* [1987] BCLC 418, an important reminder that the court only has jurisdiction to indemnify a court appointed receiver out of the assets of the company. As regards *Mace*, the facts hopefully could not be duplicated in the future because of the requirement subsequently introduced that an administrative receiver be a qualified insolvency practitioner).

Reductions of capital

There were two cases dealing with this topic, both of some practical importance. In the first, *Re Willaire System plc* [1987] BCLC 67, the court had to decide whether it could confirm a reduction of capital despite the fact that the circular setting out the resolution to reduce the company's capital contained errors. The Court of Appeal held that the reduction could be confirmed either under the court's inherent jurisdiction, or under s 137 of the Companies Act 1985, provided the error was of such an insignificant nature that no one would be prejudiced by its correction and the way in which it was to be corrected is clear. The decision in *Willaire* makes commendable commerical common sense as to refuse to give effect to a resolution, merely because the notice of the meeting suffers from some trivial technical defect, would put the company to unnecessary expense and would be the ultimate triumph of form over substance.

In the second case on reductions, *House of Fraser v ACGE Investments Ltd* [1987] BCLC 478, the House of Lords confirmed the common understanding that a reduction of capital did not constitute a variation of class rights so that there was no need to obtain the consent of the class in question either under s 125 of the Companies Act 1985, or under a standard variation of rights provision in the articles. A reduction of capital is the fulfilment of the rights of a share and not their variation.

The derivative action

The rule in *Foss v Harbottle* (1843) 2 Hare 461, and the so called exceptions to it, continue to cause difficulties as is illustrated by the decision of Knox J in *Smith v Croft (No 2)* [1987] 3 All ER 909, [1987] BCLC 355 in which over one hundred authorities were cited to the court. A shareholder, in order to bring an action on behalf of the company, has to establish, according to Knox J, a prima facie case that (i) the company is entitled to the relief claimed and (ii) that the action falls within the boundaries of one of the exceptions to the rule in *Foss v Harbottle*. On the facts he found that the plaintiff shareholders had satisfied the first requirement; the company had used its assets to finance the acquisition of its shares which he categorised as being ultra vires. Until the decision in *Smith v Croft*, the generally accepted principle has been that a shareholder has standing to bring an action with respect to an ultra vires or illegal act, but Knox J, however, added a very important refinement to this. He distinguished between past and prospective ultra vires acts and, as regards the latter, held that a shareholder would always have a personal right (derived from the contract constituted by s 14 of the Companies Act 1985) to prevent a company from entering into a transaction that is ultra vires. In addition, in such a situation it is not necessary for a shareholder to show that the wrongdoers are in control of the company. However, where a shareholder sought to recover compensation in connection with a past ultra vires act the right being asserted was that of the company and, in this situation, while a shareholder would prima facie have standing to commence an action, the right to prosecute it to a conclusion was not unqualified. Relying on authorities drawing a distinction between the abandonment of a cause of action with respect to a wrong done to the company as opposed to ratifying the wrong itself, Knox J held that a resolution of an independent organ of the company (in *Smith v Croft* it was a majority of the minority shareholders) that it was not in the interests of the company to pursue an action would preclude a derivative action by a shareholder on behalf of the company. Independence for this purpose required the organ of the company deciding to abandon the action to have no connection with the wrongdoers and that it should make its decision in the best interests of the company and not in order to protect the wrongdoers.

Smith v Croft constituted a significant reformulation of the rule in *Foss v Harbottle*. It is the first time that case law has attributed a special significance to the voice of independent shareholders or an independent organ of the company (Companies Act 1985, s 164(5)). For example, hitherto, the fact that a shareholder was interested in a transaction did not affect the validity of a shareholders' resolution carried because of the interested shareholder's votes *(North-Western Transportation Co Ltd v Beatty* (1887) 12 App Cas 589). The determination of whether the organ of the company is independent, particularly where this is claimed to be the shareholders, will often not be easy and will conflict at least in spirit with the Court of Appeal's decision in *Prudential Assurance Co Ltd v Newman Industries Ltd (No 2)* [1982] Ch 204 that the *Foss v Harbottle* point should be taken at the commencement of the proceedings and that its determination should not be allowed to devolve into a trial on the merits. It is implicit in the decision of Knox J, that the primary purpose of the fiduciary obligations imposed on directors is compensatory rather than deterrent, since where a company through an independent organ decides that the costs of an action (which can include adverse publicity and the tying up of management time) exceed any possible benefits to the company, then any action against the wrongdoers can be abandoned. What is also abundantly clear from the decision in *Smith v Croft* is that the time is now opportune for a reform of the rule in *Foss v Harbottle* which is simply failing to fulfil its function of expeditiously and cheaply sifting out those actions where a shareholder has standing to bring an action on behalf of the company from those where he does not.

Disqualification orders against directors

There have been a number of cases reported in which applications were made for orders to disqualify persons from acting as directors. *Re Dawson Print Group Ltd* [1987] BCLC 601 and *Re Stanford Services Ltd* [1987] BCLC 607 are two such cases. In the former, Hoffmann J held that mere mismanagement could not constitute grounds for a disqualification order and there had at least to be gross incompetence or a breach of the standards of commercial morality. He also held that no special significance should be attached to the fact that the company had not paid its VAT or PAYE. However, in the latter case, Vinelott J considered that special significance could be attached to the failure to make these payments as the Crown was an involuntary creditor and the directors of a company should not make use of these moneys to finance its activities. It is submitted that the position of Hoffmann J is to be preferred as the reason the Crown is an involuntary creditor is that it collects its taxes in a way that results in it having this status. Whether or not a disqualification order should be made, should be dependent on all the circumstances of the case and no special significance should be attached to the fact that the company is unable to pay a fiscal debt (which will almost invariably be the case where a company is insolvent). And in terms of commercial morality, it is not obvious why a failure to pay tax which has been collected by the company is any more culpable than a failure to pay a supplier of goods.

Liquidator: right of examination

The courts have shown a determination not to circumscribe the effectiveness of what is now s 236 of the Insolvency Act 1986. In *Re JT Rhodes Ltd* [1987] BCLC 77, Hoffmann J considered that the section should be interpreted so as to facilitate investigation of a company's affairs by a liquidator as the liquidator comes to this task without any knowledge of the company's affairs and therefore he will often need, and public policy requires that he receive, the assistance of those who were in charge of the company in order to determine exactly what has happened. Hoffmann J also indicated that the present practice of refusing to grant an order against a person against whom a liquidator was bringing an action may not be inflexible, and obviously thought that a liquidator's ignorance and his duty to the creditors might justify an order in this situation in appropriate circumstances. (See also *Re Exchange Securities and Commodities Ltd* [1987] 2 All ER 272, [1987] BCLC 425: liquidator not precluded from resiling from representations made by the company.)

Validation of dispositions made after commencement of winding up

Re a company (No 007523 of 1986) [1987] BCLC 200 involves a matter on which there is little reported authority, namely the *refusal* by the court to exercise its discretion to validate payments out of the company's bank account under s 522 of the Companies Act 1985 (now s 127 of the Insolvency Act 1986) in the case of a contributory's winding-up petition. In exercising its discretion in the case of a contributory's petition, Mervyn Davies J considered that great weight should be given to the views of the directors, otherwise a shareholder, by the simple ploy of presenting a petition, could make it impossible for a company to continue trading. However, even though the s 522 application was supported by the directors, Mervyn Davies J refused to grant it as he considered that there was 'a serious question as to the solvency of the company' and to permit it to continue to trade would be to the prejudice of the creditors. The effect of refusing to grant the order would, of course, have the inevitable effect of terminating the company's business.

An application to validate a transaction (a contract for the sale of land) was successful in *Re Tramway Building and Construction Co Ltd* [1987] BCLC 632. In this case the transaction had already been entered into before the validation order was sought, was obviously for the benefit of the creditors, and had a validation order been sought before the transaction was entered into, Scott J had no doubt that the order would have been made. In deciding whether or not to validate the transaction the question was, according to Scott J, not would the company's assets be swollen by a refusal to make the order as this would almost invariably be the consequence of refusing to validate a transaction into which the company had already entered, at least where the company has obtained a benefit but has not performed its part of the bargain. This was the position in *Re Tramway Building and Construction Co Ltd* and, as Scott J pointed out, the effect of refusing to validate the transaction would, on the facts of the case, be to confer on the other creditors of the company a windfall which was undeserved. As Scott J found that the validation of the transaction would not reduce the assets available for the creditors, according to him the relevant test to be applied in deciding whether a disposition should be validated, he granted the order sought.

Section 127 of the Insolvency Act 1986 only invalidates 'dispositions' made after the commencement of the winding up, and thus if a company has already disposed of its assets before a winding-up petition is presented, the section does not affect that transaction. This is illustrated by the judgment of Vinelott J in *Re French's (Wine Bar) Ltd* [1987] BCLC 499 where the court held that the completion of an unconditional contract for the sale of property which was specifically enforceable did not constitute a disposition as the purchaser had acquired a proprietary interest at the time the contract was entered into. However, where the contract is voidable or conditional, the carrying out of the contract might constitute a disposition and the court's approval of the transaction should therefore be sought.

Relationship between voluntary and compulsory winding up

In *Re Palmer Marine Surveys Ltd* [1986] BCLC 106, Hoffmann J considered that the court should now treat with less deference the fact that the company was being wound up voluntarily when asked to exercise its discretion to make a winding-up order. This lead was followed by Vinelott J in *Re MCH Services Ltd* [1987] BCLC 535 where he rejected any general proposition that the court had to let the voluntary winding up continue unless there were special reasons for justifying the making of a compulsory order. He held that the court should be willing to make an order where the refusal to do so would leave the majority of trade creditors with a justified feeling of unfair treatment by depriving them of the opportunity to have the affairs of the company investigated by an independent liquidator. On the facts Vinelott J found that this condition had been satisfied and granted the order sought. This recent development accords considerable weight to the views and grievances of unsecured creditors and virtually entails that if they act expeditiously after a voluntary liquidation has commenced then they should succeed in obtaining the compulsory order (on the effect of delay see *Re Medisco Equipment Ltd* [1983] BCLC 305). In a somewhat similar vein there appears to be a greater disposition to replace a liquidator who is not pursuing his duties with sufficient vigour: *Re Keypak Homecare Ltd* [1987] BCLC 409.

Administration orders

Given that an order under Part II of the Insolvency Act 1986 cannot be made if the holder of a floating charge exercises his right to appoint an administrative receiver, administration orders will probably not be made with any great frequency. The procedure, however, obviously has some role to play, as is illustrated in two recent cases. *Re Newport County Association Football Club Ltd* [1987] BCLC 582 dealt with the procedure to be followed where the company sought an extenstion of the order. Harman J held that an application for an extension of such an order should normally be made by the administrator rather than the company as he was the person most intimately connected with the operation of the company's affairs and who was in the best position to offer independent advice to the court. Of potentially greater significance is *Re a company (No 00175 of 1987)* [1987] BCLC 467 in which Vinelott J held that the court had jurisdiction to shorten the five day period of notice that the holder of a floating charge had to be given before the hearing of a petition for the making of an administration order. Vinelott J recognised that this was a jurisdiction to be invoked very rarely. Were the courts to exercise the jurisdiction with any regularity, it would undermine a basic principle of Part II, namely, that the floating charge holder should have the opportunity to appoint a receiver and prevent an administration order from being made.

Restriction on the transfer of shares

The principal purpose of Part VI of the Companies Act 1985 is to enable a company to discover the identity of the beneficial owners of its shares. Section 212 enables a public company to serve a notice on a person whom it knows, or has reasonable cause to believe, has an interest in its shares requiring disclosure of the nature of that interest. Such a notice can also be served on a person whom the company believes had an interest in its shares in the three year period preceding the notice. Where the company does not receive the information sought then it can apply to have the shares made subject to an order under Part XV of the Act which has the effect, inter alia, of restricting their transfer unless the court orders otherwise under s 456. In *Re Geers Gross plc* [1987] BCLC 253 the company had obtained a statutory restriction on shares held in the name of a nominee. The nominee petitioned to have the restriction lifted as it was proposed to sell the shares on the market and accordingly it was argued that the restriction was no longer necessary as the identity of the owner would be known after the purchase. The court refused to order the removal of the restriction. Vinelott J reasoned that the section was designed in part to enable the company to identify the persons who had acquired a beneficial interest in its shares in the three year period preceding the notice to give particulars of the ownership of the shares and this purpose could be most effectively achieved if the shares remained subject to the restriction. Also, as it lay within the power of the beneficial owner to have the restriction removed by revealing his interest, Vinelott J considered this to be a factor that should be taken into consideration in refusing to lift the restriction.

Conflict of Laws

J G COLLIER, MA, LLB
Barrister, Fellow of Trinity Hall, Cambridge

Jurisdiction: stay of action: divorce proceedings

The Domicile and Matrimonial Proceedings Act 1973 envisages that matrimonial proceedings may be commenced concurrently in respect of the same marriage in England, where one party is domiciled or has been habitually resident here for one year preceding the commencement of the proceedings, and in a foreign country. In such a case s 5(6) of that Act applies and Sch 1 para 9(i)(b) provides that the English proceedings may be stayed if it appears to the court:

'that the balance of fairness (including convenience) as between the parties to the marriage is such that it is appropriate for the [foreign] proceedings . . . to be disposed of before further steps are taken in the proceedings [in England]'

and para 9(2), that:

'In considering the balance of fairness and convenience . . . the court shall have regard to all factors appearing to be relevant, including the convenience of witnesses and any delay or expense which may result from the proceedings being stayed, or not being stayed'

These provisions have received consideration in several Court of Appeal cases, including *Shemshadfard v Shemshadfard* [1981] 1 All ER 726 and *Gadd v Gadd* [1985] 1 All ER 58 and *Thyssen-Bornemisza v Thyssen-Bornemisza* [1985] 1 All ER 328 (both discussed in 1985 All ER Rev 55–7). The House of Lords has now interpreted and applied them in *de Dampierre v de Dampierre* [1987] 2 All ER 1 where the House held that their recently stated guidelines for staying of English proceeding enunciated by Lord Goff of Chievely in *Spiliada Maritime Corpn v Cansulex Ltd, The Spiliada* [1986] 3 All ER 843 (see 1986 All ER Rev 59–63) were applicable to applications under the statutory provisions.

The husband and wife were both French nationals and were married in France in 1977. They moved to London in 1979 and in 1982 had a child; the husband bought a matrimonial home there. In 1984 the wife established a business in New York and in 1985 took the child there, informing the husband that she did not intend to return to London. So he started divorce proceedings in France alleging desertion. The wife started divorce proceedings in England alleging cruelty and adultery. The husband applied for the English proceedings to be stayed on the ground that the balance of convenience required the French proceedings to be disposed of first.

Sir John Arnold P and the Court of Appeal refused the application. The learned President applied the test laid down by Lord Diplock in *MacShannon v Rockware Glass Ltd* [1978] 1 All ER 625 at 630 and held that the wife would be deprived of an advantage in suing here, since she would be entitled to maintenance, which she might not get if the husband's French petition succeeded. The court of Appeal had doubts about the correctness of Sir John Arnold P's approach and preferred to apply the one embodied in Lord Diplock's speech in the later case of *The Abidin Daver* [1984] 1 All ER 470 at 476. Nevertheless, they took the same view, that if a stay were to be granted, the wife would lose a legitimate personal or juridical advantage.

Lord Goff of Chievely and Lord Templeman, not surprisingly in view of their speeches in *The Spiliada*, held that the wrong tests had been applied by the courts below. The weight to be given to a legitimate personal or juridical advantage is now less than it was under the old tests. The search is really for the natural forum for the hearing of the case and it is desirable that in applying his discretion under the 1973 Act, the judge should apply the same principles as those evolved in the 'forum non conveniens' cases.

In the present case the French court was clearly the natural and appropriate forum and it would not be unfair to confine the wife to her rights under French law. The parties were French nationals and the wife had severed her tenuous connection with England. She could obtain all the redress to which she was entitled under French law in the French courts.

Jurisdiction: restraining foreign proceedings

In *Spiliada Maritime Corpn v Cansulex Ltd, The Spiliada* [1986] 3 All ER 843 (see 1986 All ER Rev 59–63) the House of Lords, speaking through Lord Goff of Chievely, laid down guidelines to be followed by the courts when they are asked to exercise their discretion to permit service out of the jurisdiction under the Rules of the Supreme Court, Ord 11, r 1 or to stay an action when they have jurisdiction by reason of the presence of the defendant in England when he is served with the writ or by his submission.

In so doing the House committed English law to the doctrine of forum non conveniens, which has always applied to Ord 11 applications (see *Amin Rasheed Shipping Corpn v Kuwait Insurance Co, The Al Wahab* [1983] 2 All ER 884), and towards which the courts had been moving in cases of applications for a stay of actions since the House of Lords had 'liberalised' the law in *The Atlantic Star, Atlantic Star (owners) v Bona Spes (owners)* [1973] 2 All ER 175, through its decisions in *MacShannon v Rockware Glass Ltd* [1978] 1 All ER 625 and *The Abidin Daver* [1984] 1 All ER 470.

The same principles as those which govern the exercise of the discretion in such cases were held by the House of Lords in *Castanho v Brown & Root Ltd* [1981] 1 All ER 143, through Lord Scarman, to govern applications for an injunction to restrain a party from instituting or continuing proceedings in foreign courts. Lord Scarman reiterated the remarks of Lord Diplock in *MacShannon's* case; which, in the context of foreign proceedings, meant that the party asking for the injunction had to show that the English court was a forum to which the applicant was amenable and that it was more suitable than the foreign court and that to restrain the other party would not be likely to deprive him of a 'legitimate personal or juridical advantage' in proceeding abroad. The prospect in that case of the plaintiff's obtaining higher damages in Texas than in England was such an advantage and the House of Lords refused to restrain him from proceeding with his action there. This was applied (not very willingly) in *Bank of Tokyo v Karoon and another* [1986] 3 All ER 468 (see 1986 All ER Rev 60) by the Court of Appeal.

After the decision in *The Spiliada* one would have thought that the doctrine of forum non conveniens and Lord Goff's guidelines would now apply in such cases and that a nice symmetry now exists between applications to serve out of the jurisdiction, to stay English proceedings and to enjoin foreign proceedings.

It must be admitted that this writer has not been entirely convinced that a test which was evolved to govern the first two types of case is entirely opposite in the converse situation. When the court is asked to assume jurisdiction or to abstain from exercising such jurisdiction as it possesses, it is the master of its own proceedings. It is not so with respect to applications to restrain foreign proceedings; in doing this, the English court is in effect interfering indirectly with the jurisdiction of a foreign court and surely must move somewhat circumspectly. The danger of too liberally restraining foreign actions is demonstrated by the cases concerning admittedly different situations where there are no proceedings in England, exemplified in *British Airways Board v Laker Airways* [1984] 3 All ER 39 (see 1984 All ER Rev 241–4) of creating an embarrassing conflict between the courts of this country and of the other one concerned (see also *Smith, Kline & French Laboratories Ltd v Bloch* [1983] 2 All ER 72).

These doubts were apparently shared by Lord Goff, as Robert Goff LJ, in *Bank of Tokyo v Karoon and another* [1986] 3 All ER 468 at 483–485. And now he has turned them into law in delivering the advice of the Judicial Committee of the Privy Council on an appeal from the courts of Brunei in *SNI Aérospatiale v Lee Kui Jak and another* [1987] 3 All ER 510, where the Committee held that the principles applicable in such a case are not the same as those governing the grant of a stay of English proceedings in favour of a more appropriate foreign forum and distinguished *The Spiliada*. The court cannot restrain foreign proceedings on the sole ground that England was the natural forum. Instead, where a remedy for a particular wrong is available both in the English court and in a foreign court, the English court will, generally speaking, only restrain the plaintiff from pursuing proceedings in the foreign court if such pursuit would be vexatious or oppressive (see ibid at 522). The English court must conclude that it is the natural forum and that account must be taken of justice and injustice to the parties in restraining or not restraining the foreign proceedings. So, as a general rule 'the court will not grant an injunction if, by doing so, it will deprive the plaintiff of advantages in the foreign forum of which it would be unjust to deprive him.'

The facts of the case were somewhat complex. The respondents were the widow and administrators of the estate of a man who was killed when a helicopter crashed in Brunei. This was manufactured in France by the appellant French company (SNIAS) which had a Texas subsidiary. The helicopter was owned by a British Company and serviced by its Malaysian subsidiary (M) under contract to a Brunei company. The respondents brought proceedings against the defendants in Brunei and Texas alleging faulty design and manufacture; they sued in texas because they were advised that product liability was more favourable under Texas law and that higher damages were possibly obtainable there. Their Texas attorneys carried out pre-trial discovery of documents and examination of witnesses in Texas and France and the Texas trial was fixed for 1 July 1987. In December 1986

SNIAS applied to the Brunei court for an injunction to restrain the Texas action. (The French proceedings had been discontinued.) This was refused and SNIAS applied to the Brunei Court of Appeal, during the hearing of which both sides gave undertakings, in particular one that the SNIAS would expedite a hearing in Brunei. SNIAS also served a contribution notice on M who would accept Brunei but not Texas jurisdiction.

The Brunei Court of Appeal applied *Castanho's* case and *The Spiliada* and refused to enjoin the Texas proceedings. The Judicial Committee, rejecting this approach, and referring to earlier decisions, from the time of *Bushby v Munday* (1821) 5 Madd 297, reversed the court of Appeal.

Two features of the case call for further exposition. There is no doubt that Brunei *was* the natural forum. The fatal accident occurred there so the law governing the claim was the law of Brunei, which differed in at least three respects from that of Texas. Also, the deceased was resident in Brunei and carried on his principal business there. The respondents were resident in Brunei and witnesses of fact who lived there were likely to be called on the issue of quantum. There was nothing whatever to connect the action with Texas.

But the Court of Appeal had decided that, disregarding the question of proceedings by SNIAS against M, the natural forum had become Texas, particularly because of the work done on the case by the respondent's Texas attorneys. The court relied heavily on the '*Cambridgeshire*' factor which played a large part in persuading the English courts to allow service out of the jurisdiction in *The Spiliada*. The *Cambridgeshire* litigation, during which the application to stay further proceedings in *The Spiliada* was made, involved the same questions of fact as those in *The Spiliada* and was a test case in which many members of English lawyers and experts were engaged; a prodigious amount of preparatory work was done here and all the relevant expertise could be found in England. Moreover the parties in both actions were the same and the same P & I Club was financing both sets of proceedings and instructing the same lawyers in both of them. The activities of the Texas attorneys in the present proceedings were in no way comparable.

Then, SNIAS would be caused an injustice if the Texas proceedings were allowed to continue for the one reason that, because M had refused to submit to the jurisdiction of the Texas courts but had agreed to submit to those of Brunei, SNIAS would not be able to 'bring in' M in Texas but could do so in Brunei. (M, it was clear, was the respondents' prime target.) This would mean that SNIAS would, if held liable in Texas, then have to seek contribution in a separate action under the Brunei equivalent of the English Law Reform (Married Women and Joint Tortfeasors) Act 1935, s 6. But (a) M had already settled with the plaintiffs and might invoke this settlement against SNIAS; (b) it is not clear that s 6 applies to liability established in a foreign action, so SNIAS might have to establish their liability once again in Brunei in order to obtain contribution from M. Thus, the continuance of the Texas proceedings would be oppressive to them; the proceedings should be enjoined on terms of undertakings given by SNIAS.

So the Privy Council has disturbed what might have been thought to be the law. The English courts are, of course, bound by decisions of the House of Lords, not those of the Privy Council. But should the situation arise again before the House, it is hardly likely that it will apply *Castanho's case* rather than the latest decision, though that is one of the Privy Council.

Foreign judgment: enforcement: examination of judgment debtor

In *Interpool v Galani* [1981] 2 All ER 981, a Greek citizen now living in France faced enforcement proceedings in England of a judgment obtained against him there. The French judgment was registered in the High Court under the Foreign Jurisdiction (Reciprocal Enforcement) Act 1933. An order for his oral examination as to his assets was made under the Rules of the Supreme Court, Ord 48. During the examination be objected to answering questions as to his assets outside the jurisdiction contending that the Order should not be given extraterritorial effect.

The Court of Appeal held that the courts have jurisdiction to garnish a debt situated outside the jurisdiction of the court. Order 48 does not confer any jurisdiction in relation to enforcement proceedings outside the jurisdiction, but does do so regarding enforcement proceedings here, in relation to assets there.

Foreign arbitration award: enforcement and public policy

The Arbitration Act 1975 makes provision for the recognition and enforcement in the United Kingdom of foreign 'Convention Awards', which are arbitral awards made in pursuance of arbitration agreements in the territory of a state, other than the United Kingdom, which is a party to the New York convention on the Recognition and Enforcement of Foreign Arbitral Awards 1958. Once such an award is recognised it can be enforced in England either by action, or under s 26 of the Arbitration Act 1950 by summary judgment.

Section 5 of the 1975 Act lists eight exceptional cases in which enforcement may be refused, including, that the arbitration agreement is invalid under the law to which the parties submitted it (or if there is no such law, the law of the place where the award was made), that the award deals with a matter outside the scope of the agreement and that it would be contrary to public policy to enforce the award.

The applicability of these exceptions was, among other matters, considered by the Court of Appeal in *Deutsche Schachtbau-und Tiefbohrgesellschaft mbH v R'as Al Khaimah National Oil Co* [1987] 2 All ER 769. Two foreign companies, D and R, entered in 1976 into an oil exploration agreement. This contained an International Chamber of Commerce arbitration clause which provided for disputes to be decided by arbitration in Geneva according to a proper law of the agreement to be adopted by the arbitrators. In 1979 D referred a claim to arbitration in Geneva and obtained an award in its favour. In breach of the agreement R sued D in R'as Al Khaimah and obtained a judgment for rescission of the agreement and damages. Neither side appeared in the proceedings instituted by the other.

D applied for and was granted leave to enforce the arbitration award in England as a judgment and obtained an injunction restraining R from removing any of its assets from the jurisdiction. (With respect to the injunction see pp 56 below.) R applied for and was granted leave by Staughton J to serve a writ on D out of the jurisdiction in order to enforce its judgment, so that it could then counterclaim in D's action to enforce its arbitration award. Leggatt J refused to set aside the leave granted to D but did set aside that granted to R. R appealed.

The grant of leave to R to serve the writ on D so as to enforce its R'as Al Khaimah judgment was wrong if the agreement was governed by Swiss law and valid by that law. It was valid so R's judgment was not enforceable in England by reason of s 32 of the Civil Jurisdiction and Judgments Act 1982 which prohibits the recognition or enforcement of a foreign judgment in the United Kingdom if it results from proceedings which were contrary to an agreement to settle the dispute otherwise than by proceedings in the foreign country concerned.

With respect to the enforceability of the arbitration award in favour of D, R argued that the award dealt with a difference not contemplated by or falling within the terms of the submission or contained a decision beyond its scope. That is, that the arbitrators had exceeded their jurisdiction. It was held that they had not.

The real objection was that to enforce the award would be contrary to English public policy. This was based on the fact that the arbitrators had been allowed to choose the proper law of the agreement and that they had not selected the domestic contract law of any state but had determined that the governing law was 'internationally accepted principles of law governing contractual relations.' Sir John Donaldson MR said that where a clause (or a determination) purports to provide that a contract is governed by some system of law which is not that of England or any other state or is a serious modification of such a law, the court must ask, first, did the parties intend to create legally enforceable rights and obligations? Second, is the resulting agreement certain enough to be a legally enforceable contract? Third, is there some other reason of public policy to refuse to enforce the award?

It was held that the parties did have the requisite intention and that since there was nothing illegal about the award and it would neither be injurious to the public good or offensive to an informed member of the public, the first and third questions should be answered in favour of enforcement.

This left the court to decide whether the agreement was certain. In *Orion Cia Espanola de Seguros v Belfort Maatschappij Voor Algemene Verzekgringeen* [1962] 2 Lloyd's Rep 257, Megaw J had to consider the validity of a clause which relieved the arbitrators of compliance with judicial formalities, authorised them 'not to follow the strict rules of the law' and directed them to settle a dispute arising out of the agreement 'according to an equitable rather than a strictly legal interpretation of its terms.' He referred to *Czarnikow v Roth Schmidt & Co* [1922] 2 KB 478, CA, where it was declared that: 'the parties cannot make a question of law any less a question of law . . . by purporting that it shall be decided by some extra-legal criterion.'

Such a criterion would be the view of an individual arbitrator or some abstract principles of justice or equity. Megaw J added that an English arbitrator could apply foreign or international law. In *Eagle Star Insurance Co Ltd v Yuval Insurance* [1978] 1 Lloyd's Rep 357 the Court of Appeal discussed a clause in the same terms as that in issue in the *Orion* case and held that it was valid.

So, in *DST v Raknoc* [1987] 2 All ER 769 the same court held that the choice of law clause and the arbitrator's selection of the proper law were valid. It held that an agreement to accept terms to be determined by a third party can form the basis of a legally enforceable agreement, unlike an agreement to agree in the future.

The decision is much to be welcomed. This seems to be the first case in which it has been sought to enforce an arbitral award based on an agreement which is governed by 'general principles of law' or 'internationally accepted principles of law'. But the award in this case is not the first in which a similar chosen law has been applied by arbitrators, especially in arbitrations arising out of oil drilling concession agreements and particularly by arbitrators in arbitrations located in Switzerland. Two were referred to by the arbitrators in the present case: *Sapphire International Petroleum Ltd v National Iranian Oil Company* [1967] Int LR 136 and *Texaco Overseas Petroleum Company v The Government of the Libyan Arab Republic* [1979] Int LR 389. Another example is the award of Lord Asquith of Bishopstone in the *Abu Dhabi Arbitration* (1952) Int LR 37. Under the World Bank Convention for the Settlement of Investment Disputes between States and Nationals of Other States of 1965, the arbitral tribunal is, in the absence of a choice of law by the parties, to apply the law of a contracting state which is a party to the dispute, including its conflict rules, and such rules of international law as may be applicable. If international law is applied, this may well entail application of 'general principles of law.' An award made under the convention may be enforced in England under the Arbitration (International Investment Disputes) Act 1966 by registration in the High Court. That being so, it would have been odd if an award such as that in issue in *DST v Raknoc* has been refused enforcement.

Foreign divorce: recognition

In *Maples v Maples* [1987] 3 All ER 188 Latey J had to decide a question which had received different answers from members of the Court of Appeal in *Vervaeke v Smith (Messina and A-G intervening)* [1981] 1 All ER 55. The case concerned the recognition of a divorce obtained by the extra-judicial Jewish get (similar in its informality to the customary Islamic talaq which has enjoyed the attention of the English courts in recent years). The get, that is, a paper stating that the marriage was dissolved according to Jewish law, was delivered by the husband to the wife and accepted by her at the London Beth Din, a rabbinical religious court, in 1977. A rabbinical court in Israel later issued a 'judgment of confirmation' of the proceedings in London certifying that the requirements of the get had been complied with according to Jewish law. This did not itself purport to effect the divorce.

It was not sought to argue that the divorce could be recognised under the Recognition of Divorces and Legal Separations Act 1971 (the 1971 Act). The only provision of this Act on which recognition could have been based was s 6 (as amended) which preserves the common law basis of recognition, that the divorce is entitled to recognition if it is granted in the country of one party's domicile or in a third country and would be recognised by the law of both parties' domiciles. (This latter alternative will disappear when the Family Law Act 1986, Part II is brought into operation). No doubt reliance was not placed on this because the wife, at any rate, was held to have acquired an English domicile in 1974 and was no longer domiciled in Israel whose law would recognise the London get. (Possibly the husband also was domiciled here after 1974.)

The argument put before the court on behalf of the husband was based therefore upon the Foreign Judgments (Reciprocal Enforcement) Act 1933 (the 1933 Act), s 8 of which applies to judgments of Israel courts. Another reason was that the judgment of the Israel court could not itself be regarded as dissolving the marriage under the 1971 Act. Until fairly recently this had not, apparently, been thought to have any relevance to judgments of foreign courts concerning marital status and a dictum of Lord Reid in *Black-Clawson International Ltd v Papierwerke Waldhof-Aschaffenburg A/G* [1975] 1 All ER 810 at 817 confirms this. If it has such relevance, the 1971 Act might be outflanked if the foreign judgment granted a divorce. But in *Vervaeke v Smith* [1981] 1 All ER 55, CA, it was argued that a Belgian nullity decree could be accorded recognition under the 1933 Act. The House of Lords did not consider the point but the Court of Appeal did so, obiter, Sir John Arnold P opining that the Act does apply to judgments concerning marital status. Cumming-Bruce and Eveleigh LJJ doubted that this is so, and suggested that it only applies to money judgments in matrimonial causes. Latey J stated that although s 8 of the 1933 Act is, as Sir John Arnold P, among other judges and also the writers have said, an obscurely drafted provision, looking at the Act as a whole, it does not apply to judgments affecting marital status. Moreover, certain terms used in s 8(1), 'a judgment . . . shall be recognised . . . as conclusive between the parties thereto' and 'in all proceedings founded on the same cause of action' are inapt to describe such judgments. For the state also, not only the parties, has an interest in such judgments. And 'cause of action' is not descriptive of such proceedings. In any case, 'the cause of action' in the instant case was not the same as that in the rabbinical courts in Israel.

So, Latey J held that the 1933 Act did not apply. He held that the divorce could not be recognised here because of s 16(1) of the Domicile and Matrimonial Proceedings Act 1973 (the 1973 Act) which provides that: 'No proceeding in the United Kingdom, the Channel Islands or the Isle of Man shall be regarded as validly dissolving a marriage unless instituted in the courts of law of one of those countries.'

This provision has been the subject of some academic speculation based on whether the word 'proceeding' means or does not mean the same as 'proceedings' in the 1971 Act, ss 2–5. This need not be pursued here, for Latey J was of the sensible view that it means what it was meant to say, that an 'unofficial' or 'informal divorce' by get or talaq unaccompanied by some external official procedure which must be complied with, cannot be recognised as a divorce by English courts since it has not been obtained in a British court of law and it is immaterial that it is recognised by the law of the parties' foreign domicile. The Family Law Act 1986, s 44(1) puts this much more clearly in providing that: 'No divorce, annulment or legal separation obtained in any part of the British Islands shall be regarded as effective [in England] unless it was granted by a court of competent jurisdiction'.

The conclusion arrived at is, it is submitted, quite correct. However, the reasoning is not as clear or satisfactory as it might be. There is something missing from the middle of it. The judge seems at one point to suggest that it is the 1973 Act which forms the basis of recognition of foreign divorces (see [1978] 3 All ER 188 at 190). This is not so; that Act merely amends and supplements the 1971 Act, which is the one which contains the rules for recognition. The reason, why, given that the 1933 Act has no application, is the one mentioned above, that for the divorce having been obtained in England it could not be recognised under ss 2–5 of the 1971 Act on the basis of it being obtained in the country of one party's nationality, or habitual residence. Nor could it be recognised under s 6 on the basis of its recognition by the law of both parties' domicile since one of the parties at least was not domiciled in Israel but in England. English law could not, because of s 16(1) of the 1973 Act, recognise the divorce.

Foreign divorce: financial provision

One of the problems which arose after the enactment of the Recognition of Foreign Divorces and Legal Separations Act 1971, mainly because of the requirement that a foreign divorce must be accorded recognition on the frequently artificial basis that the foreign country has jurisdiction if one of the parties is a national of that country, was that, once the divorce was recognised, the English court had no jurisdiction to grant matrimonial, financial or proprietary relief. The injustice which this could cause was mentioned by the courts more than once, especially in *Quazi v Quazi* [1979] 3 All ER 897, HL.

Somewhat tardily, a recommendation of the Law Commission in 1982 that the court should be given such jurisdiction was enacted by the Matrimonial and Family Proceedings Act 1984, which came into force on 16 September 1985. The question before the Court of Appeal in *Chebaro v Chebaro* [1987] 1 All ER 999, which was not one of the conflict of laws itself, was whether the Act has retrospective effect so as to enable the court to grant relief to a wife in respect of a matrimonial home in England, when the marriage had been dissolved by a Lebanese divorce on 16 April 1985, five months before the Act came into force. The Court of Appeal held that the Act does have such effect and applies to all recognised foreign divorces whether obtained before or after that date.

Moveable property: situs and garnishment of debts

In *Deutsche Schachtbau-und Tiefbohrgesellschaft mbH v R'as Al Khaimah National Oil Co* [1987] 2 All ER 769 (see also p 52 above), the plaintiffs had, as judgment creditors, obtained an injunction from Bingham J restraining Shell from paying to Raknoc a trading debt worth nearly $US5m owed for shipments of oil. Raknoc and Shell objected that this debt did not constitute an asset of Raknoc 'situated within the jurisdiction' and that the injunction, which was a so-called Mareva injunction, should not have been granted in respect of it. In fact, the injunction was not really a Mareva injunction, but one granted in aid of execution of a judgment debt. The point was therefore allied to the question whether the debt could be garnished or whether a receiver could be appointed in respect of it in execution of an English judgment, for if this could not be done, no injunction could be granted.

The only relevant jurisdictional requirements for the making of a garnishee order are that the garnishee (Shell) should be 'within the jurisdiction' and that the subject matter should be a 'debt due or accruing due to the judgment debtor' (Raknoc) from the garnishee. But the courts will not, as a matter of discretion, make an order if this would lead to the garnishee having to pay the same debt twice, here and in another country: *Martin v Nadel* [1906] 2 KB 26, CA. The judgment debtor should also be within the jurisdiction, as Raknoc was not, for otherwise there might be a danger that the garnishee will have to pay him again abroad should the foreign court not recognise the English garnishee order. But if the debt is situated here and the risk of 'double jeopardy' is merely theoretical an order may be made: *Swiss Bank Corp v Boehmische Industrial Bank* [1923] 1 KB 673. In the present case, the Court of Appeal thought that the risk of Shell having to pay again was of this order, since garnishment (or attachment) of debts is recognised internationally and the court thought that most countries had the same rule of private international law, that the validity and effect of a garnishee order are governed by the lex situs of the debt.

So, was the debt 'situated within the jurisdiction'?. The answer to this was quite clear; a debt is, as a general rule, situated where it is recoverable. That is usually the place where the debtor resides because that is where he can be sued (see *Jabbour (F & K) v Custodian of Israeli Absentee Property* [1954] 1 All ER 145). Where he has more than one residence, the debt's situs is where payment is expressly or impliedly stipulated for and if there is no such place, where it would be paid in the ordinary course of business. It was argued that Shell might in the course of its business pay the debt to Raknoc in New York, so that state was the situs of the debt. However, this ignores the general rule, by which it is plain that it was in England that the debt was recoverable.

The debt could, therefore, be garnished and the grant of the injunction to restrain Shell from paying it to Raknoc was upheld.

Consumer Law

BRIAN HARVEY, MA, LLM
Solicitor, Professor of Property Law, University of Birmingham

There is little doubt that 1987 will primarily be remembered, in the world of Consumer Protection, for the Consumer Protection Act 1987. This is the first major piece of statutory reform in this area for some years. The Act (1) seeks to implement the EEC Directive on Product Liability, (2) introduces a 'general safety requirement' with regard to goods, and (3) replaces s 11 of the Trade Descriptions Act 1968 and subsidiary legislation by complex alternative provisions relating to misleading price indications.

All these provisions, when introduced, will no doubt have a significant effect on our case law. Meanwhile the All England Law Reports produced two consumer orientated cases which elucidate the meaning of 'merchantable quality'. A further case sheds valuable light on applying false trade descriptions in the sometimes seamy world of the second-hand car trade.

Merchantable quality

The decision of Rougier J in *Bernstein v Pamson Motors (Golders Green) Ltd* [1987] 2 All ER 220 provides some comfort to the disappointed buyer of a new car. Buyers are not infrequently vexed by the question of whether defects in a new vehicle amount to unmerchantability, and if so whether they can reject the car and claim damages. As the judge remarked (ibid at 222):

> 'This is the sort of dispute that has frequently come before the courts in relation to motor cars... it seems... that the practical application of the concept of merchantable quality is giving a certain amount of trouble to those engaged in the motor trading world'.

The buyer, the plaintiff, bought a new Nissan car from the defendant garage. He paid just under £8,000 in 1984. The car was hardly driven after the sale because of the plaintiff's illness but for the first hundred miles or so the car behaved perfectly. About three weeks after the purchase when the car had done a little over 100 miles, and on a longer journey than usual, the engine seized up due to the cam shaft being starved of oil. This was because a piece of sealant had entered the lubrication system and cut off the oil supply to the cam shaft. Then began a chain of events sadly familiar to many motorists. This involved the 'tedious process of recovery' by one of the official services, a cold wait, a long tow and a taxi home. From his home the plaintiff immediately rang the defendants to inform them that he was rejecting the car. This was confirmed the next day by letter. The plaintiff had the perspicacity to write saying that he did not regard the car as being 'of merchantable quality as defined by s 14 of the Sale of Goods Act 1979 and I hereby reject the car'.

The car was then repaired under the manufacturer's warranty at no cost to the plaintiff and the judge was satisfied that the repairs were competently carried out and the defect totally cured. After the repair the car was regarded effectively as good as new. The defendants then wrote to the plaintiff telling him that his car had been repaired and was ready for collection. They declined his request for refund of the purchase price on the basis that the buyer was not justified in rescinding the contract. The plaintiff, however, maintained his position and the issue was put before the court for decision.

The primary guidance for the court was the definition of merchantable quality contained in s 14(6) of the 1979 Act. This states that goods are of merchantable quality 'if they are as fit for the purpose or purposes for which goods of that kind are commonly bought as it is reasonable to expect having regard to any description applied to them, the price (if relevant) and all the other relevant circumstances'. The judge was not critical of this statutory formulation, unlike some commentators. He made the point that any attempt to forge some more exhaustive or specific definition, applicable in all cases, would soon be put to mockery by some new undreamed-of set of circumstances. But the problem has always been to apply the definition to a specific set of circumstances in the light of the predominant factor, that of fitness for the purpose for which goods of that kind are commonly bought.

Rougier J first asked the question, based on the tests in *Bartlett v Sidney Marcus Ltd* [1965] 2 All ER 753, of how the performance of the car was affected by the defect. It was clear that a car that would not move or was incapable of being driven in safety could rarely if ever be classed as being of merchantable quality. Furthermore, these tests must be applied as at the time of *delivery*. 'To that extent, therefore, there will always be an element of latency in any particular defect which is the subject of a claim for rescission' (ibid at 226). Other material considerations were: (1) the ease or otherwise with which any defect can be remedied, and (2) the time of and expense of rectification.

The next relevant factor is whether the defect is of such a kind that it is in fact *capable* of being satisfactorily repaired so as to produce a result as good as new. The judge also considered, at this point, the vexed question of an accumulation of relatively minor defects. Remarking that this must be a question of degree, Rougier J went on to say (ibid at 227), that there could come a stage when 'an army of minor, unconnected defects would be evidence of such bad workmanship in the manufacture, or on the assembly line generally, as to amount in toto to a breach of the condition of merchantability'. Then there were economic matters to consider in addition to the mechanical ones. The assumption made by the judge here was that the higher the price paid the higher the legitimate expectation of the purchaser. 'No buyer of a brand new Rolls Royce Corniche would tolerate the slightest blemish on its exterior paintwork; the purchaser of the motor car very much at the humbler end of the range might be less fastidious'.

Applying these tests to the case before him, Rougier J concluded that as at delivery the car contained a potential defect which, if it crystallized in the way that it did, would bring the car to a halt with considerable internal damage. A seizing engine halts a car much in the same way as applying the brakes, and it is possible that the defect could therefore have been dangerous. Consequential repairs were lengthy and expensive, but properly done. There was no question of any cumulative effect of a series of defects or of cosmetic defects. The situation in total, therefore, was that on delivery there was a tiny blemish, namely a blob of sealant in the wrong place which was a potential time bomb. The defect however was repairable and the car here was in fact repaired and made as good as new. Was this, therefore, a case of inevitable teething troubles or did the defect in question really render the car unmerchantable?

Rougier J seemed to have little hesitation in stating that a defect of this kind, with the results that it had, went far beyond that which a buyer must accept. Although the defect occurred by extreme mischance and reflected no general criticism of the manufacturers, the potentially unsafe condition of the car and the potential damage which could have occurred persuaded the court so to hold. It was not reasonable for the buyer of a new car of this type and price to sustain a major breakdown in the first 150 miles. The car was not of merchantable quality, still less was it fit for its purpose.

This was not, however, the end of the matter. The plaintiff had not rejected the car until approximately three weeks after delivery and it was argued on behalf of the defendants that the buyer had therefore accepted the car within the meaning of s 35 of the 1979 Act with the consequence that he is compelled to treat the breach of condition as a breach of warranty with the result that damages could be awarded only, rather than rescission (s 11(4)). The relevant part of s 35 states that a buyer accepts goods 'when after the lapse of a reasonable time he retains the goods without intimating to the seller that he has rejected them'. What was a reasonable time? By s 59, a 'reasonable time' is defined as a question of fact, which is scarcely helpful. One approach would be to ask what a reasonable time would have been to discover the particular defect which occurred. However, Rougier J rejected this approach as being suitable only to contracts of hire-purchase. The alternative approach, which commended itself here, was to ask what is a reasonable practical interval in commercial terms between a buyer receiving the goods and his ability to send them back, having regard to the nature of the goods and their function. One policy factor is the desirability of the seller being able to close his ledger reasonably soon after the transaction is complete. The answer to this test would still be variable. What would be a reasonable time in relation to a bicycle would hardly suffice for a nuclear submarine.

The court's conclusion here was that the interval of some three weeks, even discounting the period of the plaintiff's illness, was such that the buyer must be deemed to have accepted the goods within the meaning of s 35. It followed that the buyer's claim was limited to damages and these were formulted by reference to the cost of returning home, the loss of petrol, compensation for a totally spoilt day (assessed at £150) and 5 days loss of use of the car. The buyer could hardly have been satisfied with total damages amounting to a little less of £250, but this was the sum of the award.

The case is to be welcomed for the light that it throws on the circumstances in which a new car can be regarded as unmerchantable. It is scarcely reassuring to buyers however, on the question of acceptance. It may well be that the somewhat subtle interpretation adopted by the judge here, which involves ignoring the nature of the particular defect and applying a more general commercial test, is the correct one as a matter of interpretation but if it leads to the somewhat derisory award of damages in this case, it is not a comforting one for the consumer. It may be that any statutory reform of the definition of merchantability, discussed briefly below, should be accompanied by bolder and more flexible guidelines on the right to reject. There seems to be no real reason why the concept should not be considered in conjunction with the question of how long would be reasonable to discover the particular defect which rendered the car unmerchantable. The accountancy processes for cars let under hire-purchase agreements may be different but the overall economic effect is the same. In neither case has the comsumer got what he bargained for and the consequences should be that the onus of repairing and re-selling or re-letting the car should fall on the supplier.

The decision of the Court of Appeal In *Rogers v Parish (Scarborough) Ltd* [1987] 2 All ER 232 again involved the sale of a car, this time a Range Rover sold to the plaintiffs under a conditional sale agreement. The actual sale was therefore by a finance company at the instance of the dealers. The price paid was £16,000. There then followed a long series of misfortunes. After a few weeks use the vehicle initially sold had to be returned, and by agreement between the parties another vehicle of the same type was substituted for the original on the same terms. This latter vehicle proved no more satisfactory than its predecessor. About six months after delivery of the second vehicle the engine still misfired at all road speeds and excessive noise was emitted grom the gear box and the transfer box. There were also substantial defects with regards to the body work, no doubt not assisted by the fact that both vehicles had been stored in an open compound for some time before the sale. During all this time the vehicle had been subjected to a number of inspections and attempts to put it right. It had also been driven for upwards of 5,500 miles, albeit without satisfaction. Nearly six months after the transaction was initiated the buyers lost patience and gave notice to the dealers that the car was rejected.

The primary question for the court was whether the car was of merchantable quality. The Court of Appeal here echoed the judgment in *Bernstein v Pamson Motors* that if a car was capable of starting and being driven in safety from one point to the next on public roads it was not the case that it must necessarily be merchantable. The test in s 14(6) of the 1979 Act provides firmer guidelines on this. Mustill LJ (ibid at 237) first looked at the description applied to the goods. Here the vehicle was described as new. 'Deficiencies which might be acceptable on a second-hand vehicle were not to be expected in one purchased as new'. Secondly, the description was important and here 'Range Rover' sets up expectations which might not be the same as those relating to an ordinary saloon car. Thirdly, price was significant and at more than £16,000 the price level here was well above the level of the ordinary family saloon and the buyer was entitled to value for money.

The conclusion was that the defects in engine, gear box and body work in this case rendered the vehicle unmerchantable.

The court added that the existence of a manufacturers' warranty did not affect the position. Indeed, the warranty itself stated that 'your statutory rights and obligations as against the supplier are not in any way affected'. And, assuming that this case involved the buyer dealing as a consumer, liability for breach of the obligations arising, inter alia, from s 14 of the 1979 Act cannot be excluded or restricted by reference to any term of the contract (Unfair Contract Terms Act 1977, s 6).

Somewhat surprisingly the issue of whether the interval of time between delivery and rejection was so great that the buyers should be deemed to have accepted the vehicle, was not adjudicated. The Court of Appeal considered it inappropriate to allow the question of acceptance to be raised before it de novo. The order made involved a declaration that the Range Rover in question had been validly rejected by the plaintiffs. Accordingly the damages were such sums as the plintiffs paid in respect of the purchase of the vehicle together with the value of the car part-exchanged.

Before leaving the question of the definition of 'merchantable quality', it is appropriate to draw attention to Working Paper No 85 (Sale and Supply of Goods 1983) of the English and Scottish Law Commissions which has now been followed by a Report of the same name, published in May 1987. The recommendation is for a re-definition of the concept of 'merchantable quality'. The new definition should consist of two elements: the basic principle, formulated in language sufficiently general to apply to all kinds of goods and all kinds of transactions; and a list of aspects of quality, any of which could be important in a particular case. The fundamental test is proposed to be 'that the quality of the goods sold or supplied under a contract should be such as would be acceptable to a reasonable person, bearing in mind the description of the goods, their price (if relevant) and all other circumstances'. Other aspects to be considered include: (a) fitness, (b) appearance and finish, (c) freedom from minor defects, (d) safety, and (e) durability. In the draft Bill included in the Report the expression 'merchantable quality' is replaced by 'acceptable quality'. It is doubted, though, whether this semantic variation is of itself likely to be helpful in the light of the difficulties discussed in the two cases above.

False trade descriptions

Trade descriptions law has been greatly enriched by the activities of second-hand car dealers. Reducing the mileage shown on the odometer of a used car is probably the most persistent offence under the Trade Descriptions Act 1968. Anyone doing so, in the course of a business, prima facie commits an offence under s 1 of the Act. As long ago as 1978 the Director General of Fair Trading stated that in the course of making 1614 routine checks, over 50% of vehicles were found to have been 'clocked', costing purchasers an estimated £50m a year. Persistent offenders have found that their licenses to engage in consumer credit transactions have been withheld, suspended or revoked under Part 3 of the Fair Trading Act 1973.

In *R v Southwood* [1987] 3 All ER 556 the appellant was a secondhand car dealer whose stock apparently included a number of used cars with a higher than average odometer reading. In each case the appellant had turned back the odometer before selling the cars and without stating original mileage. The appellant attempted to protect himself by the well-known device of a disclaimer. Each invoice had a statement indicating that 'we do not guarantee the accuracy of the recorded mileage' and there was a similar notice in the office. Each car had a sticker on the odometer stating 'we do not guarantee the accuracy of the recorded mileage. To the best of our knowledge and belief, however, the reading is incorrect'. The adhesive disclaimer on the odometer here is in a familiar form to those to be found in many secondhand car sales yards and normally allows the seller to state that in his opinion the reading is either correct or incorrect. Here, since the odometers had been 'zeroed', the mileages must have been incorrect, the relevant wording being disingenuous in this respect.

Pausing a moment here, the practice of zeroing in the manner in question here had seemingly been blessed in a passage from the judgment of Lord Widgery CJ in *K Lill Holdings Ltd v White* [1979] RTR 120 (Divisional Court). In that case Lord Widgery CJ had said (ibid at 123):

> 'Whilst it is no business of ours to recommend or otherwise approve practices of the trade, I feel bound to say that I can see a good deal of merit in this method of winding back the odometer, because it does seem to me that, for the time being at all events, it puts the problem of a false odometer out of the reckoning because no-one will be misled by such a record'.

In that case the defendants had also placed a disclaimer as to the accuracy of the odometer inside the cab of a motor car and on a notice in their office. On the basis of this, no doubt, the practice of zeroing was thought by some members of the trade to be legitimate.

However, a parallel development in trade descriptions law had taken place as a result of the decisions of the Divisional Court in *Corfield v Starr* [1981] RTR 380 and *Newman v Hackney London BC* [1982] RTR 296. The gist of these decisions is that the effectiveness of disclaimer notices, the law relating to which is entirely the creation of the courts (since the Act itself does not mention this device), should be judged differently according to whether the offence committed prima facie lies under s 1(1)(a) or 1(1)(b) of the Act. The distinction is that s 1(1)(a) applies to any person who, in the course of a trade or business, *applies* a false trade description to any goods (an 'active' offence); whereas s 1(1)(b) applies to any person who, in the course of a trade or business, supplies or offers to supply any goods to which a false description is applied (a 'passive' offence). The distinction between the two offences is highlighted by the terms of the major defence supplied by the Act relating to what is otherwise an offence of strict liability. Section 24(1) states that it is a defence for the accused to prove that both (a) the commission of the offence was due to a mistake etc or to the act or default of another person etc *and* that (b) he took all reasonable precautions and exercised all due diligence to avoid the commission of such an offence by himself or any person under his control. This important defence is clearly inapplicable to somebody who deliberately falsifies an odometer and so commits an offence under s 1(1)(a). Did it follow, therefore, that there was also no escape by using a disclaimer notice? As Lord Lane CJ pithily observed ([1987] 3 All ER 556 at 560):

> 'this would be saying: "This is a false trade description. I assert that it is a false trade description, and because I have said that it is a false trade description it ceases to be a false trade description applied to goods, and consequently I am not guilty of a contravention of s 1(1)(a)".'

The Court of Appeal concluded that the so-called 'disclaimer' provides no defence to a person charged under s 1(1)(a).

Accordingly, it follows from this that the Court of Appeal had now laid down that a person who zeroes the odometer applies a false trade description just as much as a person who reduces it to, say, 15,000 miles. Furthermore, it is not open to a person who has actively applied a false trade description in this way to purport to disclaim it by stickers or notices. If a disclaimer were to be effective at all it could only be appropriate to a charge laid under s 1(1)(b) where the false trade description has already been applied by somebody other than the supplier in question of the vehicle. The true effect of an operative disclaimer is to negate the making of a trade description; it is not a defence once one has been made. And in principle, one cannot disclaim the consequences of one's own wrongdoing. If, on the other hand, someone buys a car with a false reading already registered, the falsity of which comes to his knowledge, his protection against a charge under s 1(1)(b) will be a suitable and candid intimation to the customer of the falsity, thereby bringing himself within s 24(1).

To illustrate the seriousness of these offences, in this case the appellant was convicted on ten counts, each alleging the contravention of s 1(1)(a) and originally sentenced to six months imprisonment. The Court of Appeal varied this only by ordering that four of the six months sentence be suspended.

Other trading law cases

The All England Law Reports necessarily present a selective account of reported litigation in trading standards law. A valuable supplement exists to practitioners involved in trading standards law in the recently launched series of Butterworths Trading Law Cases. As a tailnote and appetiser, the following decisions are worthy of note.

(a) Trade descriptions

In *R v Bow Street Magistrates' Court ex p Joseph* [1987] BTLC 116, QBD, a solicitor applied by way of judicial review to bring a private prosecution against the Law Society. He claimed that it had caused to be published an advertisement which infringed s 14(1) of the Trade Descriptions Act 1968 (a false statement as to services). It was held that the Law Society did not carry on any operation with a commercial connotation and was not therefore capable of making a statement 'in the course of a trade or business' as required by s 14 of the 1968 Act. It followed that the application to bring a private prosecution was misconceived and vexatious. The application was dismissed.

In *Best Travel Ltd v Patterson* [1987] BTLC 119, QBD, the defendants had published a travel brochure stating that a certain hotel had bar and lounge facilities which, had they enquired, they would have know not true. It followed that they were rightly convicted of recklessly making a false statement contrary to s 14(2)(b) of the 1968 Act.

In *Wolkind v Pura Foods Ltd* [1987] BTLC 181, QBD, it was held that although 'lard' is technically pig fat, a product advertised as 'Vegetable lard. 100% Vegetable Oils' and containing no animal fat did not contravene s 1 of the Trade Descriptions Act 1968. No reasonably-minded court could find that today the word 'lard' means 'pig fat' only. Furthermore, the use of the word 'vegetable' in the label was in any case sufficiently bold, precise and compelling to found a valid disclaimer and negate what might otherwise have been a false trade description.

(b) Consumer credit

In *Forward Trust Ltd v Robinson* [1987] BTLC 12, CC, the position on early repayment of a loan of £600 was considered, the early repayment being somewhat notional since the obligation arose under a default notice served on the debtor under s 87(1) of the Consumer Credit Act 1974. The question was whether judgment should be given for unliquidated damages or for a liquidated sum, particularly in the light of the statutory provision for a rebate on early settlement (see Consumer Credit (Rebate on Early Settlement) Regulations 1983). The judge held that there was nothing in Ord 9, r 8(1) of the County Court Rules 1981 to prevent the court from giving judgment in default for a liquidated sum even though that sum might be reduced in the future by the operation of the statutory rebate. The court should regard the claim as one for a total rounded-off sum which was due because of the agreement between the parties. This was a liquidated sum and it was, in any event, unlikely on the facts that the defendant would pay off the contract in such time as to qualify for a rebate. Judgment was accordingly given for the capital sum lent plus interest, less the amount already paid by the defendant.

The BTLC also include a number of reports on cases concerning sale of goods and unfair contract terms as well as on other matters of consumer protection law, the reports of which are not readily accessible elsewhere.

Contempt of Court

C J MILLER, BA, LLM
Barrister, Professor of Law, University of Warwick

A survey of the cases on contempt of court reported in the All England Law Reports for 1987 runs up against the difficulty that some of the more important were either still in progress at the end of the year or were overshadowed by cases to be reported and commented on in 1988. The Spycatcher proceedings fell into the former category (and they may fall into the latter also), whilst *Maxwell v Pressdram Ltd* [1987] 1 All ER 656, a case on the scope of the protection accorded by s 10 of the Contempt of Court Act 1981 to journalists wishing to conceal their source of information, was overshadowed by *Re an inquiry under the Company Securities (Insider Dealing) Act 1985* [1988] 1 All ER 203. Apart from these areas, there were also cases of interest on the requirements of open justice and on civil contempt.

Contempt and breach of confidence

Although, at least on a narrow view, the Spycatcher proceedings are concerned primarily with breach of confidence, they are also making an important contribution to the development of the law of contempt. As is well known, the background to this long-running saga was that intelocutory injuctions had been issued against the Guardian and the Observer, restraining them from publishing information obtained by Peter Wright in his capacity as a member of the British Security Service. The material had been published in Wright's book of memoirs, *Spycatcher*, the sales of which predictably benefitted from the publicity associated with high-profile legal proceedings. The newspapers' appeal to the House of Lords was dismissed (*A-G v Guardian Newspapers Ltd* [1987] 3 All ER 316, at 342). Currently, as the saga unfolds, the press is faring better in resisting an application to have the injunctions made permanent. At the time of writing the Attorney-General's application has been refused both by Scott J and, perhaps more surprisingly, by the Court of Appeal (*The Times* 11 February 1988). However publication is still restrained pending an appeal to the House of Lords. Should this be successful, it is to be expected that attempts will be made to follow the by now well-trodden path to the European Court of Human Rights.

Contempt of court is closely and routinely associated with breach of injunctions, but in the present case the matter arose in an unusual way. This occurred when the Independent and other newspapers, which were not directly subject to the interlocutory injunctions, published further material derived from, or attributable to, Wright's memoirs. The Attorney-General sought an order that the publishers be found in contempt of court and the issue whether such conduct was capable of amounting to a contempt was directed to be tried as a preliminary point of law. Reversing the judgment of Sir Nicolas Browne-Wilkinson, V-C, the Court of Appeal held in *A-G v Newspaper Publishing plc* [1987] 3 All ER 276 at 289, that the publication were *capable* of amounting to a contempt. Whether they were actually a contempt would, however, depend on the intent with which they were published, this being a matter to be determined by the court of first instance.

Although this decision is of considerable interest, it is not without difficulty. So far as the previous authorities were concerned it had of course long been clear that a third party might commit a contempt by assisting or procuring another to act in breach of an order or undertaking. Leading cases in point include *Seaward v Paterson* [1897] 1 Ch 545 and *Lord Wellesley v Earl of Mornington* (1848) 11 Beav 180, 50 ER 785. A modest extension of this principle was recognised by Eveleigh LJ, in *Z Ltd v A-Z* [1982] 1 All ER 556 (All ER Rev 1982, p 69), where the concern was with the position of a bank on receiving notice of a Mareva injunction. His Lordship was clear that the bank might be in contempt even though, in the absence of notice of the injunction, the person enjoined was not. The present decision extends this principle, or applies it to a new set of facts, by holding that a third party may commit a contempt even though the person enjoined is not in breach of the injunction and indeed may have made it clear that it will be reluctantly obeyed. This raises a number of related issues, of which the most important are the nature and basis of the liability incurred by the third party and the mental element which must be established.

On the first issue, the approach adopted by the Court of Appeal was to treat the conduct of the Independent as being capable of amounting to a criminal contempt on the ground that any destroying of the subject matter of the confidence would interfere with the administration of justice by depriving the Attorney-General of his claim to have the confidence protected. As Sir John Donaldson noted, 'information once published, at least on the scale achieved by publication in national newspapers, can never be truly confidential again.' In the language of the criminal law, any contempt committed by the Independent would be as a principal offender, rather than an aider and abettor. Consequently, it was not necessarily in point that those enjoined by the interlocutory injunction were not themselves in breach.

Although the view is unfashionable in some quarters, the decision on this point must surely be correct. If confidences, or for that matter secret processes, are within the protection of the law, it can hardly make sense for the courts to deny themselves the ability to make the protection effective. The difficulty lies in knowing in what circumstances the decision can be applied. Unfortunately, although a number of interesting hypothetical examples were discussed, the judgments in the Court of Appeal offer little guidance on this issue beyond suggesting that the scope of the general principle may not be confined too narowly. For example, in the judgment of Lloyd, LJ ([1987] 3 All ER 276 at 308), it may extend to any case in which conduct prevents the court from conducting the proceedings in accordance with its intention.

If the scope of the principle affecting third parties is potentially wide, it is limited in an important respect by the need to establish the appropriate mental element. Contempt has shown little consistency on this point over the years. Indeed Sir John Donaldson rightly said (ibid at 303): 'Mens rea in the law of contempt is something of a minefield.' The approach of the

Court of Appeal in the present case was to categorise the alleged contempt as one which prima facie fell within the strict liability rule of the Contempt of Court Act 1981 in that the publication tended to interfere with particular legal proceedings between the Attorney-General and the Guardian. However since these proceedings were not active at the time of publication the case could not succeed on this basis. Thereafter the court was unanimous in holding that, by virtue of s 6(c) of the 1981 Act, a contempt would have been committed by the Independent only on proof of an intent to impede or prejudice the administration of justice. In dealing with submission that recklessness would be sufficient, Lloyd, LJ said (ibid at 310):

> 'In cases covered by the Act to which the strict liability rule does not apply there is no room for a state of mind which falls short of intention. There is no middle way.
>   I would therefore hold that the mens rea required in the present case is an intent to interfere with the course of justice. As in other branches of the criminal law, that intent may exist, even though there is no desire to interfere with the course of justice. Nor need it be the sole intent. It may be inferred even though there is no overt proof. The more obvious the interference with the course of justice, the more readily will the requisite intent be inferred.'

The decision on this point has the advantage of bringing the law of contempt into line with the indictable offence based on conduct which tends to pervert the course of justice (see the discussion of *R v Selvage and Morgan* [1982] 1 All ER 96 in All ER Rev 1982, p 71). However its full implications for the mental element which must be proved in cases of summary proceedings for criminal contempt are less clear. It appears to apply to alleged contempts by publication which are of a kind which might have fallen within the strict liability rule of the 1981 Act but, because all the elements of that rule are not satisfied, do not do so. For example, if there is not the necessary substantial risk of serious prejudice to particular proceedings (see s 2(2) of the Act) or if the proceedings were not active at the time of publication (see s 2(3) of and Sch 1 to the Act), the full intent must be proved. Where such potential contempts by prejudicing particular legal proceedings are not involved, it is probable that something less than full intent will be sufficient. For example, it may be enough to prove knowledge of the substance of the order and a conscious decision to assist in its breach or frustration.

(The readers' attention is also drawn to *A-G v News Group Newspaper Ltd*, (1988) *Times* 20 February, another potentially very important case involving the Sun newspaper, which illustrates the existence of a common law jurisdiction in areas where a statutory contempt under the strict liability rule could not be established.)

An alternative way of dealing with the problems which arose in the Spycatcher case is to treat the injunctions as being directly binding on 'third parties'. Obviously there are difficulties with any such approach since the established rule, as expressed by Lord Eldon LC, in *Iveson v Harris* (1802) Ves 251, 256, is that it is not open to a court 'to hold a man bound by injunction, who is not a party in the cause for the purpose of the cause...' The question whether there are exceptions to this rule was discussed by

Balcome LJ. Having referred to his own decision at first instance in *XCC v A* [1985] 1 All ER 53 (All ER Rev 1985, p 74), he continued ([1987] 3 All ER 276 at 314):

> 'In that case I held that, in the exercise of the wardship jurisdiction, there was power to make an order (prohibiting the publication of information about the ward) binding on the world at large, when persons who were potentially subject to that order had not been parties to the proceedings in which the order was obtained... I believe that there can be another exception to the general rule which would enable the court to make an order, binding on the world at large, in the circumstances of the present case, where such an order may be appropriate to preserve the subject matter of an action pending trial. The law of contempt is but one example of the court's ability to regulate its own procedures so as to ensure that justice prevails. The rule that courts normally act only in personam is but another example of the same process. If the court needs to ensure that the subject matter of an existing action be preserved against all comers pending the trial of the action, then in my judgment the court can obtain the desired result by introducing another exception to the general rule that the court acts only in personam.'

His Lordship went on to suggest that this would be the more satisfactory way of dealing with the problem thrown up by the facts of the case.

Dealing with the same issue, Sir John Donaldson, MR disagreed and did not appear to envisage any exception to the general rule. In his judgment there was no jurisdiction, even in wardship proceedings, to make an order of the type envisaged by Balcombe J (as he then was) in *XCC v A*. The editor of a newspaper which had not been before the court could not be bound directly by the injunction as such. He could be proceeded against only on the basis that he had interfered with the administration of justice by disclosing details of the ward. Lloyd LJ, acknowledged the fundamental principle that our courts act in personam, but was, it seems, prepared to envisage 'certain very limted exceptions, of which the best established is wardship.'

Given the difference of views on this point, the law is left in a state of some uncertainty. The main problem with the approach preferred by Balcome LJ is that there are obvious objections of principle to injunctions which operate contra mundum. For example, it is by no means clear that there can be a general right to make representations against such injunctions being granted. More generally, it may be felt that such injunctions are in effect acts of judicial legislation in all but name. On the other hand, the approach has the advantage that 'third parties', being bound by and directly subject to the injunction, would be potentially liable for a civil, rather than criminal, contempt. In spite of all the difficulties, it is submitted that the balance of advantage, at least in cases involving wards, breach of confidence and secret processes, lies in adopting the approach preferred by Balcombe J.

A similar issue arose and was discussed in *Re L (a minor)* [1988] 1 All ER 418, to be commented on in next year's Annual Review.

Journalists and their sources of information

The background to *Maxwell v Pressdram Lrd* [1987] 1 All ER 656 was the long-running battle between Mr Robert Maxwell and the satirical magazine, 'Private Eye'. The Eye's allegation was that Mr Maxwell had financed trips for Mr Neil Kinnock in the expectation or hope of being recommended for a peerage. Pleas of justification and fair comment having been withdrawn and struck out, respectively, the main issue in the case was Mr Maxwell's claim for aggravated and exemplary damages. The Eye maintained that its allegations were based on information from well-placed and reliable sources which its editor, Mr Richard Ingrams, declined to reveal. Thus the stage was set for the familiar judicial dilemma which now falls to be resolved according to the terms of s 10 of the Contempt of Court Act 1981. In the context of the present case disclosure could be ordered only if it was established that it was 'necessary in the interests of justice'. Simon Brown J had declined to make the order and his decision was upheld on appeal by the Court of Appeal.

Although the decision does little more than illustrate the exercise of judgment (and not simply discretion) on a particular set of facts, there are some points of more general interest. One is the recognition by the court that a refusal to reveal (and subpoena) may arise from a genuine belief in the need to protect sources. A cynic would claim that usually it stems rather from a belief that disclosure would weaken the case. As Parker LJ noted (ibid at 667):

> 'The newspaper may be well served by revealing a source; it may equally be escaping from a difficult situation by refusing to reveal a source. But it should not be supposed that refusal indicates that the disclosure would be against the newspaper's interests. It often is not; it sometimes is.'

A further point of general interest is the insistence of the Court of Appeal that disclosure must be *necessary*, and not merely relevant and desirable, in the interests of justice. In this, of course, the court was following the decision of the House of Lords in *Secretary of State for Defence v Guardian Newspapers Ltd* [1984] 3 All ER 601. Moreover, Kerr LJ noted ([1987] 1 All ER 656 at 665), before applying the test of necessity, 'it is essential first to identify and define the issue in the legal proceedings which is said to require the disclosure of sources'. Finally, it may be noted that the press did not enjoy a similar success in the subsequent case involving the Independent newspaper journalist, Jeremy Warner. *Re an inquiry under the Company Security (Insider Dealing) Act 1985* [1988] 1 All ER 203 will be commented on in the Annual Review for 1988.

Open justice

Constraints on open justice have been one of the most marked aspects of contempt of court and associated topics to have come to the forefront of discusison in recent years. In part this has been as a result of the provisions in ss 4(2) and 11 of the Contempt of Court Act 1981. However, as *R v Felixstowe JJ, ex p Leigh* [1987] 1 All ER 551 shows, the problem can crop up in other ways.

In this case the applicant, David Leigh, an experienced journalist specialising in the criminal law, was applying for judicial review in respect of the practice of remaining anonymous of the justices of Felixstowe and surrounding areas. The clerk to the Bench had cited this practice when refusing to reveal the names of the justices who had heard an unusual and seedy case involving six adults who were accused of gross indecency with a 12-month old child in a bath. The Divisional Court granted a declaration that the policy was unlawful, but refused an order of mandamus directing that the names of the justices be disclosed. This was because the applicant, who had not been present in court at the time of the hearing, did not have the necessary locus standi to seek the order.

The point of particular interest in the case is not simply that the policy was declared unlawful, but rather the extent to which the court emphasised what Watkins LJ recognised as 'the vital significance of the work of the jounalist in reporting court proceedings'. As his Lordship noted, there was also the practical point that a policy of anonymity was inimical to scrutiny of whether a given magistrate had such an interest in the case, or association with a party to proceedings, that it was improper for him or her to sit. Moreover, others holding judicial or quasi-judicial office (and indeed jurors) had no similar shield against intrusions into their privacy. In short, and in the words of Watkins, LJ (ibid at 561), the Divisional Court found the policy 'inimical to the proper administration of justice and an unwarranted and an unlawful obstruction to the right to know who sits in judgment'. His Lordship added: 'There is, in my view, no such person known to the law as the anonymous JP.'

R v Malvern JJ, ex p Evans, R v Evesham JJ, ex p McDonagh [1988] 1 All ER 371, other important cases on open justice in magistrates courts, will be commented on in the Annual Review for 1988.

Civil contempt

As regular readers of the Annual Review will know, the procedural requirements which must be observed before a person can be committed or fined for a civil contempt have given rise to considerable difficulties over the years. These requirements are ultimately concerned to ensure that alleged contemnors have a proper opportunity to defend themselves and, if unsuccessful, knowledge of what it is that they are being imprisoned or fined for. All this seems elementary and the instinctive reaction is one of impatience that the legal professions and the courts have got things wrong on such a regular basis. However it must also be said that their task has been made no easier by requirements which had become almost excessively technical and which, it might be argued, went beyond those of procedural fairness. There is also the very important point that unpleasant consequences can ensue from failing to do things correctly, especially where non-molestation orders and domestic violence are concerned.

Such was the general background to the decision of the Court of Appeal in *Harmsworth v Harmsworth* [1987] 3 All ER 816. The wife in this case had instituted contempt proceedings in respect of alleged breaches on a non-molestation order. However her notice to show cause contained only generalised allegations of the incidents relied on and did not specify the dates and places. Moreover it made no reference to a serious assault which was subsequently relied on at the hearing. The relevant details were provided, rather, in a separate supporting affidavit sworn by the wife. The husband's appeal against committal to the Court of Appeal was successful to the extent that the order was set aside as a nullity. This was principally on the ground that the judge had wrongly taken account of the serious assault to which reference had not been made in the notice. However the Court of Appeal, relying on *Linnett v Coles* [1986] 3 All ER 652 (All ER Rev 1986, p 82) used its powers under s 13(3) of the Administration of Justice Act 1960 to substitute a new order.

A number of points of general interest emerge from this decision. The first is the need for the notice, or in the case of the High Court, the motion, to contain sufficient particulars of the breaches alleged. Although it is permissible for the particulars to be contained in a schedule or addendum to the notice, any insufficiency of particulars in the notice cannot be made good by their incorporation in a separate document. So far as the form and extent of the particulars are concerned, Woolf LJ commented ([1987] 3 All ER at 823):

> 'What is not required by the relevant rules is that the notice of the motion should be drafted as though it was an indictment in criminal proceedings. While a respondent is required to be given particulars of what is alleged to be the breach, the particulars do not need to be set out in the same way as separate counts have to be set out in an indictment, nor do they need to give the particulars that you would normally expect to be seen in a count in an indictment. Furthermore, in my view, rules of duplicity and other rules which are designed to ensure the fairness of a trial before a jury, do not apply to proceedings of a different nature which are brought in respect of an alleged contempt'

A further point of interest is that s 13(3) of the 1960 Act was used in a case in which the defect lay in the notice to show cause rather than in the committal order. However, Woolf LJ appears to have recognised that there may be a difference between the two situations in that, 'In the case of the notice, a defect can clearly materially affect the fairness of the proceedings'; so that, 'In such a situation it may not be just to make use of the powers under s 13(3).' However, as is clear from *Jelson (Estates) Ltd v Harvey* [1984] 1 All ER Rev 1984, p 65), since the respondent to the defective notice would not have been in jeopardy the court would have the power to hear a further application in correct form founded on the same contempt. The combination of these two factors should assist in discouraging unmeritorious appeals based on technicalities rather than true lack of procedural fairness.

Although procedural fairness usually requires the alleged contemnor to be served personally with the notice to show cause why he should not be committed for contempt, such service may be dispensed with in exceptional cases. Also it is possible for a contemnor to be committed to prison in his absence. Such was the position in *Wright v Jess* [1987] 2 All ER 1067 where there had been serious and repeated breaches of a non-molestation order. The Court of Appeal upheld a committal for two years (the maximum permissible term) on an ex parte application of a contemnor who had been committed on three previous occasions and given clear warning as to his future conduct. The court stressed that this course was appropriate only in exceptional cases and that the decision to dispense with service ought to have been recorded in the committal order. Clearly the respondent was a dangerous man whose conduct left little room for sympathy.

Wards of court

Finally, the attention of readers is drawn to a *Practice Direction* [1987] 3 All ER 640 concerning the disclosure of evidence concerning wards of court to persons who are not parties to the proceedings.

Criminal Law, Criminal Procedure and Sentencing

G J BENNETT, MA
Barrister, Lecturer in Law, University of Leeds

BRIAN HOGAN, LLB
Barrister, Professor of Common Law, University of Leeds

One can only guess at the degree of pleasurable anticipation experienced by readers of the *All England Annual Review* when they receive the latest volume. Where best to dip in? Contract? Land Law and Trusts? Shipping? It's all there. Twelve months of judicial wisdom neatly encapsulated and barely a cross word (decisions of the House of Lords always excepted) by any of the contributors. Some of us are surprised that a concerted effort has not been made by the readership to have the *Review* completed by Christmas. It would make an admirable stocking-filler for the lawyer and is really tailormade to fill the gap between the rituals of opening presents and the Queen's broadcast.

The section on Criminal Law, Criminal Procedure and Sentencing would be best kept, perhaps, for late evening. By that time the children will have gone to bed so it can be read without embarrassment. Also it is entirely undemanding. Just straightforward sex and violence. Not a subtlety in sight. Well, not quite. To the surprise, and probably dismay, of our readers, there's a little bit on attempting the impossible. You don't believe it? Just read on.

CRIMINAL LAW

General principles

1 Duress

We begin with the case of *R v Howe* [1986] 1 All ER 833, [1987] 1 All ER 771. The issue, it will be recalled, was whether duress, a threat of death or serious bodily harm, is a defence to murder if the person threatened succumbs to the threat and kills or is a party to the killing of another. The state of play was that the House of Lords had in *Lynch v DPP for Northern Ireland* [1975] 1 All ER 913 recognised that duress was available to a secondary party in murder but in *Abbot v The Queen* [1976] 1 All ER 140 the Privy Council had denied the defence to a principal in murder. Not an entirely satisfactory situation and in the Court of Appeal the Lord Chief Justice's proposal to resolve the anomaly was to deny it to both. That suggestion was accepted by the House of Lords and *Lynch* was overruled.

That, it might be said, is very definitely that. The House of Lords, though somewhat cavalier with its previous decisions in criminal cases, is not likely to change its mind twice. No doubt the decision will have its defenders but it leaves grotesque anomalies in its wake. The person threatened is to be acquitted of causing grievous bodily harm with intent if death does not ensue but convicted of murder and subjected to a mandatory sentence of life imprisonment if it does though the difference may turn on luck or on the skill of surgeons. The person threatened who wounds another has a complete defence to a charge of malicious wounding but, if he intends to kill, the logic of the decision is that he may be convicted of attempted murder.

In a way the case was a bad one in which to decide the issue of principle. All three defendants had, it would seem, voluntarily placed themselves under the leadership of men known to be ruthless and violent and had at no stage sought to withdraw from that liaison. *R v Sharp* [1987] 3 All ER 103 shows, and rightly shows, that duress is not available to one who joins a gang knowing that its members will use violence and that he will be expected or ordered also to use violence. Lord Lane CJ on behalf of the Court of Appeal said (ibid at 109):

'where a person has voluntarily, and with knowledge of its nature, joined a criminal organisation or gang which he knew might bring pressure on him to commit an offence and was an active member when he was put under such pressure, he cannot avail himself of the defence of duress.'

So no tears would be shed for the defendants in *Howe*. But what of the terrified passenger in an aircraft hijacked by terrorists who, out of a wellfounded fear for his own life or that of a member of his family, assists the terrorists in the murder of a member of the crew? Lord Griffiths' answer is to say that the passenger would not be prosecuted. But why ever not? It cannot be because many of us might do the same thing in the passenger's shoes since *Howe* requires us all to play the hero. Nor can it be because the passenger is merely a secondary party since *Lynch* has been overruled. Perhaps the decision to prosecute will turn on whether the defendant is regarded as a good guy or a bad guy.

In the Court of Appeal Lord Lane CJ expressed the view that if duress was to be admitted at all as a defence to murder, it should, on analogy with provocation, merely reduce the crime to manslaughter. This suggestion, it was no more than that, found no supporter among their lordships though Lord Griffiths said he might have been prepared to go down this road had murder still carried the death penalty. There was clearly no authority for this sort of halfway house solution and if it was to be introduced at all it could only be done by Parliament.

A final point on duress concerned the standard to be applied. In *R v Graham* [1982] 1 All ER 801 the Court of Appeal had approved a two-tier test in largely objective terms: (i) was the defendant, or may he have been, impelled to act as he did because, as a result of what he reasonably believed the threatener had said or done, he had good cause to fear that if he did not so act the threatener would kill him or cause him serious injury and (ii) if so, have the prosecution made the jury sure that a sober person of reasonable firmness, sharing the characteristics of the defendant, would not have responded to whatever he reasonably believed the threatener said or did by taking part in the crime.

The question was put in simpler terms to the House of Lords: does the defence of duress fail if the prosecution prove that a person of reasonable firmness sharing the characteristics of the defendant would not have given way to the threats as did the defendant? That question was answered by a unanimous Yes and Lord Mackay expressed his complete approval of the *Graham* direction.

It is entirely understandable that the question posed should have been answered in the affirmative and that an objective standard should be applied to the nature of the duress. Having said that, however, aspects of the *Graham* direction may call for reconsideration. Under the *Graham* direction the defendant is denied the defence if he honestly but unreasonably believed that his life was in danger. This contrasts oddly with the subjective approach to the defence of self-defence both by the Court of Appeal in *R v Williams* [1987] 3 All ER 411 and the Privy Council in *Beckford v R* [1987] 3 All ER 425. These two cases are considered below.

2 Parties to crime

Second-guessing the House of Lords in criminal cases is a hazardous business but your reviewers felt confident enough to predict in the last issue of the Review the outcome of *Howe* on another important point. *R v Richards* [1973] 3 All ER 1088 had decided that where a principal was convicted of a less serious offence, in that case malicious wounding, a secondary party could not be convicted of a more serious offence, in that case of wounding with intent to do grievous bodily harm, though the actus reus of the more serious offence was caused and the secondary party had the mens rea for it. In *Howe* Lord Lane CJ pointed out the absurdity of this in that it would mean that if A hands a gun to B telling B that it was loaded only with a blank and that he was to frighten X with it, A would escape conviction for murder though he knows the gun to be loaded with a live round and intended X's death. He accordingly invited the House of Lords to overrule *Richards*. This their lordships did without troubling counsel for the Crown to argue the point.

3 Mistake

R v Williams [1987] 3 All ER 411 was in fact decided in 1983 and makes a belated appearance. Its significance in the development of the criminal law is such that your reviewers took the liberty of noting it at All ER Review 1984, p 91. It has now been approved by the Privy Council in *Beckford v R* [1987] 3 All ER 425.

The issue in both cases was one on which there is a large volume of historical precedent and an impressive array of literature: where the defendant acts under a mistake of fact, is it sufficient to negative his mens rea that he is honestly mistaken or must his mistake be based on reasonable grounds?

Viewed as a matter of principle there can only be one answer that makes sense. If the defendant believes, however and whyever, that he is acting in circumstances that would, if true, make his conduct lawful, he lacks mens rea and to impute mens rea to him because there are no reasonable grounds for his mistake is to impose criminal liability for negligence.

This was essentially the view taken by Lord Lane CJ delivering the judgment of the Court of Appeal in *Williams*. Threatened, as Lord Lane put it, with the large volume of historical precedent, the answer was to be found in *R v Kimber* [1983] 3 All ER 316 (All ER Rev 1983, p 131) which had in turn applied the *Morgan* principle (*DPP v Morgan* [1975] 2 All ER 347). That principle, as it was understood in *Kimber*, was taken to require on a charge of assault that the prosecution prove that the defendant had intentionally or recklessly applied force to the victim without his consent and if the defendant in fact believed that the victim consented then the prosecution has failed to make out its case.

In *Williams* Lord Lane applied, as he saw it, the same principle where the defendant, believing that X was being attacked by Y when Y was lawfully arresting X, went to the defence of X. The trial judge was wrong, it was held, to direct the jury that the defendant was guilty of assault if he had no reasonable grounds for his belief. The reasonableness or unreasonableness of the defendant's belief is material to the question of whether the belief was held at all, but if he did so believe then the element of unlawfulness in assault was lacking. Assault is not constituted by an application of force to another but by an *unlawful* application of force and if the defendant believes he is applying force in circumstances which, if true, would make the application lawful, he cannot be convicted of assault.

Had *Williams* gone to the House of Lords in 1983 it is by no means certain that the Court of Appeal's view would have been upheld. There is much authority which supports the reasonable grounds qualification in mistake; the *Morgan* principle might have been considered inapplicable as not applying to a mistake merely as to circumstances; and there is an innate conflict of philosophy between the view of criminal liability taken in *R v Caldwell* [1981] 1 All ER 961 and in *Williams*.

The point did, however, arise for consideration by the Privy Council in *Beckford*. There the defendant, a police officer, shot dead an unarmed suspect who sought to escape. The defendant said he believed the suspect to be armed and to have fired at him and claimed to have acted in self-defence. It was held, quashing the defendant's conviction for murder, that the trial judge was wrong to rule that self-defence was available only if the defendant had reasonable grounds for believing that his life was in danger. Acknowledging that before *Morgan* the 'whole weight of authority' supported the reasonable grounds qualification in self-defence, the Privy Council approved the reasoning in *Williams* and concluded that because it is essential in crimes of violence that the violence be unlawful, the defendant is entitled to an acquittal if he belives in circumstances which, if true, would render his conduct lawful.

These are welcome developments, at least to the subjectivist, and the law is being set on a better course. Nevertheless it is permissible to wonder if the House in *Morgan* intended to go quite this far. The principle there articulated involved identifying the so-called 'prohibited act' in rape (held to be intercourse without consent) and did not necessarily extend to all the elements in the actus reus. The House was clear that it did not intend to call in question the reasonable grounds qualification to the bigamy defences. Yet, of course, if the defendant unreasonably believes that his marriage to A has been dissolved, he cannot intend 'being married to marry B and to hold that he commits bigamy is entirely inconsistent with the *Morgan* principle as that principle has been applied in *Williams* and *Beckford*. By parity of reasoning *R v Prince* (1875) LR 2 CCR 154 should be overruled because, believing the girl to be 18 years old, the defendant cannot have intended to take a 16 year-old girl out of the possession of parents. On the facts as he believed them to be, Prince's conduct was entirely lawful. But in *Morgan* Lord Hailsham was clear that nothing said in *Morgan* called *Prince* into question.

So there are some bits of the jigsaw which still do not fit. Moreover, one large piece, labelled *Caldwell*, which embraces negligence, albeit gross, as a ground of liability for an as yet undetermined number of crimes does not fit in at all well with these recent developments of the *Morgan* principle.

A third case to raise an issue of mistake was *R v Whyte* [1987] 3 All ER 416. It is established law that a person may use such force as is reasonable in the circumstances in defence of himself or another. It is also established that what is reasonable in the circumstances is to be determined objectively and it is not enough that the defendant believes his use of force to be reasonable. On the other hand, and most especially where the defendant is taken by surprise in circumstances leaving no time for reflection, it was held in *Whyte* that it is appropriate to direct a jury that if the defendant had only done what he honestly and instinctively thought was necessary that would be very strong evidence that the defensive action taken was reasonable. There was, however, no need for such a direction in the instant case where the defendant had armed himself with a lock-knife *before* having an altercation with the victim during which, as the defendant claimed, the victim struck him in the face.

4 Intoxication

R v O'Grady [1987] 3 All ER 420 was the fourth case during the year concerned with issues of mistake and self-defence but this time the issue was clouded by intoxication. The defendant and his friend having been drinking heavily went to sleep in the defendant's flat. According to the defendant's account, he awoke to find his friend hitting him and he used what he thought were a few blows to defend himself. In fact the blows struck by the defendant were very severe and inflicted serious injuries causing his friend's death. On self-defence which was raised on a charge of murder, the trial judge ruled that the defendant was entitled to rely on his drunken mistake as to the existence of an attack but not as to the amount of force necessary to repel it. The defendants conviction for murder was affirmed. The second part of this direction is obviously right. As has been shown in the discussion of *Whyte*, above, what force is reasonable in the circumstances involves an objective assessment by the jury and in that assessment the possible effect of intoxication must be discounted; if the sober man is liable if he miscalculates the degree of force permissible so must be the drunken man.

But the Court of Appeal seems to have held that the first part of the judge's direction was incorrect. The court referred to a number of cases which contained suggestions that drunkenness could be taken into account when determining what the defendant genuinely believed but said the reports of these cases left a lot to be desired and were not binding on the court. Lord Lane CJ said [1987] 3 All ER 420 at 433:

'We have come to the conclusion that, where the jury are satisfied that the defendant was mistaken in his belief that *any force* [italics supplied] or the force which he in fact used was necessary to defend himself and are further satisfied that the mistake was caused by voluntary intoxication, the defence must fail.'

This, with respect, harsh ruling was jutified by the court in the interests of public order and protecting the public. Reason recoils, said Lord Lane, from the idea that in such circumstances as these the defendant should leave the court without a stain on his character. This seems to leave out of account, as Professor Smith has pointed out ([1987] Crim LR 706), that the defendant in such a case may be properly convicted of manslaughter. Perhaps though, and since Lord Lane refers to an impeccable direction by the trial judge on the way in which intoxication may affect proof of an intent to kill, the judgment proceeds on the assumption that the jury found that the defendant intended to kill so that the choice lay only between a conviction for murder and acquittal.

Offences against the person

Indecent assault

Over the years various views of the mens rea of indecent assault have been canvassed by courts and commentators. Clearly there are two elements, one related to the assault and the other to the element of indecency. So far as the former is concerned the defendant must either intentionally or recklessly apply unlawful force to the victim (battery) or intentionally or recklessly cause the victim to apprehend an unlawful infliction of force (assault). So far as the latter is concerned the battery or assault must be accompanied by an element of indecency, and this has proved to be an elusive factor to define. In *R v Kilbourne* [1972] 3 All ER 545 the Court of Appeal held that the trial judge was wrong to direct a jury that, provided there was an assault, that assault became an indecent assault if it was accompanied by an indecent purpose. This was much too wide and the implication was that the assault must in some way display its indecent nature. On the other hand there was a ruling in *R v Pratt* [1984] Crim LR 41 that an assault in circumstances displaying indecency did not suffice if the defendant lacked any indecent purpose, so the offence was not committed where by threats the defendant forced two young boys to strip naked if his purpose was merely to ascertain whether they had stolen his property.

In *R v Court* [1987] 1 All ER 120 the defendant seized a 12 year-old girl, placed her across his knee and spanked her with his hand outside her shorts. When asked by the police why he had done so he attributed it to his 'buttock fetish'. Charged with indecent assault he sought to exclude his admission on the grounds that it was a secret motive which had not been communicated to the girl. The trial judge admitted the evidence and told the jury to convict if they found (i) that the conduct would be regarded as an affront to modesty; and (ii) that the defendant had an indecent intention.

The Court of Appeal upheld the defendant's conviction and in so doing came up with a new theory of the mens rea of indecent assault. The offence is committed by one who assaults another and knows or is reckless about the existence of circumstances which are indecent in the sense of contravening standards of decent behaviour in relation to sexual morality or privacy; and, given this, no proof of any further intention or motive was required. It followed that *Pratt* was wrongly decided; on its facts it was open to a jury to conclude that the boys had been assaulted in circumstances known to the defendant which in fact contravened decent standards of behaviour in relation to sexual morality and the fact that he may have had no sexual motive was irrelevant. It further followed that the trial judge was wrong in *Court* to rule that it was a requirement of the offence that the defendant had an indecent intention.

This was not to say that evidence of the defendant's indecent intention is always to be excluded. The court thought that the trial judge was right to admit it in the instant case because the spanking of a 12 year-old girl by a 27 year-old man might be indecent or not according to the purposes of the man. It might not be indecent if done by an uncle to his niece as part of horse-play but otherwise if it is done to afford sexual gratification. If the conduct is ambivalent, it seems that evidence of motive may be admitted provided it has probative value.

In one sense the decision may be applauded as an attempt to give precision to the definition of the mens rea of indecent assault. At least we are spared the judicial refuge of being told that it is all a matter of fact and degree. But it does, with respect, seem strange to say that a man acts indecently when no thought of indecency has crossed his mind and the decision further contemplates that he may be so convicted though it never occurred to the victim that the assault was indecent. A parallel might be drawn with the offence of blasphemy and the case of *R v Lemon* [1979] 1 All ER 898. There the defendant knew precisely what he was publishing (the poem suggesting that Christ was a homosexual) and intended to publish it but argued that he did not intend to blaspheme (to outrage Christian feelings) because he genuinely believed the poem would bring homosexuals to a greater love of Christ. It was held by the House of Lords that it sufficed that he intended to publish what he did and it was not necessary to show that he believed he was blaspheming. The two dissenting Law Lords thought that this made blasphemy a crime of strict liability. *Court* may have done the same for indecent assault.

Offences against property

1 Deception

To commit the offence of obtaining by deception contrary to s 15 of the Theft Act 1968 the defendant must of course by his deception obtain the property. It is not enough that a deception has been made but it is enough that the deception is *a* cause of the obtaining and it may be no less a cause though the defendant gives full value for the property obtained. In *R v King* [1987] 1 All ER 547 the defendants, falsely representing themselves to belong to a firm of tree specialists known to the victim, persuaded the victim, a lady of 68, to agree to pay £470 to have certain trees felled by falsely representing that these were a danger to the gas supply to, and the foundations of, her house. Fortunately a cashier at the building society where she went to draw out the money noticed her distress and the callous fraud was uncovered. Convicted of attempting to obtain £470 be deception the defendants argued on appeal that had they gone through with their scheme the full offence would not have been committed because they would have been paid the money for work which they had done and not be reason of the deception. They relied on *R v Lewis* (1922) Somerset Assizes, unreported, where a schoolmistress who obtained an appointment by falsely representing that she had a teacher's certificate was held not to have obtained her salary by false pretences since that was paid for services rendered.

It was held by the Court of Appeal that the defendants were rightly convicted. On the evidence the jury were entitled to conclude that the deceptions practised by the defendants were an operative cause of the obtaining. With respect this was correct because the victim would not have engaged the defendants but for the deception. Clearly *Lewis* would not now be followed on its facts though in such cases there may come a time when the deception is exhausted and the employee is paid only because of work done.

2 *Cheating*

While the aim of the Theft Act 1968 was to codify the law of theft and related offences and to state the law comprehensively, one exception was made. The Criminal Law Revision Committee sought to abolish the common law offence of cheating, the Revenue sought to retain it. They compromised. Cheating was abolished by s 32(1) of the Act: 'except as regards offences relating to the public revenue'.

You did not have to be a Detective Chief Superintendent to guess why the Revenue sought to retain cheating and the Revenue's highest hopes for it seem to have been realised in *R v Mavji* [1987] 2 All ER 758. The defendant had failed to make VAT returns on certain dealings in gold and the estimated tax loss was over £1,000,000. Charged, as he might have been, under s 38(1) of the Finance Act 1972 he would have been liable to a maximum penalty of two years' imprisonment and/or a fine of £1,000 or three times the value of the tax whichever was the greater. But the Revenue chose to prosecute for cheating where the penalty is at large and on conviction the defendant was sentenced to imprisonment for six years.

Affirming the defendant's conviction the Court of Appeal rejected the defendant's argument that cheating required some positive action such as a deception and that an omission to make VAT returns would not suffice. The defendant, it was held, was under a duty to make the returns and his failure to do so coupled with his intent to cheat the Revenue of the tax due to it constituted the offence.

The decision must have been greeted with loud hurras in every tax office in the land since it proved that the offence of cheating had a virtue, namely unlimited elasticity, not shared by offences under the Theft Acts. Before *Mavji* the authorities, such as they were, had at least indicated that the offence required the making of a false statement. Classically some 'artful device' has been required and it is not at all clear what artful device was practised by the defendant in *Mavji*.

3 Damaging property endangering life

In *R v Steer* [1987] 2 All ER 833 the House of Lords affirmed the decision of the Court of Appeal ([1986] 3 All ER 611; All ER Rev 1986, p 108) and for pretty well the same reasons. It is not clear why the point in the case was considered to be one of any great difficulty.

4 Forgery

Afficionados of the crime of forgery cannot but feel pleased with the outcome of the two cases which appeared in the reports this year: *R v Gold, R v Schifreen* [1987] 3 All ER 618 and *R v More* [1987] 3 All ER 825.

In *Gold* the defendants, evidently accomplished 'hackers', gained access to and use of the British Telecom Prestel database by using the numbers and passwords of authorised customers. They were charged with, and convicted of, forgery on the basis of making a false instrument with the intention of causing the computer to treat it as genuine to the prejudice of British Telecom.

While the Forgery and Counterfeiting Act 1981, s 8(1)(d) extends the definition of instrument to include 'any disc, tape, sound track or other device on or in which information is recorded or stored by mechanical, electronic or other means' and while forgery may in some circumstances be committed though no person is ever deceived (for instance by forging a cash card and causing a computer automatically to debit another's account) it was held, quashing the convictions, that the defendants had not committed forgery. What they had done was to gain access by a trick, by sending signals which caused the computer to respond in a certain way. At no stage had they made a false instrument. While the signals may have been translated to a screen and appeared there, this was only momentarily so the information was not 'recorded or stored' on the computer. This conclusion was reached 'without regret'. Life, it would seem, is complicated enough already.

Even those who have forgotten all they ever knew about forgery will remember Question 9 on the criminal law examination paper which read: "'To constitute forgery the document must not only tell a lie, it must also tell a lie about itself.' Discuss." As it turned out no candidate ever tackled Question 9. In effect the House of Lords had to answer Question 9 in *More* and produced a commendable answer to it.

The defendant had come by a cheque for some £5,000 intended for and made out to MR Jessel. With it he opened an account at a building society in the name of Mark Richard Jessel and later, by completing a withdrawal form in that name, he drew on the account. He was charged with and convicted of forging the withdrawal form.

The Forgery and Counterfeiting Act 1981 is now the exclusive source of the law of forgery and the issue is whether the defendant's conduct falls within the Act. In the Act s 9(1) provides that an instrument is false, inter alia. '(a) If it purports to have been made in the form in which it is made by a person who did not, in fact, make it in that form; or . . . (h) If it purports to have been made or altered by an existing person but he did not in fact exist.' Literally the case seems to fall within para (h); the withdrawal form was made by a person, Mark Richard Jessel, who did not in fact exist and the Court of Appeal, affirming the conviction, so held.

But people are free to adopt an alias and if Joe Bloggs adopts the stage name of Joseph Broadwood because he feels it will present a better image to the public, a letter written under the hand of Joseph Broadwood would not be a forgery. No more if Joe Bloggs opens several bank accounts in the name of Joseph Broadwood and even though his purpose is to conceal his earnings from the Revenue. No more again if he steals £5,000 from MR Jessel, pays it into one of his Joseph Broadwood accounts and draws on it in the style of Joseph Broadwood. Joe Bloggs and Joseph Broadwood are one and the same person using different names. Joseph Broadwood cannot be a fictitious person within para (h) because he is a real person who does exist. Nor is his case caught by para (a) because whenever he makes a document in the style of Joseph Broadwood the document purports to be made, not by a person who did not make it, but by a person (Joseph Broadwood alias Joe Bloggs) who did.

What the defendant did in *R v More* [1987] 3 All ER 825 is essentially indistinguishable from the foregoing examples. He had of course adopted the alias Mark Richard Jessel after he dishonestly intercepted the cheque but, as Lord Ackner said, the consistent use of the word 'purports' in s 9(1) imports a requirement that for an instrument to be false it must tell a lie about itself and since the withdrawal form clearly purported to be signed by the person who originally opened the account it was in this respect wholly accurate.

The decision corrects an error which had appeared in earlier cases (eg *R v Hopkins, R v Collins* (1957) 41 Cr App R 231; *R v Hassard, R v Devereux* [1970] 2 All ER 647) but since these cases were decided under the Forgery Act 1913 it was no doubt felt unnecessary for the House to overrule them.

Other offences

1 Controlled drugs

May a person with whom controlled drugs have been deposited and which he intends to return to the depositor be convicted of possessing a controlled drug with intent to supply contrary to s 5(3) of the Misuse of Drugs Act 1971? The answer to this question was one on which the Court of Appeal had changed its mind. In *R v Delgado* [1984] 1 All ER 449 (All ER Rev 1984, p 103), the court had taken the view that 'supply' merely required a transfer of control from one person to another but in *R v Maginnis* [1986] 2 All ER 110 (All ER Rev 1986, p 110), the court took a more restricted view and thought that a mere restoration of control by a bailee to his bailor was not properly described as a supply. A mild preference for *Delgado* was expressed in this Review (All ER Rev 1986, p 111), and a similar preference was expressed by a majority in the House of Lords ([1987] 1 All ER 907). Delivering the judgment of the majority Lord Keith said that while supply meant more than merely transferring physical control since the transfer had to be for the purpose of enabling the recipient to use the chattel for his own purposes, it was not a necessary element in a supply that it should be made from the provider's own resources. It follows that the bailor of the drugs does not supply the drugs to the bailee in handing them over only for safe custody and not for the purpose of enabling the bailee to apply for his own purposes; but the bailee supplies these same drugs when he returns them to the bailor knowing that the bailor will use them for his own purposes.

2 Official secrets

R v Galvin [1987] 2 All ER 851 is factually somewhat complex. During or shortly after the Falklands war Argentina wanted spares for its Olympus marine engines but no reputable English company was prepared to supply them though there was in fact no embargo on them. The defendant's company was approached and the defendant was willing to deal. He discovered where he could get the spares but he ran into a snag in that he needed a Ministry of Defence manual to identify the parts. To secure the manual he approached X who in turn approached Y who worked at the Old War Office Building where there was a copy of the manual in the library. It was removed by Y, passed to X who passed it on to the defendant. The defendant believed the manual was classified ('Restricted' appearing on many of its pages) but he had it photocopied and returned the original. There was no doubt that at this stage the defendant believed he was not entitled to possess the manual.

The defendant was charged and convicted under s 2(2) of the Official Secrets Act 1911 with unlawfully receiving a document knowing or having reasonable grounds to believe that it had been communicated to him in contravention of the Act. The prosecution's argument, which the trial judge accepted, was that the manual had been communicated in contravention of the Act because by s 2(1)(a) it is an offence for any person (Y in this case), having possession of a document which he has obtained while employed under a contract made on behalf of the Crown, to communicate it to any person other than a person to whom he is authorised to communicate it.

On appeal the conviction was quashed. It appeared that, though the manual was marked 'restricted', the MoD had in practice placed no restrictions on the communication of the manual and no one who had asked for it had been denied it. While Y had not been expressly authorised to communicate it, authorisation for the purposes of s 2(1)(a) could be implied as well as express. The jury should have been asked to consider whether the MoD's general dissemination of the document to anyone who might be interested did not constitute an implied authorisation for Y to communicate the document.

In short, the jury might have taken the view that communication was implicitly authorised in which case an element of the actus reus was missing and we all know that each and every element of the actus reus must be proved before the defendant can be convicted of a crime. Well, not quite. We all know, at least we are told on the highest authority, that this requirement does not apply to attempts. Here the defendant is to be judged on the facts as he supposed them to be. Apply this to *Galvin*. It is clear as clear can be that the defendant believed that Y was not authorised to communicate it. It is inconceivable that he would have paid X to procure the manual if he could have got it free.

It is therefore as plain as a pikestaff that the Court of Appeal should have substituted a conviction for the attempt. It is permissible to wonder why, and with *R v Shivpuri* [1986] 2 All ER 334 (All ER Rev 1986, p 103), still fresh in all our minds, that the Court of Appeal and counsel in the case should have missed the point. And why no shrieks from those commentators who howled in protest at the decision in *Anderton v Ryan* [1985] 2 All ER 355 (All ER Rev 1985, p 104)? Surely the hypothetical first year law student should have picked this up.

Perhaps we haven't yet reached the end of the impossible attempts saga. Watch this space.

CRIMINAL PROCEDURE

Alternative verdicts

In *R v Saunders* [1987] 2 All ER 973 the House of Lords considered a short and highly technical point on the availability of manslaughter as an alternative verdict on a charge of murder. The difficulty arose in this case because the jury was unable to agree upon the charge of murder. The judge then gave a direction that he was willing to accept a majority verdict of manslaughter. After further deliberation, the jury was unable to agree a verdict on the murder charge but unanimously found the defendant guilty of manslaughter. The appellant was thereupon convicted of manslaughter and the jury was discharged from giving a verdict on the charge of murder. The basis of the defendant's appeal was that s 6(2) of the Criminal Law Act 1967 permits a verdict of manslaughter to be returned only after a defendant has been 'found not guilty of murder.' Accordingly, it was claimed, this condition precedent had not been satisfied so that the manslaughter verdict was invalid. The House of Lords unanimously rejected this contention. Section 6(2) of the 1967 Act did not apply in the circumstances which had arisen here where a jury had not been able to agree. In this situation the common law applied and, after examining the authorities, their Lordships concluded that the course adopted by the trial judge was entirely proper.

This result no doubt accords with common sense. Indeed had the defendant been successful in his appeal he might well have found himself in a worse difficulty. On the authority of *R v Rose* [1982] 2 All ER 731 (All ER Rev 1982, p 99) the court would be entitled to order a retrial on a writ of venire de novo and the defendant would then be in jeopardy of being convicted of murder. On the facts of the case an acquital did not appear a likely possibility. Even so, the decision reveals a lacuna in the coverage provided by s 6 of the 1967 Act. The wording of cl 12(1) of the Draft Criminal Code (Law Comm No 143) follows that of s 6 of the 1967 Act. In the light of this case it would seem appropriate for the Law Commission to reconsider the draft clause.

Appeal

Two decisions are reported this year on the scope of the phrase 'criminal cause or matter' which is found in s 18(1) of the Supreme Court Act 1981. In *Day v Grant, R v Crown Court at Manchester, ex p Williams* [1987] 3 All ER 678 the Court of Appeal held that a witness summons issued out of the Crown Court or the High Court under s 2(1) of the Criminal Procedure (Attendance of Witnesses) Act 1965, requiring a person to attend and give evidence or produce documents at a criminal trial, is an order made in a 'criminal cause or matter.' Accordingly, no appeal lies to the Court of Appeal. *Carr v Atkins* [1987] 3 All ER 684 held that an order made by a circuit judge under para 4 of Schedule 1 to the Police and Criminal Evidence Act 1984 to produce or give access to special procedure material is also made in a 'criminal cause or matter' because, notwithstanding that criminal proceedings may not at that stage have been instituted, the order is made in the context of a criminal investigation. Similarly, therefore the Court of Appeal has no jurisdiction to hear an appeal against such an order.

Bail

The Practice Note [1987] 1 All ER 128 followed quickly in the wake of the Divisional Court's decision in *Schiavo v Anderton* [1986] 3 All ER 10 (All ER Rev 1986, p 112). Its purpose is to clarify the procedure to be adopted in magistrates' courts when dealing with allegations of failure to surrender to custody contrary to s 6 of the Bail Act 1976.

Bail may also arise as an issue in civil proceedings, as instanced by the Court of Appeal's decision in *R v Secretary of State for the Home Dept, ex p Turkoglu* [1987] 2 All ER 823. The impact of this decision on the jurisdiction of the High Court to grant bail in connection with proceedings for judicial review is accordingly to be found in the area of immigration law rather than criminal procedure.

Crown Court

Judicial review

Lord Bridge's willingness to alter his first impressions based on fresh arguments, so vividly illustrated in *R v Shivpuri* [1986] 2 All ER 334 when he overruled himself in *Anderton v Ryan* [1985] 2 All ER 355, is a trait which makes a more discrete appearance in *Sampson v Crown Court at Croydon* [1987] 1 All ER 609. Readers of last year's Review will recall (All ER Rev 1986, p 116) that in *Smalley v Crown Court of Warwick* [1985] 1 All ER 769 Lord Bridge had doubted the correctness of *R v Crown Court at Cardiff, ex p Jones* [1975] 3 All ER 1027. In *Sampson*, having had fresh thoughts after full argument, he described these doubts as 'unfounded' and confirmed the correctness of the earlier case. Curiously, the strict ratio decidendi of the decision in *Sampson* is unlikely to have any practical effect since the legislation on which it is based has been superseded by the rather different terms of the Legal Aid Act 1982. What makes this further decision on s 29(3) of the Supreme Court Act 1981, which gives the High Court jurisdiction over the Crown Court 'other than . . . in matters relating to trial on indictment,' of importance is the obiter guidance on how the current legislation should be construed.

It had previously been held, in *R v Crown Court at Chichester, ex p Abodunrin* (1984) 79 Cr App R 293, that a decision of the Crown Court to refuse legal aid for trial on indictment was excluded from judicial review since it clearly affected the conduct of the trial. Nevertheless, Lord Bridge expressed the view that a legal aid contribution order made under s 7(1) of the Legal Aid Act 1982 could be subject to review on an appropriate ground, for example that the order was made in the face of unchallenged evidence that the defendant's income and capital did not exceed the prescribed limits. Further, the court by which the legally aided defendant is tried retains its discretionary control over costs under s 8(5) of the 1982 Act. This provision enables the Crown Court at the conclusion of a trial to exercise a power to remit any sum due, or, if the defendant is acquitted, any sum paid or due under a legal aid contribution order. Lord Bridge expressed the view that this issue was a matter governed by the same consideration as justified the decision in *R v Cardiff Crown Court, ex p Jones* [1973] 3 All ER 1027, an integral part of the trial process, and on that ground excluded from the possibility of judicial review.

The Divisional Court's decision in *R v Crown Court at Maidstone, ex p Gill* [1987] 1 All ER 129 considered the issue of whether s 29(3) of the 1981 Act provided judicial review of a forfeiture order made against a third party under s 27 of the Misuse of Drugs Act 1971 and was noted in All ER Rev 1986, p 117. One might add that the rather imprecise statutory language which s 29(3) employs gives the court ample scope for deciding what, as a matter of policy, should or should not be amenable to judicial review. Matters which the trial court is peculiarly able to make informed decisions upon, such as arose in *Sampson v Crown Court at Croydon*, are no doubt best dealt with by the discretion of the trial court. On the other hand, the facts of *Gill* surely reveal a case where the court was right to find that judicial review was available. It would have been surprising if a forfeiture decision affecting a third party to a trial was unreviewable when a convicted defendant has a right of appeal against sentence.

Jury

Valuable guidance for trial judges on how to deal with communications from the jury was offered by the Court of Appeal in *R v Gorman* [1987] 2 All ER 435. First, if the communication raises something unconnected with the trial, for example a request that a message be sent to a relative of a juror, it can be dealt with without any reference to counsel and without bringing the jury back into court. Second, in almost every other case a judge should state in open court the nature and content of the communication which he had received and, if he considers it helpful to do so, seek the assistance of counsel. This assistance will normally be sought before the jury is asked to return to court, and then, when the jury returns, the judge will deal with their communication. Exceptionally if, as in the present case, the communication from the jury contains information which the jury need not, and indeed should not, have imparted, such as details of voting figures, then, so far as possible the communication should be dealt with in the normal way, save that the judge should not disclose the detailed information which the jury ought not to have revealed. The object of these procedures is both to ensure that there is no suspicion of private or secret communication between the court and the jury and to enable the judge to give proper assistance to the jury on any matter which is troubling them. These guidelines follow the approach previously suggested by Waller LJ in *R v Townsend* [1982] 1 All ER 509 (All ER Rev 1982, p 98) where there was a similar revelation of the jury's voting figures.

The difficulty arose in *Gorman* because the jury had sent a note to the judge indicating that they were deadlocked with a nine to three split in favour of an acquittal. Without revealing the contents of this note the trial judge discharged the jury, with the apparent acquiescence of counsel for the defendant, and the defendant was subsequently convicted by a ten to two majority at his retrial. The material irregularity alleged was that the judge should have disclosed the contents of the note to counsel before discharging the jury in the first trial, an argument which the Court rejected as the guidelines it formulated make clear. Although it is not made explicit in Lord Lane CJ's judgment the real thrust of the defendant's case was presumably that, had he known how close the first jury was to acquitting him, his counsel would not so readily have agreed to the judge's proposal to discharge the jury. On the other hand, despite feeling that the defendant was somewhat unlucky to have been ultimately convicted when he was within one vote of being acquitted at the first trial, it is difficult to see how what was done at that trial could really render the verdict in his retrial unsafe or unsatisfactory. In any event the Court also took the view, following a consistent body of authority, that they had no jurisdiction to review the discretion of a trial judge to discharge a jury. On this ground alone therefore the appeal failed.

If *R v Gorman* excites in the reader a twinge of sympathy for the defendant, *R v Ashley* [1987] 2 All ER 605 may do the same for the trial judge. After retiring for two and a half hours and failing to agree a verdict the 'very experienced circuit judge' gave the conventional direction based upon *R v Walhein* (1952) 36 Cr App R 167. This direction provides that,

> 'No one must be false to his oath, but in order to return a collective verdict, the verdict of you all, these must necessarily be argument, and a certain amount of give and take and adjustment of views within the scope of the oath . . .'

The judge may also mention the expense and inconvenience occasioned by a jury's failure to agree. Although the judge did not give the ordinary majority direction, he did indicate that a majority verdict was acceptable if they were unable to reach a unanimous verdict. Nineteen minutes later the jury returned a majority verdict of guilty.

The Court of Appeal quashed the conviction on the grounds that the judge's direction was premature. What seems to have weighed with the Court was that ([1987] 2 All ER at 608),

> 'The jury had not retired for a very lengthy period of time, particularly having regard to the issues which they had to consider. Even more important they had not been given a majority direction.'

The Court went on, however, to state that, at a proper stage in a jury's retirement, a *Walhein* direction may be given provided that it is suitably tailored to the circumstances. An example of such a case would be a long trial with many defendants when a retrial would involve both great expense and burden on the defendants. When these ingredients are combined with a lengthy retirement, possibly exceeding a day, a proper and seemly direction may be appropriate.

It is no doubt true, as the Court of Appeal acknowledged, that the *Walhein* direction was formulated before the days of majority verdicts and that care must be taken to ensure that it complies with modern conditions. On the other hand, can exception really be taken to a statement which in essence only states the obvious? As the Lord Chief Justice said of the direction in *Walhein* itself, 'That is the only way in which juries can arrive a verdict.'

More recently in *R v Smith* [1985] Crim LR 522 the Court of Appeal held upon facts difficult to distinguish from the present case that there had been nothing wrong in the way the judge had exercised his discretion in putting the matter to the jury. In that case, which is not referred to in the judgment of the Court of Appeal in *Ashley*, the jury returned with a unanimous verdict only four minutes after the judge's direction.

Equally puzzling, if one accepts the correctness of the Court's conclusion that the *Walhein* direction in *Ashley* may have put pressure on the jury so as to render the verdict unsafe and unsatisfactory, on what basis can the Court justify its use when a jury has been dead-locked for a day in a long and expensive trial? If there is pressure in the former, why is there less improper pressure in the latter? It would seem, as Professor JC Smith has observed ([1987] Crim LR 511), that, 'the defendant must put up with a risk of unfairness which, in other circumstances would invalidate his conviction.'

Postscript: The Court of Appeal further reviewed this important area in *R v Watson* (1988) Times, March 10. It is hoped to discuss this case in next year's Review.

Magistrates

1 Anonymity

It cannot often be that an important issue in criminal procedure confronts the Divisional Court with no authority directly in point to guide it, but this was the case in *R v Felixstowe Justices, ex p Leigh* [1987] 1 All ER 552. The controversial question settled by the proceedings was the legality of the policy adopted by the Felixstowe Justices, and indeed other benches, of refusing to disclose the names of individual magistrates who had adjudicated in a particular case. The justification for such a practice was stated to be to protect magistrates from unwanted approaches by public and press alike. In support of this policy the basic proposition relied upon by the respondent justices was that under common law justices had power to control proceedings in their own courts, and there was the additional consideration that undoubtedly no statute or rule explicitly required disclosure. Against this had to be set the well established principle of open justice. The Divisional Court, correctly it is suggested, emphatically chose the path of openness and declared the practice to be, 'an unwarranted and an unlawful obstruction to the right to know who sits in judgment.' The anonymous JP was not a creature known to the law. The court emphasized the need for judicial proceedings to be open to scrutiny by press and public and declared unwelcome intrusions into the private lives of judges and others to be something which must be endured, 'as a tiresome if not worse incidence of holding a judicial office.' Watkins LJ envisaged that circumstances could arise when a clerk to the justices might refuse to reveal the name of a magistrate when he reasonably believes the information is required for some 'mischievous purpose.' Generally, however, the court adopted the position that the principle of open justice could be departed from only when 'necessary in order to serve the ends of justice.' The tenor of the judgment suggests that this should only be in rare and extreme cases.

This case also provides an interesting illustration of the inter relationship between locus standi to apply for judicial review and the type of remedy being sought. The applicants' claim for mandamus to direct the magistrates' clerk to reveal the name of the justices who tried a particular case was rejected on the ground that they had insufficient interest. The applicant Leigh had not been present in court during the trial and his object was not so much to report the case as to comment upon various issues arising out of reports by others of the case. This being so, the identity of the justices who heard the case was said to be immaterial. On the other hand the same considerations did not apply to the claim for a declaration that the policy of the Felixstowe Justices was contrary to law. The court claimed a large measure of discretion in determining whether sufficient interest has been established. This application had been brought either by the applicant himself, or possibly by the press through him, as guardian of the public interest in a matter of vital concern in the administration of justice. It was not contended that the applicant was a mere busybody. On the contrary, the seriousness of his purpose was evident. Accordingly, sufficient interest had been established.

2 Bail

See Practice Note [1987] 1 All ER 128, above p 86.

3 Case stated

Magistrates are clearly empowered by s 114 of the Magistrates Courts Act 1980 to require a defendant to enter into a recognizance before they state a case for the opinion of the High Court. What *R v Newcastle JJ, ex p Skinner* [1987] 1 All ER 349 makes clear is that the court must have regard to the applicant's means before deciding whether to require any recognizance and, if so, the amount. This not very surprising conclusion was suggested by the explicit requirement to have regard to the means of the applicant to be found in the analogous passage of the Crown Court Rules dealing with an application to the Crown Court to state a case. An additional practical matter noted by the Divisional Court was that the setting of an excessive recognizance might well put undesirable pressure on an applicant to pursue an appeal which was absolutely hopeless.

In the case of *Skinner*, the applicant had been required to enter into a recognizance in the sum of £500 before the matter could be taken further. At the time he was unemployed, in receipt of Supplementary Benefit, had no capital whatsoever and had been granted Emergency Legal Aid with an anticipated nil contribution. The Court experienced little difficulty in finding that the justices had not taken the applicant's means into account in requiring the recognizance. Accordingly, the case was referred back to enable them to consider this issue.

4 Committal

Section 76(2) of the Police and Criminal Evidence Act 1984 was first revealed in *R v Oxford City JJ, ex p Berry* [1987] 1 All ER 1244 to have surprising and possibly far-reaching consequences in magistrates' courts. This provision, in effect, provides that in any proceedings where the prosecution propose to adduce confession evidence and it is represented that the confession may have been obtained by oppression or is unreliable, 'the court shall not allow the confession to be given . . . except in so far as the prosecution proves beyond reasonable doubt that the confesssion . . . was not obtained as aforesaid.' Accordingly the defendant, who claimed that his confessions were not voluntary under the terms of s 76(2), challenged their admissiblity at his committal proceedings for burglary. The magistrates, after taking advice, took the view that the admissibility of a confession was a matter for the Crown Court if there was prima facie evidence to commit for trial and the committal continued. The defendant therefore applied for judicial review of the proceedings and for an order of certiorari to quash his committal.

The Divisional Court noted that prior to the passing of the 1984 Act it would not have interfered with a committal on the grounds that inadmissible evidence had been received. Now, however, the course adopted by the magistrates amounted not only to the reception of inadmissible evidence but also to a declining of jurisdiction in a matter where there was a statutory obligation to inquire. With some reluctance the Court concluded that judicial review could go to quash a committal in the circumstances which arose in this case, but that, 'save in the exceptional case, this court should not quash any committal on this ground alone.' Indeed May LJ trembled to think what would happen if certiorari were allowed to issue in cases such as this.

The result of the case is therefore a pragmatic compromise between the almost unavoidably plain words of the statute and a result acceptable to the courts. It is perhaps a little unusual, however, that this result depends upon the willingness of the court not to issue a discretionary remedy in routine breaches of the statutory provision. May LJ is surely correct when he observes that the draftsman of s 76(2) could not have had in mind that it would affect committal proceedings before magistrates. Nor, it seems, could he have envisaged that its tentacles could reach to extradition proceedings as shown in *Re Walters* [1987] Crim LR 577, although this appears to be the inevitable effect of using a phrase as unqualified and wide as, 'in any proceedings.' Even at the best of times there is something anomalous about the notion of 'a trial within a trial' before magistrates who are judges of both law and fact (see eg *F v Chief Constable of Kent* [1982] Crim LR 682), but it is difficult to see what useful purpose can be served by the requirements of s 76(2) at committal proceedings. The obvious solution, it is suggested, is to introduce amending legislation to restrict the scope of the provision to reflect the draftsman's original presumed intention.

Helpful guidelines for the appropriate use of the procedure provided by s 76(2) of the Police and Criminal Evidence Act 1984 were provided in the later case of *R v Liverpool Juvenile Court, ex p R* [1987] 2 All ER 668. Russell LJ summarised the law in five propositions. First, the effect of s 76(2) of the

1984 Act is that in summary proceedings justices must now hold a trial within a trial if it is represented to them by the defence that a confession was or may have been obtained by either of the improper processes appearing in paragraphs (a) or (b) of the subsection. Secondly, in such a trial within a trial the defendant may give evidence confined to the question of admissibility and the justices will not be concerned with the truth or otherwise of the confession. Thirdly, in consequence of the above the defendant is entitled to a ruling on the admissibility of a confession before or at the end of the prosecution case. Fourthly, there remains a discretion open to the defendant as to the stage at which an attack is to be made on an alleged confession. A trial within a trial will only take place before the close of the prosecution case if it is represented to the court that the confession was, or may have been, obtained by one or other of the processes set out in paragraphs (a) or (b) of s 76(2). If no such representation is made the defendant is at liberty to raise admissibility or weight of the confession at any subsequent stage of the trial. 'Representation' is not the same as, nor does it include, cross-examination. Thus the court is not required to embark on, nor is the defence bound to proceed on, a voir dire merely because of a suggestion in cross-examination that the alleged confession was obtained improperly. Fifthly, it should never be necessary to call the prosecution evidence relating to the obtaining of a confession twice.

The clarification of the s 76(2) procedure in magistrates' courts in no doubt to be welcomed and certainly appears to be of benefit to the accused. Because the court will be required to make its ruling before or at the end of the prosecution case the defendant will known the strength of the case he has to meet which may better inform his decision to go into the witness box. Although Russell LJ emphasises that his rulings are confied to summary offences, it is tempting to speculate whether his view that the defence retains the option to attack a confession at any subsequent stage of the trial should not also be applied to trial on indictment (see *R v Millard* [1987] Crim LR 196). Nothing in the wording of the Act would appear to suggest a distinction on this point between the two modes of trial, although it seems any defence preference might be pre-empted by the court's power to investigate the matter of its own motion under s 76(3) of the 1984 Act.

5 Confessions

See the discussion above under 'Committal.'

6 Extradition

The central issue decided in *Government of Belgium v Postlethwaite* [1987] 2 All ER 985 related to the admissibility of evidence at the hearing.

See, for further discussion, the article on Extradition, p 128 below.

7 Procedure and bias

In *R v Liverpool City JJ, ex p Topping* [1983] 1 All ER 490 (All ER Rev 1983, pp 160, 202), the Divisional Court quashed a conviction where the magistrates were aware of other charges against the defendant and failed to give proper consideration to the issue of bias. The decision also expressed views on the propriety of issuing magistrates with computerised sheets which showed other unconnected charges pending against the accused. Similar issues arose in *R v Weston-super-Mare JJ, ex p Shaw* [1987] 1 All ER 255, although the approach taken by the court on the latter issue was significantly different.

In *Shaw* the defendant appeared before the justices to answer seven charges. A plea of not guilty had previously been entered to a charge under s 5(2) of the Criminal Law Act 1967 and the remaining six charges involved an unrelated escapade with a motor scooter. The defendant's solicitor noticed the court list posted on the notice board which listed all seven charges against him and that copies of this list had been placed before each justice. She submitted that the justices should not try the charge of wasteful employment of the police because knowledge of the six other charges would lead to a reasonable suspicion of bias. The magistrates rejected this application and convicted the defendant. The appeal to the Divisional Court sought an order of certiorari to quash the conviction and a declaration that the practice of producing for the justices a court list in the way it was done here was a practice contrary to law.

The court refused to issue certiorari on the grounds that, in substance, the magistrates had applied the correct test to themselves on the issue of bias. Even if the language used was 'less than felicitous,' Mann J 'would not flaw the decision by reference to the language employed.' This test was to be found in *R v Liverpool JJ, ex p Topping* and was, would a reasonable and fair-minded person sitting in court and knowing all the relevant facts have a reasonable suspicion that a fair trial for the applicant was not possible? On the issue of a declaration the court similarly found against the defendant. What makes this part of the decision curious is that form here apears to take its full revenge on substance. The rather intricate discussion of the nature of the 'court sheets' seems to overlook the point that it is their contents rather than their status which matters (see 'Knowing The Outstanding Charges On A Not Guilty Plea' (1986) 150 JP 805). This discussion is partly occasioned by the Court's reluctance explicitly to overrule *Topping* whilst stating a preference for their later decision in *R v Weston-super-Mare JJ, ex p Stone* unreported, 19 November 1984 which arguably conflicts with the earlier decision. The result of the decision at least appears to be that it is generally not unlawful to list all charges related or unrelated against a single defendant which are for hearing on the same day and for the justices to see that list. This proposition is qualified, however, by the observation that there may well be occasions when it would be 'most undesirable' for unrelated charges to be listed together, but the 'good sense' of the clerk should enable him to identify those occasions. Even so, at the end of the day it is said to be for the justices themselves to determine whether in any case they should disqualify themselves by reference to the test for ostensible bias.

8 Road traffic

Cracknell v Willis [1987] 3 All ER 801 is an important decision of the House of Lords on the offence of driving with excess alcohol under s 6(1) of the Road Traffic Act 1972. Much of the judgment is concerned with the issue of the admissibility of evidence relating to the reliability of the Intoximeter. In essence it was decided that a driver who had provided specimens of breath for a Lion Intoximeter machine is entitled to adduce evidence which, although not direct evidence of the machine's malfunctioning, nevertheless provides material from which it may be inferred that the machine was unreliable. It would not be altogether surprising if some amendment of the legislation was considered in the light of this decision if it proves to have opened up a promising, or at least arguable, line of defence in such cases. In addition, the House of Lords overruled earlier authorities and decided that the offences prescribed by ss 6 and 8(7) of the Road Traffic Act 1972 were mutually exclusive. Nevertheless, in assessing the penalty for the s 8(7) offence the magistrates are entitled to take into account any evidence which indicated the motorist's consumption of alcohol, and that would include the analysis of the first breath specimen if he unreasonably refuses to provide a second specimen.

9 Summary trial

As an example of argument based upon statutory construction at its most involved and intricate it would be difficult to improve upon *Kemp v Liebherr–GB Ltd* [1987] 1 All ER 885. The details of the inquiry may be spared the reader. The general point decided by the court was that, subject to any time limit that may be specified in the enactment creating the offence, a magistrates' court has jurisdiction to try an information alleging the commission of an offence which is triable either way notwithstanding that the offfence was committed more than six months before the information was laid. This was the case because by virtue of Sch 1 to the Interpretation Act 1978 an offence triable either way is an 'indictable offence,' and hence s 127(2) of the Magistrates Courts Act 1980 applies to exclude it from the time limit for the trial of summary offences laid down by s 127(1) of the 1980 Act.

SENTENCING

Forfeiture

1 Order against a third party

See *R v Crown Court at Maidstone, ex p Gill* [1987] 1 All ER 129, above p 87.

2 Wireless telegraphy apparatus

Records and cassettes seized at pirate radio stations are often, it seems, the most valuable items to be found at such stations and their forfeiture is therefore likely to be the most effective deterrent against this activity. Such forfeiture is likely to be more difficult to justify after the decision by the House of Lords in *Rudd v Secretary of State for Trade and Industry* [1987] 2 All ER 553 that records and cassettes used by such a radio station do not constitute 'wireless telegraphy apparatus' for the purpose of the Wireless Telegraphy Act 1949 and so cannot be liable to forfeiture under s 143(3) of that Act. Furthermore, the word 'use' in s 1 of the Act is to be construed according to it ordinary meaning and not in the sense of 'available for use.' Accordingly, in a charge under s 1(1) of the 1949 Act the prosecution must persuade the court to draw the inference that the apparatus had in fact been used by the defendant during the relevant period if it is to prove the offence. Lord Goff based his judgment on a principle whose appearance in the House of Lords is always to be welcomed, that words in a criminal statute should be give a narrow rather than a broad construction.

Guidance for sentences

1 Cheating the Revenue

Fraud on an enormous scale and the problems for sentencing which this may pose is a topic which readers will remember arose in the case of *R v Garner* [1986] 1 All ER 78 (All ER Rev 1986, p 122). By 1987 prosecutors had clearly became more ingenious in bringing charges and in *R v Mavji* [1987] 2 All ER 758, which is discussed above at p 81, the stratagem of using the common law offence of cheating the Revenue opened up new sentencing possibilities. Accordingly, after dealing with the appeal on the substantive law, the Court of Appeal commented briefly on the appropriateness of the sentence. In particular, it was claimed by the appellant that the sentence of six years imprisonment on the cheating count was excessive having regard to the two year maximum of the alternative statutory offence. The Court disposed briefly of the contention. This was a serious case in which the defendant had deliberately set out to avoid the payment of value added tax on a massive scale. The total amount of tax avoided may have been in the region of £1,240,000. The common law offence of cheating was said to be reserved for serious and unusual cases and the provisions of s 38(1) of the Finance Act 1972 ought not to inhibit a judge from imposing what would otherwise be a proper sentence. Notwithstanding that the defendant was a family man of good character it could not be said that the sentence was wrong in principle or excessive.

2 Detention and youth custody

Before the decision in *R v Fairhurst* [1987] 1 All ER 46 difficult problems had arisen out of the relationship between s 53(2) of Children and Young Persons Act 1933 and the Criminal Justice Act 1982 which introduced the concept of youth custody. Many of these difficulties are now resolved by this important case which lays down detailed guidelines for sentences. Anyone concerned with this area could do no better than consider the comments of Professor Thomas in [1987] Crim LR 64. Further helpful guidance on the application of *Fairhurst* can be found in subsequent cases to which those interested should refer. These include, *R v Taylor* [1987] Crim LR 649; *R v Clews* [1987] Crim LR 586; *R v Smith and Roberts* [1987] Crim LR 425; *R v Pawar* [1987] Crim LR 279; *R v Brown and Chung* 8 Cr App R (S) 417.

3 Social security fraud

Guidelines on appropriate sentences in cases of obtaining welfare benefits by fraud are set out by the Court of Appeal in *R v Stewart* [1987] 2 All ER 383. In cases involving professional fraud the length of the sentence imposed should depend on the scope of the fraud. A carefully organised and large scale fraud may well merit an immediate term of two and a half years imprisonment or more. As in all fraud cases, there may be mitigating circumstances and in particular a proper discount should be given for a plea of guilty. In other cases, the factors influencing sentence may include, (a) a guilty plea, (b) the amount and length of time involved (bearing in mind that a large total may represent a very small weekly amount), (c) the circumstances in which the offence began (thus there is a distinction between a legitimate claim which later became false and one that was false from the beginning), (d) the use to which the money was put, (e) the offender's previous character, (f) matter special to the offender, such as illness, disability etc, and (g) any voluntary repayment of the amounts overpaid. Before sentencing the offender the court should consider, (a) whether a custodial sentence is really necessary, (b) if so, whether the court can make a community service order as an equivalent to imprisonment, or whether it can suspend the whole sentence, and (c) if not, what is the shortest sentence the court can properly impose. Deterrence should not play a large part in this sort of sentencing. If immediate imprisonment is necessary a short term of up to twelve months will normally suffice in a contested case where the overpayment is less than £10,000. Where no immediate custodial sentence is imposed and the amount of overpayment is below £1,000 or thereabouts, a compensation order may be of value but usually only where the defendant is in work.

This is an important guideline decision on benefit fraud, although it must be borne in mind, as Lord Lane CJ indicated, that the overwhelming majority of such cases will be dealt with by magistrates and will never reach the Crown Court. Doubtless those that do will be of the more serious kind and this decision appears to represent a significant shift away from earlier decisions of the court, such as *R v Burns* 5 Cr App R (S) 370, which suggested that an immediate sentence of imprisonment was likely in such cases. In particular the court indicated that a community service order 'may be an ideal form of punishment in many of these cases.'

Employment Law

IAN SMITH, MA, LLB
Barrister, Senior Lecturer in Law, University of East Anglia

Until its latter part, 1987 appeared to be a year of solid if unexciting progress in employment law, with a standard amount of case law on significant topics such as continuity of employment, trade union victimisation, internal trade union law, health and safety and the inevitable movements in equal pay, with this case law being largely overshadowed by the impending Employment Bill, published in October. However, the end of the year saw perhaps the most important decision on unfair dismissal law in the decade since *W Devis & Sons Ltd v Atkins* [1977] 3 All ER 40, HL. The case is *Polkey v A E Dayton Services Ltd* [1987] 3 All ER 974, HL, in which some of the most fundamental points arose for consideration, hence the disproportionate space given to it in this short chapter, at the expense of certain other cases—all cases are equal, but some are more equal than others, with *Polkey* certainly falling into that category.

Contracts of employment—remedies

In *Miles v Wakefield Metropolitan DC* [1987] 1 All ER 1089 the question arose as to the propriety or otherwise of an employer's response to industrial action falling short of a strike. A superintendent registrar of births, deaths and marriages had refused to work his usual three hours on a Saturday morning (out of a total working week of 37 hours) as part of industrial action against the council, who thereupon withheld 3/37ths of his weekly salary. The registrar sued to recover the amounts withheld. This was one of a series of recent cases on the point; in particular, in *Sim v Rotherham Metropolitan BC* [1986] 3 All ER 387 (see All ER Rev 1986, p 125) Scott J had held that in such a case an employer had the right to deduct—prima facie the employee could sue for his wages, but that was subject to a counter-claim by the employer and by making the deductions in advance all that the employer was doing was exercising a right of equitable set-off. In the instant case, however, there was a complication—the Court of Appeal ([1985] 1 All ER 905) had found for the plaintiff because, as an 'office holder' rather than an ordinary employee, the ordinary rules did not apply. The House of Lords reversed that decision on the basis that his position was directly analogous to that of an ordinary employee; that, however, then begged the question—what *are* the ordinary rules? Lords Templeman and Oliver, giving the principal speeches, reached the same conclusion as in the previous cases (especially *Sim*) but by simpler reasoning. In an action for wages an employee must establish that he was ready and willing to work (ie wages are remuneration that has to be earned); if that willingness is absent (wholly or, as here, partly) then the employer may deduct the appropriate amounts from the employee's pay and the employee will be unable to sue for those amounts because of, in effect, his failure to provide the contractual consideration. On this reasoning, there is no need to invoke ideas of claim and counter-claim (and equitable set-off) in damages actions. The case leaves open two points: (i) whether the subtleties of *Sim's* case may still be relevant to a case where the facts are more complicated than here (eg where there is a 'go-slow' or 'withdrawal of goodwill', with no definable refusal to work a set number of hours, so that quantification of the deductible amounts becomes more difficult); (ii) whether an employee engaged in such conduct as a 'go-slow' could claim remuneration for work actually done on a quantum meruit basis (their lordships being split obiter on this point). Once again, however, these are only questions as to the reasoning in such a case; the end result is what is important to employers faced, especially, with 'guerilla' action such as that seen in the prolonged industrial action in state education (an example adverted to in the speeches).

Contracts of employment—the employer's duty of care

The duty of care upon an employer is usually thought of as an element of the laws relating to health and safety, ie to care for the physical well-being of existing employees. However, the judgment of Tudor Evans J in *Lawton v BOC Transhield Ltd* [1987] 2 All ER 608 shows an interesting extension of such ideas to the giving of a reference to an *ex*-employee. The defendant employer wrote an unfavourable reference on an ex-employee, the plaintiff, resulting in the loss of further employment. The plaintiff sued for damages based upon the defendant's negligence in providing an inaccurate reference. The plaintiff lost his case, but the important point is that he did so *on the facts* (ie that the reference was not negligently written, there being factual backing to the defendant's opinions); the validity of the cause of action itself was accepted by the judge. The position therefore is that, although an employer is under no obligation to give a reference, if he does so he is under a duty of care to the *subject*. The significance of this last point is that the cause of action must arise otherwise than under *Hedley Byrne & Co Ltd v Heller & Partners Ltd* [1963] 2 All ER 575, which would only give an action to the *recipient* of the reference (provided there was reasonable and foreseeable reliance on it by that recipient employer). This case is therefore more akin to the extension of such principles (allowing third party rights) in cases like *Ministry of Housing and Local Government v Sharp* [1970] 1 All ER 1009 and *Ross v Caunters (a firm)* [1979] 3 All ER 580, and to the wilder and least hospitable regions of the little-followed decision of the House of Lords in *Junior Books Ltd v Veitchi Co Ltd* [1982] 3 All ER 201. These points are considered in the chapter on Tort, but from the employment law point of view it might be queried whether as a matter of policy it is desirable to place potential disincentives on the giving of references (an indispensible element of many recruitment policies); however, arguably this is merely one aspect of the larger (and more controversial) question of how confidential such references should be (whether or not stored on computer)—after all, a subject cannot sue on a reference unless he knows what is in it! The opposite argument is that a decision such as this does not prevent an employer from writing a bad reference, only a negligently-written bad reference; in that context, it is important to bear in mind the actual result of the case.

Continuity of employment—aggregation of separate contracts

The need for an employee to be able to establish continuity of employment for the purposes of claiming statutory rights is well known. The provisions of the Employment Protection (Consolidation) Act 1978, Sch 13, para 9 preserve continuity through certain 'hiccoughs', especially a 'temporary cessation of work' (para 9(1)(b)). The leading case on that paragraph is *Ford v Warwickshire CC* [1983] 1 All ER 753, HL (see All ER Rev 1983, p 178) where it was used to establish continuity between a teacher's annual fixed-term contracts, from September to July, so that after eight such contracts she could claim to have eight years of continuity of employment. However, for *any* time to count in the first place there must normally be employment for 16 hours or more per week (see para 4); in *Surrey CC v Lewis* [1987] 3 All ER 641 an attempt to achieve this by a *further* aggregation (of a kind not covered by *Ford*) failed. The applicant (claiming both a redundancy payment and unfair dismissal) was a teacher employed on a term-by-term basis to teach in three separate colleges, all run by the same authority (though with separate contracts). While it appeared that she could use *Ford* to run the separate terms together, she still could not show employment for 16 hours per week unless she could aggregate the hours worked under all three contracts and rely on the total number of hours. The Court of Appeal allowed her to do so, applying the principle of the Interpretation Act 1978, s 6 that the singular generally includes the plural (so that 'contract of employment' in Sch 13 could be read as 'contracts of employment'). However, the House of Lords reversed this decision and upheld the employer's appeal—in spite of the general principle of s 6 of the Interpretation Act, as a matter of interpretation Sch 13 was to be construed as showing a contrary intention; indeed, according to Lord Hailsham LC the whole scheme of the legislation under which the applicant was claiming was based upon rights under *one* contract of employment. The applicant therefore lost, and this extension of the *Ford* principle was clearly disapproved. This reinstates the decision of the EAT, but it is to be noted that the EAT had sounded a note of caution, that this decision could tempt unscrupulous employers to attempt to circumvent the legislation by the use of separate contracts (each for less than 16 hours per week). At the end of his speech (ibid at 653) Lord Hailsham refers to this, expresses the same concern and states that an industrial tribunal should be able to deal with the problem, either (i) by looking at the substance of the relationship rather than at its form and finding in reality one contract, or (ii) by finding a unifying 'umbrella' contract of employment embracing the individual contracts (as in *O'Kelly v Trusthouse Forte plc* [1983] 3 All ER 456, see All ER Rev 1983, p 172).

Statutory protection for trade union membership or activities

The case of *National Coal Board v Ridgway* [1987] 3 All ER 582 establishes important points of interpretation of the Employment Protection (Consolidation) Act 1978, s 23 which protects union members from 'action short of dismissal' taken against them by their employer on the grounds of their union membership or activities. One tends to think of this section applying typically where an individual is victimised personally for his activities, but this case showed a role for the section in a more collective sphere of inter-union rivalry. After the miners' strike and the breakaway of the UDM from the NUM, problems arose over bargaining rights at certain pits. A pay rise was negotiated with the UDM but rejected by the NUM; at the colliery in question, the rise was paid to UDM members but not to NUM members. Two of the latter complained to an industrial tribunal that this constituted a breach of s 23, ie 'action [short of dismissal] taken against him as an individual by his employer for the purpose of... preventing or deterring him from being... a member of an independent trade union, or penalising him for doing so.' The tribunal found for them but the EAT allowed the appeal in a judgment that seemed, at least in part, concerned that s 23 *should* not apply to large-scale collective disputes such as this. It was accepted that there was 'action' and that it was 'penalising' members of the NUM; however, the EAT avoided applying the section on two grounds: (i) the action had to be taken against them as individuals, but here the action was against the union itself (with only incidental effects on members); (ii) the section only outlawed action to prevent an employee being a member of *any* trade union whatsoever, not to prevent membership of a particular union (here, the NUM). However, on further appeal, the Court of Appeal allowed the applicants' appeal and held that the section applied. Both of the above grounds were disapproved: (i) there was action taken against them as individuals because (May LJ dissenting) the action against the union also affected them directly through their pay packets, and that was sufficient under the section; (ii) the protection in the section, on its proper construction, applied to penalising membership of a particular union as well as membership of unions generally. The court therefore accepted the possible application of s 23 to inter-union disputes. It may be noted that the issues in the pit in question had in fact been resolved by the time the case came to the Court of Appeal, but the appeal was heard anyway, its NUM backers being obviously concerned to have the EAT reasoning overturned, as in fact happened.

Unfair dismissal—the correct approach

In 1977 the House of Lords laid down the cardinal principle of unfair dismissal law that the tribunal must look at the facts as known to the employer as at the date of dismissal and judge the reasonableness of his actions on that basis (*W Devis & Sons Ltd v Atkins* [1977] 3 All ER 40); that gave rise to a complication where dismissal was followed by an internal appeal, and this point was resolved last year by the House of Lords in *West Midland Co-operative Society v Tipton* [1986] 1 All ER 513 (see All ER Rev 1986, p 129). The House of Lords have now, in *Polkey v A E Dayton Services Ltd* [1987] 3 All ER 974, given further consideration to the very basics of an unfair dismissal action and applied the approach in *Devis v Atkins* to another, and even more important, area.

In the early years of unfair dismissal law after its inception in 1971, considerable emphasis was placed on *procedural* fairness (ie the employer must have a good reason to dismiss *and* must adopt a fair procedure, especially in relation to warnings and hearings; see *Earl v Slater & Wheeler*

(Airlyne) Ltd [1973] 1 All ER 145, NIRC). This was important in changing employers' attitudes towards dismissal, having a so-called 'normative' effect on industrial relations (it may be put crudely in these terms—like the law of murder, unfair dismissal law is there not to convict many employers of unfair dismissal, but to try to reduce the incidence of unfair dismissals). One possible result of this (and the speed with which most employers came to terms with the new procedural requirements placed on them) is that for many years now employers have won between 65% and 75% of all industrial tribunal cases heard against them. However, during this decade there has been a perceptible move away from a strict view of procedural requirements, to an extent that many employment lawyers have expressed a desire for a swing back of the pendulum. This movement has been partly a question of general attitude and approach (particularly in the Court of Appeal), but was also aided by one important principle evolved over several cases, but generally known as the rule in *British Labour Pump Co Ltd v Byrne* [1979] ICR 347, EAT—put simply, it meant that even where there had been a definable breach of procedure in dismissing (eg no hearing given) a tribunal might still decide to 'forgive' that breach (and hold the dismissal to have been fair) if satisfied that the employee would still probably have been dismissed even if the procedure had been followed and that that dismissal would then have been fair. The 'coach and pair' effect of this on the law on procedural fairness is easy to imagine.

It was argued that *Byrne's* case was inconsistent with the *fons et origo* of *Devis v Atkins* on two grounds: (i) it took into account matters (and speculative matters at that) occurring after the date of dismissal; (ii) it entailed looking at the injustice (or lack of it) done to the employee rather than applying the true test of looking at the reasonableness of the employer's actions. There was particularly strong criticism of it in the EAT by Browne-Wilkinson P in *Silliphant v Powell Duffryn Timber Ltd* [1983] IRLR 91, but at the end of the day he felt he had to follow it since it had been consistently applied and, more particularly, had been approved by the Court of Appeal in *W & J Wass Ltd v Binns* [1982] ICR 486.

The point arose for consideration in *Polkey* quite neatly. The applicant employee was dismissed without warning for redundancy and sent home immediately; the employers had been faced with what is known inelegantly as a redundancy situation but had made no efforts at prior consultation with any of those potentially affected. The industrial tribunal held that, although there had been a breach of normally-expected procedures on a redundancy (especially the usual requirement of consultation, as set out in the old Industrial Relations Code of Practice), that breach could be forgiven under *Byrne's* case because it appeared likely that the applicant would still have been dismissed even if there had been proper consultation; the dismissal was therefore fair. That decision was upheld by the EAT and the Court of Appeal, but was reversed by this landmark decision of the House of Lords in which *Byrne's* case is overruled as being contrary to *Devis v Atkins* and the statutory test as set out in the Employment Protection (Consolidation) Act 1978, s 57(3); moreover 'all decisions supporting it [ie *Byrne's* case]' are overruled, including the decision of the Court of Appeal in *W & J Wass Ltd v Binns* and important statements are made on the proper approach by a tribunal.

The leading speech was given by Lord MacKay LC ([1987] 3 All ER at 975 et seq) and four particular points from it are worth setting out:

(i) A tribunal should look at what the employer did, not at what he might have done ([1987] 3 All ER at 976):

> 'Where there is no issue raised by ss 58 to 62 the subject matter for the tribunal's consideration is the employer's action in treating the reason as a sufficient reason for dismissing the employee. It is that action and that action only that the tribunal is required to characterise as reasonable or unreasonable. That leaves no scope for the tribunal considering whether, if the employer had acted differently, he might have dismissed the employee. It is what the employer did that is to be judged, not what he might have done.'

(ii) Under s 57(3) the correct approach is for the tribunal to look at the reasonableness of the employer's actions, *not* at the injustice (or, as here possibly, the lack of it) to the employee. In making this point, Lord Mackay adopted the following passage from Browne-Wilkinson P in *Sillifant* (ibid at 979):

> 'The choice in dealing with s 57(3) is between looking at the reasonableness of the employer or justice to the employee. *Devis v Atkins* shows that the correct test is the reasonableness of the employer; the *British Labour Pump* principle confuses the two approaches.'

Lord Mackay added (ibid at 983):

> 'In my opinion, therefore, the additional reasons given by the Court of Appeal in the present case for supporting the *British Labour Pump* principle involve an impermissible reliance upon matters not known to the employers before the dismissal and a confusion between unreasonable conduct in reaching the conclusion to dismiss, which is a necessary ingredient of an unfair dismissal, and injustice to the employee which is not a necessary ingredient of an unfair dismissal, although its absence will be important in relation to a compensatory award.'

(iii) Following on from that final point, injustice (or otherwise) to the employee may be relevant in *fixing compensation*.

Again, a passage from *Sillifant* is cited (ibid at 978):

> 'It [ie the *British Labour Pump* principle] introduces just that confusion which *Devis v Atkins* . . . was concerned to avoid between the fairness of the dismissal (which depends solely upon the reasonableness of the employer's conduct) and the compensation payable to the employee (which takes into account the conduct of the employee whether known to the employer or not).'

(iv) Lack of a warning or consultation will not automatically make a dismissal unfair, but procedural regularity or otherwise will be a factor for the tribunal to consider. There may be cases where (for example) a redundancy dismissal without consultation will be fair *but* that will be because the employer took a deliberate decision on the facts at the time of dismissal not to consult (which is later judged to have been reasonable), *not* merely because of an argument that with hindsight it actually made no difference (ibid at 976):

'On the other hand, in judging whether what the employer did was reasonable it is right to consider what a reasonable employer would have in mind at the time he decided to dismiss as a consequence of not consulting or not warning. If the employer could reasonably have concluded in the light of the circumstances known to him at the time of dismissal that consultation or warning would be utterly useless he might well act reasonably even if he did not observe the provisions of the code. Failure to observe the requirements of the code relating to consultation or warning will not necessarily render a dismissal unfair. Whether in any particular case it did so is a matter for the industrial tribunal to consider in the light of the circumstances known to the employer at the time he dismissed the employee.'

It is probably the case (particularly in the light of point (iv)) that there will never be a return in full to the heyday of procedural unfairness of the mid-1970s, but this decision remains of great significance in its reaffirmation of basic principles and in ridding unfair dismissal law of the distortions caused in recent years by the approach in *British Labour Pump v Byrne*.

Unfair dismissal—deciding questions of fact

In the case of *Morris v London Iron & Steel Co Ltd* [1987] 2 All ER 496 the Court of Appeal decided a short but important point on the burden of proof in unfair dismissal actions. The industrial tribunal had at the end of the day found it impossible to decide (in the face of conflicting testimony) whether the employee applicant had been dismissed or had resigned and so fell back on the burden of proof—as this lay upon the employee (on the question of establishing dismissal), this meant that the tribunal found against him. On appeal, the EAT held that this recourse to the burden of proof was incorrect, the tribunal being under an obligation to decide on facts one way or the other. However, on further appeal, the Court of Appeal upheld the industrial tribunal's approach. May LJ, giving judgment, held that rare cases can arise where in all conscience a tribunal cannot decide a point of fact, and in such a case recourse to the burden of proof is proper (indeed, to do anything other would be a breach of judicial duty). However, he pointed out that this approach was not to be adopted lightly (ibid at 501):

'. . . [I]t should not be thought that a swift reliance on where the burden of proof lies and a failure to decide issues of fact in the case ought in any way to be considered an easy or convenient refuge for anybody who does find it difficult to make up his mind in a particular case.'

Unfair dismissal—compensation and payments made by the employer

Where an employee is dismissed with a payment in lieu of notice and is later successful in an action for unfair dismissal, is the tribunal (in fixing compensation) to deduct that payment in lieu from the compensation awarded to the employee? If the matter is looked at in terms of causation and the requirement to mitigate damage (Employment Protection (Consolidation) Act 1978, s 74(4)), then the payment should be deducted (thus avoiding double compensation); however, from a wider industrial relations standpoint it could be argued that the employee should be entitled to notice payments come what may (for example, if an employee dismissed with wages in lieu finds a job in what should have been the notice period, the employer cannot claim part of the notice payment back). This point arose in *Addison v Babcock FATA Ltd* [1987] 2 All ER 784. The industrial tribunal deducted the notice payment, but the EAT (following *Finnie v Top Hat Frozen Foods* [1985] ICR 433, EAT) held that this was incorrect – that in the interests of good industrial practice the employee ought to be entitled to his payment in lieu automatically. Reversing that decision (overruling *Finnie*) and restoring that of the tribunal, the Court of Appeal held in effect that the duty to mitigate (thus avoiding double compensation) took precedence, and so notice payments *are* to be deducted. This decision is of considerable practical importance, as it can be seen as encouraging (or, at least, not discouraging) attempts by the employer to settle cases without recourse to a tribunal.

Expanding this last point, the case has now been construed as of *general* effect, ie applying to *any* termination payment made by the employer; such a payment is to be deducted from compensation. There was in fact an ex gratia payment (as well as the payment in lieu of notice) in *Addison*, but because of the peculiar circumstances surrounding it, its deductability was not a live issue before the Court of Appeal. However, in the subsequent decision of the EAT in *Horizon Holidays Ltd v Grassi* [1987] IRLR 372 it was held that the *principle* in Addison applies generally to all termination payments (with payments in lieu being, in effect, merely one example).

Equal pay—the general material difference defence

A claim for equality of pay may be defeated by the defence under the Equal Pay Act 1970, s 1(3) that, although there is like work, the lower rate of pay is due to a 'genuine material difference' other than sex justifying the variation. Clearly, it is a matter of great significance as to whether the courts are to construe this defence narrowly or widely. Until the decision of the House of Lords in *Rainey v Greater Glasgow Health Board* [1987] 1 All ER 65 it had been construed relatively narrowly, in one respect in particular— since the early decision of the Court of Appeal in *Clay Cross (Quarry Services) Ltd v Fletcher* [1979] 1 All ER 474 it appeared established that the difference in question had to be personal to the applicant and her male comparator (eg in terms of him being more experienced, better qualified, more efficient in the job or, as a special category, him being 'red–circled' for historic factors); this meant that external factors would not be enough, which in particular ruled out 'market forces' (the fear being the simple defence that 'I gave the man more because he asked for it and would not come for less'). That interpretation has now been held to be incorrect by the House of Lords. The applicant was one of a number of male and female prosthetists employed in the national health service; when a decision was made to expand that particular area it could only be done by tempting private prosthetists into the service by paying salaries greater than those paid to the existing employees. All the 'entrants' on the higher salaries happened to be men; the applicant claimed equality of pay with one of them. It was clear that they were engaged on 'like work' but the question was whether the method of entry (dictated by market forces) was a genuine material difference within s 1(3). The House of Lords held that it was, and dismissed the applicant's claim. Stating that dicta in *Clay Cross* by Lord Denning MR and Lawton LJ were too wide, Lord Keith giving judgment held that the difference does *not* have to be personal, so that it is open to a tribunal to find that an external, economic factor justifies a pay difference (especially where, as here, it is fortuitous that the comparator is male and the applicant female—the evidence here showed that if one of the entrants had been female she would also have been paid at the enhanced rate) (ibid at 72):

> 'In the present case the difference between the case of the appellant and that of [the male comparator] is that the former is a person who entered the national health service... direct while the latter is a person who entered it from employment with a private contractor. The fact that one is a woman and the other a man is an accident. The findings of the industrial tribunal make it clear that the new prosthetic service could never have been established within a reasonable time if [the comparator] and others like him had not been offered a scale of remuneration no less favourable than that which they were then enjoying. That was undoubtedly a good and objectively justified ground for offering him that scale of remuneration.'

Arguably, this decision makes the 'genuine material difference' defence in s 1(3)(i) more akin to the special 'genuine material factor' defence in s 1(3)(ii) which applies to an equal value claim and which the government deliberately widened in order to admit 'market forces' arguments.

Equal pay—equal value claims

Claims for equal pay for work of equal value are still in their infancy, and cases on the construction of their complicated statutory provisions are only now coming to the higher courts. Two Court of Appeal cases were reported this year, one on the application of equal value laws, the other on the end result of a successful claim. The former went in the applicant's favour and the latter against her.

In *Pickstone v Freemans plc* [1987] 3 All ER 756 the female applicants were warehouse operatives claiming that their work was of equal value to that of a male checker warehouse operative. However, this claim failed in the EAT on the wording of the Equal Pay Act 1970, s 1(2)(c): 'where a woman is employed on work which, *not being work in relation to which para(a) or (b) above applies*, is... of equal value to that of a man in the same employment.' Section 1(2)(a) applies to 'like work' and the point in this case was that men *were* employed as warehouse operatives (ie on like work); as a matter of construction, the EAT held that this meant that there could be no equal value claim under s 1(2)(c). On further appeal to the Court of Appeal, this was held to be correct, as a matter of English law. However, the court went much further and held for the applicants; there may be no claim under the statute but there is under EEC law because the general right to equal pay for like work or work of equal value is also contained in Art 119 of the Treaty of Rome which (a) is directly applicable and (b) is not subject to any such restriction as that contained in s 1(2)(c). In a judgment of importance to constitutional law as well as employment law, the Court of Appeal therefore held that the applicants could succeed under EEC law even though they could not succeed under domestic law.

In the second case, *Hayward v Cammell Laird Shipbuilders Ltd* [1987] 2 All ER 344 the applicant (a cook) had succeeded in establishing that her work was of equal value to that of certain male shipyard workers. The point at issue in this, the most newsworthy equal value claim to date was the *effect* of that decision. She claimed that it meant that she was entitled to the same basic pay and overtime pay as her male comparators; the basis of this approach is that each and every term relating to pay must be equal (or, at least, no less advantageous). However, the complication in the case was that the facts showed that, although worse off in terms purely of pay, the applicant enjoyed quantifiably better terms of employment than her comparators on meals and meal breaks, paid holidays and sick pay. In the light of this, the employers argued that the correct approach was to look at *all* terms as a 'package' and see whether the applicant was in a worse position overall. The industrial tribunal took the latter 'package' approach; this decision (with its refusal to make an unqualified declaration that basic and overtime rates should be the same as those of her comparators) was upheld first by the EAT and then by the Court of Appeal. One irony of the decision is that support for the 'package' rather than the 'individual terms' approach was taken from the wide approach to 'pay' in EEC law (in particular under Art 119) by virtue of which other terms and benefits can be taken into account under the umbrella heading of pay; normally that construction works in the applicant's favour, but here it had a distinct boomerang effect and it may be anticipated as a result of this case that even where entitlement to equal pay for work of equal value has been established there will still be major disputes over what equal pay actually means on the facts of the case—an equal value claim involves cross-job comparisons where it is quite likely that the applicant and the comparator will have significantly different terms of employment on all sorts of matters.

Trade unions—judicial intervention in internal matters

The decision of Harman J in *Hamlet v General Municipal Boilermakers and Allied Trade Union* [1987] 1 All ER 631 shows a degree of judicial restraint in matters concerning the internal government of a union which has not always characterised court decisions in the past (particularly under the last Master of the Rolls). The plaintiff union member lost an election for a full-time post and his complaint of breach of the rules to the union's executive council was dismissed as was an appeal to the general council. He sought court declarations that there had been irregularities and that the internal appeal decision was void for breach of natural justice. The judge struck out his statement of claim as disclosing no reasonable cause of action—applying the old rule in *Dawkins v Antrobus* (1881) 17 Ch 615, the courts are not to sit as appeal bodies from decisions of private clubs; whilst a court may in an extreme case find an internal decision perverse, it should not interfere on lesser arguments (eg allegations that the internal body had failed to take into account relevant considerations, or had taken into account irrelevant ones) and so the plaintiff's only remedies were internal. As to natural justice, the judge considered that there is no rule that a member of a body which had sat at first instance is necessarily debarred from sitting on an appeal on the same matter (particularly where that is provided for in the union rules).

The question of *how* to interpret such rules arose in *Jacques v Amalgamated Union of Engineering Workers (Engineering Section)* [1987] 1 All ER 621. There have been differences of approach in the past (most dicta being in favour of a wider, less legalistic mode of interpretation, but with dicta by Lord Dilhorne in *British Actors' Equity Association v Goring* [1978] ICR 791, HL to the effect that different canons of construction are not to be used). The interest in this case is the statement by Warner J that the wider approach is to be taken ([1987] 1 All ER 621 at 628):

> 'There are, of course, in those dicta differences of emphasis and of formulation, but not, I think, differences of principle.... The effect of the authorities may I think be summarised by saying that the rules of a trade union are not to be construed literally or like a statute, but so as to give them a reasonable interpretation which accords with what in the court's view they must have been intended to mean, bearing in mind their authorship, their purpose and the readership to which they are addressed.'

Industrial disputes—strike ballots

Strike ballots are now compulsory in the case of official action by virtue of the Trade Union Act 1984, s 10. In *Monsanto plc v Transport and General Workers' Union* [1987] 1 All ER 358 the Court of Appeal had to decide upon the important question of how long a ballot result in favour of industrial action remains operative. A ballot in favour of action was held on 6 May 1986 and the action commenced resulting in dismissal of temporary workers (whose hiring had precipitated the dispute) on 30 May. On 10 June a branch meeting called off the action pending negotiations (but with the intention of reimposing it if there was no satisfactory outcome); on 23 June it was decided to recommence the action in the absence of such an outcome. The company sought to restrain this recommenced action on the basis that it was not supported by a fresh ballot. The judge at first instance granted an injunction but it was discharged on appeal by the Court of Appeal. The proper construction of s 10 was that provided the industrial action was commenced within four weeks of the ballot (s 10(3)(c)), there did not have to be a fresh ballot if the union had merely suspended the action during negotiations (a not uncommon happening, particularly where an employer refuses to negotiate until action is lifted), *provided* the dispute continues to be the same dispute as that in respect of which the ballot was held. On the facts, that was so here; although the temporary workers at the heart of the dispute had been dismissed by 23 June, the continuing dispute was over the repercussions of the industrial action already taken and the question of temporary workers generally. While this reading of s 10 is to be welcomed (and possibly contrasted with the stricter approach, in a different context, in *Shipping Company Uniform Inc v International Transport Workers' Federation* [1985] ICR 245) it could lead to courts in the future being faced with difficult decisions of fact as to what is the 'same' dispute.

Postscript

Two cases were reported which follow on from decisions commented on in previous reviews. In *Bristow v City Petroleum Ltd* [1987] 2 All ER 45 the House of Lords held that the protection of the Truck Act 1896, s 1(1) could after all apply to a deduction from a shop worker's wages in respect of a stock or till deficiency (reversing the decision of the Divisional Court [1985] 3 All ER 463 (see All ER Rev 1985, p 141) and following the later decision of that same court in *Sealand Petroleum Co Ltd v Barratt* [1986] 2 All ER 360); however, as pointed out in All ER Rev 1986, p 135 the point is now of little significance as the Truck Acts have been repealed and replaced by the new and different provisions of Part I of the Wages Act 1986. Secondly, in the long-running saga of *Thomas v University of Bradford* [1987] 1 All ER 834 the House of Lords reversed the decision of the Court of Appeal (All ER Rev 1986, p 135, upholding the decision of Whitford J All ER Rev 1985, p 143) and held that the plaintiff university lecturer's complaint of dismissal contrary to her contract of employment (which incorporated parts of the university's charter, statutes, etc) lay within the exclusive jurisdiction of the university visitor and so could not be brought before the ordinary courts.

Finally, two cases are reported concerning the application of industrial safety laws. In *R v Mara* [1987] 1 All ER 478 the Court of Appeal held that the Health and Safety at Work Act 1974, s 3 (duty to persons other than employees) applied where a cleaning company left equipment on the premises of a customer, a defect in the equipment causing the electrocution of an employee of the customer. In *R v A I Industrial Products plc* [1987] 2 All ER 368 the Court of Appeal held that a single operation such as the demolition of a kiln could not constitute a 'process', which connoted instead some manufacturing process or continuous or regular activity carried on as a normal factory operation. Although this arose in the context of the Asbestos Regulations 1969, the term 'process' is also used in the Factories Act 1961, s 175(1) (definition of 'factory') and so the case may be of wider application.

Evidence

ADRIAN A S ZUCKERMAN, LLM, MA
Fellow of University College, Oxford

Burden of proof—a matter of substance

A plaintiff who takes his grievance to a court of law is bound to feel hard done by when he is sent away because the judge cannot make up his mind whether it is the plaintiff or the defendant who is right in his factual contentions. This was the feeling with which the employee who had sued his employer for dismissal left the industrial tribunal in *Morris v London Iron and Steel Co Ltd* [1987] 2 All ER 496. He did, however, find solace in the Employment Appeal Tribunal where it was decided, by majority, that in failing to determine the issue of whether the employee had been dismissed or whether he had resigned, as the employer contended, the industrial tribunal failed 'in its duty as a tribunal of fact'. The Court of Appeal disagreed. May LJ held that while the trier of fact had to make every effort to resolve the dispute one way or another, there was 'no absolute obligation on the industrial tribunal to reach a finding of fact' (ibid at 502). In those cases, and the hope was expressed that they would be rare, where the tribunal of fact finds it impossible to determine which party's evidence to prefer, the tribunal is entitled 'to fall back on the onus of proof which lay on the employee to prove that he had in fact been dismissed' (ibid at 502).

Inevitably, there are situations where the evidence advanced by the parties produces an impasse so that the trier of fact is unable to decide which of the opposing factual contentions to accept. Rules of burden of proof are designed to deal with this problem. If the law stipulates that the plaintiff must prove his case on the balance of probabilities, it does so in order to indicate which of the parties to litigation would lose if the relevant factual contentions are not established. To that extent the Court of Appeal is right in its decision. But there is another dimension to the problem that arose in the present case.

The imposition of the burden of proof on this or that party is an exercise in risk allocation: allocating the risk of losing the case in the event of the evidence being inconclusive. The law-maker's decision about the burden of proof is essentially determined in the light of the principles that govern the given substantive field of law. In the criminal law the general rule is that the prosecution must prove guilt beyond reasonable doubt. This reflects the weight and importance that attach to the public interest in the protection of the innocent from conviction (see on this point the comment on *R v Hunt* [1987] 1 All ER 1, in All ER Rev 1986, p 148). However, the fact that we have a general rule for criminal cases does not mean that we must have one general rule for all civil cases. Although it is generally assumed that in civil cases the plaintiff must prove his claim on the balance of probabilities, this is no more than a provisional starting point. In different branches of the law different risk distribution may be called for, depending on the policies of that branch of law and on the aims of its provisions. The trouble is that all too often the courts lose sight of this and take the general principle to determine the burden conclusively, without any thought about whether this is in accord with the substantive law in question.

In the case under consideration the Court of Appeal may be forgiven for not questioning the assumption that the burden of proof (as distinguished from the burden of adducing evidence) lay on the employee, seeing that counsel for the employee did not see fit to raise the point. What is, however, doubtful is the criticism which the Court of Appeal directed to the decision of Browne-Wilkinson J in *Khanna v Ministry of Defence* [1981] ICR 653. In that case the applicant contended that he had been discriminated against by his employers because of his race. The industrial tribunal felt unable to decide whether the allegation was correct or incorrect and decided against the applicant on the ground that he had failed to discharge his burden of proof. On appeal Browne-Wilkinson J said that:

> 'either the tribunal accepts the evidence of the board members that they were not motivated by racial considerations (in which case the claim fails) or it does not (in which case the claim is established by reason of the unavoidable inference the industrial tribunal has found)'.

The result of this view is, in effect, that when the tribunal is in doubt whether an employee was discriminated against, it should decide in favour of the employee. Such a rule may well be consonant with the purpose and the policies of the anti-discrimination law in question and Browne-Wilkinson J's view on this matter cannot be dismissed without careful consideration of the substantive law on the point.

In the absence of such consideration it is doubtful whether the decision in *Morris v London Iron and Steel Co Ltd* [1987] 2 All ER 496 can be regarded as authority on the incidence of the burden of proof in proceedings concerned with wrongful dismissal as well as in discrimination proceedings. The place for such consideration, it should be borne in mind, is the industrial relations law and not the law of evidence.

Contrary to the assumption that there cannot be an absolute duty on the judge to decide between two competing contentions on an issue of fact, *Scott v Martin* [1987] 2 All ER 813, shows that there is a way of imposing such a duty. It involves the simple device of describing the issue as one of law rather than one of fact. The issue in this case was whether a right of way conferred in a conveyance referred only to the road in question or also extended to its verges. The trial judge dismissed the plaintiff's claim to the right over the verges on the ground that he had failed to prove that on its true construction the conveyance conferred a right over the verges. Speaking for the Court of Appeal, Nourse LJ said (ibid at 817) that it is not correct 'to say that the burden of proof on a question of construction lies on the plaintiff. A question of construction is a question of law, in respect of which no burden lies on either side.'

But in what sense is the construction of a conveyance a question of law? The parties to a conveyance are free to grant a right of way over any land they choose and, within the bounds of legality and recognised property rights, the court has to give effect to what they stipulate. Hence the content of the right of way is not determined by the general law but by the parties. The question 'What did the parties stipulate in their conveyance?' sounds like a question of fact. The precise question here was: What did the parties mean by the words 'private road called Allerton Garth'? Nourse LJ accepted that (ibid at 817) 'if the plaintiff relies on surrounding circumstances as an aid to construction, the onus is on him to prove these circumstances'. To be admissible such surrounding factual circumstance must be relevant to some issue and, one would have thought, this issue must be an issue of fact.

Although one may quibble about Nourse LJ's characterisation of the issue, he is however correct in his basic attitude: in issues of this kind the judge cannot take refuge in the rules concerning the burden of proof, he must determine which of the competing interpretations is the best.

Corroboration

A consistent reaction against formalism seems to be emerging in the law of corroboration. In 1986 the House of Lords decided that a corroboration warning 'does not involve some legalistic ritual to be automatically recited by the judge'; *R v Spencer* [1986] 2 All ER 928 at 937; All ER Rev 1986, p 158. This year the Privy Council takes up the cue. In *A-G of Hong Kong v Wong Muk-ping* [1987] 2 All ER 488, counsel for the accused contended that when the trial judge administers a corroboration warning in respect of an accomplice, he must tell the jury that the accomplice must be independently credible before any question of corroboration can arise. On this view, the jury must approach the matter in two stages. It must first consider whether, apart from the corroborative evidence, the accomplice is credible. If he is not, it must reject his evidence and avoid any reliance on it. Only if the jury has found the testimony credible, it need consider whether it is corroborated.

This contention was derived from Lord Morris's speech in *DPP v Hester* [1972] 3 All ER 1056 at 1065, and from Lord Hailsham's speech in *DPP v Kilbourne* [1973] 1 All ER 440 at 452. Lord Hailsham attempted to resile from this view in *Boardman v DPP* at [1974] 3 All ER 887 at 906–907, but this did not deter counsel for the accused in the present case. It is to be hoped that the Privy Council will have succeeded in putting the matter to rest once and for all.

Lord Bridge explained ([1987] 2 All ER 488 at 492) that a witness' credibility can be meaningfully assessed only by considering how well it fits in with the circumstances of the case and that 'it is dangerous to assess the credibility of the evidence given by any witness in isolation from other evidence in the case which is capable of throwing light on its reliability.' He concluded (ibid at 494) that if

> 'the presence or absence of corroborative evidence may assist a jury to resolve, one way or the other, their doubts as to whether or not to believe the evidence of a suspect witness, it must . . . be wrong to direct [the jury] to approach the question of credibility in two stages as suggested'

by the accused's counsel.

Still more important is the Privy Council's reiteration of Lord Reid's view in *DPP v Kilbourne* [1973] 1 All ER 440 at 456, that there

> 'is nothing technical in the idea or corroboration. When in the ordinary affairs of life one is doubtful whether or not to believe a particular statement one naturally looks to see whether it fits in with other statements or circumstances relating to the particular matter; the better it fits in, the more one is inclined

to believe it. The doubted statement is corroborated to a greater or
lesser extent by the other statements or circumstances with which it fits in'

(to similar effect see *R v Turner* (1975) 61 Cr App R 67 at 83 per James LJ).
This is plain common sense. The reason why counsel for the accused was
able to pursue a different view all the way up to the Privy Council lies in the
theory that corroboration is not merely a matter of common sense but one
regulated by rules of law. As long as this theory has some life left in it, our
courts will continue to have to address themselves to the kind of counter-
intuitive argument with which the present case was concerned.

Hearsay—the continuing retreat

Few, if any, will deny that the law of hearsay is a morass of mindless
technicalities. Yet it continues to survive. Of all the nonsensical theories
that fester in this field one of the most damaging is the theory that the courts
may do nothing to modify the rule but must await the legislature's pleasure
to introduce reform. The chief source of this theory is the notorious *Myers v
DPP* [1964] 2 All ER 881. However, that case was decided in the expressed
expectation that Parliament will be stirred into action. In fact Parliament
only passed the modest Criminal Evidence Act 1965, frustrating the
expectations of wide scale reform.

Successive All ER Annual Reviews have plotted the progressively
narrowing scope of the hearsay rule; see All ER Rev 1982, p 131; All ER
Rev 1983, p 204; All ER Rev 1985, p 160. Notwithstanding the frequent lip-
service paid to *Myers*, the courts have resorted to a variety of devices for
side-stepping the hearsay rule where they feel that exclusion runs in the face
of both policy and common sense. It is entirely right and proper that the
courts should do so. The hearsay rule is the creature of the common law.
The contents of the rule are not to be found in a crisp piece of legislation but
have to be distilled from many, and at times irreconcilable, authorities.
These authorities inevitably reflect the judicial concerns of their time and
these, in turn, have to be taken into account in interpreting judicial rulings
of the past. When new situations arise against a wholly different social and
technical background the old rulings cannot automatically be regarded as
conclusive.

This is reflected in *R v Cook* [1987] 1 All ER 1049 (another instance is
provided by *R v Andrews* [1987] 1 All ER 513 discussed below). The issue in
this case was whether a photofit picture constructed under the direction of a
witness to the crime was admissible in evidence. Objection was taken on the
ground that it amounted to hearsay evidence. In a sense this is correct as D J
Birch showed when commenting on a previous case of this kind in [1982]
Crim L Rev 748. The photofit is constructed on the basis of statements
made by the witness; such statements would be clearly inadmissible
hearsay; therefore the photofit must also be inadmissible.

However, this is not the right approach. The photofit is not just, not even
mainly, a statement. Language is a notoriously inadequate tool for
capturing the appearance of a person seen by a witness and conveying the
subtle and complex detail perceived by the witness. It is precisely for this
reason that we have an identification parade; otherwise it would be enough

for the witness to describe at the trial his impressions of the person he claims to have seen. A photograph does capture that which language cannot and, for this reason, has always been admissible. Drawing an analogy to photographs Watkins LJ held ([1987] 1 All ER 1049 at 1054):

'We regard the production of the sketch or photofit by the police officer making the graphic representation of a witness's memory as another form of camera at work, albeit imperfectly . . . the photofit is not a statement in writing . . . or anything resembling it in the sense that this very old rule against hearsay has ever been expressed to embrace.'

This is surely right, for if a photofit picture consisted of a statement, the witness could just repeat his statement and we would have no use for the photofit picture. In truth this kind of picture consists of that which no statement, however rich and intricate, can transmit: a likeness. The picture is produced not just from verbal description but by piecing together different facial ingredients or by guiding the hand of the artist. Suppose that the artist draws a nose and the witness says: 'It was not like this, but bigger'. The artist then modifies the nose and the witness assents. Although the witness's statement helped the artist fashion the nose, it can hardly be suggested that the drawing represents the witness's statement or that that statement is a description of the nose which the artist depicted. The artist's product transcends the verbal communication of the witness, just as a photograph transcends all possible verbal description of its subject.

The rationale of the hearsay rule is that the risks of mistaken perception, of faulty memory, of inaccurate narration and of mendacity cannot be tested by cross-examination when reliance is placed on an out of court statement. This rationale does not hold good in the present situation. The photofit picture represents far more accurately and fully than anything that the witness can say at the trial the mental picture that the witness obtained of the person identified. Of course there may be weaknesses in the witness's perception of the object but the witness in this case was called by the prosecution and the quality of her observation of the accused could be tested by cross-examination. As for the danger that the witness's memory was faulty, this was largely to be dismissed because the picture was constructed shortly after the incident. If, in addition, the possibility of misunderstanding by the photofit artist is excluded by the nature of the process of constructing the picture, then the picture cannot be said to be in any way inferior to direct evidence by the witness at the trial but, on the contrary, far superior.

The crucial question turns therefore on this: is the procedure by which a photofit representation is constructed sufficiently advanced to capture the image that the sight of the subject left in the witness's mind? If the answer is 'yes', then the picture should not be held inadmissible merely because the technique did not exist and, consequently, was not catered for when the hearsay rule was first being elaborated over a century and half ago. Watkins LJ's ruling represents a triumph of good sense and he deserves our thanks.

Another case reported this year involves the converse situation of that in *Cook*. Whereas in *Cook* the court was concerned with a picture produced from a description by a witness, in *Taylor v Chief Constable of Cheshire* [1987] 1 All ER 225, the issue concerned the admissibility of a witness's description of what he had seen in a picture. The accused was charged with shoplifting. He was allegedly filmed in the act by a concealed video camera but the video recording was subsequently destroyed accidentally. The prosecution called witnesses who had seen the film and who testified that the person whom the film showed stealing was the accused. It was held that their testimony did not infringe the hearsay rule.

If, as we have just seen, the pictures on the film (duly authenticated) would have been admissible as original evidence, the witnesses' account of what they had seen in the film was not hearsay either. However, due to the fact that much of the court's attention was devoted to dealing with admissibility, little consideration was paid to the much more difficult problem of reliability.

Identification evidence is notoriously difficult to assess and all too often turns out to be unreliable. In the instant case the problem of identification was doubly problematic because the incident lasted only a few seconds. On this point Ralph Gibson LJ said (ibid at 225):

'As with the witness who saw directly, so with him who viewed a display or recording, the weight and reliability of his evidence will depend on assessment of all the relevant considerations, including the clarity of the recording, its length and, where identification is in issue, the witness's prior knowledge of the person said to be identified, in accordance with well established principles.'

The principles referred to in this dictum are those of *R v Turnbull* [1976] 3 All ER 549, as McNeill J made clear. However, it is not enough that the court should just reiterate that care has to be taken in the assessment of evidence. It is not easy to safeguard against mistake and the most honest witnesses can lead the most conscientious jury to grave injustice, as the Devlin Committee on Evidence of Identification demonstrated in 1976. The courts must show their commitment to reliability by taking care in the admission of evidence in the first place.

In the instant case it was unsatisfactory to say that the trier of fact will have assessed reliability by reference to the quality of the recording because the recording was not available in court; there was only the word of the witnesses on the matter. Consequently the weakness of the Divisional Court's judgment lies in its failure to deal adequately with the question of whether an identification based on a brief video recording was of sufficient weight to justify admissibility and, indeed, whether there was sufficient material before the court (such as information about the angle and distance from which the pictures were taken and samples of recordings made by the photographic equipment in question) to arrive at an informed conclusion on this point. In the absence of such consideration it is impossible to have confidence in the conviction that the Divisional Court upheld.

Res gestae

It was suggested earlier that, although often ignored, the *Myers* theory that the hearsay rule may not be modified by the courts is harmful. Both these propositions are borne out by *R v Andrews* [1987] 1 All ER 513. The case was concerned with that branch res gestae according to which statements made during, or immediately after, an event and in the excitement of involvement in it are admissible as evidence of facts stated therein. At one time this idea was thought to have crystalized into a strict rule of law and this gave rise to sterile technicality. Contemporaneity was treated as a technical requirement. In order to ascertain whether a statement was part of an event much learning was devoted to the identification of an 'event' and to the nature of the connection between words and events.

This formalist approach reached its nadir in *Bedingfield* (1897) 14 Cox CC 341, where, on a charge of murder by cutting a woman's throat, the accused's defence was that the woman committed suicide. To refute this defence the prosecution proposed to call evidence that the deceased woman rushed out of the accused's room with her throat cut, cried 'See what Bedingfield has done to me', and immediately died. The evidence was held inadmissible because it did not form part of a relevant event. The cry, as Cockburn CJ put it, 'was something stated ... after it was all over, whatever it was, and after the act was completed.'

It is only relatively recently that the law has shed some of the more spurious technicalities that have haunted the present topic. We owe this mainly to the Privy Council decision in *Ratten v R* [1971] 3 All ER 801. The accused pleaded accident to a charge of murdering his wife with a shotgun. The accused, his wife and their children were alone at home. According to the evidence the wife was alive at 1.12 pm and dead by 1.20 pm on the day in question. A telephone operator was called by the prosecution who testified that at about 1.15 pm on that day she plugged into a certain number in response to a call from that telephone number, that a woman's voice, which sounded hysterical and frightened, asked for the police and immediately hung up. That number was the accused's telephone number. The defence objected to the telephonist's testimony on the ground that it amounted to hearsay. Rejecting this contention the Privy Council held that the evidence did not infringe the hearsay rule because the caller's statement was admitted as a fact relevant to the issue of whether a telephone call was made from the accused's home during the critical time, and because the call tended to rebut the accused's defence of accident since the caller's voice betrayed fear. (The House of Lords in *R v Blastland* [1985] 2 All ER 1095 at 1103, approve *Ratten* on this basis.)

The Privy Council took matters further and held that even if the caller's statement had been adduced as proof of facts stated in it, it would still have been admissible as res gestae. It is on this point that the judgment made its most important contribution, in that it settled that the test of admissibility was really a test of probative weight and not of conformity to some technical definition. As Lord Wilberforce put it ([1971] 3 All ER 801 at 808):

> '... hearsay evidence may be admitted if the statement providing it is made in such conditions (always being those of approximate but not exact contemporaneity) of involvement or pressure as to exclude the possibility of concoction or distortion to the advantage of the maker or disadvantage of the accused.'

Lord Wilberforce was unequivocal in rejecting the previous technical approach under which, as he put it (ibid at 806): 'concentration tends to be focused on the opaque or at least imprecise Latin phrase rather than on the basic reason for excluding the type of evidence which this group of cases is concerned with.'

However, matters were not allowed to rest there and *Myers* returned to haunt the House of Lords in *R v Andrews* [1987] 1 All ER 513, where counsel for the accused contended that *Ratten* amounted to an extension of the *Bedingfield* principle and was, as such, a breach of the *Myers* vow not to create new exceptions. Indeed, the facts of *Andrews* were indistinguishable from those of *Bedingfield*. Fortunately, the House of Lords found the strength to ignore the *Myers* vow. This was done on the basis that two of the parties to the vow in *Myers*, Lords Reid and Hodgson, were also parties to *Ratten*. As a result admissibility now depends on probative value, as the test formulated by Lord Ackner clearly suggests ([1987] 1 All ER 513 at 520):

> '(1) The primary question which the judge must ask himself is: can the possibility of concoction or distortion be disregarded? (2) To answer that question the judge must first consider the circumstances in which the particular statement was made, in order to satisfy himself that the event was so unusual or startling or dramatic as to dominate the thoughts of the victim, so that his utterance was an instinctive reaction to that event, thus giving no real opportunity for reasoned reflection. . . .'

The decision in *Andrews* does more than any recent decision to shift the basis of the hearsay rule from a fixed definition to a test of trustworthiness. Broadly speaking, hearsay statements of eye witnesses are admissible if their reliability is secured by intense and unselfconscious involvement in an event (for illustration see *R v Nye and Loan* (1977) 66 Cr App R 252; the position is similar in the USA: 6 Wigmore, Chad Rev, Ch 59). In its generality *Andrews* makes other exceptions redundant. If, for instance, spontaneity and involvement can be proved it is unnecessary to rely on the exception of dying declarations as to the cause of death (see *R v Turnbull* (1984) 80 Cr App R 104).

Lastly, *Andrews* reduces the House of Lords' commitment to the *Myers* principle of no judicial change. Since the change brought by *Ratten* in overruling *Bedingfield* took place after *Myers*, it follows that *Myers* cannot prevent judicial change.

Refreshing memory

One of the oldest devices for avoiding the consequences of the hearsay rule is the device of refreshing memory. In *R v Britton* [1987] 2 All ER 412, the accused consulted in the course of his testimony a note in which he recorded the events in question shortly after their occurrence. Counsel for the prosecution was naturally given a copy of the note and he used it in cross-examination. However, in doing so he did not confine himself to matters upon which the accused testified in chief but questioned the latter on other matters arising from the note. The Court of Appeal decided that the trial judge's refusal to admit the note in evidence was contrary to the rule whereby a document, that has been used by a witness for refreshing memory, becomes evidence in the case if the cross-examiner strays beyond the parts relied upon by the witness and questions him on other parts of the document (see Newark and Samuels, Refreshing memory, [1978] Crim L Rev 408, 411).

But the question immediately arises: is not the admission of the note in evidence contrary to the hearsay rule? Using a well-worn fiction Lord Lane CJ answered this question by saying (ibid at 415) that the note is admitted 'solely to show consistency in the witness producing them [the notes], and they are not to be used as evidence of the truth of the facts stated' therein. I have argued elsewhere that the distinction between relevance to the issue and relevance to credibility is largely illusory; All ER Rev 1982, p 128. In a case such as the present the idea that the document is relevant to consistency and nothing more is clearly weak. Since the witness did not assert in-chief the facts which are introduced in cross-examination, since these matters are in no way part of the accused's case, his testimony does not need to seek support in consistency.

The truth is that where a witness cannot remember the matters contained in the note, it is the note itself and not his testimony that constitutes the real evidence in the case. Such a witness is nothing more that an conduit for the introduction of the contents of the document in evidence. The very structure of the rules governing the use of documents for the purpose of refreshing memory reveals an underlying assumption that the documents may well constitute evidence of the facts they proclaim. Why otherwise is it required that the document should have been made at the time of the reported event or soon afterwards? (*A-G's Reference No 3 of 1979* (1979) 69 Cr App R 411. Indeed, as Newark and Samuel point out, the less the witness could be expected to remember the greater the insistence on contemporaneity: [1978] Crim L Rev 408–409.) Why else must the document have been made by the witness himself or under his supervision? (*R v Mills*; *R v Rose* (1962) 46 Cr App R 336.) Why must either the original of the witness's record, or a verified copy of it, be produced? (*R v Kwol Si Cheng* (1976) 63 Cr App R 20; *Phipson on Evidence*, 13th ed, 780.) If there is no special significance in the witness consulting the document in the witness-box, why should not all these rules apply equally where the witness has consulted the documents just before entering the box? Why is it, as the court said in *R v Richardson* (1971) 55 Cr App R 244, that a 'line is drawn at the moment when a witness enters the witness box'? (see also *Owen v Edwards* (1983) 77 Cr App R 191).

These requirements make sense only if the document itself, quite apart from the witness's recollection, plays a central role in the inference to the fact in issue. Only then does it make sense to insist on safeguards concerning the provenance of the document. In many cases the fiction does no harm since the document is allowed in by the back door, but its harmful potential remains, as is illustrated by *R v Sean Lyndon* [1987] Crim L Rev 407, and commentary by D J Birch.

Civil Evidence Act 1968

Three points arising from *Rover International Ltd v Cannon Film Sales Ltd (No 2)* [1987] 3 All ER 986, deserve notice.

First, the Channel Islands and the Isle of Man are 'beyond the seas' for the purpose of s 8(2) of the Civil Evidence Act 1968. Hence, a statement made by a person living in these islands is admissible under the Act.

Secondly, the procedure of the 1968 Act may not be used for introducing expert evidence. Documents containing an expert opinion must be introduced in accordance to the procedure laid down by RSC Ord 38.

Lastly, Harman J refused to exercise his discretion to allow the introduction of some documents, containing witness statements, in relation to which the notice provisions were not observed.

Conviction as evidence of the commission of the offence

According to the rule in *Hollington v Hewthorn* [1943] 2 All ER 35, a criminal conviction was an opinion and as such was inadmissible in subsequent proceedings as proof that a person had committed the offence of which he was convicted. If A was charged with receiving stolen goods from B, the prosecution could not rely on the fact that B had been convicted of the theft of the goods in question. This rule was thought to produce unnecesary and wasteful litigation and to create an undesirable risk of conflicting decisions on the same issue. It was abolished therefore in civil proceedings by s 11 of the Civil Evidence Act 1968. The Police and Criminal Evidence Act 1984, s 74, makes a similar provision for criminal proceedings.

This last provision was considered in *R v Robertson and Golder* [1987] 3 All ER 231, in which the Court of Appeal dealt jointly with two separate appeals. It was argued that s 74 should be confined to cases where the commission of an offence by a third party was an essential ingredient of the offence with which the accused is charged; eg on a charge of receiving it is essential to prove theft by another. The Court of Appeal rejected this argument holding that the wording of the section does not justify such restriction.

Section 74(1) makes a conviction admissible 'for the purpose of proving, where to do so is relevant *to any issue in those proceedings*, that that person committed that offence' (emphasis added). On the wording of the section the Court of Appeal's conclusion is unassailable. But the section presents grave potential for injustice. This potential was exposed by Professor J C Smith in his commentary on the similar case of *R v O'Connor* [1987] Crim L Rev 260. This case is referred to in *Robertson* but, unfortunately, the Court of Appeal did not see fit to address the points made in the commentary. The main source of injustice is the effect that s 74 has on the burden of proof. Once B's conviction is proved in A's trial then, according to s 74(2), B 'shall be taken to have committed that offence unless the contrary is proved' by A. This constitutes a reversal of the criminal burden of proof and imposes on the accused the heavy task of disproving a conviction to which he was not a party and which, being a stranger to the events leading to that conviction, he may be ill placed to discharge. Suppose that A is charged with receiving stolen goods. The prosecution adduces B's conviction for the theft of the goods. A who, let us suppose, did not receive the goods from B, may lack all means of challenging the conviction of a total stranger to whose trial he was not privy. Suppose that A does find evidence that contradicts B's conviction and adduces it at his own trial. The jury must be directed that if at the end of the day they are in doubt if B stole the goods they must nevertheless convict the accused.

The seriousness of this injustice is intensified when it is realised that a conviction resulting from a plea of guilty has the same effect as one that follows from a trial, as has been decided in the case under consideration. There are two reasons why it is particularly unjust to impose on an accused a burden to disprove a conviction resulting from a plea of guilty. First, it is known that persons plead guilty for all sorts of reasons, including plea bargaining. Secondly, where a conviction results from a trial the accused in the subsequent case will be able to consider the evidence adduced at the previous trial and this may help him disprove the validity of the conviction (for the means of challenging the effect of a previous conviction see my note in (1971) 87 LQR 21). Where a conviction was based on a plea of guilty, however, the subsequent accused would in many, if not most, cases not even know how to start challenging that conviction.

Indeed, it might happen that the previous conviction fully proves the accused's offence in the subsequent trial. This was, as Professor Smith pointed out, the situation in *R v O'Connor* [1987] Crim L Rev 260. The accused was charged alongside B with conspiracy. B pleaded guilty. B's conviction was held admissible at the accused's trial. Since B's conviction of conspiracy with the accused imposed on the accused the burden of proving the contrary, the effect was that from the start the accused had to prove that he was not guilty.

Describing the nature of this burden in relation to the comparable provision in s 11 of the Civil Evidence Act 1968, Lord Denning MR wrote (*McIlkenny v Chief Constable of West Midlands* [1980] 2 All ER 227 at 237):

> 'How is a convicted man to prove "the contrary"? That is, how is he to prove that he did not commit the offence? How is he to prove that he was innocent? Only, I suggest, by proving that the conviction was obtained by fraud or collusion, or by adducing fresh evidence. If the fresh evidence is inconclusive, he does not prove his innocence. It must be decisive, it must be conclusive, before he can be declared innocent.'

Such a burden in criminal cases clearly runs in the face of the famous 'golden thread' of English law which demands that a person must not be convicted of a criminal offence unless his guilt has been proved by the prosecution beyond all reasonable doubt.

The Court of Appeal accepted that trial judges had a discretion, under s 78 of the Police and Criminal Evidence Act 1984, to exclude a conviction where its admission 'would have such an adverse effect on the fairness of the proceedings that the court ought not to admit it'. However, Lord Lane CJ ([1987] 3 All ER 231 at 237) confined the discretion to cases where 'its [the previous conviction] effect is likely to be so slight that it will be wiser not to adduce it'. Yet, for the reasons just given, the most pressing need for exclusion is where the likely effect of the previous conviction is great and not the other way around. Professor Smith is probably right in observing that it is unlikely that the courts would use the discretion under s 78 for the purpose of wholesale exclusion of that which is made admissible by s 74. Consequently the matter requires legislative intervention and the correct solution would be to provide that proof of a previous conviction merely imposes on the accused a burden of adducing evidence and not a burden of persuasion. Whether a similar modification of s 74(3), which deals with the accused's own previous conviction, is required is a different matter.

Confessions

It used to be the case that at common law a confession was admissible if it was voluntary. To establish voluntariness the prosecution had to prove that the suspect was not induced to speak, when he would have preferred to keep silent, by promise of advantage or threat of harm emanating from a person in authority (see *Ibrahim v R* [1914] AC 599; *DPP v Ping Lin* [1975] 3 All ER 175). This definition was rather narrow and technical but its purpose was clear: to protect the right of the suspect to decline to make any statement.

Section 76 of the Police and Criminal Evidence Act 1984, has altered this rule. It establishes a new rule consisting of two mutually independent tests: oppression and credibility. However, as I have argued in (1986) 102 LQR 43, since the new test is silent on the right of the suspect to refuse to answer police questions, the protection of the suspect's privilege against self-incrimination is thrown into confusion and this, in turn, is liable to make both the task of the police and of the courts very difficult. This difficulty is exemplified by recent decisions.

In *R v Fulling* [1987] 2 All ER 65, the accused was suspected of having committed a fraud on an insurance company. She was arrested and exercised her right to say nothing. Despite her assertion of the privilege against self-incrimination she was not spared from persistent questioning, but she persevered in her refusal to make a statement. These facts were not in dispute. The following day she made a confession. The accused contended that she confessed only because the police told her that her lover was having an affair with a woman whom the police had also arrested and who was being held in the cell next to the accused. According to the accused, she was deeply upset by this revelation, she found the proximity to her rival unbearable and she confessed because she wanted to escape from the place. The police denied these allegations. The confession was challenged on the ground that it had been obtained by oppression. Section 76(2)(a) of the 1984 Act provides that the prosecution must prove beyond reasonable doubt that the confession was not obtained 'by oppression of the person who made it'. The trial judge found it unnecessary to make a finding of fact regarding the accused's allegations since in his view even if the accused's allegations were entirely correct, the conduct of the police did not amount to oppression.

It will not come as a surprise to those who have followed the case law concerning the privilege against self-incrimination to read that the Court of Appeal has upheld the judge's decision. The trial judge held that 'oppression' means something above and beyond that which is inherently oppressive in police custody and must import some impropriety ([1987] 2 All ER 65 at 68–69). According to the Lord Chief Justice 'oppression' in s 76(2)(a) should be given its ordinary dictionary meaning. The *Oxford English Dictionary* gives three definitions to this word. The third runs as follows: 'Exercise of authority or power in a burdensome, harsh, or wrongful manner; unjust or cruel treatment of subjects, inferiors, etc; the imposition of unreasonable or unjust burdens.' The Lord Chief Justice adopted this definition. One of the quotations given by the dictionary is: 'There is not a word in our language which expresses more detestable wickedness than *oppression*'. His Lordship quoted it and went on to say that (ibid at 69): 'it is hard to envisage any circumstances in which such oppression would not entail some impropriety on the part of the interrogator.' He upheld the judge's decision that this was neither a case of impropriety nor of oppression.

There are many objections that can be raised against this interpretation. A perfunctory reference to a dictionary entry can hardly provide the guidelines for the conduct of interrogation that the police and the courts require. It is not self-evident that in our society the word 'oppression' represents the most 'detestable wickedness'. It may be that the second dictionary definition, for the rejection of which no explanation was given (perhaps because it was described as late Middle English, although the same definition is subject to no such qualification in more modern dictionaries; see *Chambers Twentieth Century Dictionary*; *Longman Pocket English Dictionary*), captures more accurately what is meant by oppression in the present context. This definition states: 'The feeling of being oppressed or weighed down; bodily or mental uneasiness or distress'. These words capture exactly what the accused claimed that she felt. But even if the restrictive definition adopted by his Lordship is the correct one, should we not expect some explanation as to why the alleged police conduct was not 'unjust or cruel treatment of subjects'? Should we not be told why this conduct involves no impropriety? The answers do not seem to be self-evident and it seems unlikely that we could glean from a dictionary the meaning and nature of 'injustice' and of 'impropriety' in the interrogation of suspects.

Leaving apart these important queries, there is something still less satisfactory in this decision. The suspect had an unquestionable right to decline making any statement to the police. She asserted this right. On the assumed facts, the police did not like the suspect's insistence on her rights. To overcome this unfortunate obstacle, it was alleged, the police invented a story which was calculated to distress and confuse the suspect to such an extent that she would forego her right and speak. Indeed, her second period of questioning, after the alleged imputations of unfaithfulness, started with the following questions and answers:

> 'Q. You have obviously got a lot on your mind, are you finding it difficult? A. Yes.
> Q. Would I be right in saying that you want to talk about this but every bone in your body is telling you shouldn't? A. Something like that.'

If the accused's account of her interrogation was correct, it must follow that the police set out to trick the suspect into foregoing the privilege that she had so strenuously maintained. Yet the protection of the accused's right against self-incrimination played no part whatsoever in the Lord Chief Justice's reasoning.

Seeing that the courts themselves pay scant attention to the suspect's privilege against self-incrimination it is unfair to criticise the police for employing trick and subterfuge to overcome a suspect's reliance on his right to refuse to co-operate with his interrogators. This happened in *R v Mason* [1987] 3 All ER 481. The police suspected the accused of arson and arrested him although they had no evidence whatsoever. In order to get the accused to talk the police told him and his solicitor that they had found the accused's fingerprints at the scene of the crime, a concocted allegation, whereupon the accused was advised by his solicitor to make a statement. The trial judge refused to exercise his discretion under s 78 of the Police and Criminal Evidence Act 1984, and exclude the confession holding that (ibid at 483):

> 'I have no doubt that this defendant was well aware of his right to remain silent and could have remained silent, with his solicitor being present, had he chosen that alternative. But he did not choose that alternative; he chose to give the interview . . . I see nothing in his doing that which adversely affects the fairness of the proceedings.'

The Court of Appeal disagreed. It rejected the argument that s 76 was exhaustive regarding to the admissibility of confessions and held that a judge always had a residual discretion under s 78 to reject a confession. Watkins LJ went on to hold that the trial judge had wrongly exercised his discretion because he did not give due consideration to 'the deceit practiced on the appellant's solicitor' (ibid at 484). He concluded with the hope

> 'never again to hear of deceit such as this being practiced on the accused person, and more particularly possibly on a solicitor whose duty it is to advise him, unfettered by false information from the police' (ibid at 485).

Alas, the police know only too well that unfettered legal advice is only too likely to be a counsel of silence. In *R v McIvor* [1987] Crim L Rev 409, the police prevented the accused, who was charged with conspiracy to steal dogs, from seeing a solicitor on the ground that the offence was a serious arrestable offence and that access to a solicitor might 'prejudice enquiries', in accordance with s 58(8) of the Police and Criminal Evidence Act 1984. Sir Frederick Lawton, sitting in the Crown Court decided that the theft of 28 dogs worth £880, in relation to which the accused was charged, did not amount to a serious arrestable offence and that it was improper of the police to refuse access to a solicitor because the accused would be advised to remain silent.

All the three cases discussed have one thing in common: the employment of trickery or other devices calculated to induce the suspect to speak when he would rather rest on his privilege to withhold a statement. In *R v Mason* [1987] 3 All ER 481, and in *R v McIvor* [1987] Crim L Rev 409, the confession was excluded but not in *Fulling*, even though in the latter case the trick created psychological pressure of a particularly acute and cruel nature (on the assumed facts). The court's attitude in *Fulling* seems inconsistent with the courts' position in the other cases. It is possible to reconcile them by saying that in the two cases in which the confession was excluded the accused was denied access to a solicitor whereas in the case in which it was admitted the suspect was pressurised into waiving the privilege without denial of access to a solicitor. However, since the access to a solicitor is intended to help the suspect insist on his rights, this distinction cannot adequately explain the differential treatment.

What this inconsistency really reflects is the irreconcilable tension between the privilege against self-incrimination and the function of the police to bring offenders to justice. If the police accord the suspect and his solicitor an unfettered opportunity to insist on the suspect's right not to make any statement, the suspect will decline to do so, especially where he senses that the evidence in the police hands is not overwhelming. If this happens frequently the police, and the public, will lose an important source of proof of guilt. Faced with this conflict between the privilege and the need to secure evidence of crime the courts give contradictory messages to the police. When the violation of the suspect's privilege is not blatant, the courts are prepared to turn a blind eye. When the violation is conspicuous, they feel obliged to exclude the confession and criticise the police.

This state of affairs is unsatisfactory. The solution lies in one direction only: in the elimination of the conflict. One way of achieving this is to remove the privilege while at the same time providing that only statements made in the presence of the suspect's solicitor, or some other unbiased and independent person, will be admissible. No sanction ought to exist against a suspect refusing to answer police questions, but the trier of fact will be free to attach to any refusal such probative weight as the circumstances may justify. Under this arrangement the police will not have to resort to tricks, the suspect will be free from undue pressure and abuse, and the courts will have a much more reliable record of the conduct of the interrogation and its outcome.

Before leaving this topic two procedural points should be noted. *R v Oxford City Justices, ex p Berry* [1987] 1 All ER 1244, effectively gives examining magistrates discretion not to subject a confession to the s 76 admissibility tests in committal proceedings. *R v Liverpool Juvenile Court, ex p R* [1987] 2 All ER 668, decides that in summary proceedings the magistrates must hold a trial within a trial in order to determine the admissibility of a confession under s 76 of the 1984 Act, if the accused demands it. On the duty to hold a voir dire at a jury trial see *R v Millard* [1987] Crim L R 197.

Legal professional privilege

By contrast to the half-hearted support that the courts have given to the privilege against self-incrimination legal professional privilege seems to have been an object of continual extension and fortification. *Guinness Peat Properties Ltd v Fitzroy Robinson Partnership* [1987] 2 All ER 716 widens the latter privilege in two respects: it stretches its scope and it consolidates recent limitations on the incidence of waiver.

The plaintiffs sued the defendants, a firm of architects, for the faulty design of a building. When the plaintiffs notified the defendants of their displeasure with the design, the defendants informed their insurers of the complaint and of their reactions to it (this document will be referred to as 'the letter'). They were bound to do so by the provision of the insurance policy in order to take the benefit of the policy. The first issue in the case was whether this letter was covered by legal professional privilege.

The Court of Appeal decided that it was. The court was aware that it was bound by the House of Lords decision in *Waugh v British Railways Board* [1979] 2 All ER 1169, where it had been decided that a document would be privileged only if the dominant purpose for which it came into existence was submission to a legal advisor for advice and use in litigation. Here the document was prepared by the defendants not for submission to a legal adviser but in order to be able to claim under an insurance policy. Slade LJ held ([1987] 2 All ER 716 at 722, 724) that the intention of the person who composed the document was not conclusive and that its main purpose must be viewed 'objectively'. By using an 'objective' test his Lordship was not in the least excluding a test of subjective intention. He simply meant the purpose of the document should be decided not by examining the intention and purpose with which the defendants wrote it but, instead, the intention and purpose for which the insurers required it (ibid at 722–4). He held that since the insurers required it for seeking legal advice on whether to settle the claim or resist it, the document was privileged.

However, this conclusion was not enough since the insurers were not parties to the litigation. To overcome this difficulty, his lordship relied on *Buttes Gas and Oil Co v Hammer (No 3)* [1980] 3 All ER 475 at 502, where Brightman LJ held that

> 'if two parties with a common interest and a common solicitor exchange information for the dominant purpose of obtaining legal advice in respect of a contemplated or pending litigation, the documents . . . are privileged'.

The practical effect of this decision is to accord legal professional privilege to all insurance relationships. Any communication which a person sends to his insurers seems to become privileged because an insurance company always contemplates litigation. It is doubtful whether such an extension is necessary in the interests of justice; especially at a time when the courts are resisting demands for similar privileges from other quarters. To bar access to evidence a justification has to be found in some public interest. When considering the scope of legal professional privilege in *Waugh v British Railways Board* Lord Wilberforce found it necessary to consider at the outset the interests of the due administration of justice. In the instant case the Court of Appeal did not find it necessary to consider the public interest.

More disturbing still is the decision on the second issue in the case. At the discovery stage the defendants' solicitors inadvertently failed to claim privilege for the letter and on two separate occasions they allowed the plaintiffs' solicitors to inspect it. When they realised that the plaintiffs were relying on this letter in their expert evidence they sought an order restraining the plaintiffs from relying on it. Following the decision in *Goddard v Nationwide Building Society* [1986] 3 All ER 264, the Court of Appeal approved the order restraining the plaintiff from using the letter in evidence. I argued in All ER Rev 1987, p 160, that that decision was based on confusion between two doctrines: the doctrine of confidence and the doctrine of privilege. Confidence should be protected by an injunction but once confidential information has come out through the fault of the person entitled to confidence or his representatives, there is no more confidence to protect. The doctrine of privilege does not alter this position.

Slade LJ thought otherwise. He laid down three principles. First, where solicitors inadvertently fail to claim privilege, 'the court will ordinarily permit them to amend the list . . . at any time before inspection of the document has taken place' ([1987] 2 All ER 716 at 730–731). Secondly, once the document is inspected by the opponent, 'the general rule is that it is too late for the party who seeks to claim privilege to attempt to correct the mistake by applying for injunctive relief (ibid at 731). However, this rule is subject to two qualifications (ibid at 731):

'If... [the opponent or his solicitor] either (a) has procured inspection of the relevant document by fraud, or (b) on inspection, realises that he has been permitted to see the document only by reason of an obvious mistake, the court has power to intervene for the protection of the mistaken party by the grant of an injunction.... Furthermore... it should ordinarily intervene....'

In deference to public opinion the Court of Appeal decided, following *Great Atlantic Insurance Co v Home Insurance Co* [1981] 2 All ER 485, that where the inadvertent disclosure of a privileged document has taken place at the trial, its use in evidence will not be restrained. But it is difficult to see why disclosure during the trial should have a different effect from disclosure during the discovery stage. In both instances evidence has come out and no principle of fairness or of the effectiveness of litigation demands its exclusion.

Nor was the effect of this decision on the interests of the administration of justice considered. It may be accepted that all communications for the purpose of preparing a case for litigation are privileged, but it by no means follows that the administration of justice is well served by the suppression of known evidence that can help the court reach a correct decision on the issue. Suppose, for the sake of argument, that the letter to the insurers in the instant case contained an admission that the plaintiffs' claim is justified. The plaintiffs would know of this as would, presumably, the court. Yet the case has to be fought as if there was no such admission. And if, for any reasons, the decision went against the plaintiff, he would feel unjustly treated. Public respect for the courts is unlikely to be enhanced in such situations. Suppose, further, that in his evidence at the trial the writer of the letter testifies and gives an account inconsistent with his statement in the letter. Would the injunction prevent the plaintiff from exposing perjury? If the answer is that it would, then it follows that equitable relief can help iniquity. Slade LJ spoke of protecting 'the mistaken party', but surely it is not the business of the law to help a party to litigation mislead the court and induce it to reach a conclusion that is at variance with the truth. If the answer is that the plaintiff is not prevented from exposing perjury, then it follows that the defendant may not in his evidence contradict the contents of the letter. And if this is the case, there seems little reason why the plaintiff should not be allowed to use it in the first place.

From a practical point of view the present decision complicates the process of discovery and reduces its efficacy. Discovery often involves enormous quantities of material. Until the decision in this case a party could assume that if his opponent has not claimed privilege in respect of a certain document and has produced it for inspection, he could rely on this document. Parties can no longer make this assumption. They can no longer be sure that they will be able to use all the documents that they have seen. In the instant case the plaintiffs' experts prepared their opinions on the basis of the defendants' letter, only to discover that they were not allowed to do so and that they must, presumably, submit new opinions.

Before leaving this topic it should be noted that in *R v Crown Court at Inner London Sessions, ex p Baines & Baines* [1987] 3 All ER 1025, Watkins LJ cast doubt on whether conveyancing matters are subject to legal professional privilege.

Press immunity

In *Maxwell v Pressdram Ltd* [1987] 1 All ER 656, the plaintiff sued the defendants, a magazine, its publisher and its reporter, for libel. The defendant journalists refused to disclose the sources of their information. These were relevant to the assessment of aggravated and exemplary damages. The trial judge refused to make an order requiring the defendants to disclose the sources. The relevant provision is s 10 of the Contempt of Court Act 1981:

> 'No court may require a person to disclose...the source of information contained in a publication for which he is responsible, unless it be established to the satisfaction of the court that disclosure is necessary in the interests of justice....'

Following the decision in *Secretary of State for Defence v Guardian Newspapers Ltd* [1984] 3 All ER 601, All ER 1985, p 157, the Court of Appeal has decided that the burden lies on the party seeking disclosure to persuade the court that it is 'necessary in the interests of justice'. The party seeking disclosure has to identify the issue to which the information sought is relevant and persuade the courts that the public interest in protecting journalistic sources was outweighed by the interests of the litigant in the litigation.

The Court of Appeal approved of the trial judge's decision that the matter of aggravated damages or exemplary damages could be dealt with by an appropriately strongly worded direction to the jury and that, although a direction might not be as good as evidence, there was no justification to order disclosure.

Special procedure material

Section 9 of the Police and Criminal Evidence Act 1984 empowers the court to make an order allowing the police access to 'excluded material' and to 'special procedure material'. These terms are defined by ss 11 and 14 of the 1984 Act to include, inter alia, personal records acquired in the course of trade or business, journalistic material held in confidence, and material held in the course of business under an express obligation of confidentiality. An application under such order has to be made in accordance with Sch 1 of the 1984 Act which, in para 7, requires that the application by the police be made 'inter partes'. It has been held in *R v Crown Court at Leicester, ex p DPP* [1987] 3 All ER 654, that the only parties to such an application are the police and the person or institution in whose custody the material is thought to be. It was not necessary, it was held, to notify the person suspected or charged in connection to that material.

Everything else being equal, one would have thought that fairness requires that the person entitled to the material should be notified because usually only he will be able to contest the application by the police. The reason given by Watkins LJ for dispensing with notice to the person interested in the material was that if a suspect was notified, he might influence the person or institution in possession of the material to dispose of it. This reason is unconvincing. A bank served with a notice of such application is free to notify its client. Indeed, it is difficult to see how it can resist the order and make representations without the consent of the client and an undertaking by the latter to bear the legal costs.

In *R v Crown Court at Inner London Sessions, ex p Baines & Baines* [1987] 3 All ER 1025, on being notified of an application under s 9 the solicitors seem to have sought their clients' instructions. Here Watkins LJ singled out the risk of interference with evidence as reason for holding that when a party is notified of an application it is not incumbent on the police to provide notice of the evidence upon which it will rely at the hearing. Lack of notification could well undermine the opponent's ability to resist the application. Realising this, his Lordship held that such a party may seek adjournment in order to deal with the evidence presented at the hearing. But if this is the case, why should he not be notified of it in the first place?

Furthermore, excluded materials and special procedure materials are usually kept by institutions and by professional people and these are highly unlikely to co-operate in the destruction of evidence. Hence dispensing with notice to the party most affected by applications for access to material is both unfair and unnecessary.

Proof of intoxication

In *Gumbley v Cunningham* [1987] 3 All ER 733, the Divisional Court was confronted with the following problem. An accident occurs at 9 pm. The driver involved is breathalised and provides a specimen of urine or blood at 11 pm. The analysis of the specimen shows that he had consumed alcohol but its proportion in the driver's blood is below the proscribed proportion. May the prosecution prove by expert evidence that, on the basis of the proportion of alcohol detected at 11 pm, it must have been above the proscribed limit at 9 pm?

The question was answered in the affirmative by Mann LJ who proceeded to add that (ibid at 737–738):

> '... the prosecution should not seek to rely on evidence of back calculation save where the evidence is easily understood and clearly persuasive of the presence of excess alcohol at the time when the accused person was driving.'

It is difficult to see why such a rider is called for when it is the function of expert witnesses to help the court resolve issues that require specialised knowledge. It is precisely because scientific matters are sometimes complicated that experts are required. Of course if the trial judge is left in doubt at the end of the day he must acquit, but the complicated nature of the expert opinion, as distinguished from its reliability, should not be a consideration in admissibility.

For another case on the breath-testing device, see *Cracknell v Willis* [1987] 3 All ER 801 (discussed at pp 93, 94 above) in which the House of Lords overruled *Hughes v McConnell* [1986] 1 All ER 268 (All ER Rev 1986, p 151).

Extradition

I M YEATS, BCL, MA
Barrister, Lecturer in Law, Queen Mary College, University of London

Government of Belgium v Postlethwaite [1987] 2 All ER 985 was newsworthy rather than remarkable. The appellant sought the surrender to Belgium of 26 English soccer supporters to face charges of manslaughter arising out of events in the Heysel stadium in 1985 before the final of the European Cup Championship. The respondents resisted, relying on art V of the Extradition Treaty with Belgium (TS 7 (1902) Cd 1008), which provides: 'If within two months, counting from the date of arrest, sufficient evidence shall not have been presented, the person arrested shall be set at liberty.'

The courts have previously, in considering the equivalent provisions in other treaties, had to determine the meaning of 'arrest' and 'presented' or the equivalent terms. Now they had to construe 'evidence'. Did evidence presented within two months merely have to be sufficient in content or did it also then have to be in a form which was legally admissible? The House of Lords held that the latter was not always necessary.

The magistrate reached his decision on the basis of Belgian evidence and English evidence. It was not argued that the Belgian evidence alone justified surrender. The evidence taken in Belgium from Belgian witnesses was presented in the form required by the Extradition Act 1870. The statements of 75 English witnesses were furnished to the magistrate. These complied with the conditions prescribed in s 102(2)(a) and (b) of the Magistrates' Courts Act 1980, which allows a written statement in committal proceedings to be 'admissible as evidence to the like extent as oral evidence to the like effect'. Section 102 however imposes two further conditions:

> '(c) before the statement is tendered in evidence, a copy of the statement is given, by or on behalf of the party proposing to tender it, to each of the other parties to the proceedings; and (d) none of the other parties, before the statement is tendered in evidence at the committal proceedings, objects to the statement being so tendered.'

These conditions cannot be satisfied until the committal proceedings have begun and proceeded far enough to allow the statements to be tendered without objection or oral evidence to be given. In *Postlethwaite* the statements had been produced within two months but the committal proceedings had not then started. The Divisional Court with much reluctance felt driven to the conclusion that, the evidence not being in admissible form, the requirements of art V had not been satisfied and the surrender had to be refused. The House of Lords was able to avoid this inconvenient outcome by holding that at least in these circumstances the evidence did not have to be in admissible form.

Article V merely requires that sufficient evidence be presented within two months, not that its sufficiency be established within two months. So, where oral evidence is relied on, the committal proceedings must continue long enough within the two months for 'sufficient evidence' to be given by the witnesses, but do not have to be concluded within the period (*Beese v Governor of Ashford Remand Centre* [1973] 3 All ER 689). Further, the sufficient evidence need only be produced to the Foreign Office and not to the magistrate within the period (*Government of the Federal Republic of Germany v Sotiriadis* [1974] 1 All ER 692). This is because, as the House of Lords has now again confirmed, the purpose of art V is to ensure that the requesting state does not delay in producing the evidence to the state whose extradition machinery it has activated. Therefore, if the foreign state has done all it can to comply, it would run counter to the objectives of extradition arrangements if it were to be frustrated by delays on the part of the requested state, eg, because a magistrate was not available at the appropriate date, or by distinctive features of its procedure such as the conditions imposed by s 102 of the Magistrates' Courts Act 1980.

Two ways out of the difficulty inherent in the Divisional Court's view were suggested: first (implied by the Divisional Court but not relied on by counsel) that the English witnesses should have been asked or where possible obliged to give their evidence in Belgium so that, duly authenticated, it could be despatched to England in support of the application for surrender; second (advanced by counsel), that those acting on behalf of the Belgian government should have ensured that the proceedings before the magistrates had started and progressed far enough for sufficient evidence to be tendered within two months. The House of Lords found the possible consequences even of the latter argument 'wholly unacceptable', although it would appear to be necessary where oral evidence is to be given as in *Beese v Governor of Ashford Remand Centre*.

The House was therefore able to re-affirm the principle that an extradition treaty should be construed not as a domestic statute but as a contract between sovereign states, so as to promote international arrangements for the suppression of crime. The only substantial difficulty was the *Sotiriadis* case [1974] 1 All ER 692, which was prayed in aid by both sides. On the one hand, in holding that the evidence was required to be presented to the Foreign Office and not necessarily to the magistrate within two months, the majority referred to a desire not to penalise the requesting state because of delays in English administrative or judicial procedures. On the other hand, as Lord Bridge of Harwich conceded in *Government of Belgium v Postlethwaite* [1987] 2 All ER 985 at 996:

> 'the House in *Sotiriadis's* case proceeded on the implicit assumption that the "evidence" required to be produced by the relevant provision of the German extradition treaty in a case where the only evidence relied on by the requesting state consisted of depositions and statements on oath taken in the requesting state, meant such evidence as duly authenticated'.

In fact, on the majority view in *Sotiriadis's* case, this assumption was irrelevant; it would have been material if production had had to be to the magistrate, since English translations were furnished to him, but not the authenticated documents, within the prescribed period. But, even making this assumption, Lord Bridge preferred the inelegance of holding that 'evidence' meant different things according to the category of evidence relied on. There is in any case a considerable difference between the two kinds of evidence. The evidence taken in the requesting state, as in *Sotiriadis*, can be put in admissible form by that state and the form of authentication required is prescribed directly by s 15 of the Extradition Act 1870. The English evidence in *Postlethwaite* could not be put in admissible form by the requesting state, and the conditions for admissibility were prescribed by domestic legislation indirectly made applicable to extradition proceedings.

Family Law

SM CRETNEY, DCL, FBA
Solicitor, Professor of Law, University of Bristol

Financial relief

The Matrimonial and Family Proceedings Act 1984 was intended to ensure, first, that priority be given to the welfare of children affected by divorce, and secondly that greater emphasis be given to the importance of the parties becoming self sufficient. The Act also reformulated the statutory reference to 'conduct': the court is now required 'in particular' to have regard to a number of matters, which include 'the conduct of each of the parties, if that conduct is such that it would in the opinion of the court be inequitable to disregard it': Matrimonial Causes Act 1973, s 25(2)(g).

Children's welfare not paramount

Decisions in the year under review have done something to clarify the interpretation of these legislative provisions. The most important is perhaps *Suter v Suter and Jones* [1987] 2 All ER 336 which involved a consideration of all three matters. The facts were that, after divorce, the wife continued to live in the matrimonial home with the two children, who were aged 14 and 8. The co-respondent—a dockyard labourer earning some £7,000 per annum—slept there with the wife every night. Their relationship was a comparatively stable one, but he made no financial contribution to the household expenses. However, he continued to pay £12.00 a week to his mother for a room in her house, and he returned to her house for breakfast every day. On these facts, the trial judge ordered the husband to transfer his interest in the former matrimonial home (subject to a mortgage of some £20,000) to the wife and ordered him to make periodical payments for the two children totalling £200 a month and periodical payments of £100 per month to the wife until both children had attained the age of 18.

The Court of Appeal held that the judge had been wrong in thinking that the statutory provision requiring 'first consideration' to be given to the welfare of children of the family required him to treat their welfare as the 'over-riding or paramount consideration'. That would indeed be the proper approach if the court were concerned with the children's custody or upbringing (Guardianship of Minors Act 1971, s 1) but in deciding on the financial orders to be made after divorce Parliament had not made welfare the paramount factor, over-riding all othe considerations pointing to a just result. The court should therefore consider all the circumstances 'always bearing in mind the important consideration of the welfare of the children, and then to try to attain a financial result which is just as between husband and wife'. It follows that the courts are not to make financial orders (or indeed ouster orders: *Richards v Richards* [1984] AC 174) which ordinary people would regard as unjust.

Children and the clean break

How far are the interests of the children relevant in deciding whether or not to impose a 'clean break', ie an order terminating the financial dependence of the one party on the other? In *Suter v Suter and Jones* the trial judge followed dicta of Ormrod LJ to the effect that the 'clean break' could not be appropriate where there were young children: *Pearce v Pearce* (1980) 1 FLR 261; *Moore v Moore* (1981) 11 Fam Law 109. But the Court of Appeal held that judgments in pre-1984 cases must be read in the light of the specific provision introduced in that year which require the court to consider in every case whether it would be appropriate that the financial obligations of each party towards the other be terminated as soon after the grant of the decree as the court considers just and reasonable. Specifically, if the court does decide to make a periodical payments order it must consider whether it would be appropriate to require those payments to be 'made or secured only for such term as would in the opinion of the court be sufficient to enable the party in whose favour the order is made to adjust without undue hardship to the termination of his or her financial dependence' on the other party; and there might (said Sir Roualeyn Cumming-Bruce [1987] 2 All ER 336 at 340) be cases in which such an adjustment could be made notwithstanding the fact that there were young children. On the facts of the present case, however, there were too many uncertainties to predict the development of events over the next ten years. The court was not able to predict with confidence whether the wife would have the opportunity to adjust herself to changed conditions; and in those circumstances the judge was right to refuse to terminate the husband's financial obligations towards his wife altogether. The right order would be for a nominal amount (variable upwards if circumstances changed), since the husband should not be expected to pay more than was just for his wife's support.

In contast *S v S* [1987] 2 All ER 312 was a case in which the direction to give first consideration to the children's welfare indicated a 'clean break'. The most important factor in the judge's decision was that to terminate the wife's periodical payments order would remove the sole remaining source of serious dispute between the parents, and thereby promote the welfare of their children.

Effects of cohabitation

The legislation provides [MCA 1973, s 28(1)] that orders made in divorce or nullity proceedings shall not extend beyond the remarriage of the party in whose favour the order is made; and a party who remarries is debarred from subsequently applying for financial relief: MCA 1973, s 28(3). But what is to happen if one party simply lives with a third party in a marriage-like relationship? In *Atkinson v Atkinson* [1987] 3 All ER 849 the husband, a man of financial substance, agreed to pay to his former wife, after a marriage of some 22 years, maintenance at the rate of £5,500 per annum. A house was also bought for her. Shortly after the divorce the wife became friendly with a nurseryman, and they set up house together. The trial judge was satisfied that the wife's decision not to marry was 'financially motivated to a very large extent'; but felt constrained by authority to the effect that cohabitation would only be relevant insofar as it resulted in some diminution of the wife's needs, either on account of financial support given by her cohabitee or because it was simply cheaper for people to live together in a joint household rather than to live separately: see ibid at 852, per Waterhouse J. The judge stated expressly that, if he had not felt so constrained, he would have reduced the periodical payments to a nominal sum, the reduction to take effect by gradual stages over a period of two or three years; but, as it was, only a small reduction in the order to £4,500 per annum could be justified. The husband appealed, arguing that cohabitation was relevant on a basis much wider than its impact on the wife's financial needs. He urged that it was a circumstance or change to which the court should have regard within the terms of the legislation governing applications for variation or discharge. It might be right only to take the financial implications of cohabitation into account where the relationship was comparatively casual: see *S v S* [1986] 3 All ER 566 at 573–4. But it would be wrong to do so where the relationship was in practical terms difficult to distinguish from marriage.

The case thus raised the fundamental question of whether an ex-wife who cohabits permanently with another man should be in a financially better position than an ex-wife who remarries. The Court of Appeal refused to equate the position of an ex-wife who remarries with that of one who cohabits. A cohabitant, unlike an ex-wife who remarries, does not acquire any right of support against her new partner; and remarriage ([1987] 3 All ER 849 at 857, per Waterhouse J) is dealt with separately in the legistlation. The underlying policy is that the acquisition of a new matrimonial status and new matrimonial rights against another man are crucial features. It is not open to the courts to add a gloss to those provisions by equating cohabitation, however defined, with remarriage. All the circumstances should be considered on a variation application [MCA 1973, s 31(7)(a)] and the 'variety of human folly' (ibid at 857) is, of course, infinite. There might thus be cases in which an ex-wife's conduct in the context of cohabitation (such as financial irresponsiblity or sexual or other misconduct), would make it necessary and appropriate that a periodical payments order be discharged or reduced to a nominal amount; but there is no statutory requirement that the court give decisive weight to cohabitation, and to do so would impose 'an unjustified fetter' on the freedom of an ex-wife to lead her own life. In substance, therefore, the court accepted the arguments which had weighed with the Court of Appeal in *Duxbury v Duxbury* [1987] 1 FLR 7. An ex-wife should have freedom to chose for herself how she spends the money which, in effect, she had earned during the marriage. *Suter v Suter and Jones* [1987] 2 All ER 336 reinforces the view that cohabitation is relevant to the extent that it involves or should reasonably involve, financial support; and in that case it was held that the wife should be expected to receive financial support from a cohabitee who was in a position to contribute at least a sum equivalent to the rent of the room which he occupied. It was this factor which justified the court in reducing the wife's claim to a nominal amount. In effect, therefore, the court has imposed an obligation to maintain on a cohabiting partner.

Conduct

In both *Suter* and *Atkinson* the court held that a wife's conduct was such that it would be inequitable to disregard it. In *Atkinson* the court accepted that the conduct was a matter to be taken into consideration, but only amongst all the circumstances. In the result, no further reduction was ordered. But in *Suter* the periodical payments which she would otherwise have received were reduced. *Kyte v Kyte* [1987] 3 All ER 1041 is one of the rare cases in which a wife's conduct seem to have been the main factor influencing the outcome. The wife had actively assisted (or alternatively she had taken no steps to prevent) her husbands's attempt at suicide. Her motives included an appreciation of the financial gain which she would make by reason of his death. She had also been guilty of 'wholly deceitful conduct' in relation to her association with the co-respondent; and in those circumstances it was right that the wife should not receive periodical payments, but be limited to the transfer of the matrimonial home and a small lump sum.

The clean break—when does final mean final?

The modern practice, it has been said, is to favour the 'clean break' wherever possible; but when is such an order to become final and irrevocable? The difficulty of this question was dramatically illustrated by *Bader v Bader (Caluori intervening)* [1987] 2 All ER 440, where the Divorce Court by consent made a clean break order under which the husband was to transfer all his interest in the matrimonial home to the wife within 28 days in full and final settlement of all claims made or capable of being made by the wife. However, some five weeks later the wife killed her two children and committed suicide. She left a will giving her property to her mother. Was the husband (who had not yet executed the transfer of his interest in the house) obliged to convey it to her executors? The county court judge held that he was not; he granted the husband leave to appeal against the original order, allowed the appeal, and set aside the order on the ground that it had been vitiated by a common mistake, ie that the wife and children would continue to live for an appreciable time in the former matrimonial home. But the Court of Appeal ([1986] 2 All ER 918—albeit speaking with three different voices (see All ER Rev 1986, p 168), by a majority restored the original order. The House of Lords agreed that the judge had been right, and that the husband's appeal had properly been allowed.

As suggested in last year's *Review* the case highlights an underlying dilemma of the modern law: where is the line to be drawn between, on the one hand, achieving finality in litigation and, on the other hand, avoiding manifest injustice to those involved in a particular case? However on one view, it was not necessary to confrom this policy issue squarely, since (it was argued) the wife's death had caused the divorce suit to abate, with the result that no court thereafter had any jurisdiction to entertain the husband's application for leave to appeal.

Abatement

Lord Brandon of Oakbrook (with whose speech all the other Law Lords expressed agreement) examined the case law relating to abatement in detail. He accepted the view (expounded by Sir John Arnold P in *Purse v Purse* [1981] 2 All ER 465) that, although there would be many cases in which death rendered it meaningless to continue proceedings in relation to a marriage which had thereby been brought to an end, it was wrong to conclude that the death of a party always and necessarily deprived the court of jurisdiction to entertain an appeal. The real question (said Lord Brandon) is not whether the divorce suit abates, but whether further proceedings in the suit can or cannot be taken; and the answer to that question depends on the nature of further proceedings, the true construction of the relevant statutory provisions, and (in appropriate cases) the applicability of s 1(1) of the Law Reform (Miscellaneous Provisions) Act 1934 (whereby causes of actions survive for the benefit of a deceased person's estate). In Lord Brandon's view the purpose of the statutory right of appeal against financial orders was to enable unjust decisions to be set aside or varied; and the fulfilment of that purpose would not be made any the less necessary or desirable by the death of one of the parties to the cause in which the decision had been made. Accordingly the husband was entitled to apply for leave to appeal against the order.

When should a case be re-opened?

Did the court act correctly in granting him leave and allowing the appeal? Lord Brandon stated a number of conditions to be satisfied if leave to appeal is to be given. First, there must have been new events since the making of the order which invalidate the basis or fundamental assumption on which the order had been made to such an extent that an appeal would be 'certain' or 'very likely' to succeed. It follows from this that the court cannot treat the question of leave to appeal separately from the question of the merits of the appeal. Secondly, the new events in question must have occurred 'within a relatively short time of the order having been made'. That period is not capable of being precisely stipulated, but Lord Brandon regarded it as 'extremely unlikely that it could be as much as a year. Indeed, in most cases it would be no more than a few months'. Thirdly, the application for leave to appeal out of time 'should be made reasonably promptly in the circumstances of the case'. Finally, it might also be that the applicant would have to satisfy the court that leave to appeal would not prejudice third parties who had, in the meantime, acquired, in good faith and for valuable consideration, interests in property forming the subject matter of the relevant order. On the facts of *Bader* there could be little doubt that these conditions were all satisfied: the appeal was accordingly allowed.

It should be noted the *Bader* was concerned with an event which had not occurred at the date when the original order was made. Presumably the existing case-law which allows an order to be set aside on the ground of eg, non-disclosure (see *Robinson v Robinson* [1982] 2 All ER 699 at 700 as approved in *Livesey v Jenkins* [1985] 1 All ER 106 at 117, per Lord Brandon] remains unaffected: in such cases the court has a discretion, not to be lightly exercised: see *Edgar v Edgar* [1980] 3 All ER 887, to set aside the order if the interests of justice so require.

Financial orders and the Revenue

A court *order* whereby a parent is required to make periodical payments to his child is effective to transfer that income to the child for tax purposes. (In contrast, an out of court *agreement* whereby the parent undertakes to make payments to his infant and unmarried child would be caught by the parent's settlement provisions of the Income and Corporation Taxes Act 1970, s 444(2): *Harvey v Sivyer* [1986] Ch 119). As a result, the financial consequences of divorce are not as catastrophic as would otherwise be the case for the relatively highly taxed parent, since income on which he had been paying tax at 60% or more will not be taxed at all in the child's hands insofar as it is within the single person's nil rate band (£2,335 in 1987–8). The child's legal guardian, usually the custodial parent, may then defray the expenses of the child's maintenance, education, and so on, out of the payments.

Clearly, such income could properly be applied in paying for the child's education; and a practice developed whereby the court order might provide for payments direct to the child's school in settlement of the fee. Such an order would be effective for tax purposes: see *Practice Direction (Minor: Payment of School Fees)* [1983] 2 All ER 679. In *Sherdley v Sherdley* [1987] 2 All ER 54 a father who *himself* had custody and care and control applied for a school-fees order against himself. Wood J held that although he had jurisdiction to make such an order, he was not prepared to exercise it. In taking this decision he was apparently following a policy adopted for some years by the judges of the Family Division. The Court of Appeal dismissed the father's appeal: the court also accepted that there was jurisdiction to make such orders, but agreed that the jurisdiction should not be exercised. In particular, the court expressed concern that the scheme would be ineffective to save tax since the 'reality' was that the father would simply be discharging his own liability. Indeed Sir John Donaldson MR thought that the word 'sham' might be appropriately used: *Furniss v Dawson* [1984] 1 All ER 530.

The father's appeal to the House of Lords succeeded; and the rule now seems to be that the court had indeed jurisdiction to make such orders, and that a spouse may properly seek an order against himself, provided that he had good cause to do so: *Simister v Simister* [1987] 1 All ER 233. It would be wrong to discriminate against children whose welfare required that they live with their father. The House also rejected the suggestion (made by Balcombe LJ in the Court of Appeal) that the such orders should not be made because the husband's application could give rise to no issue on which the court could adjudicate: in dealing with financial provision for children there is always an issue (now reinforced by the statutory requirement to give first consideration to their welfare) which it is for the court to resolve, since such matters cannot be settled simply by the agreement of the parties.

No limitation to school fees

The reasoning of the speeches in the House of Lords is not limited to maintenance payments made specifically for school fees. Does this mean that a custodial parent who has an income should always seek a court order in order to maximise tax relief: see the suggestion made in (1987) 84 Law Soc Gaz 3177?

It is suggested that there may be a case for the exercise of caution in this respect. This is because the question whether the court has jurisdiction to make the order, and the question whether the order will be effective to operate as a transfer for tax purposes of the payer's income to the child are two separate and distinct issues; and it must be a prerequisite of a transfer which is to be effective for tax purposes that the income is not simply to be applied to defray the payer's own contractual common law obligations. Hence, it cannot be assumed that tax relief will be available if (for example) the income is merely applied in meeting the normal costs of food, clothing etc. which would fall under a parent's common law duty to maintain the child. Orders whereby payments are to be made direct to the child's school in settlement of the fees have normally required the child to enter into a contract with the school: see *Practice Direction (Minor: Payments of Schools Fees)* and this provision, although treated with, possibly unwarranted, scorn in some of the Court of Appeal judgments, no doubt meets any objection on these grounds.

It should be noted that in the year under review it has become clear that the Revenue interpret orders of the type 'until X obtains the age of 17 or ceases full time education...' as terminating on whichever of these events happens first. For the future, the words 'whichever is the later' will be inserted: *Practice Direction (Minor: Maintenance: School Fees)* [1987] 2 All ER 1084.

The right to life

English courts, perhaps because of the lack of any written guarantee of basic human rights in our domestic law, seem comparatively rarely to become involved in the resolution of disputes about basic moral issues. But this year, the House of Lords had been invited to consider, on two occasions, what is perhaps the most fundamental of all moral and philosophical issues: the right to life. In the event, however, the decisions of the courts avoided any discussion of those underlying issues.

Sterilisation of the mentally handicapped

In *Re B (a minor)(wardship: sterilisation)* [1987] 2 All ER 206, the question was whether leave should be given for the sterilisation of a young woman who was some months short of her eighteenth birthday. She was an epileptic who had limited ability to understand and express herself. She did not understand the relationship between sexual intercourse and pregnancy; and she suffered from extremes of mood. She was incapable of giving an informed consent to contraceptive treatment or indeed to medical treatment of any kind. However, she had been showing signs of sexual awareness and sexual drive; and the local authority (in whose care she had been for some fourteen years) was concerned at the risk that she would become pregnant. The medical advice pointed towards sterilisation as the only effective way whereby this risk could be avoided.

The local authority accordingly made the child a ward of court, and sought leave for a sterilisation operation to be performed. The Official Solicitor, acting on the ward's behalf, submitted that the problem should be dealt with by a birth control procedure stopping short of sterilisation. Bush J gave leave for the operation on the basis that it was the only possible decision for the future welfare of the ward. His decision was unanimously upheld by the Court of Appeal and by the House of Lords.

The Lord Chancellor, Lord Hailsham of St Marylebone, denied that the case involved any issue of public policy. It was not about eugenics; it was not about the convenience of those who had to care for the ward or the anxieties of her family. It was about what would be in the best interests 'of this unfortunate young woman and how best she could be given the protection' essential to her future well being, so that she may lead as full a life as her intellectual capacity allowed. On the evidence (said Lord Hailsham) there could be no doubt that sterilisation was the right solution. Sterilisation may indeed involve 'the deprivation of a basic human right, namely the right of a woman to reproduce' (*Re D (A Minor) (Wardship: Sterilisation)* [1976] 1 All ER 326 at 332, per Heilbron J); but it is only meaningful to talk in terms of such a right when reproduction would be the result of an informed choice.

The case clearly established that the wardship court has jurisdiction to order sterilisation on a minor (even, it would appear, if the minor is of full mental capacity). It also appears to be the case that in deciding whether leave should be given the court will have regard only to the interests of the ward, and not to the interests of unborn child, or the community generally. No doubt leave will only be given as a last resort.

The case does however expose some gaps in the law. Firstly, what would the position be had the person concerned been over the age of eighteen? The House of Lords refused to given any guidance on whether the courts had a jurisdiction, perhaps derived from the parens patriae powers over the mentally incapable, in relation to adults. (Subsequent first instance decisions: *T v T* [1988] 1 All ER 613 and *Re X* (1987) *The Times*, 4 June suggest that declarations can be granted in such cases to protect doctors and others against the risk of legal action). Secondly, Lord Templeman expressed the view that sterilisation should never be carried out without the leave of a High Court judge. This is at variance with the traditional understanding that a parent has the right to give a valid consent to medical procedures; and it is not altogether clear whether Lord Templeman's views relate only to sterilisation, or whether they extend (as logic would suggest should be the case) to other extremely important surgical procedures. There is an interesting contrast between the approach upholding parents' rights in relation to the provision of contraceptive treatment and advice for their children which Lord Templeman favoured in the landmark decision of *Gillick v West Norfolk and Wisbech Area Health Authority* [1985] 3 All ER 402 and the present decision in which he considered that the autonomy of the family unit should not be respected. Possibly the case raises as many questions as it answers.

Abortion—whose decision?

In *C v S* [1987] 1 All ER 1230 a pregnant unmarried woman satisfied the requirements laid down by the Abortion Act 1967 and intended to have her pregnancy terminated. The putative father sought an injunction restraining her from undergoing a termination operation. His application was rejected by Heilbron J. The Court of Appeal heard the appeal within an hour of the judgment at first instance, and unanimously dismissed the putative father's appeal. The Appeal Committee of the House of Lords refused him leave to appeal. None of the courts involved sought to address the underlying moral and philosophical issues. Instead, the decision turned largely on procedural matters and in particular on the question of standing.

The father brought the action in his own name, and in that of the foetus, who was said to sue by his father and his friend. It was unanimously held that the foetus could have no standing to bring an action. It is only on birth that a child attains the status of a legal person. So could the putative father sue in his own right? He claimed that he had standing 'based on his personal interest, which he does not put as high as a legal right', and also because he claimed that the proposed termination would encompass a threatened crime under the Infant Life (Preservation) Act 1929 concerning the life of his child.

But Heilbron J and the Court of Appeal held on the facts that a foetus of a gestational age of between 18 and 21 weeks could not properly be described as being 'capable of being born alive' for the purposes of s 1(1) of the Act, and that accordingly the action was bound to fail. The father did not pursue his claim based on his standing simply as a father. This was partly because of the decision in *Paton v Trustees of BPAS* [1978] 2 All ER 987 (which had denied a husband any right enforceable at law or in equity to stop his wife having an abortion), and partly because the father of an illegitimate child has in principle no rights whatsoever over that child beyond a right to apply to the court for custody or access. Even if the father had been able to show that the proposed termination would constitute a criminal offence, he might, by reason of the decision of the courts in *Gouriet v Union of Post Office Workers* [1977] 3 All ER 70 still have had difficulty in making out the requisite standing.

The practical result of the decision seems to be that provided the requirements of the Abortion Act 1967 are satisfied, a mother is to be the sole judge of whether her infant child should be allowed to be born or not.

Surrogacy—the legal implications

The welfare principle which was given such wide scope in the sterilisation case discussed above has also been adopted as effectively the sole criterion for dealing with the custody of children conceived as the result of a surrogacy arrangement: see *Re C (A Minor) (Wardship: Surrogacy)* [1985] FLR 486 where Latey J held that the artificial methods used in arranging the conception were irrelevant, and that it would in the circumstances be best for the child that the commissioning parents have care and control.

In *Re an adoption application (surrogacy)* [1987] 2 All ER 826 the commissioning parents wanted fully to integrate a child conceived as a result of a surrogacy arrangement into their family, and accordingly applied for an adoption order. They had made payments to the birth mother (although it seems that these payments were not sufficient even to cover her loss of earnings and expenses); and the question therefore arose whether an adoption order could be made, given the provisions of s 22(5) of the Children Act 1975 which prohibit the making of an adoption order where payments have been made or given in consideration of the making of arrangements for the adoption of the child.

Latey J held that the payments which had been made did not fall within that statutory prohibition. He was strongly influenced by the fact that the parties only began to 'turn their minds in any real sense to adoption and the legalities' after the child had been born. In any event, the court has power to authorise the making of payments or rewards, and Latey J considered that such authorisation could be given not only prospectively but also retroactively. In exercising its discretion to authorise payments the court would balance all the circumstances of the case: the welfare of the child is the first consideration, but must nevertheless be weighted against 'the degree of taint of the transaction for which authorisation is asked'.

On the circumstances of this case the judge would 'without hesitiation' exercise the discretion by authorising the payments and making the adoption order. But the judge took the opportunity to warn that, although surrogacy arrangements were not as such against the law as it stands, they almost inevitably involved pitfalls, obstacles, anxiety, and distress.

The State and the family

When is the State to be entitled to take over the care of a child from the parents? It is difficult to imagine a more important issue, involving as it does questions of fundamental human rights.

In English law, there are two relevant procedures. First, a local authority may make any child a ward of court, and the court will thereafter resolve all questions relating to the child's legal custody by reference to his welfare. In particular, the court may commit a ward to the care of a local authority if there are, as there almost always will be, 'exceptional circumstances making it impracticable or undesirable' for the ward to be or to continue to be under the care of his parents or any other individual: Family Law Reform Act 1969, s 7. Alternatively, the local authority may bring care proceedings in the juvenile court. On such an application, the court must first of all find that one of a number of primary conditions has been proved. It must then satisfy itself that the child is in need of care or control which he is unlikely to receive unless the court makes an order. Finally it must consider what order (if any) it is appropriate to make, having regard to the child's welfare: Children and Young Persons Act 1933, s 44(1).

In both wardship and care proceedings, therefore, the child may be removed from his family; but the consequences of the removal are very different. If the child is warded, all important steps in his life must be referred to the court for decision—so that, for example, the court would have to decide whether or not the child should be placed for adoption, and whether in order to prepare for the adoption its parents should cease to have access to him. On the other hand, once a care order is made the local authority is firmly in control of the child's future, subject only to the parent's right to apply to the juvenile court for the discharge of the order, or (in certain circumstances) to apply to the court if the local authority terminate (rather than merely restrict) access. The case of *D v Berkshire CC* [1987] 1 All ER 20 was really about which of these two jurisdictions should be used.

The facts were dramatic. A child had been born to a drug addict. The baby was suffering from drug withdrawal symptoms. This was because the mother, who had been addicted to hard drugs for 10 years, and was still so addicted at the date of the hearing, had persisted during pregnancy in taking drugs in excess of those prescribed notwithstanding the fact that she knew that this could injure the child. The father was also addicted to hard drugs.

The child had never been in the care and control of her parents; and there was no doubt that the child was in need of care which the parents were unable to provide. The question was whether (as the local authority claimed) the conditions laid down by the Children and Young Persons Act 1969 for the making of a care order had been satisfied, or whether the case was one (as the parents claimed) which should, and indeed could only, be dealt with under the wardship jurisdiction.

The underlying issue was thus whether the local authority should be put wholly in control of the child's future under a care order, or whether the parents should be able to retain the right to have their views put to the High Court before any important issue was decided. This involved deciding the specific issue, which the House of Lords ultimately resolved in favour of the local authority, whether the primary condition (that the 'child's proper development' was being avoidably prevented or neglected or his health was being avoidably impaired or neglected) was satisfied or not.

The House of Lords held that, although the mere apprehension of harm is insufficient to make out the statutory ground, the court can properly look to the past, even before the child's birth, in deciding whether a child 'is being' ill treated; and the court may also look to the future as a part of the process of determining whether, in the absence of intervention, the situation would be likely to continue.

This decision re-enforces the utility of the care order procedure as 'a most important and valuable power giving a local authority the ability . . . to obtain . . . orders for the care and protection of children' (ibid at 30, per Woolf LJ); but it also demonstrates the remarkable paradox that the lowest court in the judicial hierarchy is given power to make what will often seem to be an irreversible decision, potentially depriving the parent of all links with his child, whereas the wardship jurisdiction always give the parent the opportunity of a judicial hearing before any irreversible step relating to the child's future was taken. In *A v Liverpool City Council* [1982] AC 363 the House of Lords effectively removed many vitally important questions about the exercise of local authority powers and duties in relation to children who are subject to care orders from direct supervision by the court, and decided that these decisions had been entrusted by Parliament to the local authority. There is clearly still a lot of feeling that the parents' position is not adequately protected by the procedures which are available for questioning local authority decisions.

Nonetheless, in all cases affecting the custody of children, the wardship court retains a potential jurisdiction. In *Re D (a minor)* [1987] 3 All ER 717 the local authority started care proceedings in respect of an intellectually and linguistically handicapped child on the basis that this was the only way in which they could deal with the parents' tactics which had impeded them in assessing the child's needs. The parents then started wardship proceedings. It appears that the local authority did not object to this course, and the care proceedings were adjourned sine die. The wardship judge committed the child to care, and ordered that he attend a special boarding school. The father wished to question that decision; and paradoxically he did so by arguing that the local authority had improperly surrendered its statutory powers under the Education Act to the court. The Court of Appeal rejected this argument: it was true that the legislation laid down a comprehensive code relating to the education of children, but the court retained its wardship jurisdiction and would only decline to intervene if the result of its intervention would be to create a conflict or the risk of such conflict between the court and the local authority. In this case, there was no such conflict, and no material on which leave to apply for judicial review could properly be given.

Adoption or custodianship?

The concept of custodianship stems from the Report of the Houghton Committee on Adoption of Children: Cmnd 5107, 1972. The Committee thought that there should be a procedure whereby foster parents, and others who were caring for a child on a long term basis, could obtain formal legal recognition of their relationship with the child, and protection against claims to remove the child made by the birth parent. The Committee also considered that adoption was an unsatisfactory legal institution in cases in which the applicant was a step-parent or relative of the child: adoption in such cases could distort family relationships, and result in concerned relatives being deprived of a proper involvement in the child's life.

The relevant provisions of the Children Act 1975 were only brought into force some 10 years later; and three decisions in the year under review suggest that the utility of custodianship is likely to be limited.

First of all, in *Re A (a minor) (adoption: parental consent)* [1987] 2 All ER 81 the Court of Appeal held that the onus was on those who opposed adoption and favoured custodianship as an alternative to establish that custodianship would better serve the interests of the child than adoption. Moreover, the fact that parents were willing to agree to the making of a custodianship order did not mean that they were necessarily reasonable in withholding their agreement to an adoption. On the facts of the case, where a five year old girl had been severely battered at the age of five months, and subsequently had no significant relationship with her birth parents, the parents were unreasonable in withholding their agreement to adoption. An adoption order was made.

The facts of *Re S (a minor)* [1987] 2 All ER 99 are even more striking, since the application was by the child's grandfather and his wife. Adoption in such a case would have the effect of making the child's biological grandfather its legal father, and the biological mother the child's legal sister. Given these factors, the local authority favoured custodianship rather than adoption, on the basis that adoption would not enhance the quality of the relationship which the child had with the applicants, and that it could confuse his perception of family relationships. But the Court of Appeal rejected this view. The court considered there to be two advantages tipping the scales in favour of adoption. First, adoption would give greater legal security for the actual relationships on which the child had become totally reliant, and adoption would minimise the risk of those relationships being disrupted by the mother (or anyone else). Secondly, the making of an adoption order would reduce (rather than increase) the risk of emotional confusion or the onset of insecurity when the child was introduced to the facts about his birth parentage. In effect, the Court of Appeal took precisely the opposite view of the advantages and disadvantages of adoption in such a case from that taken by the Houghton Committee.

These two cases have been concerned with the underlying policy of the law. The third case, *Re M (a minor) (custodianship: jurisdiction)* [1987] 2 All ER 88 reveals what must surely be a technical flaw in the legislation. The Children Act 1975, s 37(2) seems to provide in general terms that the court may make a custodianship order in favour of applicants for an adoption order if it is of the opinion that custodianship would be more appropriate. However, this jurisdiction only arises if the parents have agreed to adoption or if the court has decided that it can dispense with the parents' consent (for example because that agreement is being unreasonably withheld). In cases where the parent has refused to agree to adoption this leads to the absurd result that the court will often first have to find that no reasonable parent could have refused agreement but then go on to decide, notwithstanding this finding, that custodianship would be better in the child's interest. Hence, where a judge had refused to dispense with parental agreement to the adoption of a child by parent who had not seen him for some 23 months, it was held that he had had no jurisdiction to make a custodianship order on that application.

The Court of Appeal held that the judge should on the facts have dispensed with agreement, since there was no prospect of a successful reintroduction of the child to his birth parents. However, although this finding, paradoxically, would give the court jurisdiction to make a custodianship order, the Court of Appeal decided that the appropriate course would be to remit the case for trial of the issue whether those favouring custodianship had discharged the onus of establishing that it was to be preferred to adoption. This exercise seems rather artificial.

Land Law and Trusts

P J CLARKE, BCL, MA
Barrister, Fellow of Jesus College, Oxford

Contracts for sale: the rule in *Re Forsey and Hollebone's Contract*

Vendors should be honest; purchasers should be careful; registration in the Land Charges Register of an interest registrable under the Land Charges Act constitutes notice to a purchaser. Three seemingly simple propositions: but how do they relate to each other? *Rignall Developments Ltd v Halil* [1987] 3 All ER 170 (Thompson (1987) 84 LSG 2434, Wilkinson (1987) 137 NLJ 1178 and [1987] Conv 393, Harpum [1987] Conv 291) attempts to provide some of the answers.

In *Rignall Developments*, the plaintiff contracted to buy a house from the defendant at auction, completion to take place on 31 December 1985. Under the terms of the contract, (i) the purchaser was deemed to have made local searches and inquiries and to purchase with knowledge of everything that they would have disclosed; (ii) the purchaser was deemed to purchase with 'full knowledge and notice' of all such matters, and was precluded from raising any objection or requisition in relation to such matters. Unbeknown to the purchaser there were entries on the Local Land Charges Register relating to an improvement grant, which the purchaser might have to repay. The plaintiff refused to complete, and the defendant served notice on him to do so. Within four months, the entry was removed, and the plaintiff then sought to complete; this the defendant refused to permit unless the defendant paid interest from the contractual completion date. This seemingly small issue went to trial: and the result turned on whether the plaintiff was entitled to object to the entries on the register, despite the terms of the contract.

Millett J's judgment (which it is understood is being appealed) may be summarised as follows: (i) there is a rule in equity that, if there is a defect in title or an incumbrance of which the vendor is aware, the vendor cannot rely on express conditions such as those in *Rignall* unless full and frank disclosure is made: *Nottingham Patent Brick and Tile Co v Butler* (1885) 15 QBD 261; (ii) the obligation to repay the grant was a real liability which could bind successive owners; (iii) the purchaser had not been imprudent in not inspecting the register before auction: a purchaser, reading the conditions of sale would have thought that although there were entries, they were the 'usual sort . . . which would not adversely affect the value of the property': *Faruqi v English Real Estates Ltd* [1979] 1 WLR 963; (iv) even if the purchaser had not been prudent, the vendor still had an obligation of candour; (v) the Law of Property Act, s 198(1) as amended by the Local Land Charges Act 1975, deems the registration of any instrument or matter in any local land charges register to constitute 'actual notice of such instrument or matter, and of the fact of such registration, to all persons and for all purposes connected with the land affected'; in *Re Forsey and Hollebone's Contract* [1927] All ER Rep 635 knowledge and notice were equated and a purchaser thus bound; this decision, however, was wrong: it forced purchasers to make inquiries when it was inconvenient or impracticable to do so; it was incorrect to equate 'actual notice' (s 198) with the state of mind required for terms to be implied into an open contract. The defendant was therefore obliged to make a full and frank disclosure of the existence of the registered charge, and, not having done so, she had not shown a good title before the charge was removed.

Re Forsey and Hollebone's Contract has long had a bad press. Before 1969, it applied not only to local land charges but to land charges generally. However, so far as 'national' land charges was concerned, the Law of Property Act 1969, s 24(1) provided that a purchaser's knowledge of registered land charge at the time of contract is to be determined by 'his actual knowledge', irrespective of LPA 1925, s 198 (see Emmet on Title. 1.013). The Act, however, left the position unaltered for local land charges, and, as Millett J pointed out in *Rignall Developments*, many local authorities are now unable to return local searches in a reasonable time. Moreover, in auction sales, the position may be that the purchaser has no realistic chance to inquire of the local authority beforehand. Against this background, where the scales seem more heavily weighed against a purchaser, the rule in *Re Forsey and Hollebone's Contract* looks unjust. The rule itself is open to several fundamental objections (see Harpum [1987] Conv. at 293–4); first, a purchaser's notice (ie that which for legal purposes he is taken to know) is irrelevant as between the vendor and the purchaser himself: only when a purchaser actually knows of a latent incumbrance does a vendor not have to disclose it: *Sakkas v Danford* (1982) 46 P & CR 290. Second, how does *Re Forsey and Hollebone's Contract* fit in with the rule that a vendor who expressly contracts to sell free of incumbrances cannot adduce evidence that a purchaser knows of such incumbrance: *Re Gloag and Miller's Contract* (1883) 23 ChD 320? Third, it undermines the vendor's duty to make disclosure prior to contract: this is necessary because a vendor will not be able to investigate title prior to contract, and because he, the purchaser, needs to know all the facts when deciding whether to buy the property and, if so, at what price. Millett J clearly disliked *Re Forsey and Hollebone's Contract*. He thought its reasoning was 'unsound'; but in any event he was able to distinguish it. The local land charge in *Re Forsey and Hollebone* was irremoveable and was unknown to the vendor; in *Rignall Developments* it was removable and the vendor knew about it.

How far will *Re Forsey and Hollebone's Contract* continue to be regarded as good law? For the moment at least, conveyancers would be unwise to assume that local land charge searches are unnecessary before contract: however many academic writers believe that *Re Forsey and Hollebone's Contract* is bad law, and however cogently it has been criticised by Millett J, it has not yet been overruled. Moreover, if the vendor himself and his solicitor are ignorant of a local land charge, an exclusionary clause as in *Rignall Developments* may still be effective.

Vendors, however, should be truthful: indeed, it may be prudent for them to make their own local searches which can be shown to a purchaser; although this may occasionally cause an unpleasant surprise to the vendor himself, such a surprise is surely better earlier rather than later—especially if coupled with the threat of withdrawal from a bargain and the risk of litigation.

Where is all this leading? The Government Conveyancing Committee in 1985 made recommendations which would increase the burden on vendors. This approach could lead to a vendor of property being under an obligation to disclose all material facts—whether he knew they were material or not. Will the maxim be caveat vendor rather than caveat emptor?

Sale of registered land: covenants for title; plans

A J Dunning & Sons (Shopfitters) Ltd v Skyes & Son (Poole) Ltd [1987] 1 All ER 700 (Sydenham [1987] Conv 214) raises a number of interesting points on the sale of registered land. The facts are simple—the law less so. The defendants were registered proprietors of property at Poole, and purported to transfer as beneficial owners 'all that freehold property edged with red on the plan annexed hereto being another part of the property registered at HM Land Registry under Title Number P 7608'. The defendants, however, had transferred part of the land (the yellow land) included within the red-edged land to an earlier purchaser. When the true facts emerged, the purchaser sought damages against the vendor for breach of covenants of title. The trial judge found for the plaintiffs; the Court of Appeal (Sir John Donaldson MR dissenting) allowed the appeal and found for the defendants. Dillon LJ (with whom Croom-Johnson LJ agreed) first considered what the transfer vested in the purchaser: like many questions of construction the matter was one of impression, and Dillon LJ regarded the colouring on the plan as trumping the reference to the title number. The intention was that the reader of the document would rely on it; a reference to 'another part' of the number would not, as such, help a purchaser: he would not know to which part the document was referring, save by reference to the document. Sir John Donaldson MR, dissenting (ibid at 709), took a broader view, emphasising that '[r]egistration of land titles have only a limited utility if it is not clear to what land the registered title and other particulars relate': the primary unit was the registered parcel or an indicated part of it. The plan therefore did not have the overriding importance given to it by the majority; it was intended to indicate what land had been (i) sold to a third party, (ii) sold to the purchasers and (iii) retained by the defendants. The yellow land was therefore not included. There is much to be said for Sir John Donaldson MR's approach: first, an attempt should be made to reconcile the plan and the document, and second, every attempt should surely be made to give the greatest importance to the Land Registry title.

The case has other points of interest, on which all three judges agreed. Covenants for title apply to registered land (see particularly Land Registration Rules 76 and 77): the fact that in transactions affecting land the language is of 'transfer' rather than 'conveyance' was not considered. *Dunning* shows that these covenants can be useful. Second, the vendor was *not* the beneficial owner of the yellow land, but was expressed to convey as such: he was therefore liable on these covenants. This sensible and robust approach has not always been followed (see eg, Harman J in *Pilkington v Wood* [1953] Ch 770 at 777), but is to be applauded. Third, the purchaser's right to inspect 'the register' only meant a right to inspect the register in respect of the relevant individual title held by the vendor; it did not mean 'the global register' relating to all registered land. Reasonable enough: for are purchasers (unless they fear difficulties) going to expect to look at other titles? And surely, until the Law Commission's proposals to open the register are accepted, could not a purchaser obtain information to which he had no right, which might harm his vendor or, indeed, a third party?

The Court of Appeal in *A J Dunning & Sons (Shopfitters) Ltd v Sykes & Sons (Poole) Ltd* [1987] 1 All ER 700 were thus unable to agree how to construe a transfer of registered land where the plan and the title number conflicted, the majority giving the plan precedence over the title number. In *Scott v Martin* [1987] 2 All ER 813, a differently constituted Court of Appeal had to consider the vexed question of how to construe a conveyance where the plan and the description conflicted. In 1958, planning permission was given for construction of five houses and for an estate road, which was required to have a 13 foot carriageway with a 3 foot verge on either side. A conveyance of one of the houses in 1962 contained a reference to a right of way over and along 'a private road called Allerton Garth', which was not further defined, save that a schedule to the covenant distinguished between repair of the 'road' and making good damage to the 'grass verges'. A plan attached to the conveyance, 'for the sake of more particular identification only and not of limitation delineated on the plan annexed...' showed the road as consisting of an inner strip with adjoining strips, these corresponding approximately in width to the road and the verges. The plaintiffs purchased the land the subject of the 1962 conveyance; the defendants claimed that they could incorporate the verge into their property, thus destroying the plaintiffs' alleged right of way. The Court of Appeal emphasised that the case involved a question of construction and thus a question of law; therefore there was no burden of proof on either side. Only if surrounding circumstances were relied on did a problem concerning the burden of proof arise. Nourse LJ emphasised that it was permissible to look at the plan if the terms of the parcels were not clear. That seems entirely in accord with principle: as *Emmet on Title* states (19th edn, 15.012, '[t]he effect is that the plan may be looked to for elucidation but not contradiction of the verbal description; *Wiggington & Milner Ltd v Winster Engineering Ltd* [1978] 3 All ER 436.' However, Nourse LJ appears to express himself in an unusual way: 'I reject the submission of counsel... that you can only look at it [ie the plan] if the written terms of the conveyance are not clear. It is the terms of the parcels which have to be looked at first. If they are not clear, you can look for assistance to the plan just as much as you can to any of the other written terms'. The final part of the passage is clear, the former less so.

Surely a description of land is as much a term of a conveyance as any other term? Balcombe LJ was even more blunt: the plan was vital, he said, as without the plan, it was impossible to understand the shape of the plot. The case is thus in accord with the trend of recent authorities such as *Wiggington & Milner Ltd v Winster Engineering Ltd;* if the verbal description in a conveyance is incomplete, the phase 'for identification only' has no talismanic significance. The moral, hinted at by Balcombe LJ, is that a draftsman should think what he is doing, rather than mechanically to use a standard–form precedent. Are the standards of conveyancing thus expected to rise? If so, will there be even more actions for professional negligence?

Sale of land: the rule in *Bain v Fothergill*

Sometimes a rule of law justified at the time of its creation becomes sanctified by the House of Lords and maintains an existence which changed circumstances make it impossible to justify. A good example is the rule in *Flureau v Thornhill* (1766) 2 Wm Bl 1078, applied by the House of Lords in *Bain v Fothergill* [1874–80] All ER Rep 33. This rule, which Lord Westbury is alleged to have said arose in connection with defects in title concealed in deeds 'difficult to read, disgusting to touch and impossible to understand', provides that if a vendor is not able to show title to land he has agreed to sell, the purchaser will recover his deposit and expenses, but not damages for loss of his bargain, providing always that the vendor is without fault. Two cases in 1985, *Ray v Druce* [1985] 2 All ER 482, All ER Rev 1985, p 189 and *Sharneyford Supplies Ltd v Edge and Barrington Black & Co* [1985] 1 All ER 976, All ER Rev 1985, pp 189–190 followed the rule. The latter case, in particular, showed the arbitrariness of the rule: the defendant had contracted to sell to the plaintiff a maggot farm in Yorkshire (being registered land); the price was £8,500 and 20 years' supply of maggots, worth over £100,000. The farm was occupied, as the defendant believed, by occupants whom he could evict; they turned out to be protected tenants, and the defendant had declined to buy them out for £12,000. Mervyn Davies J applied the rule in *Bain v Fothergill*: the plaintiffs thus were awarded £472 instead of the £131,544 they would have received under ordinary principles of contract. This was described in All ER Rev 1985, p 190 as 'surprising, indeed harsh', and it is pleasing to see that the Court of Appeal ([1987] 1 All ER 588, Harpum [1987] CLJ 212, Evans and Rank (1987) 84 LSG 26) have reversed Mervyn Davies J. All three judges, Balcombe, Kerr and Parker LJJ, heartily disliked the rule: in an age when registered title was the norm, a rule based on the difficulties of deducing unregistered title was anomalous. The Law Commission's Working Paper 98, recommending abolition of the rule, was judicially applauded.

However, the Court of Appeal regarded themselves as bound by the voices of infallibility in the House of Lords, and, almost with tears in their eyes, had to accept the rule. However, they were able to apply an exception, which, although difficult logically to justify, enabled them to avoid the rigours and injustice of the rule. The rule applied, according to the House of Lords in *Bain v Fothergill* itself, even though the vendors knew of the defect—provided they were not fraudulent. However, in *Day v Singleton* [1899] 2 Ch 320, the Court of Appeal had held that the rule did not apply where the vendor had not used his best endeavours to remedy the defect in his title: this could be regarded as equivalent to bad faith, thus ousting the rule. Moreover, *Malhotra v Choudhury* [1979] 1 All ER 186 indicated that the vendor had the onus of showing that he had used his best endeavours. The Court of Appeal (differing from Mervyn Davies J) considered the vendors had not satisfied that onus; therefore the exception applied, the rule was thus excluded, and substantial damages were awarded.

One point was left open by the judges in *Sharneyford Supplies Ltd v Edge and Barrington Black & Co*: was the vendor obliged to try to buy out the occupier? Balcombe LJ thought not: virtually every interest-holder could be bought out if the price were sufficiently attractive. Parker LJ, however, thought that this was incorrect: he drew the analogy between the vendor's duty to redeem a mortgage (*Re Daniel* [1916–17] All ER Rep 654) and the facts before him. However, as Harpum points out, this analogy is false: a mortgage can be redeemed at a known price, whereas a tenant's demands may be entirely unreasonable. Certainly, if Parker LJ were right, the rule in *Bain v Fothergill* would virtually cease to exist, as few defects could not be removed by offering the holder of the impeding interest a large enough sum! Perhaps that is what Parker LJ intended: neither he nor his brethren liked the rule, and he may have regarded its emasculation to be almost as good as its removal.

Although the Court of Appeal gave leave to appeal to the House of Lords, the case has apparently been settled ([1986] CLJ at 215). We shall have to wait for another occasion, or for legislation, to witness the demise of the rule: it must be hoped that it will not be 'an unconscionable time a–dying'.

Sale of land: rescission

29 *Equities Ltd v Bank Leumi (UK) Ltd* [1987] 1 All ER 108 was briefly noted in All ER Rev 1986, p 201. A vendor wished to rescind a contract for sale of a leasehold interest under condition 11(5) of the National Conditions of Sale (20th edn) because a licence to assign had not been obtained at the contractual date for completion, even though it was likely that the licence would be granted later. Knox J held that the date of completion was material ([1986] 2 All ER 873); the Court of Appeal took a broader view: can 'it fairly be said as a question of fact that the licence cannot be obtained'? ([1987] 1 All ER 108 at 113). Since it was likely that the licence was obtainable in the future, the contract could not be rescinded and the purported rescission was thus ineffective. This seems entirely in accord with commonsense.

One point, however, was left open. Under condition 22 of the National Conditions of Sale (20th edn) would the vendors be able to give a notice, where the landlords are not refusing to grant their licence, but are being dilatory in granting it? Why should a vendor be locked in to a contract? Knox J's solution at first instance meant that neither side would be committed, the vendor being able to rescind under condition 22 (*Shires v Brock* (1977) 247 EG 127, *Jneid v Mirza* [1981] CA Transcript 306), and the purchaser being likewise entitled under condition 11(5). If, however, as the Court of Appeal have now held, a purchaser may not be entitled automatically to rescind, why should a vendor under condition 22 be treated differently? By analogy, it would appear that condition 22 should be similarly construed, but authority, as outlined above, is at present to the contrary.

Trustees for sale, the Land Registration Acts and the rights of occupiers

The All England Review 1986 contained a critique of *City of London Building Society v Flegg* [1986] 1 All ER 989, All ER Rev 1986, pp 186–190, and it was there commented, 'Perhaps the best thing about *Flegg* is that an appeal to the House of Lords is pending'.

The appeal has now been heard ([1987] 3 All ER 435) (Harpum [1987] CLJ 392, R J Smith (1987) 103 LQR 520, Swadling [1987] Conv 457, P H Kenny (1987) 84 LSG 1952, Greed, (1987) 84 LSG 1957) and the House of Lords have, more or less, fulfilled expectations. Order has been restored; whether the layman would think that justice has been achieved is, however, a moot point. In *Flegg* (as the case will hereafter be called) the facts were as follows: 'Bleak House' (*sic*) was bought by Mr & Mrs Flegg and by their daughter and son-in-law, Mr & Mrs Maxwell-Brown, as a house in which they all intended to live. All contributed to the price, but notwithstanding their solicitor's advice, the Fleggs were not registered as co-proprietors, the names of the Maxwell-Browns alone appearing on the register. The conveyance to them contained an express trust for sale regarding them (and them alone) as beneficial joint tenants, and also give them full powers to mortgage the property. Indeed, a mortgage with the Hastings and Thanet Building Society (later paid off) was raised, with the full authorisation of both the Maxwell-Browns and the Fleggs. Later, the Maxwell-Browns moved out, leaving the Fleggs in sole occupation of the property. The Maxwell-Browns then further mortgaged the property to the City of London Building Society, who did not know about the Fleggs, and who, on default by the Maxwell-Browns, sought to obtain possession of the property. The Fleggs argued that thay were entitled as equitable tenants in common to remain in the house and that they were protected by the Land Registration Act 1925, s 70(1)(g). The Court of Appeal accepted their arguments; they regarded it as irrelevant that the disposition was made by two registered proprietors, and held that as the Fleggs were tenants in common in occupation, the Law of Property Act 1925, s 14 protected their rights notwithstanding the overreaching provisions of the Act. The House of Lords unanimously rejected these arguments: a long speech was given by Lord Oliver and a shorter one by Lord Templeman; Lords Bridge, Mackay of Clashfern and Goff concerned.

First, their Lordships assumed that the Fleggs had interests under a tenancy in common, even though there was a declaration of trust that did not refer to them ([1987] 3 All ER 435 at 438), cf *Goodman v Gallant* [1986] 1 All ER 311, All ER Rev 1986, p 190, where the only two beneficiaries appeared on the documents as such. Second, they stated that all tenancies in common after 1925 took effect behind a trust for sale, even though, as Lord Oliver implied ([1987] 3 All ER 435 at 443) the Law of Property Act 1925 did not by itself achieve this: the reference to the Settled Land Act 1925, s 36(4) (cf *Bull v Bull* [1955] 1 All ER 253) makes this clear. Whatever the reasoning, however, the argument that a tenancy in common can take effect behind a bare trust, which the Court of Appeal toyed with in *Williams & Glyn's Bank Ltd v Boland* [1979] 2 All ER 697, has now been laid to rest.

Given, then, that the rights of the beneficiaries were under a trust for sale, how should they be characterised? The House of Lords distinguished the nature of the rights before and after the overreaching process. Previously, Lord Wilberforce, in *Williams & Glyn's Bank Ltd v Boland* [1980] 2 All ER 408 had stated that to describe the interest of a wife under a trust for sale as merely being an interest in the proceeds of sale was 'just a little unreal'. However, in *Flegg*, Lord Oliver seems to have rescued, or at least resuscitated, 'conversion-orthodoxy'; he approved the judgment of Cross LJ in *Irani Finance Ltd v Singh* [1970] 3 All ER 199 which emphasised the doctrine of conversion, and criticised the House of Lords in *Boland* for not regarding it of sufficient importance. Having emphasised the doctrine, however, he admitted that, where a beneficiary had an interest ([1987] 3 All ER 435 at 446): 'an incident of that beneficial interest is, or may be according to the agreement between the beneficiaries or to the purpose for which the trust was originally created, the enjoyment of the property in specie either alone or concurrently with the other beneficiaries'. It followed therefore, that in any dispute between beneficiaries *inter se* or between a beneficiary and a trustee, a right to occupy might exist: cf *Bull v Bull*. However, the right to occupy as such was not 'free-standing' (ibid at 446). As Lord Oliver had earlier said (ibid at 443): '. . . pending the exercise of the trustees powers, [the interests of beneficiaries holding as tenants in common] retain, by judicial construction, some of the incidents of legal interests which they replaced.' Two comments may be made on this. First, the 'purpose' doctrine may be useful in at least two contexts; where the court is being asked to exercise its discretion under the Law of Property Act 1925, s 30 (*Jones v Challenger* [1960] 1 All ER 785, *Bedson v Bedson* [1965] 3 All ER 307, *Williams v Williams* [1977] 1 All ER 28, *Re Evers' Trust* [1980] 3 All ER 399), and where a beneficiary is trying to prevent a sale (*Bull v Bull* [1955] 1 All ER 253, cf *Barclay v Barclay* [1970] 2 All ER 676). Second, the Law of Property Act 1925, s 14 (see p 152 below) may have relevance here to protect the beneficiary's right to occupy, until overreaching of the beneficiary's interest occurs.

However, their Lordships in *Flegg* emphasised that this was not relevant once overreaching had taken place. On the facts of the case, the overreaching machinery operated to transfer the beneficiaries' rights to the equity of redemption and to the moneys advanced by the Building Society; moreover, the overreaching occurred when the charge was executed, rather than when it was registered ([1987] 3 All ER 435 at 454). Even, therefore, if the interests of the Fleggs had included the right to occupy before overreaching took place, that right to occupy ceased to exist once overreaching occurred. It will be noted that there is no automatic link between conversion and overreaching: the doctrine of conversion characterises the interests of beneficiaries before sale or mortgage; the machinery of overreaching tells us about the nature of their interests after the sale or mortgage takes place. This, in part, enabled the House of Lords in *Flegg* to reconcile their decision with that in *Boland*. Quite simply, in *Boland* as the disposition was by one trustee, there was no overreaching.

This left two questions for consideration: first, what effect did the Law of Property Act 1925, s 14 have on the case; and, second, what was the relevance of the Land Registration Act 1925, s 70(1)(g). Lord Oliver felt unable to say what s 14 achieved; he thought it might have been designed to protect those who had acquired or were acquiring title by adverse possession (in which case it would be otiose) or to protect rights of, for example, statutory tenants under the Rent Acts (though it is hard to credit the framers of the 1925 legislation with such foresight in view of the limited nature of Rent Act-type protection at the time). However, it was clear that it did not enlarge whatever interests an occupier had; it merely protected those that existed. It is on this point that assertion may be seen to have taken over from argument. The Court of Appeal gave s 14 a wide meaning, based on a literal interpretation of what it said: the House of Lords seemed determined to restrict s 14 almost to the point where it has no role to play (the misplacing of s 14 in the 1925 consolidation was explained in 41 Conv (NS) 419). Neither view is logically correct or incorrect; it is very much a matter of impression. The House of Lords (rightly, in view of the importance of the overreaching machinery) have given s 14 a narrow meaning, but the decision on the policy adopted should be emphasised.

This left the problem of the Land Registration Act 1925, s 70(1)(g). It is trite law that the rights of those in occupation which paragraph (g) protect have to be rights which are conventionally regarded as 'affecting a purchaser finding a person in occupation of the land': *National Provincial Bank Ltd v Ainsworth* [1965] 2 All ER 472 at 503, per Lord Wilberforce. The rights in *Boland* were such rights, because overreaching had taken place; the rights in *Flegg* were not, because there had been no overreaching. Once again, the change effected by the overreaching machinery is crucial.

A few miscellaneous points remain. First, the courts seemed determined to treat the Law of Property Act 1925, s 14 and the Land Registration Act 1925, s 70(1)(g) as similar. Second, it should be remembered that *Flegg* was a case where the trustees for sale were given by the transfer powers of absolute owners, whereas trustees for sale (who by the Law of Property Act 1925, s 28(1) are given the powers of a tenant for life and trustees of a settlement) can only mortgage for very limited purposes: Settled Land Act 1925, s 71. Third, the case involved overreaching a beneficiary's interest in favour of a mortgagee rather than a purchaser. If a purchaser, as is the norm, will want vacant possession, there should be no difference, logically speaking, but one can never be sure, especially as in *Irani Finance Ltd v Singh* [1970] 3 All ER 199 it was suggested that a beneficiary's consent may be impliedly required prior to sale with vacant possession, and that an application under the Law of Property Act 1925, s 30 might enable dispensation from this requirement to occur. In registered land, would a restriction which included the consent of a beneficiary to be obtained be sufficient to protect a beneficiary? In unregistered land, the Law of Property Act 1925, s 26(1) achieves this result: cf *Re Inns* [1947] Ch 576 and *Re Herklots' Will Trusts* [1964] 2 All ER 66.

Finally, reference should be made to Lord Templeman's analysis of the 1925 legislation as effecting ([1987] 3 All ER 435 at 440) 'a compromise between . . . the interests of the public in securing that land held in trust is freely marketable and . . . the interests in beneficiaries in preserving their interests under trusts'. How *Boland* fits in to that compromise is not altogether clear: the answer is presumably that the magic of overreaching makes all the difference. But a layman, purchasing a house, would never think that it would matter whether he or she was buying from joint proprietors or a single proprietor; the 1925 legislation, however, makes the distinction crucial. Should the legislation itself be reconsidered?

Contributions to the matrimonial and non-matrimonial home

Flegg's case (p 149 et seq above) dealt with the rights of beneficiaries under trusts for sale against third parties; *Winkworth v Edward Baron Development Co Ltd* [1987] 1 All ER 114 (Warburton [1987] Conv 217) deals with the question whether a wife had an equitable interest in property or in its proceeds of sale; *Turton v Turton* [1987] 2 All ER 641 (Warburton [1987] Conv 378) considers the appropriate date, and method, of valuing the shares of those who contribute to property. *Winkworth* is a case where the result seems clear, but the method of achieving it is less obvious. The facts were as follows: Mr and Mrs Wing acquired the two shares in Edward Baron Development Co Ltd for £115,000 and became the company's directors. That £115,000 was paid from the company's bank account. The company acquired a house, which the Wings then occupied as their home. Although the company's account was then in credit, withdrawals by Mr Wing made the company's bank account overdrawn, and the title deeds of the house were held by the bank as security. The Wings' previous house was sold, and the balance of the proceeds of sale, £8,600, was paid into the company's bank account. Mr Winkworth advanced £70,000 to the company and took a legal charge on the house; Mr Wing forged Mrs Wing's signature on the relevant documents, Mrs Wing being ignorant of the husband's dealings with the company's bank account. The company went into liquidation, and Mr Winkworth sought possession of the house against the Wings; Mr Wing did not oppose the order, but Mrs Wing did, alleging that she had an equitable interest in the house following the payment of the £8,600 into the company's bank account. The Court of Appeal found for Mrs Wing by a majority, holding that the payment of the £8,600 was referable to paying off part of the existing mortgage on the property. The House of Lords (the sole speech being given by Lord Templeman) held that the money was paid to the *company*, not to the Wings, and therefore the Wings had acquired no interest. Mrs Wing was not entitled to the assistance of equity; as a director she had broken her duties, and there was no argument which would justify the creditors being disadvantaged.

Lord Templeman clearly regarded the appeal as unmeritorious: but, as Warburton points out, his remarks may be symptomatic of 'a less liberal approach to claims by women to an equitable interest in the family home' ([1987] Conv at 219): cf *Burns v Burns* [1984] 1 All ER 244 (All ER Rev 1984, pp 167–69), *Midland Bank plc v Dobson and Dobson* [1986] 1 FLR 171, *Grant v Edwards* [1986] 2 All ER 426 (All ER Rev 1986, pp 192–95).

Turton v Turton is a case which confirms the hitherto accepted view of the law, but also appears to extirpate some undesirable heresies. An unmarried couple purchased a house in 1972, with an express declaration of trust for themselves as joint tenants. The couple separated in 1975 (when the property was worth £10,000) and the property was sold in 1986 (when it was worth £35,000). What were the shares to which the parties were entitled? What was the date of valuation? The former question was easily resolved: *Goodman v Gallant* [1986] 1 All ER 311 (All ER Rev 1986, pp 190–92) provided that, unless there were a claim for rescession or rectification, the express declaration of trust was decisive of the parties interests. The second question was more complex; the purpose of the trust had come to an end in 1975, but sale was delayed for 11 years. *Hall v Hall* [1982] 3 FLR 379 suggested that the date of separation, when the purpose came to an end, was relevant; *Gordon v Douce* [1983] 2 All ER 228 (All ER Rev 1983, pp 351–352) (probably) and *Walker v Hall* [1984] FLR 126 (certainly) suggested that the date of realisation was what mattered. *Bernard v Josephs* [1982] 3 All ER 162 (All ER Rev 1982, pp 169–71) was not relevant, as there the separation had triggered off the demand for sale; and it was agreed that the relevant time was the date of sale or notional sale. The Court of Appeal in *Turton v Turton* declined to follow *Hall v Hall*, holding, seemingly as an absolute rule, that the date of valuation must be the date of sale (or other realisation of the parties interests). As far as an *express* declaration of trust was concerned, this is inevitable, because to hold otherwise would be to rewrite the conveyance; the same rule, moreover, applied to cases where there was no declaration of trust, partly because (though this was not articulated by the Court of Appeal) an implied or constructive trust gives rise to a statutory trust for sale. One problem might arise: it is possible that the quantum of the interests under such trusts may vary from the position that existed when the trust first arose (cf *Gissing v Gissing* [1970] 2 All ER 780 and *Bernard v Josephs* [1982] 3 All ER 162). This *could* mean that a valuation at sale could be disadvantageous to one party compared with valuation at the earlier date of separation; but the reality, with house prices increasing at rates well above those of inflation, is that a lowering of the share may well not mean less money. It is, of course, always open to parties to provide expressly that a particular date for valuation is to be adopted.

One final point may be made. A court may well refuse an application under the Law of Property Act 1925, s 30 to sell the property, thus protecting the interest of a beneficiary in occupation. This is entirely separate from the valuation of the right when the property is later sold.

Leases and licences

In 1985, *Street v Mountford* [1985] 2 All ER 289, All ER Rev 1985 pp 190–196) was hailed as a land-mark case, but subjected to considerable criticism. The nub of the case may be found in Lord Templeman's speech [1985] 2 All ER 289 at 293f–j:

> 'An occupier of residential occupation at a rent is either a lodger or a tenant. The occupier is a lodger if the landlord provides attendance or services which require the landlord or his servants to exercise unrestricted access to and use of his premises . . . if, on the other hand, residential accommodation is granted for a term at a rent with exclusive possession, the landlord providing neither attendance nor services, the grant is a tenancy . . .'

The inference commonly drawn from Lord Templeman's speech in general, and from that passage in particular, is that occupation licences will be extremely rarely found, and that the courts will not be able to depart from the view that occupation plus periodic payment will create a lease, not a licence.

Street v Mountford has already given use to a considerable number of cases reported primarily in the Estates Gazette: *Royal Philanthropic Society v County* [1985] 2 EGLR 109, *Bretherton v Paton* [1986] 1 EGLR 172, *Crancour Ltd v Da Silvaesa* [1986] 1 EGLR 80, *London & Associated Investment Trusts*

Ltd v Calow [1986] 2 EGLR 80, *Dresden Estates Ltd v Collinson* [1987] 1 EGLR 45, *Dellneed Ltd v Chin* [1987] 1 EGLR 75. *Brent People's Housing Association v Winsmore* (1986) noted 281 EG 996, *Brooker Settled Estates Ltd v Ayres* [1987] 1 EGLR 50, *Smith v Northside Developments Ltd* (1987) 283 EG 1211. These cases are impossible briefly to summarise: they display varying approaches to the lease/licence problem, but do make it clear that Lord Templeman's speech has apparently exacerbated rather than simplified the difficulties that hitherto existed. *Hadjiloucas v Crean* [1987] 3 All ER 1008 is a reserved judgment of the Court of Appeal which an attempt is made to analyse what Lord Templeman said, and to chart a way forward. (The case will need to be read in conjunction with the decision of the Court of Appeal in *AG Securities v Vaughan*, when a full report is available; the case is at present reported in [1988] NLJ Practitioner 23). In *Hadjiloucas v Crean*, Miss Crean and Miss Broderick agreed to rent a flat; they signed separate but identical documents purporting to be licences (this was in 1984, before *Street v Mountford*), expressly indicating that the licences were separate and that the licensee was not to have exclusive possession. Each lady was responsible for the whole rent. Miss Broderick left, and she, without consulting Miss Crean, agreed with the landlord that Miss Rollins should take her (ie Miss Broderick's) place. Miss Rollins left; Miss Crean applied to the Rent Officer to fix a fair rent, and the landlord sought possession. The county court judge held that Miss Crean was a licensee, and ordered possession. Purchas LJ began by emphasising that Lord Templeman in *Street v Mountford* was dealing with a single occupation, where exclusive possession was conceded. How far could the law laid down in this situation be applied elsewhere? If there was a sham, the question was easy. If there was not a sham, the true contractual effect of the agreement had to be found 'eliminating any artificial provisions' ([1987] 3 All ER 1008 at 1014). 'In the final analysis each case must be considered on its own facts to see whether in the case of multiple occupancy, a joint tenancy has been created' (ibid at 1016). The factual matrix was important (ibid at 1017), and as the county court judge had not considered the matter suffciently fully the issue would have to be referred back to him. Mustill LJ reached the same conclusion by a slightly different route. He began by indicating that there were a number of situations where a document should not be taken at face value: (i) where rectification was available, (ii) where there was no intention to create a legal obligation, (iii) where there was a sham and (iv) where the document reflects the agreement, but the language and/or the description of it placed it in the wrong legal category (*Street v Mountford* was an example of (iv)). Exclusive occupation or possession was the prerequisite of a tenancy, but it did not therefore follow that every occupation or possession was necessarily exclusive. The ordinary rules of the law of contract will be used to determine whether there is an intention to confer exclusive occupation; thus the way the parties conducted themselves while the agreement was in force was not relevant. Sir Roualeyn Cumming-Bruce concurred with both judgments.

Several points emerge from the case. First, as Mustill LJ points out 'in this field, each case turns on its own facts' ([1987] 3 All ER 1008 at 1023). The amount of reported litigation on the subject since *Street v Mountford* had tended to suggest this conclusion, but it has now been judicially confirmed.

Second, the circumstances in which agreement was made—the factual matrix—must be considered. Third, there is no presumption that in joint occupancy there is a joint tenancy, two parallel tenancies, or two licences. Such a choice cannot exist where there is a single occupier: there the choice is 'tenancy or licence', and, as *Street v Mountford* shows, a tenancy will be the more likely result. The virtually infinite number of variations on the theme of multi-occupancy however makes a presumption of a tenancy inappropriate in these situations. Fourth, *Street v Mountford*, it appears, is not to be construed as if it were a statute, a point already made by Ralph Gibson LJ in *Crancour Ltd v Da Silvaesa* [1986] 1 EGLR at 82j. Fifth, the remark of Purchas LJ in *Crancour Ltd* (ibid at 88k) that 'a skilled draftsman must, in appropriate circumstances, be allowed to succeed' seems implicitly to be followed in *Hadjiloucas v Crean*; if parties can make an agreement which both on its face and on the facts of the case does not create a lease, so be it. This also seems consistent with the approach of Fox LJ in *AG Securities v Vaughan* [1988] NLJ Practitioner 23. Coupled with this is the necessary implication that it is possible for a licence to exist where there is no provision for attendance or services: this had already been hinted at by Ralph Gibson LJ in *Crancour v Da Silvaesa*, and accepted by the Court of Appeal in *Brooker Settled Estates Ltd v Ayers* [1987] 1 EGLR 50. How far this fits in with Lord Templeman's tenant/lodger dichotomy is hard to see. Sixth, an uncertainty still remains as to what is 'an artificial device' to avoid the Rent Acts: Mustill LJ regards it as another description of a sham (*Hadjiloucas v Crean* [1987] 3 All ER 1008 at 1022); Purchas LJ regards the two concepts as separate: ibid at 1017. It may be that the two are similar but that a suspicious court, while reluctant to find a sham, would regard the documentary evidence before it as artificial, and thus fit to be struck down: shades of *Furniss v Dawson* [1984] 1 All ER 530. Nothing in the case relates to arrangements concerning non-residential property: as Judge Paul Baker QC, sitting as a Deputy Judge of the High Court said in *London & Associated Investment Trust Ltd v Calow* [1986] 2 EGLR 80 at 84: 'there might be special cases of some sort for trading properties, areas in shops and so forth, or stalls in markets, and there might be difficulties with agricultural properties, where licencees are frequent'. *Dresden Estates Ltd v Collinson* [1987] 1 EGLR 45 and *Smith v Northside Developments* (1987) 283 EG 1211 support this verdict: in both these cases, the courts were prepared to find a licence of business premises rather than a lease.

The outlook for litigant and judge alike looks hazardous. First, the parties must produce detailed evidence of the transaction, its circumstances, and 'the factual matrix' in which it was made. Second, the written agreement must be considered and construed, with the possibility that it may be upset. Third, as 'each case turns on its own facts', the judge cannot easily raise by analogy from the facts of reported cases, but must argue from principle. The chimaera of simplicity looks as far away as ever.

Estoppel interests

In the All England Review 1986, in noting *Grant v Edwards* [1986] 2 All ER 426 (All ER Rev 1986, pp 192–95), it was commented that there were clearly similarities between the law of proprietary estoppel and the law of constructive trusts. This point again arose in *Re Basham (dec'd)* [1987] 1 All ER 405 (Hayton [1987] CLJ 217, Martin [1987] Conv 211). Mr Basham married the plaintiff's mother when the plaintiff was 15. The plaintiff, over a period of about thirty years had helped to run the family business (a series of public houses and a service station) without being paid, on the understanding that she would inherit from Mr Basham. The plaintiff and her husband had lived very near Mr Basham and had for years done everything Mr Basham wished, including sorting out a boundary dispute, laying carpets, and cleaning his house. Moreover, the husband refused a job with a tied cottage so that he could stay near Mr Basham. The plaintiff thought she would inherit at least the cottage; Mr Basham, however, died intestate. On his intestacy the property passed to his nephews and nieces, and the plaintiff claimed an interest in the estate. The facts are not, therefore, unusual, but the approach of Mr Edward Nugee QC, sitting as a Deputy Judge of the High Court, was. The problem, from the plaintiff's point of view, was how to formulate her claim; no contract was alleged (presumably what the plaintiff was to receive was uncertain) and therefore the doctrine of part performance could not be invoked; further, if there was an estoppel or a constructive trust, in respect of what property did it operate and when did it arise?

As far as estoppel is concerned the law is in a state of flux; after all, in *Crabb v Arun DC* [1975] 3 All ER 865, Scarman LJ asked the questions (i) is there an equity, (ii) what is its extent?, (iii) how can it best be satisfied? Likewise, in *Taylor Fashions Ltd v Liverpool Victoria Trustees Co Ltd* [1981] 1 All ER 897 Oliver J adopted a general approach based on unconscionability, rather than on the five probanda in *Willmott v Barber* (1880) 15 Ch D 96. If this approach is followed, there is no need to link estoppel to existing property, or to a present right; a promise relating to the estate of a person not yet dead can be brought within it. Nugee QC was prepared to adopt this view, where (i) there was detriment by A, and (ii) the belief known to or encouraged by B, 'that A has or *is going to be given* [writer's italics] an interest in or over B's property' ([1987] 1 All ER at 410b); he thus awarded the plaintiff the whole of Mr Basham's estate. That part of the judgment is surprising enough: estoppel is now seemingly without any boundaries save those which a judge, on the facts of the case before him, may consider appropriate.

However, the judge went on to hold that proprietary estoppel can give rise to a constructive trust. He regarded a common thread as running through proprietary estoppel, mutual wills, secret trusts and the acquisition of interests in the matrimonial home. As indicated, *Grant v Edwards* hinted at this, by extending the requirement of detriment into the sphere of constructive trusts, whereas in *Re Basham*, constructive trusts are extended into proprietary estoppel. What is not clear is why the constructive trust is vital. Is it simply to bolster an argument that might itself not be sufficient (cf *Re Sharpe* [1980] 1 All ER 198)? Certainly the use of a constructive trust to protect against a third party an otherwise unprotected contractual licence supports this view (cf *DHN Food Distributors Ltd v London Borough of Tower Hamlets* [1976] 3 All ER 462), though the recent case of *Ashburn Anstalt v Arnold* (1987) 284 EG 1375 emphasises that 'the court will not impose a constructive trust unless it is satisfied that the conscience of the estate owner is affected' (ibid at 1384). In *Re Basham* it is difficult to see whose conscience was affected: the testator was dead, and his administrators, the statutory next of kin, were, it appears, unaware of what had transpired. The reference to *Re Cleaver* [1981] 1 All ER 1018, although concerned with a 'floating' constructive trusteeship, emphasised that the trusteeship is imposed on the recipient, whose conscience, in that case, was affected.

The constructive trust is thus fast becoming 'an unruly horse', and there seems no serious attempt to bridle it. Once again, formalities are being subverted, and the idea that a will is necessary to pass property on death is further undermined. Is this really satisfactory? Surely, as Jill Martin suggests ([1987] Conv at 214) if the plaintiff were to succeed, an application under the Inheritance (Provision for Family and Dependants) Act 1975 by her as a 'child of the family' might have been more appropriate. The plaintiff might not have received, as she did under Nugee QC's judgment, the whole of the estate, but the result would not have been unfair to her (because it was not clear that she expected everything to be left to her), and legal principle would have remained intact.

The other case on proprietary estoppel is the decision of the Privy Council in *A-G of Hong Kong v Humphreys Estate (Queen's Gardens) Ltd* [1987] 2 All ER 387. Lord Templeman, giving the judgment of the Board, considered the authorities on estoppel, from *Ramsden v Dyson* (1866) LR 1 HL 129 to *Taylor Fashions Ltd v Liverpool Victoria Trustee Co Ltd* [1981] 1 All ER 897, and held that, for A to claim an estoppel against B (i) there had to be an acting by A to his detriment, (ii) a creation or encouragement of a belief or expectation by B, and (iii) a reliance on that by A. As these were not shown, there was no estoppel. The case thus follows the orthodox, traditional, doctrine of proprietary estoppel.

The mortgagee's right to possession

In most recent years, the power of the court to exercise its discretion in respect of a mortgagee's right to possession has fallen for judicial consideration. The Administration of Justice Act 1970, s 36 (as amended by the Administration of Justice Act 1973, s 8) provides that, where the mortgaged property is, or includes, a dwellinghouse, the court has a discretion to postpone the mortgagee's right to possession if it appears that the mortgagor was likely to be able to pay within a reasonable period any sums due under the mortgage. *Citibank Trust Ltd v Ayivor* [1987] 3 All ER 241 was a new problem in this context, though one that has arisen elsewhere in the law of mortgages. The mortgagors, who were in default, were prosecuting a counterclaim against the mortgagee in respect of information in the mortgagee's survey report that was not shown to them. It is clear that the mortgagee's right to possession is not to be defeated by the existence of a counterclaim: *Barclays Bank plc v Tennet* [1984] CA Transcript 242, and *Mobil Oil Co Ltd v Rawlinson* (1982) 43 P & CR 221 (All ER Rev 1982, p 179). Mervyn Davies J held, first that the existence of the counterclaim might be an admissible consideration in the court's exercise of its discretionary power under the Administration of Justice Acts. Second, the judge then went on to say that the existence of the counterclaim did not mean that the defendants were likely 'to be able within a reasonable period' to pay off the arrears. Third, even if the counterclaim were successful, the judge did not believe himself justified in concluding that the moneys would be used to pay off the arrears. With respect, the first and third points are difficult to follow. The Act gives a wide discretion to the court: the question is 'is the mortgagor likely to be able within a reasonable period' to clear the arrears? Imagine a mortgagor, with a terminally ill and mentally incompetent relative who has made a will in the mortgagor's favour. Surely, in such a case the court might be satisfied that a staying of the order for possession would be justified. If that is within the Act, and there is surely nothing to prevent it, then a valid counterclaim could likewise be relevant. Mervyn Davies' J second point, however, is a difficult one: how is a judge to estimate the chances of success, and, if successful, the question of damages, when all the facts are not yet known? Surely, if there is a genuine dispute, the best course would be to stay the order for possession, order prosecution of the counterclaim as a matter of urgency, with the mortgagee having the right to re-apply for possession. Possession, once ordered, will mean the dispossession of the mortgagors and sale of the property; staying an order is unlikely to have such draconian effects on the mortgagee. The third point, ie that even if the mortgagors succeeded in their counterclaim, they would not necessarily use the damages to pay off the arrears, could surely be dealt with by an undertaking to pay off the arrears from the damages if awarded; if no damages, or inadequate damages, were awarded, the matter would then come back to the court. Mervyn Davies J admitted that he made the order for possession without enthusiasm ([1987] 3 All ER at 246); it is submitted that he need not have made it at all.

Perpetuities: the rule in *Andrews v Partington*

Re Tom's Settlement [1987] 1 All ER 1081 contains a clear exposition by Sir Nicolas Browne-Wilkinson V-C of the rule in *Andrews v Partington* [1775–1802] All ER Rep 209; as the relevant settlement was made in 1955, the provisions of the Perpetuities and Accumulations Act 1964 were not considered. As is well-known, the rule in *Andrews v Partington* provides that, subject to a contrary intention, 'automatically and artificially' ([1987] 1 All ER at 1084) a class closes when the first member of the class would be entitled to claim his share. In the case before him, the Vice-Chancellor found two factors which evinced a contrary intention: first, there was a 'closing date' specifically referred to in the instrument; second, the settlement made it clear that persons who might not be born at date of the operation of the class-closing rule were to take at the 'closing date'. As a result, *Andrews v Partington* did not apply, and certain capital transfer tax advantages were lost: the 'automatic and artificial' operation of the rule would have gained them.

Condition precedent and subsequent

Re Tepper [1987] 1 All ER 970 (Arnheim (1987) 131 SJ 1472) raises again the vexed questions of the construction and validity of gifts subject to conditions precedent and subsequent. Beneficiaries under a will were to receive income on their attaining the age of 25, provided, inter alia, that they did not marry outside the Jewish faith. Scott J held that these gifts were subject to conditions of defeasance, and that the beneficiaries had to know, with certainty, and from the outset, the exact event which, if it happened, would divest their interest. The judge was, however, prepared to allow extrinsic evidence of the Jewish faith as practised by the testator and his family to be adduced, to see if the expression in the will could be sufficiently clarified. This last point, although perhaps generous, calls for little comment: it can be regarded as an example of the judge attempting to place himself in the testator's armchair (see *Bowes v Cook* (1880) 14 Ch D 53 at 56, per James LJ), and equipping himself with the evidence to do so. The main points, however, are, first, whether the judge was correct in regarding the gift as being one subject to a condition subsequent, and, if so, whether he applied the correct test of certainty. The terms of the will have elements of both conditions precedent and conditions subsequent: if someone *was* within the Jewish faith and married inside the Jewish faith and attained 25, the three requirements in the will had been fulfilled, and it could surely be said that these were conditions precedent to his taking; if, however, someone aged 25 or over and within the Jewish faith, marries outside the Jewish faith, there is a condition subsequent. However, as Cross J pointed out in *Re Lowry's Will Trusts* [1966] 3 All ER 955 at 960: 'I must, of course, remember that the court in any case of doubt construes the condition as a condition subsequent rather than a condition precedent' (in view of the test for validity for conditions precedent and subsequent, this seems surprising). The point was clearly one of difficulty, and the presumption may have made the difference. As far as the test for validity is concerned, the judge followed closely and carefully the orthodox view: the test for validity where a condition precedent was involved was that laid down by Evershed MR in *Re Allen* [1953] 2 All ER 898 at 901: 'All that the [claimant] has to do is . . . is to establish . . . that he satisfies the condition or qualification'. It did not matter that there might be persons who either did or did not satisfy the condition. For conditions subsequent, the test was much stricter: as Lord Russell stated in *Clayton v Ramsden* [1943] 1 All ER 16 at 18: 'conditions of defeasance . . . should be framed so that the persons affected . . . can from the outset know with certainty the exact event on the happening of which their interests are to be diverted'. In *Re Tepper* itself, Scott J admitted [1987] 1 All ER 970 at 978) that *Re Tuck* [1978] 1 All ER 1047, where the tests seemed to be regarded as similar, was 'difficult to understand'.

Powers

By her will, Mrs Poulton left property to her daughter 'to be divided amongst her [ie her daughter's] relatives at her discretion'. Her daughter, by her will, left property to her distant cousins's children, who would not have been statutory next-of-kin. In *Re Poulton* [1987] 1 All ER 1068, the questions were (i) how the gift should be construed, and (ii) was the gift in the daughter's will valid? The courts have commonly regarded such a gift in the terms of Mrs Poulton's will as a power to select amongst any relative, with a trust in default for statutory next-of-kin (*Wilson v Duguid* (1883) 24 Ch D 244, *re Deakin* [1894] 3 Ch 565). This approach was based on a distinction, made obsolete by statute in 1874, between exclusive and non-exclusive powers. However, as the Court of Appeal in *Re Ganloser's Will Trusts* [1951] 2 All ER 936 had pointed out, the construction in *Wilson v Duguid* was an artificial one to save a gift from failing. Warner J therefore construed 'relatives' as meaning 'all relatives, however remote'; since there was a power of selection, the gift was valid. Presumably this was because the power had been validly exercised in favour of those who were clearly relatives; it did not, apparently, matter that the property might have been given to persons of whom it could not be said with reasonable certainty whether they were or were not 'relatives' in the broad sense: cf *McPhail v Doulton* [1970] 2 All ER 228 and *Re Baden's Deed Trusts (No 2)* [1972] 2 All ER 1304.

Charity: 'ultra vires'

It is well established that one charity cannot give property to another, unless the recipient charity is expressly or impliedly a purpose or object of the donor charity: *Baldry v Feintuck* [1972] 2 All ER 81. In *Rosemary Simmons Memorial Housing Association Ltd v United Dominions Trust Ltd* [1987] 1 All ER 281, the plaintiff charity gratuitously guaranteed the obligations of a non-charitable body: this was held to come within the principle laid down in *Baldry v Feintuck*.

Landlord and Tenant

PHILIP H PETTIT, MA
Barrister, Professor of Equity, University of Buckingham

Common law

In *Celsteel Ltd v Alton House Holdings Ltd (No 2)* [1987] 2 All ER 240 the Court of Appeal has affirmed the decision of Scott J reported in [1986] 1 All ER 598 and discussed in All ER Rev 1986, pp 201, 210, 242. The question raised was one of the construction of a common form covenant for quiet enjoyment by which the landlord, Alton House, covenanted that the tenant, Mobil, should peaceably hold the demised premises 'without any interruption by the Landlord or any person lawfully claiming through under or in trust for the Landlord'. Alton House had purchased the freehold from C, who had previously granted numerous leases of flats in the premises. Were the tenants of the flats 'claiming under' Alton House so as to make Alton House liable under the covenant to Mobil? It was held that though they might be described as 'holding' under Alton House, they did not 'claim' under it, ie claim a lawful right to interrupt Mobil's occupation of the demised property. The tenants derived their rights from C, and in asserting and establishing their rights they did not need to refer to Alton House at all. Their rights were created by virtue of a title paramount to Alton House, which had effect in priority to Alton House's title and was superior to it. Fox LJ, with whose judgment the other members of the court concurred, added that the recommendations of the Law Commission's 'Report on Obligations of Landlords and Tenants' (Law Com No 67 (1975) para 37) do not envisage any change in the law in this respect.

The main interest of *Kumar v Dunning* [1987] 2 All ER 801 relates to the test to be applied to decide whether a covenant touches and concerns the land. The facts were that the underlessor granted the plaintiff underlessee a licence to assign, under which sureties covenanted with the underlessor to guarantee payment of the rent. The underlessor assigned the leasehold reversion to H and B, and the assignee of the underlease went into liquidation leaving unpaid arrears of rent. It was agreed that the plaintiff, the original underlessee, was liable to pay the rent to H and B as assignees of the reversion, and that, having paid the rent, he was entitled to be subrogated to the rights of H and B. Accordingly he was only entitled to succeed in his action against the sureties if H and B, as assignees of the immediate reversion, were entitled to recover the rent from the sureties. It was assumed that there had been no express assignment to H and B of the benefit of the surety covenant contained in the licence.

There was, of course, neither privity of contract nor privity of estate between H and B and the sureties. The benefit of the covenant could, however, run with the land at law to H and B, but only if the covenant touched and concerned the land. If it did, it would be enforceable against the covenantors. The same principles apply in this sort of case as to cases between landlord and tenant in deciding whether a covenant touches and concerns the land.

Browne-Wilkinson V-C, with whose judgment the other judges agreed, began by quoting the well-known test formulated by Bayley J in *Mayor of Congleton v Pattison* (1808) 10 East 130 that to touch and concern the land '... the covenant must either affect the land as regards mode of occupation, or it must be such as per se, and not merely from collateral circumstances, affects the value of the land.' His comment was that although this test is certain, its exact meaning when applied to different sets of circumstances is very obscure. He then proceeded, before discussing the authorities, to state his impression that in principle a covenant by a third party guaranteeing the performance by the tenant of his obligations should touch and concern the reversion as much as the tenant's covenants themselves, whether the covenants related to the land itself (eg repair and user covenants) or were mere covenants for the payment of money (eg rent and insurance). This in his view was consistent with justice and common sense. Where a lease has been assigned on the terms that sureties will guarantee the performance of the lease, they and not the original tenant should be primarily liable in case of default by the assignee. This is undoubtedly so where the reversion has not been assigned, and should be no different where it has. Yet, he observed, in all but one of the cases decided at first instance (and in that one the question was left open) including the recent case of *Coastplace Ltd v Hartley* [1987] 2 WLR 1299 it has been held that a surety covenant does not touch and concern the land.

Browne-Wilkinson V-C then discussed the question whether a surety covenant affects the value of the reversion 'per se and not merely from collateral circumstances'. He thought the test proposed by Best J in *Vyvyan v Arthur* [1814–23] All ER Rep 349 a sound one, one moreover which had been approved by the Court of Appeal and the House of Lords in *Forster v Elvet Colliery Co* [1908] 1 KB 629, sub nom *Dyson v Foster* [1908–10] All ER Rep 212. He summarised the position by saying first that the acid test whether or not a benefit is collateral is that laid down by Best J, namely 'is the covenant beneficial to the owner for the time being of the covenantee's land, and to no one else?' Secondly that a covenant simply to pay a sum of money is a covenant capable of touching and concerning the land provided that the existence of the covenant and the right to payment thereunder effects the value of the land in whomsoever it is vested for the time being. Applying these principles to the case before him he had no hesitation in holding that a covenant by a surety securing the performance of a tenant's covenants in a lease touched and concerned the land.

The case which caused the judge the greatest difficulty was *Dewar v Goodman* [1908–10] All ER Rep 188, another House of Lords decision. He attempted to draw a distinction between this case and *Dyson v Foster* but ended by saying that he suspected that they were in fact irreconcilable which left him free to choose between them and to decide in favour of *Dyson v Foster*.

Browne-Wilkinson V-C did not find any difficulty in distinguishing *Hua Chiao Commercial Bank Ltd v Chiaphua Industries Ltd* [1987] 1 All ER 1110 where the Privy Council was concerned with a five year lease of premises in Hong Kong granted in 1979 by L to T. The lease required T to pay L a liquidated sum as a deposit, to be 'returned' at the expiration of the term if there was no breach of covenant, but otherwise to be forfeited without

prejudice to L's right of action. In 1982 L assigned the reversion to P an
subsequently went into liquidation. There having been no breach c
covenant, on the expiry of the lease T claimed return of the deposit from F
The question therefore was, did the burden of the covenant to return th
deposit run with the reversion? It would only do so if it touched an
concerned the land. It was held it did not. It did not per se affect the nature
quality or value of the land either during or at the end of the term, nor did
per se affect the mode of using or enjoying that which was demised. Th
obligation to return the deposit was a personal obligation to repay mone
which the landlord had received in the capacity of payee rather than in th
capacity of landlord. Accordingly L's obligation to return the deposit wa
personal to it and did not pass to P as assignee of the reversion. Likewise
was the original tenant who was entitled to the return of the deposit and no
any assignee of the term there might have been. The decision that th
benefit of the covenant to repay could not touch and concern the land wa
entirely consistent with the test laid down by Best J because someone othe
than the owner for the time being of the term could take the benefit of it.

In *Bass Holdings Ltd v Morton Music Ltd* [1987] 2 All ER 1001 the Court c
Appeal reversed the decision of Scott J reported in [1987] 1 All ER 389
though on most points the Court of Appeal were in entire agreement wit
the first instance judgment. The question of law which arose as
preliminary issue concerned the validity of the exercise by the tenants of a
option for a further lease from the plaintiff landlords. The right of th
tenants to exercise the option was subject to a condition precedent: '. . . if
shall have paid the rent hereby reserved and shall have performed an
observed the several stipulations on its part herein contained and on its pa
to be performed and observed up to the date thereof. . .' The tenants ha
committed breaches of positive covenants to pay rent and water rates, an
of a negative covenant not to apply for planning permission without th
consent of the landlords. The lease had in fact been forfeited, but the tenan
had obtained relief against forfeiture and been reinstated unconditionall
before the purported exercise of the option. At that time there was n
subsisting cause of action in relation to breaches by then wholly in the pa
whose effect was spent.

Scott J at first instance observed ([1987] 1 All ER 389 at 395): 'If th
condition is to be construed literally according to its strict language, th
submissions of counsel for the [landlord] are, in my view, correct'. I
agreeing with this on appeal, Bingham LJ said that on a strict interpretatio
of the condition, any breach of covenant, even if wholly in the past, wou
deprive the tenant of his right to exercise the option, and, indeed, b
thought that there would be much to be said for this view in the absence c
authority. However authorities going back in particular to *Grey v Fri*
(1854) 4 HL Cas 565 establish that spent breaches will not destroy th
tenant's right to exercise the option, though, of course, subsisting breache
will. As Nicholls LJ observed the contrary view, which he called the 'neve
any breach' construction, would mean that in practice the condition wou
be impossible of fulfilment in almost all cases of buildings containing a fu
range of repairing and other covenants by a tenant. Further even in lease
where the tenant's covenants were far less far-reaching, the 'never an
breach' construction would lead to much uncertainty for tenants and the

ssigns. If a renewal option (or a break option) given to a tenant is to have
any real meaning the 'no subsisting breach' construction must be applied,
though it would of course be open to the parties by express language to
make it clear that any breach at any time would deprive the tenant of his
right. The only expression of judicial opinion the other way is to be found
in the judgment of Griffith LJ in *Bassett v Whiteley* (1983) 45 P & CR 87. In
the view of all three members of the Court, and this is surely right, the short
obiter dictum cannot stem or divert the strong current of judicial authority
to the contrary.

Up to this point there was no disagreement between Scott J and the Court of
Appeal. Scott J, however, had drawn a distinction between positive and
negative covenants. The breach of a positive covenant, he said, is in a real sense
capable of remedy—the act required to be done can be done late. In the case of a
negative covenant, however, he thought that once broken by the doing of a
positive act it could not be undone: the covenant had not been performed and
observed. The Court of Appeal unanimously rejected this distinction which
was unsupported by authority, save by decisions on s 146 of the Law of
Property Act 1925 which were not regarded as relevant. The Court of Appeal
could see no reason for applying a 'no subsisting breach' construction to
positive covenants, but a 'never any breach' construction to negative
covenants. Most importantly they thought that to draw such a distinction
would distract attention from the commercial core of the contract and direct it
to what might often be matters of form. There was no basis for the distinction
from the point of view of the sensible commercial construction of the clause.

In *Post Office v Aquarius Properties Ltd* [1987] 1 All ER 1055 a 22½-year lease
had been granted of commercial premises in 1969 which contained a fairly
standard repairing covenant. As a consequence of a structural defect the
basement was ankle deep in water for some five years as a result of a rise in the
level of the water table. This had now dropped and the basement was dry. The
substantial question was whether work to make the basement waterproof
should the water table rise again came within the tenant's repairing covenant.

As Judge Paul Baker QC observed in *Elite Investments Ltd v TI Bainbridge
Silencers Ltd* (1986) 280 EG 1001, *Ravenseft Properties v Davstone (Holdings) Ltd*
[1979] 1 All ER 929 'exploded the notion which had been current up to then
that remedying an inherent defect could never be a repair; it is always a matter
of degree'. However, as pointed out in *Quick v Taff Ely BC* [1985] 3 All ER
321, this does not mean that any work to eradicate an inherent defect in a
building must be a work of repair if, as a matter of degree, it does not amount
to a renewal or improvement of the building. It must be established that there
is disrepair before any question arises as to whether it would be reasonable to
remedy an inherent defect when doing the repair. Disrepair connotes a
deterioration from some previous physical condition. The Court of Appeal
applied *Quick v Taff Ely BC* in *Post Office v Aquarius Properties Ltd*, where the
structural defects complained of by the landlords had existed from the time
when the premises were originally built. There was no evidence that the
water which had come into the basement because of the original defects had
done any damage to the premises, whether to plaster on walls, or to the
flooring, or to electrical or other installations. There was accordingly no
disrepair and no liability on the repairing covenant.

The court chose to leave open the question of what the liability of the tenant would be if the water table were to rise again and actually cause damage to, say the plaster work or electrical fittings. The *Ravenseft Properties* case, approved in *Quick v Taff Ely BC*, where the stone cladding was insecure and dangerous because of an inherent design defect, establishes that the obligation to repair may involve curing an inherent defect. These cases, together with *Post Office v Aquarius Properties Ltd* were again considered and applied by the Court of Appeal in *Stent v Monmouth DC* (1987) 54 P & CR 193. Here it was said that if the only defect in the door had been that it did not perform its primary function of keeping out the rain, and the door had been otherwise undamaged and in the condition it was in when the letting began, there would have been no defect for the purpose of a repairing covenant, even though in layman's terms a door which does not keep out the rain is a defective door, and one which is in need of some form of repair or modification or replacement. However the factual position was that damage undoubtedly did occur to the door and the door frame, which had led to repairs from time to time and even the replacement of the door in 1977. None of this cured the problem of water penetration, which was finally solved by the installation of a purpose-built, self-sealing aluminium door in 1983. It was held that in these circumstances the repairing covenant gave rise to an obligation to make good the design defect which caused the collection of water which caused the rotting.

It may be noted that the statement of Slade LJ in [1987] 1 All ER at 1061 c 4/5 is correct, but that the date on p 1056 e 1 should read 1985.

The primary question that had to be decided in *Ashton v Sobelman* [1987] 1 All ER 755 was whether the actions of the head landlord constituted forfeiture of the head lease by peaceable re-entry. The premises were in the possession of a subtenant and the purported forfeiture was carried out by the head-landlord's solicitor handing the subtenant a letter which stated that the rent under the head lease was in arrears and that the head landlord was accordingly entitled to forfeit the head lease by peaceably re-entering the premises and re-taking possession. This was to be done by (1) peaceably re-entering the premises, (2) changing the locks on the front door, and, (3) instructing the subtenant to pay all future rent to the head landlord. The subtenant was assured that his position would not be prejudiced and that the head landlord was 'not in any way challenging [the subtenant's] right to remain in occupation of the premises under the provisions of the Underlease under which you are the present Lessee . . . you will become [the head landlord's] direct Lessee.'

Reliance was placed by counsel on the statement in *Woodfall's Law of Landlord and Tenant* (28th edn, 1978) vol, 1 para 1–1899: 'Peaceable re-entry may be effected by the forfeiture landlord accepting as tenant a subtenant who is already in occupation. . . .' but the judge did not think that the proposition was justified by the case cited as authority, *London and County (A and D) Ltd v Wilfred Sportsman Ltd* [1970] 2 All ER 600, for in that case the defendants had never been the subtenants of the head tenants whose lease was held to have been determined by re-entry. In his judgment in that case Russell LJ referred to *Baylis v Le Gros* (1858) 4 CBN S 537 as 'a case in which there was sufficient re-entry by acceptance of a subtenant already in occupation as tenant of the forfeiting landlord'. The judge in *Ashton*

Sobelman, however, after a careful consideration of the facts of the earlier case, concluded that *Baylis v Le Gros* did not go so far, and that the most that could be derived from it was that a landlord may affect a re-entry against his tenant by an arrangement with an existing subtenant under which the subtenant is to remain in occupation as the tenant of the landlord on the terms of a new tenancy. This was insufficient for the defendant in *Ashton v Sobelman* where the head landlord had assured the subtenant that his underlease would continue, a position which was wholly inconsistent with the determination by forfeiture of the head lease. The decision might, perhaps, be different if the subtenant is offered a new tenancy on the terms of the old one, though in practice it would be safer to start forfeiture proceedings.

The secondary question, which did not arise in view of the decision on the first, was whether if the head lease had been forfeited it would have been a proper case for relief against forfeiture. The judge was clearly right on the facts on holding that it would have been a proper case for relief.

In *City and Metropolitan Properties Ltd v Greycroft Ltd* [1987] 3 All ER 839 the tenant company had acquired a leashold flat in 1982, at which time the landlord was in serious breach of the lessor's structural repairing covenant. In 1983 the tenant attempted to sell the flat by auction, but it did not reach its reserve and was withdrawn. In August 1984 the tenant brought an action claiming specific performance of the repairing covenant. After the repairs were done the tenant sold the lease in December 1984 and amended its writ to claim consequential damages from the landlord for damage sustained while it was the tenant. The four heads of damage claimed were (1) the costs of the abortive sale, (2) the tenant's running loss on the flat while the disrepair was delaying its resale, (3) loss of executive time in dealing with the landlord and the local authority in getting the repairs done and (4) loss of opportunity to make profits with the proceeds of the flat while sale at a suitable price was impeded by the disrepair.

The landlord's first defence was that the tenant having assigned his lease could not thereafter recover damages from the landlord for breaches of the landlord's covenant committed while the tenant held the lease. It had previously been held by the Court of Appeal in *Re King (decd), Robinson v Gray* [1963] 1 All ER 781 and *London and County (A and D) Ltd v Wilfred Sportsman Ltd* [1970] 2 All ER 600 that the effect of s 141(1) of the Law of Property Act 1925 was to make a statutory transfer of the whole benefit of a tenant's covenant to an assignee of the reversion, so that the assignor can no longer sue. This changed the previous law under which the assignor and not the assignee could sue for breaches of covenant committed before the assignment, not being breaches of a continuing character. It was argued that this principle of *Re King* should apply by analogy to an assignment of the lease. The judge, however, held that this was not so, pointing out that the language of s 142(1) dealing with the running of the obligation of the lessor's covenants is significantly different from the language of s 141. He accepted that there was a possibility in some circumstances that a landlord might be sued by both assignor and assignee, but he did not think that this would be likely to lead to injustice. Certainly on the facts of the case before him, where the repairs had been done before the assignment, there was no possibility of a successful claim by the assignee.

The second defence of the landlord was that all the heads of damage claimed were too remote. Before considering the defence in general, the judge considered its application to the claim for the costs of the abortive sale. He cited *Calabar Properties Ltd v Stitcher* [1983] 3 All ER 759 for the proposition that the tenant was entitled to quantify its damage by selling the flat in its state of disrepair and then suing the landlord for the difference between the price it fetched and the value it would have had if the repairs had been done. While this is right, it is not entirely clear how it led to the very reasonable conclusion that there should be an inquiry as to damages where the tenant would have an opportunity to establish that the auction costs were properly recoverable as damages.

Turning to the second defence in general the judge again referred to *Calabar Properties Ltd v Stitcher* where Stephenson LJ said that speculative damages for loss of rental on capital value could be recovered if the landlord knew that the flat was bought as a speculation. He decided to give the tenant the opportunity at the inquiry to establish either that the landlord had actual knowledge that he had bought as a speculation, or that the parties must be taken to have comtemplated that the lease would be treated as an item of commerce. The tenant might then be able to persuade the inquiry that he should recover for executive time spent in administering the lettings and so forth. The judge warned that even if a loss was established the tenant would need to show why the large profit he made on the ultimate sale of the lease should not be set off against it.

Finally the judge said that heads (2) and (4) should in any event be disallowed. Head (2) he referred to as an attempt to recover as damages something which is more like costs but is not recoverable as costs. As to head (4), he accepted counsel's admission that it was a cheeky claim.

Business tenancies under Part II of the Landlord and Tenant Act 1954

In *Harmond Properties Ltd v Gajdzis* [1968] 3 All ER 263 the Court of Appeal had felt free to decide that a common law notice to quit is valid if it is given by a duly authorised general agent, even though the name of the person on whose behalf the notice is given is not named. This decision was held to be irrelevant in *Morrow v Nadeem* [1987] 1 All ER 237 where the question was stated to be whether the notice of termination of a tenancy under s 25 of the Landlord and Tenant Act 1954 required the name of the landlord to be stated.

The question arose in a case where one Alfred Danzig was the controlling shareholder and sole director of G D Investments Ltd. Of the 1,000 shares issued by the company, 999 were held by him and the remaining share was held jointly by him and his wife. G D Investments Ltd was the landlord, but the s 25 notice, which otherwise complied with the statutory form, was signed by solicitors as agents for Alfred Danzig. The tenant addressed the counter-notice to the solicitors as 'Solicitors and Agents for Alfred Danzig', and instituted proceedings for a new tenancy naming Alfred Danzig as respondent. Subsequently G D Investments Ltd transferred its interest to Mr Nadeem, who took steps to be substituted as respondent. The fact that the notice, counter-notice and application all referred to Alfred Danzig and not the landlord, G D Investments Ltd, was brought out and the response of the tenant was to challenge the validity of the original notice on this ground.

The Court of Appeal, reversing the decision at first instance, held that the prescribed form envisages that it will be completed with the name and address of the competent landlord. What is contemplated is that the notice will give the tenant sufficient information to enable him to serve a counter-notice and apply for a new tenancy. This includes information as to the identity of the landlord. The test is that stated by Barry J in *Barclays Bank Ltd v Ascott* [1961] 1 All ER 782 previously approved by the Court of Appeal in *Tegerdine v Brooks* (1977) 36 P & CR 261, namely 'whether the notice given by the landlord has given such information to the tenant as will enable the tenant to deal, in a proper way, with the situation (whatever it may be) referred to in the notice'. Save perhaps in an exceptional case a notice will be invalid if it does not include the name and identity of the competent landlord. The notice in the case before the court not merely failed to name the correct landlord, but was misleading in a most material respect in that it incorrectly represented that Mr Danzig was the landlord. The court was unimpressed by the argument that it was a mere technicality that the landlord was not mentioned in terms, when it was Alfred Danzig in all but name.

It was further argued that if the notice was invalid the invalidity had been waived. This argument was shortly and convincingly rejected. The error in the notice was not such as to put the tenant on enquiry regarding who was the landlord, and when the error came to her attention she took the invalidity point with reasonable promptness. She could not be treated as waiving a defect of which she was unaware.

The moral to be drawn from this case is to take the utmost care to ensure that statutory forms of notice are completed with precision.

Residential tenancies

In *South Northamptonshire DC v Power* [1987] 3 All ER 831 the claimant had lived with the tenant as husband and wife for some three years before her death. Less than 12 months before her death the tenant became a secure tenant of the premises of which the local authority was claiming possession, and moved into them with the claimant. On the death of the tenant the local authority claimed possession, and whether or not it could succeed depended upon whether the claimant could establish that he had 'resided with the tenant throughout the period of twelve months ending with the tenant's death' (s 30(2)(b) of the Housing Act 1980 now replaced by s 87 of the Housing Act 1985). This is, of course, virtually identical language to the transmission provisions in Sch 1 para 3 of the Rent Act 1977: '. . . residing with [the tenant] . . . for a period of 6 months immediately before his death . . .' save for the difference in the specified period.

As Woolf LJ observed, on a literal construction of the Act the claimant would be entitled to succeed. The court, however, accepted the local authority's argument that the Act imposed a requirement of residence not only with the person who, until his or her death, had been the tenant, but also residence at the premises in question with that particular person for 12 months, during which he or she was the tenant. In so deciding the court claimed to be following the Rent Act decisions of *Edmunds v Jones* (1952) [1957] 3 All ER 23 n and *Collier v Stoneman* [1957] 3 All ER 20, which it said had settled the law along these lines. Leave to appeal to the House of Lords having been refused, it seems that in practice the point must now be taken to be settled, whether or not it was before, in the terms that the connection which is required to establish a succession is a double one, both a family one and a residential one in the premises in question to which the succession is claimed.

In *Brooker Settled Estates Ltd v Ayers* (1987) 54 P & CR 165 O'Connor LJ referred to the tortured question as to whether an occupant is in occupation as licensee or as a tenant, and to Lord Templeman's speech in the House of Lords in *Street v Mountford* [1985] 2 All ER 289 as an attempt to introduce some order into the law for the guidance of the judges who have to deal with the problem. Unfortunately *Street v Mountford* has not turned out to be a magic wand which enables the right answer to be found without anxious thought, and there are particular difficulties in cases involving multiple occupancy (there was a sole tenant in *Street v Mountford*), or where there is uncertainty as to whether exclusive possession has been granted (conceded in *Street v Mountford*).

These difficulties were demonstrated in *Hadjiloucas v Crean* [1987] 3 All ER 1008. Space will not permit the long discussion which this case perhaps merits, but this may be unimportant for although leave to appeal to the House of Lords was refused, it was granted in one of the last cases to be reported in 1987, *A G Securities v Vaughan* (1987) *Times*, 28 December, which will give the House of Lords an opportunity to give further guidance in this area.

In *Hadjiloucas v Crean* two ladies, the appellant and B, agreed with the respondent to rent a furnished two-roomed flat. They were each given copies of separate but identical documents purporting to be licences, which gave each a licence to share the flat with one other person to be separately licensed 'to the intent that the licensee shall not have exclusive possession'. The rental was for six months and each occupant was responsible for the whole rent of £260 per month. B left after two months and arranged with the respondent for R to take her place. She was granted a licence for the remaining four months but then left, after which the question arose as to the appellant's status. The Court of Appeal agreed with the rejection by the county court judge of the argument allegedly based on *Street v Mountford* that in all cases involving residential premises the occupier must either be a tenant or a lodger and that there is no room for a person enjoying some intermediate interest in the premises. They said that each case must be considered on its own facts to see whether, in the case of multiple occupancy, a joint tenancy has been created, and they did not think that the judge had made a sufficiently close examination of the factual matrix in order to determine whether the agreement between the appellant, B and the respondent created a joint tenancy so as to grant them together exclusive possession as against the outside world, or whether they created two separate licences under which neither the appellant nor B had exclusive possession. The case was accordingly remitted to the judge for a retrial.

There was some minor difference of view between Purchas and Mustill LJJ in relation to shams, though neither of them expressed any disagreement with the county court judge's opinion that the agreement in question was not a sham. In relation to Lord Templeman's discussion of *Somma v*

Hazelhurst [1978] 2 All ER 1011, *Aldrington Garages v Fielder* (1978) 37 P & CR 461 and *Sturolson & Co v Weniz* (1984) 272 EG 326, Purchas LJ said that *Somma v Hazelhurst* was clearly a sham but that the other two cases were in a different category ([1987] 3 All ER 1008 at 1014): 'With respect to Lord Templeman the peremptory association of these two cases with *Somma's* case ought not to be used as an authority for describing the latter two cases as "sham cases" as might be thought from the expression "for the same reasons" which appears in Lord Templeman's speech.' Mustill LJ, however, (ibid at 1023), seems to have accepted that all three were shams, though noting that no reasons were given by the House of Lords for that view in relation to the latter two cases.

Lord Templeman's statement that 'the court should, in my opinion, be astute to detect and frustrate sham devices and artificial transactions whose only object is to disguise the grant of a tenancy and to evade the Rent Acts' has also been slightly differently interpreted. Purchas LJ (ibid at 1017), referred to this as requiring the court to be 'astute to prevent the exclusion of the protection of the Rent Acts being achieved by an artificial device [sic] *even if these are [sic] not a sham*', (author's italics) while Mustill LJ (ibid at 1022) said he understood Lord Templeman's reference to an artificial device [sic] as 'another description of a sham'.

Agricultural holdings

The main point of interest in *Watts v Yeend* [1987] 1 All ER 744 relates to the construction of the proviso to s 2(1) of the 1948 Act. The general effect of the subsection is that the grant of an interest less than a tenancy from year to year, or of a licence, in relation to agricultural land takes effect as an agreement for the letting of the land for a tenancy from year to year, which means that it enjoys the protection of the Act. What the proviso does is to exclude from the operation of the subsection '. . . an agreement for the letting of land, or the granting of a licence to occupy land, made (whether or not the agreement expressly so provides) in contemplation of the use of the land only for grazing or mowing during some specified period of the year. . .'

The Court of Appeal has now, first, confirmed the significance of the word 'contemplation' as emphasised by Denning LJ, as he then was, in *Scene Estate Ltd v Amos* [1957] 2 All ER 325. The object of the word, he said, was 'to protect a landlord who has not expressly inserted a provision that it is for grazing only or for mowing only or that it is for a specified part of the year: when nevertheless both parties know that that is what is contemplated'.

Secondly the Court of Appeal has confirmed that the Scottish decision of *Mackenzie v Laird* [1959] SC 266 applies equally in England. The question at issue there was whether in the absence of definite terminal dates it can be said that what was in contemplation was 'some specified period of the year'. It was held that fixed or specific dates for the beginning and end of the period are not essential: it suffices if the period is so named or described as to be identifiable by persons versed in agricultural matters. What the proviso is excepting is the use of land only for grazing or mowing and these uses are in essence seasonal, and what is meant by 'grazing season' or 'seasonal let' is unambiguous and well understood in farming circles.

Leasehold Reform Act 1967

All the other Law Lords present agreed with the speech of Lord Templeman in *Dixon v Allgood* [1987] 3 All ER 1082 dismissing the tenant's appeal against the Court of Appeal decision that he was not entitled to acquire the freehold of the premises he occupied as his residence under the Act. As is well known the Act provides for enfranchisement in the case of dwelling-houses let under a long lease at a low rent, ie less than two thirds of the rateable value. The two cottages, which had been converted into one in 1977, first appeared in the valuation list on 9 May 1966 and 6 February 1967 respectively at values of £42 and £34 making a total of £76. The rent of £52 a year was not less than two thirds of this figure. Subsequently the tenant erected garages and a domestic store room on the forecourt of the building which was separately rated on 22 December 1971 at £24. The aggregate rateable value of the cottages including the garages was therefore £100, and the rent was less than two thirds of this figure.

It is clear that if the Act applied the tenant would be entitled to purchase not only the 'house', ie the cottages he occupied, but also the 'premises', defined by s 2(3) as referring to 'any garage, outhouse, garden, yard and appurtenances which at the relevant time are let to him with the house and are occupied with and used for the purposes of the house or any part of it. . .' However in determining whether the Act applied one looks, for a definition of 'low rent', at s 4 which first refers to two thirds of the rateable value of the property on the appropriate day, and then in (a) defines 'appropriate date' as: 'the 23rd March 1965 or such later day as by virtue of section 25(3) of the Rent Act 1977 would be the appropriate day for purposes of that Act in relation to a dwelling-house consisting of the house in question.'

Lord Templeman confirmed the distinction which had been made by Slade LJ in the Court of Appeal, where he had pointed out that there was a 'clear and unequivocal difference' between s 1 entitling the tenant to purchase 'the house and premises', and s 4(1)(a) requiring the appropriate day to be determined in relation to a dwelling house 'consisting of the house in question'.

Lord Templeman went on to explain that this decision was in line with the general scheme of the Act. As he pointed out, by fixing 23 March 1965 as the appropriate day for houses rated before that day, the 1967 Act indicated clearly that events taking place after 23 March 1965 resulting in an alteration of rateable value were to be ignored. If the cottages had been rated at £76 on that date the Act would not have applied and the position would not have been affected had the tenant subsequently erected the garages as a result of which the rateable value of the hereditament had been increased to £100, whether by increasing the rateable value of the cottages or raising a separate rateable value for the garages. In the present case the tenant likewise could not improve his position under the 1967 Act by erecting the garages after the appropriate day which was not later than 6 February 1967 when the rateable value was £76.

Medical Law

ANDREW GRUBB, MA
Barrister, Fellow of Fitzwilliam College, Cambridge

Consent

Abortion

Whose decision should it be to undergo an abortion? In February, the courts were asked to decide whether the father of an unborn child could obtain an injunction to prevent his girlfriend undergoing an abortion without his consent. In *C v S* [1987] 1 All ER 1230 Heilbron J, the Court of Appeal and, ultimately, the Appeal Committee of the House of Lords in refusing leave to appeal, held that the father's consent to the abortion was unnecessary and refused an injunction. The parents were unmarried students studying at Oxford University. After a brief affair, Miss C discovered she was pregnant. In accordance with the terms of the Abortion Act 1967 and the Abortion Regulations 1968 (as amended) (SI 1968 No 390) two doctors certified that 'the continuance of the pregnancy would involve risk... of injury to the physical or mental health of the pregnant woman... greater than if the pregnancy were terminated' (s 1(1)). The father sought to establish his locus standi to seek an injunction on two separate bases.

(a) The unborn child's claim

First, he argued that he had the right to prevent the abortion on behalf of the unborn child itself suing as next friend. In all aspects of the law, the unborn child is not conceded legal personality. A few examples of this will suffice: (1) the law of homicide does not protect the unborn child (*Commonwealth v Edelin* (1976) 359 NE 2d 4) (the criminal law); (2) at common law an unborn child has no action for pre-natal death and an action for pre-natal injuries was contingent on live birth (*Watts v Rama* [1972] VR 353. See now Congenital Disabilities (Civil Liability) Act 1976, s 1(1)) (the civil law); (3) a foetus does not enjoy the protection of constitutional provisions entrenching 'a right of life' (*Borowski v A-G of Canada* (1987) 4 DLR (4th) 112, semble *Paton v United Kingdom* (1980) 3 EHRR 408) (public law).

The best authority that the father could muster to support his argument was the extraordinary case of *Mullick v Mullick* (1925) LR 52 Ind App 245 where the Privy Council granted an Indian Idol locus to participate in legal proceedings. In *Paton v BPAS Trustees* [1978] 2 All ER 987 Sir George Baker P reaffirmed that the common law did not concede legal personality to the unborn child when refusing an application by a husband for an injunction to prevent his wife's proposed abortion. Heilbron J in *C v S* followed this view, relying on the Canadian cases of *Medhurst v Medhurst* (1984) 46 OR (2d) 263 and *Dehler v Ottawa Civic Hospital* (1979) 101 DLR (3d) 686. She concluded ([1987] 1 All ER at 1234) that 'a child, after it has been born, and only then in certain circumstances based upon his or her having a legal right, may be a party to an action brought with regard to such matters [as arise before birth]. In other words, the claim crystallises on the birth, at which date, but not before, the child attains the status of a legal persona, and thereupon can [complain about those matters].'

(b) The father's own claim

Secondly, the father sought to establish locus standi based upon his own right to refuse consent to the abortion. An amendment proposed to the Medical Termination of Pregnancy Bill, which subsequently became the 1967 Act, would have granted the husband this right but it was defeated in the House of Commons. Few jurisdictions would contemplate intrusions into the mother's freedom of choice, certainly in the early stages of pregnancy (*Roe v Wade* (1973) 35 L Ed 2d 147; *Planned Parenthood v Danforth* (1976) 428 US 52). There are good practical reasons for this. Would the court require the mother to carry the child to term against her wishes? If so, how would the court supervise its order? The court could not effectively prevent her from potentially harming the child by abusing herself (for example, with alcohol, drugs or by smoking).

Perhaps having considerations of this sort in mind, Sir George Baker held in *Paton* that a husband had no right at law or in equity which the court could protect. In *C v S* the father accepted this, but he argued that it did not prevent him seeking an injunction to prevent an *illegal* abortion. *Paton* was distinguishable because the husband had been seeking an injunction to prevent a *lawful* abortion.

This argument raises two issues. Was the proposed abortion unlawful and, if so, did the father have locus standi to prevent a criminal offence being committed? Both Heilbron J and the Court of Appeal mainly concerned themselves with the first of these questions.

(i) Locus standi

The simple answer to the father's claim was that he lacked the necessary locus standi to enforce the criminal law since he was not seeking to enforce a private right (*Gouriet v UPOW* [1977] 3 All ER 70; applied in the case of abortion: *The League for Life in Manitoba Inc v Morgentaler* [1985] 4 WWR 633).

Indeed, the father's difficulty ran even deeper. It is generally regarded as the province of the Attorney-General alone, as guardian of the public interest, to ask the civil courts for their aid to enforce the criminal law. The courts are not wholly accommodating even to the Attorney-General because the individual is deprived of trial by jury and exposed to potentially far greater penalties for contempt of court than he might suffer at the hands of a criminal court for his offence. Therefore, once the court determined that the father had no private right, the action should have been dismissed *in limine* for lack of locus standi.

However both Heilbron J and the Court of Appeal were content to decide the father's case on its merits. Was the proposed abortion unlawful?

(ii) The criminal law

Although the abortion came within the terms of the Abortion Act, the father argued that it was illegal because it amounted to the offence of child destruction under the Infant Life (Preservation) Act 1929. Section 1(1) makes it an offence for

> 'any person who, with intent to destroy the life of a child capable of being born alive, by any wilful act causes a child to die before it has an existence independent of its mother.'

The Abortion Act provides a defence to the crime of doing an act 'with intent to procure a miscarriage' contrary to ss 58 and 59 of the Offences Against the Person Act 1861 but it has no effect on a doctor's potential criminal liability under the 1929 Act (s 5(1) of the 1967 Act). The evidence was that Miss C was about 18 weeks pregnant. Was her unborn child 'capable of being born alive'? It is generally assumed that abortion is lawful up to 28 weeks. This is derived from s 1(2) of the 1929 Act which raises a presumption that a 28 week old foetus is 'capable of being born alive'. But this does not exclude the possibility that a younger foetus might come within the terms of the Act.

Heilbron J had before her the evidence of medical experts some of which regarded an 18 week foetus as alive because it would show 'real and discernible signs of life' (affidavit of Mr Norris) while others disagreed taking the view that even though between 18 and 21 weeks the 'cardiac muscle is contracting and a primitive circulation is developing... lung development does not occur until after 24 weeks gestation' (affidavit of Professor Newton). Therefore, the necessary indicia of life were missing. Until 24 weeks there would be no possibility that a foetus could survive naturally or with reasonable medical intervention outside the womb.

In the end, Heilbron J rejected the view that every 18 week old foetus came within the 1929 Act as not 'a realistic one'. Beyond this the judge does not offer a precise legal interpretation of the 1929 Act. She was content to dismiss the father's action because there was insufficient evidence before the court as to the condition of *this* foetus or of the doctor's state of mind to satisfy the court that an offence would be committed.

The Court of Appeal held that the meaning of the 1929 Act was a legal question for the court and not for the medical profession. In order to be 'capable of being born alive' a foetus had to be capable of 'breathing either naturally or with the aid of a ventilator'. The court accepted the medical evidence that an 18 week foetus of normal development had no lungs and was incapable of breathing. Since there was no evidence that the foetus was other than of normal development for one of 18 weeks, the court held that if could not be proved that any offence would be committed if the pregnancy were terminated.

Although the Court of Appeal did not say so, it appeared to accept that a foetus must have the capacity to survive in order to come within the 1929 Act. It remains to be seen for how long? Perhaps, to breath and die would not do but a foetus that had a reasonable prospect of survival would be 'capable of being born alive'.

It is clear after *C v S* [1987] 1 All ER 1230 that the widely held belief that abortion is lawful up to 28 weeks gestation cannot stand in the face of the

Court of Appeal's decision. Of course, difficulties of proof will always arise but a doctor who performs an abortion when the foetus is of normal development within the age range of 24–28 weeks risks a prosecution under the 1929 Act *even if the terms of the Abortion Act have been complied with.*

As a matter of caution, the medical profession would be well advised to exercise restraint in relation to any foetus aged over 20 weeks. But, only if it can be proved beyond reasonable doubt that the foetus had the capacity to survive and, *importantly,* the doctor was aware of this, will a prosecution stand any chance of success.

Sterilisation

In April, the court was asked to authorise a sterilisation operation upon a 17 year-old severely mentally retarded girl under its inherent wardship jurisdiction. After considerable acrimonious coverage in the media, the House of Lords (affirming the Court of Appeal) in *Re B (a minor) (wardship: sterilisation)* [1987] 2 All ER 206 gave their authorisation because the sterilisation was in the 'best interests' of the girl. The facts of the case were tragic. Lord Hailsham set them out in his speech (ibid at 212):

> 'The ward in the present case is of a mental age of five or six. . . . She does not understand and cannot learn the causal connection between intercourse and pregnancy and the birth of children. . . . She would not understand, or be capable of easily supporting, the inconveniences and pains of pregnancy. As she menstruates irregularly, pregnancy would be difficult to detect or diagnose in time to terminate it easily. Were she to carry a child to full term she would not understand what was happening to her, she would be likely to panic, and would probably have to be delivered by Caesarian section, but, owing to her emotional state, and the fact that she has a high pain threshold she would be quite likely to pick at the operational wound and tear it open. In any event, she would be "terrified, distressed and extremely violent" during normal labour. She has no maternal instincts and is unlikely to develop any. She does not desire children, and, if she bore a child, would be unable to care for it.'

In addition to this, the girl's condition made her very sexually active but with none of the inhibitions normally present. As a consequence, she was extremely vulnerable and there was a significant risk that she might become pregnant. Not surprisingly, the House of Lords acted to stop this possibility. Treating the case, in the words of the Court of Appeal, as one of 'last resort' the House of Lords saw no alternative. Lord Hailsham stated (ibid at 212): 'To incarcerate her or reduce such liberty as she is able to enjoy would be gravely detrimental to the amenity and quality of her life.' Also, the House of Lords rejected the alternative of a contraceptive drug regime as ineffective in her case since it would be impossible to ensure she maintained it. As a social worker stated in her evidence 'if [the girl] is . . . in one of her moods . . . there is no way' that she could be made to take the pill.

The House of Lords distinguished the earlier case of *Re D (a minor) (wardship: sterilisation)* [1976] 1 All ER 326. In that case Heilbron J had refused to authorise a sterilisation operation on a young girl suffering from

Soto's Syndrome which resulted in severe mental impairment. Heilbron J held that (ibid at 332):

'The type of operation proposed is one which involves the deprivation of a basic human right, namely the right of a woman to reproduce, and therefore it would, if performed on a woman for non-therapeutic reasons and without her consent, be a violation of such right.'

Lord Oliver thought *Re D* was 'plainly a right decision'. However the Law Lords distinguished it as a case where the evidence showed that in time the girl would mature sufficiently to make a choice for herself. As Lord Oliver said ([1987] 2 All ER at 219):

'the right to reproduce is of value only if accompanied by the ability to make a choice and in the instant case there is no question of the minor ever being able to make such a choice or indeed to appreciate the need to make one.'

In the result, the House of Lords saw its role as *parens patriae* in wardship proceedings as a protective one which could best be achieved by authorising the operation.

A number of limitations on the court's power are contained in the speeches in *Re B*. First, the sterilisation in *Re B* was for therapeutic purposes. It was clear from the evidence that the girl's 'best *medical* interests' justified the operation. Although Lords Hailsham, Bridge and Oliver rejected the distinction between therapeutic and non-therapeutic sterilisations as likely to mislead and confuse and, ultimately, was irrelevant to the court's determination, it is precisely the distinction which they applied.

'Therapeutic', in this context, must be taken to cover current or foreseeable health needs; this would necessarily include prophylactic measures. The decision of the Canadian Supreme Court in *Re Eve* (1986) 31 DLR (4th) 1 is explicable on this basis because the sterilisation operation appears to have been proposed because it would be beneficial to the prospective grandparents. The evidence indicated that the risks of pregnancy for Eve were no greater than for any other girl. The court in refusing to consent to the procedure, refused to give its imprimatur to a sterilisation operation for 'social' purposes.

In *Re B*, Lord Oliver confirmed that he would not have authorised an operation in similar circumstances and Lord Bridge considered *Re Eve* to be correct on its own facts. Lord Bridge thought that *Re B* had nothing to do with lightening 'the burden which must fall on those who have the care of the ward' (ibid at 213). Consequently, an English court will require evidence of particular detriment to the ward's health if pregnancy occurs before authorising the procedure. Convenience for her, or her family, alone will not do. This is a significant restriction. In addition, it is certain that the court would not give its consent to a procedure to be performed for pure 'eugenic' reasons. Lords Bridge and Oliver said so. There is absolutely no prospect of an English court proclaiming, as Holmes J did in the United States Supreme Court in *Buck v Bell* (1927) 274 US 200, that 'three generations of imbeciles are enough'.

Secondly, the court is only likely to give its authority if there is little or no prospect of the ward herself consenting to the procedure at some later stage, ie where she is permanently incompetent. Certainly, in this situation the court will be less likely to authorise an irreversible procedure preferring, perhaps, a 'holding procedure' which is nevertheless effective for the time being. So much is clear from the court's general acceptance of the decision of Heilbron J in *Re D*.

Thirdly, Lord Templeman indicated that before a sterilisation operation may be performed on an incompetent young girl, the court must give its permission in wardship proceedings. While it is easy to see why an application to a judge of the Family Division who is 'selected for his or her experience, ability and compassion' might be desirable, it is not easy to understand why it is legally essential. Lord Templeman thought that a doctor might face 'criminal, civil or professional proceedings' if the court's wardship jurisdiction was not sought. Surely, if the medical procedure is in the girl's 'best interests' then her parents may consent on her behalf? Otherwise the court, which must always act as a 'wise and prudent parent' (*R v Gyngall* [1893] 2 QB 232), would have the power to act in a way which no 'wise and prudent parent' could lawfully act by consenting to the sterilisation. Sterilisation may be a major step in a young girl's life but so are many others aspects of a child's youth and we willingly concede the prima facie right to determine all of these to the parents. Why not the decision to undergo a sterilisation?

One final point. *Re B* raises the issue of whether the court retains any power, akin to wardship, to authorise treatment on a 'ward' who has attained majority. In the Court of Appeal it was common ground that it did not. But by the time the case had reached the House of Lords counsel had discovered the Canadian Supreme Court decision of *Re Eve*. There, the girl was aged 25 but the Supreme Court held, at least in principle, that it retained a parens patriae jurisdiction to take care of incompetent adults.

In *Re B* counsel argued that this meant that the court need not act now on the eve of the girl's eighteenth birthday but could wait and see how circumstances progressed and, if necessary, a further application could be made to the court later if the sterilisation operation procedure was then thought to be in her 'best interests'. The House of Lords rejected the argument that it was acting in haste because it was in the girl's best interests to undergo the procedure now whether or not the court retained a power after her majority. Lord Hailsham said he found the reasoning of the *Eve* court 'extremely helpful' but he did not examine whether it was correct. Lord Oliver assumed the parens patriae existed but declined to determine the matter without full argument.

The problems facing the English courts, some of which are procedural, in recognising this power over incompetent adults is discussed elsewhere (see Grubb and Pearl [1987] CLJ 439, 458 et seq). It seems that, in principle, the Crown does have such a power but that it was delegated to the judges by Royal Warrant and the last such Warrant was revoked in November 1960 after the Mental Health Act 1959 came into force. Therefore, the power exists but the judges have been disarmed, at least, temporarily (see *T v T* [1988] 1 All ER 613).

In the wake of *Re B*, applications have been made in three cases for declarations that proposed sterilisation or abortion procedures on mentally retarded adult girls would not be unlawful (*T v T* supra, *Re X The Times* 4 June, 1987 and unreported decision of Latey J referred to in *Law Magazine*

29 May 1987). Each of the declarations sought was restricted to the civil liability of the doctor and excluded his potential criminal liability. In each case a declaration was granted on the basis that the doctor was justified in acting out of 'necessity' or in a case of 'emergency' since the particular girl's health was at stake and there was no-one else with legal power to consent on her behalf (quaere whether this defence is not equally applicable in a criminal case?).

Malpractice

Duty of care

In *Gold v Haringey HA* [1987] 2 All ER 888, the Court of Appeal held that a doctor's duty of disclosure of the risks of reversal of a female sterilisation operation and the availability of alternative procedures was to be determined by means of professional practice. Since the doctor had complied with *a* practice accepted as proper by a responsible body of medical opinion in not telling Mrs Gold that there was a risk of between 20–60 per 10,000 of these operations naturally reversing themselves, he had not been negligent.

Like all professionals a doctor owes a duty of care to his client to come up to the standards of the 'ordinary skilled man professing to have that special skill' (*Bolam v Friern HMC* [1957] 2 All ER 118 at 121, per McNair J, approved in *Whitehouse v Jordan* [1981] 1 All ER 267 and *Maynard v West Midland RHA* [1985] 1 All ER 635). All this is elementary; what is remarkable about professional malpractice in the case of a doctor is that the courts have uniquely conceded to the medical profession the right to determine when there has been a breach of that duty (*Sidaway v Board of Governors of the Bethlem Royal Hospital and the Maudsley Hospital* [1985] 1 All ER 643 at 649, per Lord Scarman).

However, when the case concerns a negligent failure to warn a patient of an inherent risk of injury in a medical procedure or of an alternative procedure that is available, it is less clear why professional opinion should be determinative of what the patient should, as a matter of law, be told by the doctor. Obviously, the range of risks and alternatives is a medical-technical question but what information *ought* to be volunteered is not so obviously such a question. As a consequence, a majority of the House of Lords (Lords Bridge, Keith and Templeman) in *Sidaway* held that a doctor's duty to volunteer information should not exclusively be determined by reference to medical practice, although that would be important and often crucial. Lord Diplock held that a doctor's duty should *always* be determined by reference to medical practice. It is strange that in *Gold* the Court of Appeal only relied on the speech of Lord Diplock (see [1988] CLJ 12).

In *Gold*, Lloyd LJ distinguished two earlier cases where the failure to disclose reversal rates had been held negligent. The decision of Ognall J in *Jones v Berkshire HA* (unreported 2 July 1986) was a case where the defendant had admitted negligence and the Court of Appeal's earlier decision in *Thake v Maurice* [1986] 1 All ER 479 was explained as a special case where the only evidence of professional practice was the defendant's own usual practice of disclosing the risk of reversal. Lloyd LJ said that in the absence of any counter-balancing expert evidence, the doctor was rightly held to be negligent.

Lloyd LJ stated that the trial judge in *Gold* was wrong to reject the *Bolam* test as exceptional. What the trial judge saw as exceptional about *Bolam* was not the 'reasonable doctor' test, but that reaching his objective counterpart's standards could be established if he acted in a way which was approved by a responsible body of medical opinion. This, as we have seen, *is* exceptional in the case of doctors and, following the majority view in *Sidaway*, it has no application *as a rule* in negligent advice cases.

Indeed, in cases of purely contraceptive advice, where sterilisation is sought for social or economic reasons, there is no reason for the court to place such a heavy reliance upon professional practice. In so far as professional practice is relevant after *Sidaway*, it is because of the court's concern to take account of the therapeutic nature of the medical procedure and the doctor's general duty to act in the best interests of his patient.

Causation

(a) Kay v Ayrshire and Arran Health Board [1987] 2 All ER 417

Andrew Kay was admitted to hospital suffering from pneumoccocal meningitis. In order to treat this very dangerous bacterial infection of the membranes surrounding the brain, a doctor injected intrathecally a quantity of penicillin. However, he negligently injected 30 times the correct dose. Fortunately, the mistake was spotted before it proved fatal. Nevertheless, the child suffered convulsions, paralysis on one side of his body and deafness. In an action brought on behalf of the child, it was alleged that the overdose had caused or materially contributed to his disabilities. The question arose whether the deafness had been caused by the overdose or by the meningitis.

Deafness is a common side-effect of meningitis and the medical evidence at the trial was that it had never been caused by penicillin alone. However the trial judge found that the penicillin had materially contributed to the deafness because it had reduced the boy's natural resistence to the bacterial infection. This was a factual theory which had not been suggested by (or to) any of the expert witnesses at the trial. As a consequence, the House of Lords held that the trial judge's theory could not stand. Causation, in this context, was a question of medical evidence. The judge was not entitled to determine the case on a theory which he had invented without any scientific support. The House of Lords held, tragically, that the balance of evidence showed that meningitis was the sole cause of the deafness.

Even so, the plaintiff argued that the decision of the House of Lords in *McGhee v NCB* [1972] 3 All ER 1008 helped to establish causation. The House of Lords in *Kay* rejected the application of *McGhee* without questioning the correctness of the decision itself. The House of Lords held that the plaintiff had failed to establish the necessary factual basis. Lord Keith explained how *McGhee* could not help ([1987] 2 All ER at 421):

'Had there been acceptable medical evidence here that an overdose of penicillin administered intrathecally was known to increase the risk that the meningitis, which the penicillin was intended to treat, would cause deafness, the decision would have been in point. It would be immaterial that medical science was unable to demonstrate the precise mechanism whereby the risk was increased. But as it is, there is in the instant case no such medical evidence.'

Had there been this evidence to 'incriminate the overdose' (per Lord Ackner) then, as Lord Griffiths put it, the effect of *McGhee* would have been that (ibid at 422):

'when there are two competing causes, namely meningitis and penicillin, the law should presume in favour of the plaintiff that the tortious cause was responsible for the damage.'

(b) *Hotson v East Berkshire AHA* [1987] 2 All ER 909

Stephen Hotson fell out of a tree at school. He badly injured his hip. Through the negligence of the doctors at the hospital where he was taken, the injury was not discovered for five days. The injury to his hip joint where the blood vessels had been damaged meant that he would suffer from permanent disability for the rest of his life. In his action, he claimed that the failure to treat him promptly caused his permanent disability. In other words, he argued that 'but for' the doctor's negligence he would have made a complete recovery. The trial judge, Simon Brown J ([1985] 3 All ER 167), found that even if he had been treated there was a 75% chance that he would have suffered the permanent disability. However, looking at it from another point of view, the judge held that the plaintiff had a 25% chance of recovery. Because of the doctors' negligence, the plaintiff had lost that chance since it had become 100% certain that the disability would result. Consequently, the judge held that although the doctors had not caused the disability they had caused the plaintiff to lose a 25% chance of recovery and he awarded the plaintiff a quarter of the damages he would otherwise have recovered. The Court of Appeal upheld Simon Brown J's judgment ([1987] 1 All ER 210).

On further appeal to the House of Lords, the defendant's appeal was allowed. Lord Bridge explained the reasoning of their Lordships ([1987] 2 All ER at 913):

'... the judge's findings of fact ... are unmistakably to the effect that on a balance of probabilities the injury caused by the plaintiff's fall [produced the permanent disability]. This amounts to a finding of fact that the fall was the sole cause of the [permanent disability].'

The House of Lords determined that there never was a chance that the plaintiff would recover because it was more likely than not, on the judge's findings (the 75% chance), that the damage was already done before the doctors' negligence occured. The 25% chance was, therefore, at best a statistical and hypothetical chance which the judge ruled out. Lord Ackner put the plaintiff's claim in perspective (ibid at 921):

'The debate on loss of a chance cannot arise where there has been a positive finding that before the duty arose the damage complained of had already been sustained or had become inevitable.'

The trial judge, in effect, had made two inconsistent findings. Once he had determined that it was 75% likely that the injury would have resulted whatever the doctors had done, he had determined the causation issue against the plaintiff because '[a]nything which is more probable than not [the court] treats as certain' (per Lord Diplock in *Mallett v McMonagle* [1969] 2 All ER 178 at 191). What the judge had done was to confuse a statistical chance (1 in 4 children do not suffer permanent disability if treated promptly) with the issue of which statistical group (the one or the three) the plaintiff actually fell into. The judge's 75% finding put the plaintiff in the three, and therefore, for him, the losing group. Lord Bridge was of the view that a judge in a personal injury case should struggle to make a finding on a balance of probabilities if he could do so.

What of the 'loss of a chance' case? The Court of Appeal held that a 'chance of recovery' was, in itself, a valuable asset which the courts could compensate in damages if a plaintiff lost it. The court had relied on the well-known case of *Chaplin v Hicks* [1911] 2 KB 786 where damages were awarded for a lost chance of appearing in a beauty contest and also the solicitors' negligence case (eg *Kitchen v Royal Air Force Association* [1958] 2 All ER 241) where damages for the lost chance of winning a legal action founded a claim in damages. The reasoning of the Court of Appeal is open to objection on principle and there is a considerable weight of authority against such an action (see (1987) 50 MLR 241, 256 et seq).

Lord Bridge left open whether a plaintiff could recover when causation could not be established but it could be said that there was a statistical chance, less than even, that he would not have suffered the injury 'but for' the defendant's negligence. However, he remarked that there were 'formidable difficulties in the way of accepting the analogy' with cases such as *Chaplin v Hicks* and *Kitchen*.

Lord MacKay saw 'loss of a chance' as the other side of the coin of the problem in *McGhee*. While *McGhee* stood, there might be something in the 'loss of a chance' argument. However, *McGhee* allows the court to infer that the defendant's negligence 'caused or materially contributed' to the plaintiff's injury. If the court is prepared to make this inference the plaintiff recovers all his damages. Lord MacKay gave the following example based upon the facts of *McGhee* ([1987] 2 All ER at 916):

'... say that it was established that of 100 people working ... without facilities for washing at the end of their shift 70 contracted dermatitis: of 100 people working ... when washing facilities were provided for them at the end of the shift 30 contracted dermatitis ... [after *McGhee*] it was reasonable to infer that there was a relationship between contraction of dermatitis in these conditions and the absence of washing facilities.'

But, as Lord MacKay pointed out, in this example the plaintiff would prove that the defendant's negligence 'materially contributed' to his dermatitis. To see this example as a 'loss of a chance' case would be to fall into the same trap as the trial judge in *Hotson* by giving the statistical figures (a 30% chance of avoiding dermatitis) undue emphasis. Once the inference is made that the plaintiff suffered the dermatitis because of the defendant's negligence the figures become irrelevant. There is no 'lost chance'.

McGhee was not a 'loss of a chance' case. The damage which triggered the cause of action was the dermatitis. In a pure 'loss of a chance' case, the plaintiff recovers a proportion of the damages he would recover if he had proved causation. On this view, the injury would not be the dermatitis but the 'lost chance' itself. Only if the inference could not be drawn would this be a 'lost chance' case. Here statistics are being used as *evidence* of causation in much the same way as circumstantial matters might be. Lord MacKay seemed to realise this when he said (ibid at 916):

> 'Unless and until this House departs from the decision in *McGhee* your Lordships cannot affirm the proposition that in no circumstances can *evidence* of loss of a chance . . . found a successful claim in damages.'

But, this gives no support to the Court of Appeal since their decision was that a 'lost chance' was an asset which founded an action in damages in itself; this was how the plaintiff had put his case. If statistical chances are only matters of evidence, then the law has not moved in *Hotson*.

(c) Pre-trial disclosure of medical reports

Until *Naylor v Preston AHA* [1987] 2 All ER 353, the practice in medical negligence actions had been that pre-trial disclosure of the expert evidence which each party will rely on at the trial was not made to the other side. This was a practice which differed from the disclosure of expert evidence in all other cases. The effect was two-fold. First, it discouraged settlement of cases since each side did not know the strength of the opposing experts. Secondly, if the case went to trial each side might be taken by surprise and, as a result, the proceedings might be prolonged unduly and at greater than necessary expense.

In *Naylor* the Court of Appeal took the opportunity to radically change the practice of litigation in this area. The court held that pre-trial disclosure should be the norm in the future. The court reasoned that the old rule accepted by the Court of Appeal in *Rahmam v Kirkless AHA* [1980] 3 All ER 610, had been established at a time when disclosure of reports in medical negligence actions came within RSC Ord 38, r 37, while all other professional negligence actions came within RSC Ord 38, r 38. Since the amendment to the Rules of the Supreme Court in 1980, medical negligence actions have also come within RSC Ord 38, r 38 and so the court was not bound by the restrictive interpretation of r 37 in *Rahman*.

The Court of Appeal held that r 38 gave a wide discretion to the court to order mutual disclosure. Sir John Donaldson MR said ([1987] 2 All ER at 360):

> '[N]owadays the general rule is that, whilst a party is entitled to privacy in seeking out the 'cards' for his hand, once he has put his hand together, the litigation is to be conducted with all the cards face up on the table. Furthermore, most of the cards have to be put down well before the hearing. . . . It is the product of a growing appreciation that the public interest demands that justice be provided as swiftly and economically as possible.'

A little later in his judgment he acknowledged the value of settlement in the administration of justice (ibid at 360):

'[A]nything which enables the parties to appreciate the true strength or weakness of their positions at the earliest possible moment and at the same time enables them to enter on a fully informed and realistic discussion designed to achieve a consensual resolution of the dispute is very much in the public interest.'

In addition to these arguments, Glidewell LJ identified a number of changes in the law and practice since *Rahman*. First, he noted the changes in RSC Ord 38, rr 37, 38. Secondly, it was now standard practice for the clinical and nursing notes and other medical records of a patient to be disclosed at an early stage of the litigation (see the Supreme Court Act 1981, s 33). Thirdly, Glidewell LJ observed that it was now the practice under RSC Ord 38, r 38 to order disclosure of reports in other cases of professional negligence and there was no reason, in principle, to have a different rule in medical cases.

Should disclosure be contemporaneous or sequential? The Court of Appeal thought, as a general rule, it should be contemporaneous. However, in an exceptional case sequential disclosure might be ordered if the particulars of negligence are:

'So vague that it would be unfair to the defendants to expect their experts to deal with them until such time as the plaintiff had disclosed, either by further particulars or by his own expert's reports, exactly what his case was.' (per Sir Frederick Lawton at 367).

The Court of Appeal recognised that in some circumstances disclosure would not be ordered. Two situations are suggested in the judgments of Glidewell LJ and Sir Frederick Lawton. First, where disclosure might allow the plaintiff or his experts to trim their evidence. This would only arise where either (i) there was substantial dispute of primary fact or (ii) the plaintiff's experts have based their opinions on clinical findings which the defendants can prove are wrong. Secondly, where the defendants have evidence that the plaintiff is suffering from a non-existent illness or is exaggerating his symptoms or that his disability is due to an earlier trauma which he failed to disclose to the defendants. The court thought that here the defendant should be allowed the opportunity to take the plaintiff by surprise at the trial if the evidence was to have any effect at all. These situations seem to include not only the dishonest plaintiff but also genuine 'compensationitus'.

On final point on *Naylor*. Sir John Donaldson MR returned to a view he had expressed in *Lee v South West Thames RHA* [1985] 2 All ER 385 that a doctor owes his patient a duty of candour to explain if a medical procedure goes wrong exactly what happened. He pointed to the analogous duty of the legal profession to advise their client to seek independent legal advice if it appears that the client has a valid negligence claim against the lawyer. There is some authority both in favour of such an action (*Gerber v Pines* (1934) 79 SJ 13) and against it (*Daniels v Heskin* [1954] IR 73). However, such an action is fraught with difficulty.

First, if a doctor has such a duty it does not sit well with the rather limited duty of disclosure prior to the medical procedure. Indeed, on one view of the law, it may only be the duty to disclose which the court will accept without reference to medical practice.

Secondly, if breach of the duty is to give rise to more than professional sanction, then the action must lie in the tort of negligence. What is the plaintiff's damage? Clearly, it cannot be the medical injuries because they have already happened. In a legal malpractice action, the loss of a valuable cause of action is an accepted loss sounding in damages (see *Kitchen v Royal Air Force Association* above). But can it really be said that a doctor has a duty to advise about a possible legal action in the same way? If he does, why stop at imposing liability on doctors.

Professional responsibility

The General Medical Council, which is an independent statutory body first created in 1858, is responsible for the registration of doctors; it gives guidance on the ethical responsibilities of the profession and exercises disciplinary powers over doctors. Under the Medical Act 1983, s 35 the GMC has power to discipline a doctor who has been guilty of 'serious professional misconduct'. If the Professional Conduct Committee so finds a doctor, it ultimately has the power to erase a doctor's name from the medical register and so prevent him practising.

Serious professional misconduct

In *Doughty v General Dental Council* [1987] 3 All ER 843, the Privy Council was concerned with the meaning of 'serious professional misconduct' in s 25(1) of the Dentists Act 1957 (see now Dentists Act 1984, s 27(1)). Doughty was a registered dentist who was found guilty by the General Dental Council (the dental equivalent of the GMC) of 'serious professional misconduct'. He exercised his right of appeal to the Privy Council. The allegations were (i) that he had failed to retain the radiographs of various patients and had not submitted them to the Dental Estimates Board when required, (ii) that he had failed to exercise proper skill in treating patients and (iii) that he had failed to complete treatment that was required by patients.

The Privy Council held that he had properly been found guilty of 'serious professional misconduct' in respect of each of these independent allegations, notwithstanding it could not be shown that Doughty had been dishonest in his opinion that the treatment was proper, or in determining that he had done all that was necessary. Lord MacKay distinguished the well-known remarks of Lord Jenkins in *Felix v General Dental Council* [1960] 2 All ER 391 at 400 that dishonesty was essential in professional disciplinary proceedings. Lord MacKay thought that these remarks had been made in a case where dishonesty was an issue and, therefore, they should not be taken to be of general application.

It is probable that the Privy Council in *Felix* had not intended to suggest that dishonesty had to be proved in every case. Take, for example, a case of continuing neglect of a patient which takes place over an extended period of time, the GMC has always been entitled to consider this as amounting to 'serious professional misconduct'.

This is, of course, different from the point made by Lord MacKay in *Doughty* that a finding of guilt does not 'import any moral stigma' (see also *R v Pharmaceutical Society of Great Britain ex p Sokoh, The Times,* 4 December 1986). Would the average medical practitioner take the same view?

The second reason give by Lord MacKay for distinguishing Lord Jenkins' view in *Felix* is more significant. In *Felix*, the Privy Council was interpreting the wording of the Medical and Dentists Acts that the practitioner must be found guilty of 'infamous conduct in a professional respect'. Until *Doughty*, the accepted view had been that when these words were changed by the Dentists Act 1983 and by the Medical Act 1969 to 'serious professional misconduct', no change in meaning was intended. The GMC in its 'Professional Conduct and Discipline: Fitness to Practise' states that 'the Council intended that the phrases should have the same significance' (April 1987 para 8). Indeed, the case law bears out this view (*Marten v Royal College of Veterinary Surgeons' Disciplinary Committee* [1966] 1 QB 1). In *R v General Council of Medical Education and Registration* [1930] 1 KB 562 at 569 Scruttons LJ said that 'infamous conduct' 'means no more than serious misconduct judged according to the rules written or unwritten governing the profession'. It is a matter of some surprise, therefore, that in *Doughty* the Privy Council held that a change had occurred.

Lord MacKay pointed out that the change in wording had been accompanied by an enlargement of the potential penalties which could be imposed, particularly the power to impose less severe penalties than erasure. This militated in favour of the view that the statutory remit of the GDC (and, of course, of the GMC) in disciplinary cases had been enlarged also.

Lord MacKay has given support to the well-known shift in the approach of the GMC to consider cases of medical negligence as within their statutory remit. His explanation of the meaning of 'serious professional misconduct' is strangely reminiscent of the famous *Bolam* test ([1987] 3 All ER at 847):

> 'What is now required is that the Council should establish conduct connected with his profession in which the dentist concerned has fallen short, by omission or commission, of the standards of conduct expected among dentists and that such falling short as is established should be serious.'

Two matters should be noted. First, not every case of negligence will amount to serious professional misconduct, nor should it since the GMC is concerned with protecting the public from *incompetent* doctors not those who are merely negligent in a given case (see the GMC's own view in the Blue Book, para 38). In determining whether *misconduct* had arisen Lord MacKay stated (ibid at 848) that the GDC had to determine whether 'the dental treatments critisised as unnecessary would be treatments that no dentist of reasonable skill exercising reasonable care would carry out.' In other words, negligent conduct might amount to 'professional misconduct' but would not be necessarily 'serious'.

Lord MacKay pointed out that in determining whether misconduct was *serious* the GDC should have regard to such things as the number of patients in respect of whom the dentist failed to keep proper records, the number of patients in respect of whom the dentist is alleged to have acted without due skill and the number of treatments criticised and the nature and extent of the failure to complete the treatments properly. No suggestion here that a single act of negligence will be viewed as 'serious professional misconduct'. As we shall see shortly, usually these cases concern a course of conduct in respect of one or more patients which, when taken together, can be seen as 'serious'. Of course, a single very grave act of negligence could be 'serious' but this would be an unusual case.

Secondly, a doctor need not fear professional sanction if he is not negligent, which, as *Bolam* shows, he cannot be unless 'no reasonable practitioner' would act as he did. These are precisely the words used by Lord MacKay to test whether Doughty had been guilty of misconduct. Otherwise, the Privy Council would have introduced without legislation, the changes intended in relation to doctors to be effected by the Medical Act 1983 (Amendment) Bill introduced by Nigel Spearing MP in 1984. This would have given the GMC power in cases of unacceptable professional conduct falling short of serious professional misconduct.

While *Doughty* does not suggest negligent treatment will in future be the staple diet of the GDC or the Professional Conduct Committee of the GMC, it does suggest that it is included on the menu in an appropriate case. Adultery, abuse of professional privilege, improper advertising and canvassing and, even, gross incompetence will remain the main courses even after *Doughty*. But for how long?

Duplicity and reasons in the GMC

In *Gee v General Medical Council* [1987] 2 All ER 193 the House of Lords held (overturning a majority decision of the Court of Appeal [1987] 1 All ER 1204) that the rule of procedure applicable in criminal cases that a charge must only allege a single crime (the rule against duplicity) did not apply to charges before the Professional Conduct Committee of the GMC. The House of Lords came to this conclusion on two grounds.

First, unlike a criminal offence, an allegation of 'serious professional misconduct' would often involve a course of conduct or series of events spanning a period of time. A combination of similar or different instances of behaviour might together be 'serious professional misconduct' although individually they would not. This made it impractical to apply the rule against duplicity to the proceedings of the GMC.

Secondly, duplicity would only be relevant if the procedure before the Professional Conduct Committee required the doctor to answer to a single finding of guilt as in a jury case. But that was not the procedure which consisted of a two stage process. Having heard the evidence, the PCC was required under the statutory regulations (General Medical Council Preliminary Proceedings and Professional Conduct Committee (Procedure) Rules, SI 1980 No 858) to make a finding of the facts which they found proved against the doctor. Thereafter, the doctor was entitled to make representations as to whether these facts amounted to 'serious professional misconduct'. Providing the PCC clearly indicated which facts it found proved and which it did not, the House of Lords thought that the doctor would not be prejudiced, as he would be in a criminal trial, if two or more allegations were made in a particular count where the jury could only return a single verdict of guilty or not guilty.

Lord MacKay pointed out that the PCC at 'half-time' was under a duty by virtue of r 30(1) of the Regulations to 'specify with sufficient particularity which facts have been... proved.' His Lordship agreed with the earlier views of Lord Griffiths in *Datta v General Medical Council* (unreported 27 January 1986) that the 'delphic' finding of the PCC in *Datta* that 'you are not guilty of serious professional misconduct in respect of those other facts alleged which have not been proved' (cited by Lloyd LJ in the Court of Appeal) was simply not good enough.

In any event, the House of Lords held that, on the facts the charges against Dr Gee were not bad for duplicity since the charges alleged a course of conduct which amounted to a single allegation of 'serious professional misconduct'. The House of Lords decision accords with the earlier Privy Council case of *Peatfield v General Medical Council* [1987] 1 All ER 1197.

Gee is interesting for a number of reasons. First, it did not come before the courts in the usual way by an appeal to the Privy Council by a doctor because he had been erased from the register by the PCC of the GMC. Instead, Dr Gee brought an 'application for judicial review' seeking to stop proposed proceedings being brought against him. This 'pre-emptive strike' strategy may prove more common in the future. If a justiciable issue of law can be found the court can entertain the doctor's action. For instance, the Court of Appeal in *Gee* had ordered the PCC to provide further and better particulars of the charges against the doctor in order for the doctor to 'know in advance what is the standard against which he is to be judged' (per Lloyd LJ). Such requests, if the GMC does not change its practice, may become a matter of course in the future, especially if the GMC turns its attention to the negligent but not really incompetent doctor.

Conceivably, the court may hear cases which do not involve erasure and which are brought after a finding of 'serious professional misconduct'. Or will the court view the statutory appeal as creating an exclusive avenue for redress after the event?

After *Gee*, the GMC must not only know its own rules but it must read the administrative law textbooks. The effects may be considerable. Traditionally, the Privy Council has been slow to interfere with the PCC on matters of professional judgment (eg *Bhattacharya v General Medical Council* [1967] 2 AC 259). But, as Mann J pointed out at first instance in *Gee*, in judicial review proceedings ([1987] 1 All ER 1204 at 1217):

> '[w]here the court is confronted with the threat either of an ultra vires act or of procedural impropriety in the area of public law it will intervene... reticence is not appropriate when the court is confronted with allegations of illegality and procedural impropriety.'

Practice and Procedure

ADRIAN AS ZUCKERMAN, LLM, MA
Fellow of University College, Oxford

Compulsory process

The popularity of interlocutory orders directed at an opponent and requiring him, on pain of contempt of court, to take, or refrain from, certain actions is such that it is useful to find a term that would refer to all the different procedures involved in these matters. Such a term would draw attention to the need to consider not only each separate procedural device but also their cumulative effect, especially on the liberty of defendants. The term 'compulsory process' will henceforth be used for this purpose.

The writ ne exeat regno

Last year, in *Columbia Picture Industries v Robinson* [1986] 3 All ER 338 ([1986] All ER Rev, p 225), Scott J warned against the oppressive potential of Anton Piller orders. This year Leggatt J has voiced misgivings about the writ ne exeat regno in *Allied Arab Bank Ltd v Hajjar* [1987] 3 All ER 739.

The plaintiff had lent a large sum of money to a company. The defendant was a guarantor. The plaintiff brought an action for damages against the defendant alleging fraudulent conspiracy in that the defendant and others procured the dissipation of the borrowed money. When the defendant happened to be in England, he was served with a writ ne exeat regno ordering him to be detained unless he raise £36m as security. Being unable to do so he was remanded in jail overnight. The following day he appeared in court and was released only on giving undertakings to disclose his assets, deposit his passport and refrain from leaving the country without leave of the court or of the plaintiff's solicitors. After his release the defendant applied for the discharge of the order on the ground that it should never have been made.

Arrest under a ne exeat regno writ seems to be a survival of the old procedure of imprisonment for debt which was largely abolished in 1838. Some limited powers of arrest did however survive, subject to the conditions laid down by s 6 of the Debtors Act 1969 which, as explained by Megarry J in *Fenton v Callis* [1968] 3 All ER 673 at 679, are that:

'(i) The action is one in which the defendant would formerly have been liable to arrest at law. (ii) A good cause of action for at least £50 is established. (iii) There is a "probable cause" for believing that the defendant is "about to quit England" unless he is arrested. (iv) "The absence of the defendant from England will materially prejudice the plaintiff in the prosecution of his cause".'

The plaintiff's argument was essentially this. The power of arrest for debt under the 1869 Act still exists. Equity follows the law, therefore the courts should use this power in support of the equitable remedy of a Mareva injunction. Leggatt J found this argument unappealing. Indeed, if his Lordship had accepted it, he would effectively have revived arrest for debt. Instead, Leggatt J decided to place the most restrictive interpretation on this anachronistic power. He held that since a Mareva injunction was a remedy in aid of execution it did not amount to 'prosecution of an action'. As the primary purpose of the writ in the instant case was the enforcement of a Mareva injunction, it followed that the fourth of the above conditions was not fulfilled and a writ should not have been issued.

Moreover, Leggatt J decided that the first condition was not satisfied either because the plaintiff was seeking damages rather than trying to enforce a debt and, hence, the action was not one in which a defendant would formerly have been liable for arrest at law. Lastly, his Lordship held that the writ ne exeat regno was confined to equitable claims and here the plaintiff's claim was at law.

The importance of a restrictive interpretation for the protection of defendants from oppressive practices is underlined by the facts of the present case. The plaintiff could have obtained a summary judgment against the defendant on his guarantee. They refrained from doing so and sued for damages in order to avail themselves of interlocutory procedures which, they believed, would not otherwise have been available to them as judgment debtors. Once the order was issued and the defendant arrested, the plaintiff was in a position to extract various undertakings from him as the price of his release. Indeed, having just spent 'one of the most distressing and humiliating nights in his life' (ibid at 741), the defendant was probably willing to be very accommodating to gain his freedom. Lastly, Leggatt was convinced that if the judge who made the order had the benefit of argument, the writ would never have been issued.

Leggatt J discharged the writ and ordered an inquiry into damages to be paid by the plaintiff to the defendant. Seeing that the writ and the concomitant indignities to which the defendant was subjected were without justification, there was no good reason why his compensation should not have been assessed on the discharge of the writ ne exeat regno. However, Leggatt J decided that the question of compensation should be dealt with after the trial. A decision of compensation at that stage is likely to be affected by the outcome of the trial. If that happens and the defendant's damages are substantially reduced, the deterrent effect of damages will be much weakened and a plaintiff with a strong cause of action might still be tempted to harass his defendant in the hope that winning the case will in effect wipe out the defendant's remedy.

Subject to this reservation, it has to be acknowledged that Leggatt J's judgment greatly reduces scope for the kind of oppression which was involved in the present case.

Mareva injunctions

A gap in the protection of defendants from the damaging effects of Mareva injunctions is revealed by A-G v Wright [1987] 3 All ER 579. The Attorney General brought an action against the trustees of an educational charity and sought an interlocutory injunction to restrain one defendant from disposing of various properties and moneys. The question arose whether the injunction should be made subject to the condition that the Attorney General provide a cross-undertaking in damages. A Mareva order is usually subject to such an undertaking in order to protect the interests of defendants whose liberty may turn out to have been unjustly restricted. When the injunction is sought by the Crown there is a further consideration; in Hoffmann J's words (ibid at 581):

> '...[that] Crown officials should not be inhibited from performing their duty to take action to enforce the law by the fear that public funds may be exposed to claims for compensation by people who have thereby been caused loss.'

Although Hoffmann J obvserved that not 'everyone will find this particularly attractive', he did not feel able, on the authorities, to hold that the Crown must always give such an undertaking. Nor, on the other hand, was he disposed to hold that the Crown was always dispensed from the cross-undertaking. He decided that the imposition of an undertaking must depend on the circumstances. Hoffman J found that, unlike the situation in *F Hoffman-La Roche v Secretary of State for Trade and Industry* [1974] 2 All ER 1128, where no cross-undertaking was required, there was no presumption in the present case that the defendant's conduct was unlawful. Furthermore, as the Attorney General was pursuing the interests of a particular charity Hoffmann J concluded that it was proper to require an undertaking from the charity, limited to its funds, as a condition for granting the injunction.

It is doubtful whether it is ever justified to dispense with such an undertaking. The principle that servants of the Crown must not be inhibited in pursuing the public interest in no way demands that an individual should go without compensation when the Crown's action unjustly harms him. After all, the fact that Crown servants need to drive cars in the course of their service does not entail that the crown should be exempt from liability for road accidents. It is in the public interest that the Attorney General should feel free to take proceedings to protect the public interest but the burden of injustice, should there be one, must be shouldered by the public at large and not by the individual who through no fault of his own happens to be the subject of interlocutory proceedings.

The scope for Mareva injunctions has received further extension in *DST v Raknoc* [1987] 2 All ER 769. D and R were foreign oil companies with no English connection. D brought arbitration proceedings against R in Geneva under Swiss law and obtained a substantial award. When D discovered that Shell, a UK company, had bought some oil from R and owed the latter money, D brought proceedings in England to satisfy the arbitration award out of money owed by Shell to R and obtained a Mareva injunction restraining Shell from paying its debt to R.

The Court of Appeal accepted that a Mareva injunction could be granted in aid of a judgment creditor. This point has been similarly decided in *Orwell Steel (Erection and Fabrication) Ltd v Asphalt and Tarmac (UK) Ltd* [1985] 3 All ER 747 (All ER Rev 1985, p 225). (Another case this year has held that a judgment debtor could be ordered, in the exercise of the court's inherent jurisdiction, to provide information about his assets within the jurisdiction even where there was no danger that he would conceal or dissipate them and where a Mareva injunction would be inappropriate; *Maclaine Watson & Co ltd v International Tin Council (No 2)* [1987] 3 All ER 886.)

The main issues in *DST v Raknoc* [1987] 2 All ER 769 was, however, whether the trading debt owed by Shell to R was an asset situated within the jurisdiction. Shell and R contended that since the money owed would normally have been paid in the USA in dollars, the debt was not effectively situated within the jurisdiction. Donaldson MR held that there were three critical questions to be asked in order to determine the present issue.

First, whether R could have sued Shell in this country, had the latter defaulted on its obligation. In the instant case the answer was clearly in the affirmative. The second question was whether the debt owed by Shell to R could be taken in execution of an English judgment, by garnishment or appointment of a receiver, in favour of D; for, clearly, it would not be right to maintain an injunction if the debt could not be so taken. Order 49, r 1, provides the answer to this question by laying down that a judgment creditor may attach the debt owed by a person within the jurisdiction ('the garnishee') to the judgment debtor. Since D's award was enforceable in this country he would be entitled to avail himself of the garnishment procedure (see also *SCF Finance Co v Masri (No 3)* [1987] 1 All ER 194 discussed below). The last question was whether a garnishment order would operate to discharge the garnishee from his liability to the judgment debtor; if this were not the case and the judgment debtor could still sue the garnishee for the debt in this or any other country it would not be fair to subject the garnishee to the risk of having to pay his debt twice over. Donaldson MR decided that as the garnishment procedure had international recognition, there was no risk that Shell might have to pay twice. It was accordingly held that the Mareva injunction had been rightly granted.

However, the matter did not end there, for after judgment in the Court of Appeal it transpired that a judgment in respect of the same debt had in fact been obtained by the judgment debtor against Shell in a foreign country. The Court of Appeal granted Shell leave to appeal to the House of Lords.

Whether or not Shell was exposed to double jeorpardy in respect of its debt was a question of fact and clearly no Mareva order should be made in England if Shell was liable to pay under a foreign judgment. But this question of fact brings out the question of principle involved: to what extent ought English courts to issue Mareva injunctions to prevent dissipation of assets when the parties and the subject matter of their dispute have nothing whatever to do with this country. The reason why company D turned up on the doorstep of our courts is, presumably, because the news of the Mareva jurisdiction had reached it in its foreign abode. However, we should not disregard the possibility that the same piece of news may deter other companies from doing business in this country lest their assets be seized for reasons that have little to do with their operations in England. The House of Lords would do well to hold that in circumstances such as these there is no justification for exercising the essentially discretionary Mareva jurisdiction. In the absence of fraud, the enforcement of foreign judgments between parties with no connection with this country should take its course without the help of the Mareva jurisdiction. (See also *Interpool Ltd v Galani* [1987] 2 All ER 981, discussed below.)

In one respect the courts have abided by their self-imposed restraint in relation to the Mareva jurisdiction. In *Allied Bank Ltd v Hajjar* [1987] 3 All ER 739, dicussed above, Leggatt J refused to uphold an order, issued in aid of a Mareva injunction, to disclose assets in so far as it concerned the foreign assets of the defendant. He thus followed in this respect *Ashtiani v Kashi* [1986] 2 All ER 970 (All ER Rev 1986, p 229).

Butt v Butt [1987] 3 All ER 657, allows defendants who have consented to give an undertaking, in lieu of an injunction, not to dispose of their assets to apply subsequently to have their undertakings discharged on the grounds of material non-disclosure by the plaintiff at the earlier ex parte stage.

Anton Piller orders

Ever since the introduction of the Anton Piller search procedure the question has been looming of whether a plaintiff who, in the course of executing an Anton Piller order in an action brought to remedy one wrong, has discovered evidence of another wrong may use this evidence to remedy the latter wrong? This question was the issue in the House of Lords decision in *Crest Homes plc v Marks* [1987] 2 All ER 1074. In 1984 the plaintiff obtained an Anton Piller order against the defendant in pursuit of a breach of copyright action and executed it. In 1985 the plaintiff suspected fresh breaches on the part of the defendant and obtained another order. When executing this last order he discovered evidence suggesting that the defendant breached the 1984 order by failing, on that occasion, to disclose certain documents. The plaintiff applied for permission to use the documents discovered under the 1985 order in contempt proceedings.

The House of Lords accepted that the discovery of documents by one party to another is always subject to an implied undertaking given to the court not to use the documents so disclosed, or information derived from them, for any collateral or ulterior purpose. It further accepted that such undertaking prevents the party giving it from using the discovery material in any legal proceedings other than the proceedings in which discovery is obtained. Lastly, the House accepted that the court will not normally discharge a party from his undertaking and will not allow the use of the documents even for the purpose of legal proceedings. While a general prohibition on making free with information obtained in discovery is sensible, the extension of this prohibition to the use of the discovery material in evidence is both ill-supported by authority and harmful to the interests of justice.

The authorities mentioned in support of the proposition that the implied undertaking prevents use in evidence were *Alterskye v Scott* [1948] 1 All ER 469; *Riddick v Thames Board Mills Ltd* [1977] 3 All ER 677; *Home Office v Harman* [1982] 1 All ER 532. The first case was not concerned with the admissibility in evidence of discovered material. It merely held that, since the court will imply an undertaking, a litigant seeking discovery will not be required to give an express one. Nor was the *Harman* case concerned with the use of discovered material in evidence (for a discussion of the decision see All ER Rev 1982, p 222). Only the *Riddick* case dealt with the use of discovery material in other proceedings. However, the decision of inadmissibility in that case was determined by very special considerations: first, by a desire to remedy the shortcomings of the law of defamation and, second, by the fact that the plaintiff was in effect attempting to re-open a dispute between himself and the defendant which had already been settled in the litigation on which the document in question had been discovered (see discussion in my paper 'Privilege and public interest', in *Crime Proof and Punishment*, Tapper ed, 1981, 256).

More importantly, there are weighty reasons of policy for regarding a ban on the use of evidence as unsatisfactory. The reason given for the present rule was that a ban on collateral use encourages discovery. This reason is weak. The main inhibition on the discovery of unfavourable materials is the fear of loss in the litigation in which discovery is claimed. It is true that, if the information in question is harmful to the litigant's position in the immediate litigation, fear of losing a future litigation adds to the resistance to discovery. It may also be true that, where the information is not harmful to the litigant's immediate position, the fear of future adverse use of the information creates a resistance where none would otherwise have existed. But all this is rather speculative and therefore the fear of harm in future litigation must be at best marginal.

Even if there is reason to fear increased resistance, the risk that this will inhibit the discovery process is insufficiently strong to overcome the harm to the interests of justice which the present rule creates. It must be accepted as axiomatic that the suppression of evidence which can help the court to ascertain the truth harms the interests of justice. Access by the court to such evidence is doubly important where the evidence is known to the party whose case it supports.

The unattractive consequence of the ban on use in evidence is illustrated by the facts of the case under consideration. The defendant contended that, since the material discovered under the 1985 order was subject to the usual undertaking, it could not be used to prove his disobedience of the 1984 order. Were this argument to succeed, Lord Oliver observed, the defendant could, by putting himself in contempt of court, successfully resist discovery of relevant documents at any stage of the proceedings ([1987] 2 All ER 1074 at 1082). Lord Oliver found two grounds on which to avoid this result. One ground was special to this particular case; ie that the 1984 and the 1985 actions were in substance a single set of proceedings and the proposed use of the evidence was therefore not at all for a foreign purpose but, on the contrary, employed to enforce the 1984 order. The second ground has far wider application. Lord Oliver held that (ibid at 1081):

> 'that obligation [not to make collateral use] can be of little relevance in relation to the seizure of documents and materials under an Anton Piller order, the whole purpose of which is to gain possession of material evidence without giving the defendant the opportunity of considering whether or not he shall make disclosure at all.'

Not only does this finding open the way to the use in evidence for any purpose of information obtained under an Anton Piller order, but it also weakens the general ban on collateral use. This is so because the reason given by Lord Oliver is not confined to Anton Piller orders but holds good in relation to discovery orders generally. The doctrine of discovery was developed precisely for the purpose of gaining access to material evidence without giving the defendant the option of suppressing it.

The House of Lord's judgment leaves intact the rule that the implied undertaking is directed to the court and that the court's permission must be sought for the use of the information in other proceedings, subject to the court's power to refuse permission where the use of the information might cause injustice. However, it is hard to see how the courts could possibly withhold permission if, unlike the position in the *Riddick* case, a party wishes to use the information to establish a just and reasonable cause of action.

Discovery

Documents not in possession of a deponent

A party is entitled to demand inspection of a document upon which his opponent has relied in his pleadings or affidavits: RSC Ord 24, r 10. But what happens if the opponent has no possession, custody or power in respect of a document mentioned in his pleadings or affidavits? In *Rafidain Bank v Agom Universal Sugar Trading Co Ltd* [1987] 3 All ER 859, the Court of Appeal decided that even in such a situation the court had jurisdiction to order production for inspection and that the deponent's lack of possession of, or control over, the document is only relevant in the exercise of the discretion whether or not to make an order under Ord 24, r 11. Nourse LJ explained that, where a party has relied on a document he did not possess, he should nevertheless bear the burden of procuring it rather than leave its search to the party who has not relied on it. This is consistent with the assumption behind Ord 24, r 10 to the effect that it would be unjust for a party both to rely on a document in his pleadings and refuse access to it to his opponent. However, the pursuit of these sensible aims does not justify ordering a party to do the impossible, especially where a failure to comply with the order results in the striking out of a defence and in judgment against the party affected; as happened in the present case. Fairness can be achieved in a more balanced fashion.

In this case the defendant was sued by the plaintiff bank for the return of £12m on the grounds that payment was procured by fraud. In his defence the defendant relied on an argreement between the goverment of Iraq and a Kurdish organisation whereby that sum was to be paid by the former to the latter as compensation. It was this agreement which formed the object of the order. Clearly, if at the trial the defendant fails to produce a document upon which he had relied in his pleadings, the judge would be unlikely to give much credence to its existence and to what extent the defendant's defence would be undercut and the plaintiff's interests protected. It may well be that on the facts of the present case it was right to order production in view of the close connection between the defendant and the organisation who possessed it. But this does not justify a rule authorising an order where no such relationship exists and where the party against whom the order is made is powerless to secure production.

Nourse LJ found support for the view that absence of possession and control do not go to jurisdiction in the fact that Ord 24, r 11(1), under which the order of inspection was made, does not include the words possession, custody or power', which by contrast do appear in r 11(2) of the same order. He concluded that, whereas under the latter provision an order for production can be made only against a party who is in possession, or has control, of the document, the jurisdiction under the former is not subject to such a restriction. The difference in phraseology may, however be explained on other grounds. Order 24, r 11(1) empowers the court t order production against parties who have to give inspection under rr 9 an 10. Rule 9 deals with a party who has served a list of documents under rr or 3. Rules 2 and 3 deal with parties who have, or have had, 'possession custody or power' over the relevant documents. Consequently th enforcement power under r 11(1), and not just of r 11(2), is clearly meant t be directed to parties in possession or control of the document in question

Furthermore, the terminology of r 10(2), which confers the right c inspection, also makes it clear that the same applies to a party whose duty c disclosure arises from reliance on a document in the pleadings. It provid that, upon being served with notice to disclose the documents, such a part must make provision for inspection by the other party over the document 'or such of them as he does not object to produce'. As a matter of usage, th words 'object to produce' cannot be used to describe the position of a part who has no possession or control of a document and has no way c producing them even if he wants to do so. It follows that as a matter c construction, as well as of policy, there is no justification for ordering party to do the impossible.

Discovery against strangers

In *Norwich Pharmacal Co v Customs and Excise Comrs* [1973] 2 All ER 943 948 the House of Lords decided that 'if through no fault of his own a perso gets mixed up in the tortious acts of others so as to facilitate the wrongdoing he may incur not personal liability but he comes under a dut to assist the person who has been wronged by giving him full informatio and disclosing the identify of the wrongdoers.' In *Ricci v Chow* [1987] 3 A ER 534, the Court of Appeal refused to extend this rule.

The plaintiff felt libelled by a magazine article. He did not know th identity of the writer, publisher or printer but he suspected that th defendant did and sought from him disclosure of their identify. Since th defendant had nothing to do with the printing and publication of the artic and had not faciliated its preparation the Court of Appeal accepted that n order of disclosure could be made against him.

The right of a potential plaintiff to discover suspected defamator material was also considered in *Huddleston v Control Risks Informatic Services Ltd* [1987] 2 All ER 1035. The plaintiff suspected that the defendan had compiled a report that contained defamatory material. He applied for a order pursuant to s 33(1) of the Supreme Court Act 1981 and RSC Ord 2 r 7A, directing the defendants to allow them to inspect the report. Th section empowers the court to order 'the inspection, photographin preservation, custody and detention of property which appears to the cou to be property which may become the subject matter of subseque proceedings'.

Hoffmann J rejected the application. He observed that subs (1) of s contained no limitation upon the parties who were entitled to the ord whereas subs (2) of the same section, which empowers the court to ord disclosure against third parties in respect of 'documents... which a relevant to any issue arising or likely to arise' in litigation, is confined

laims of personal injuries or death. This difference lead him to conclude
hat the former is concerned with the medium while the latter with the
nessage (ibid at 1037):

> 'If the question will be concerned with the medium, the actual physical object
> which carries the information, the application is to inspect "property" within
> s 33(1). If the question will be concerned with the message, the information
> which the object conveys, the application is for discovery and can be granted
> before writ only in the limited classes to which s 33(2) applies.'

n the case before him Hoffmann J held that there was no jurisdiction to
nake the order because the plaintiff was clearly concerned with the contents
·f the document and because he did not fulfil the conditions of subsection
2). He further held that, even if he was wrong on the point of jurisdiction,
ιe would refuse the application as a matter of discretion on the grounds that
here was no evidence that the report was defamatory and that the making
·f the order would violate the defendant's right of privacy.

   The extent to which a court would help a prospective plaintiff to obtain
lisclosure from strangers in cases of personal injury and fatal accident was
onsidered in *O'Sullivan v Herdmans Ltd* [1987] 3 All ER 129. Section 32 of
he Administration of Justice Act 1970 (equivalent to s 34 of the Supreme
:ourt Act 1981) empowers the courts of Northern Ireland to make
liscovery orders in cases of personal injury against third parties who possess
locuments relevant to the plaintiff's action. On an appeal from Northern
reland the House of Lords decided that an order of discovery was not
ubject to the limitation that the material was 'necessary either for disposing
airly of the case or for saving costs'. Nor was the party seeking discovery
imited to situations where it was impractical for him to conduct his case
vithout seeing the documents in question. On the contrary, the House of
.ords decided, discovery should be made at the earliest possible
·pportunity so as to enable the parties to prepare their cases and consider
ettlement.

   Williams v Williams [1987] 3 All ER 257 reveals a lacuna in the Bankers'
looks Evidence Act 1879, s 9 which, despite its amendment in 1979, does
ιot provide for the inspection of cheques and paying-in slips. The act
pplies to books and other records. Bundles of cheques and of slips, it was
eld, cannot be held to be records. The Court of Appeal recommended the
lteration of the law so as to apply to cheques and other documents collected
y banks in the course of their business.

Employment of adviser in discovery

he litigation in *Davies v Eli Lilly & Co* [1987] 1 All ER 801 was in effect a
·st case against the manufacturers of the drug Opren. Discovery by the
ιanufacturers involved an enormous number of documents, the assessment
·f which gave rise to highly complex scientific and statistical problems. To
elp with the analysis of the documents the plaintiffs employed the services
·f a person who, while not having a scientific specialisation, had suitable
·aining and qualifications for the task of sorting out and digesting the
iscovered material. Both the trial judge, Hirst J, and the Court of Appeal
ccepted the principle that solicitors could retain the services of a person

who was not an expert to undertake inspection on their behalf, provided that the party seeking the appointment persuades the court that such employment is essential to the preparation of the case and provided that the court is satisfied that there would be no breach of confidentiality in respec of the documents inspected. If the opponent objects to the appointment, it i for the opponent to show that the proposed person is unsuitable or could not be relied upon to abide by the duty of confidentiality.

Extension of validity of writs

The House of Lords has considered the principles governing the extension of the validity of writs under RSC Ord 6, r 8 when the result of such extension is to extend the limitation period. It held in *Kleinwort Benson Ltd v Barbrak Ltd* [1987] 2 All ER 289, that the power to extend validity is now confined to 'exceptional circumstances' but could be exercised whereve: there are 'good reasons' for doing so. When determining whether to allow an extension, the court has to take into consideration not only the reason: for the delay in serving the writ but also to balance the hardship to the plaintiff, were extension to be refused, against the hardship to the defendant, were an extension to be allowed. If at the time of the application both the writ and the limitation period have expired, the applicant has to show good reason why he had not applied before the expiry of the writ and why the defendant should be deprived of his limitation right.

In the present case the delay was motivated not only by the plaintiff's desire to save his own costs but also those of the defendants. For this and other reasons peculiar to the case the House of Lords reinstated the original order extending the writ.

Amendment of pleadings

The cardinal principle concerning amendments of pleadings is, in the word of May LJ in *Atkinson v Fitzwalter* [1987] 1 All ER 483 at 490: 'that all amendments should be allowed so as to ensure that the real matters in controversy are before the court, provided that can be done withou injustice to the other side.' Injustice can spring from different sources and as we shall shortly see, we cannot hope that by obeying one rule we will counteract all of them.

As a general principle an amendment of pleadings has retrospective force in the sense that it takes effect not from the time that it is made but relates back to the original date of the pleadings. If this were not the case, the court would be encumbered by different layers of pleadings, each having its own relevant date and its own temporal consequences. However, the theory o relating back causes difficulty where the amendment seeks to add a cause o action which has accrued after the service of the pleadings. Consequently i was thought that an amendment may not add a cause of action which post-dates the original writ; *Eshelby v Federated European Bank Ltd* [1932 1 KB 254.

In *Tilcon Ltd v Land and Real Estate Investment Ltd* [1987] 1 All ER 615 a party to a contract counterclaimed for damages for breach. He was allowed to amend and add a claim in respect of the termination of the contract which took place after his original claim on the grounds that the facts giving rise to the claim for termination occurred before the issue of the original claim. It was also decided that the claim for termination did not constitute a new cause of action but merely went to the issue of remedy and did not breach the rule against adding a new cause of action. Thus the Court of Appeal left unaffected the generality of the rule in the *Eshelby* case.

The *Eshelby* limitation makes little sense. Where it is desirable that the new cause of action should be tried together with the old one, the plaintiff can issue a new writ and apply for the new action to be heard with the old one. If it is desirable to try two cases together, it ought to be possible to achieve this result by the simple device of amendment. While the rule of relating-back is sensible in most circumstances, it is only a rule of convenience and it should not be allowed to become a source of inconvenience.

Indeed, the House of Lords has deviated from the relating-back rule in *Ketteman v Hansel Properties Ltd* [1987] 2 WLR 312, where it was decided that an amendment to add a defendant takes effect not retrospectively but on the date on which he is joined. This decision was designed to protect the new defendant from losing an accrued limitation period (see discussion of this point in All ER Rev 1982, p 229).

In *Atkinson v Fitzwalter* [1987] 1 All ER 483 the Court of Appeal refused to endorse a rule that an allegation of fraud cannot be added by way of an amendment. It embraced the principle that amendments, however late, should be allowed if justice so requires, provided that the other party be financially compensated for any inconvenience. However, as May LJ put it (ibid at 490): 'the more serious the allegation that is made, then the more clearly satisfied must the court be that indeed no prejudice is caused which cannot be compensated for in some satisfactory way or another before allowing the amendment.'

Interim payment

Rules of the Supreme Court, Order 29, r 10, provides that a plaintiff may apply for interim payment. Rule 11 of the same order authorises the court to make an order in respect of 'damages which in the opinion of the Court are likely to be recovered by the plaintiff'. Rule 12 authorises the court to order the defendant to make an interim payment if the court is satisfied 'that, if the action proceeded to trial; the plaintiff would obtain judgment against the defendant for a substantial sum of money apart from any damages or costs'. In an action based on a contract of sale the vendor can sue for damages for breach, where ownership in the subject matter of the contract has not passed to the purchaser, and for the price where it has. But what if it is not clear whether the property has passed?

On an application for interim payment by the plaintiff vendor in *Shearson Leham Bros Inc v Maclaine Watson & Co Ltd* [1987] 2 All ER 181 the issue was whether the plaintiff would be able to sue for the price, as he sought to do, or only for damages. Bingham J could not say with confidence that the plaintiff would obtain judgment for the price and he therefore decided that the plaintiff was not entitled to interim payment under r 12. Nor, by the same token, could Bingham J feel sure that the plaintiff would be able to obtain damages and he therefore felt unable to order interim payment under r 11 either. The result was that although it was clear that the plaintiff would obtain judgment for either the price or for damages he could not benefit from interim payment.

The Court of Appeal decided that such a result was entirely inconsistent with the purpose of the jurisdiction to award interim payment. It held that where a plaintiff makes alternative claims and the court is satisfied that he would obtain judgment on one or the other, the court can order interim payment on the basis of the lower of the alternative sums in respect of which he was suing. On the question of construction Nicholls LJ observed (ibid at 190):

> 'Although the power given by each rule is a separate power, the underlying purpose of the two rules is the same: to mitigate hardship or prejudice . . . which may exist during the period from commencement of an action to the trial. Further, the underlying task of the court under each rule is the same: ordering an interim payment of such amount as is just, having regard to all the circumstances. Accordingly, when construing each rule, the court should be slow to adopt a construction which would . . . defeat the evident purpose of both rules . . .'

It is hoped that the same enlightened approach will be followed in the interpretation of other rules of the Supreme Court.

Disclosure of expert evidence

In *Naylor v Preston Area Health Authority* [1987] 2 All ER 353 the Court of Appeal reviewed the principles governing the disclosure of expert evidence generally and, in particular, disclosure of expert opinion in cases of medical negligence. The court's views are largely reflected in the new, and much simplified, rr 37 and 38 of Ord 38 which came into force on 1 October 1987.

The basic principle is one of general disclosure. Where a party applies to be allowed to produce oral expert evidence he must disclose the substance of the evidence to his opponent, unless the court considers that there are special reasons for not doing so. The new r 38 makes available a procedure for 'without prejudice' meetings of experts representing both sides in order to clarify the issues on which there is disagreement between them. As a result of the Court of Appeal's decision and the new rules, the doctrine expressed in *Rahman v Kirklees Area Health Authority* [1980] 3 All ER 610 that the courts should not ordinarily order compulsory disclosure of experts' reports in medical negligence cases, is discarded.

Appeal without lis

The issue in *Ainsbury v Millington* [1987] 1 All ER 929 was whether a court had jurisdiction to issue an injunction excluding a joint tenant from a local authority tenancy. By the time it had reached the House of Lords, the tenancy had come to an end and no further dispute existed between the parties. Despite the fact that there were conflicting authorities on the point and that the issue was one of considerable importance to family lawyers, the

House of Lords refused to entertain the appeal. Lord Bridge explained (ibid at 930–31):

> 'It has always been a fundamental feature of our judicial system that the courts decide disputes between the parties before them; they do not pronounce on abstract questions of law when there is no dispute to be resolved.'

Furthermore, Lord Bridge stresssed that where the parties are legally aided, as was the situation in the present appeal, it is the duty of counsel and solicitors either to ensure that the appeal is withdrawn or apply to the court for directions.

An inflexible rule that where the lis has disappeared, the appeal will not be entertained is not necessarily desirable. In the case under consideration the issue had been taken to the House of Lords because the law was unclear. The litigation in the courts below had been conducted at public expense and further expenses had already been incurred for its argument in the House. All this outlay will have to be undertaken afresh, probably again with legal aid funds, when the issue resurfaces, as it is bound to do.

A somewhat different approach was adopted by a majority of the Court of Appeal in *National Coal Board v Ridgeway* [1987] 3 All ER 582. In that case the lis had mainly been resolved before the appeal. Although the Court of Appeal managed to detect some outstanding issues it seems that what really prompted Nicholls and Bingham LJJ to entertain the appeal was the view that the latter explained as follows (ibid at 604):

> '. . . the board [the respondents] submitted that these [the appellants'] were not genuine claims but mere pretexts designed to keep the appeal alive. . . . that does not, however, even if true, entitle this court to brush the claims aside as being illegitimate or of no consequence. . . . The tribunal's decision [below] and the EAT contain rulings on questions of legal principle which will or may affect a significant number of other cases. The parties have spent time and money litigating these questions up to this level. Much of that time and money would have to be spent all over again if, in any later case raising the same questions, it were sought to challenge the existing ruling of the EAT. That would not in my view be creditable to our legal system.'

The trouble is that as long as the House of Lords declines to subscribe to the same policy much time and money may well have to be spent all over again in cases of this kind.

Costs

Security for costs

The Court of Appeal has denied the existence of a rule that security for costs must not be ordered against a foreign plaintiff if there is a co-plaintiff within the jurisdiction: *Slazengers Ltd v Seaspeed Ferries International Ltd* [1987] 3 All ER 967. Furthermore, it was held that in ordering such payment under Ord 23, r 1 the court had discretion to make an order for a portion of the expected costs.

In that particular case there were a large number of plaintiffs, many of them outside the jurisdiction, but the Court of Appeal decided that no order of security was necessary because all the plaintiffs stood together and were supported by their insurers and underwriters who had ample funds to meet any costs that might be awarded against the plaintiffs.

Browne-Wilkinson V-C's judgment in *Porzelack KG v Porzelack (UK) Ltd* [1987] 1 All ER 1074 serves as a reminder that an order directed to a foreign plaintiff to provide security for costs is by no means automatic. He explained that in deciding whether to make such an order considerable weight is to be given to the fact that the Civil Jurisdiction and Judgments Act 1982, which embodies the European convention on the enforcement of judgments within the EEC, provides improved facilities for enforcement abroad and thus reduces the need to rely on security for costs. There were further factors that influenced Brown-Wilkinson V-C in refusing to make an order: the fact that security on the scale demanded by the defendant would stifle the action and the consideration that by using the plaintiffs' brand name, to which they had no right, the defendants were creating confusion between the plaintiffs' goods and their own.

Respondents to appeals who seek to obtain security for costs would do well to bear in mind Sir John Donaldson MR's decision in *A Co v K Ltd* [1987] 3 All ER 377 where he refused to make an order for securing the appeal costs of the respondent, who was the successful plaintiff below, because of late application; and this despite the fact that there was little prospect of the respondent recovering his costs, even if the appeal was dismissed, from the foreign appellant.

Costs in 'class' action

The litigation involving the drug Opren has given rise to another Court of Appeal judgment this year: *Davies v Eli Lilly & Co* [1987] 3 All ER 94. When discussing discovery above, it was mentioned that the issues in the case were highly complex and involved extensive research and preparation. There was also a highly complicated procedural problem caused by the large number of plaintiffs; some 1500. In countries that make arrangements for class actions the number of parties does not give rise to special diffiiculties, but English law makes no such arrangements. Here there are normally two options open to litigants when several actions raise identical issues: they can either apply for the actions to be tried together or allow them to be litigated separately. On this occasion it was both impractical to try 1500 actions together and unacceptable to litigate the same issues 1500 times over. Hirst J came up with the eminently sensible solution of choosing 'lead actions' and litigating in them the issues which were common to all, or virtually all, of the 1500 claims. For all practical purposes a 'lead action' would settle the common issues for all litigants; though whether the findings would be binding as issue estoppel on all the plaintiffs must be subject to some doubt.

The 'lead actions' solution inexorably gave rise to the question: who would bear the costs of the lead actions? An individual plaintiff chosen for the purpose would be clearly unable to find the enormous resources necessary to challenge the defendant drug company effectively; to have done so on a shoe-string would certainly not have satisfactorily resolved the issues for all plaintiffs. Nor was it just to choose a plaintiff who was legally aided because, in the event of such plaintiff winning, the legal aid fund would have first call on the amount recovered by him and his damages would be likely to be wiped out by the costs incurred over and above the sum (including costs paid by the defendant) recovered by the plaintiff.

To overcome this problem, which threatened the success of the 'lead actions' idea, Hirst J ordered that the costs incurred by the plaintiffs in the lead actions should be borne by all the plaintiffs equally (giving freedom to the parties to apply for variation of the order should later circumstances demand it).

The power to order a non-party to pay costs was established by the House of Lords in *Aiden Shipping Co Ltd v Interbulk, The Vimeria* [1986] 2 All ER 409, but the plaintiffs appealed on the ground that such order could not be made before the action and in advance of the costs being incurred. To make out this contention counsel for the plaintiffs relied on Ord 62, r 3. No reading of the rule or its predecessors lends support to this argument and the Court of Appeal was right to give it a short shrift.

The real practical risk in this litigation was, as Sir John Donaldson MR pointed out, that 'the costs will be out of proportion to any benefit which is likely to be obtained' ([1987] 3 All ER 94 at 100). Hirst J's order went some way to reduce this risk, though the same could not be said of the appeal against it.

Award of gross sum by the judge in lieu of taxed costs

As we have just seen, one of the hazards of litigation is that, although successful, the plaintiff may still be out of pocket at the end of the day. In certain cases this is highly unjust and the courts have power to prevent it by, for instance, making an order under Ord 62, r 9(4)(b) (now Ord 62, r 7(4)(b)) for payment of a gross sum 'instead of his [the party's] taxed costs'. This was done in the matrimonial dispute of *Leary v Leary* [1987] 1 All ER 261. The wife applied for financial provision. Booth J found that, due to the husband's persistent failure to disclose his financial position, an inquiry had to be pursued which was out of proportion to the end result. She felt that the wife should in no way be in debt as a result of the husband's actions. The wife's solicitors had submitted an itemised schedule of the costs of the suit and Booth J ordered the husband, without warning him of her intention to do so, to pay the full amount of the costs, amounting to £32,000, as a fixed amount.

The Court of Appeal approved the order and held that although in the ordinary case the judge ought to inform the parties of the intention to make such an order, so as to give the party affected an opportunity to make representations, the judge's failure to do so in the instant case did not prejudice the husband. The reason for this being, first, that, even had the judge given notice of her intention, the husband would not have been allowed to query every item of the costs (as he intimated in his notice of appeal that he wanted to do) because this would have defeated the purpose of the gross sum procedure which is to avoid the expense and delay involved in litigation arising out of taxation. The second reason was that even after the order the husband was free to apply to the judge to make submissions in case certain aspects have been overlooked.

Payment into court

The case of *John Laing Construction Ltd v Dastur* [1987] 3 All ER 247 illustrates the difficulties faced by plaintiffs in recovering the costs of their efforts to secure payment in respect of an undisputed claim. The plaintiffs' car was damaged in an accident for which the defendant was undeniably liable. The plaintiffs' solicitors wrote to the defendant's insurers claiming £132.50 in respect of repair, £5 in respect of loss of use, and £28.80 in respect of costs. They indicated that they were prepared to settle for this sum and that if the defendant did not pay, they would take their claim to the county court and sue for interest too. The defendants tendered £137.50 but were not prepared to pay the costs. The plaintiffs sued for the loss and for interest. The defendants paid £137.50 into the court and pleaded tender under CCR Ord 9, r 12.

Tender is a defence only in respect of liquidated claims. Damages in respect of the cost of repairs arising out of a road accident would not be a liquidated claim but for CCR Ord 1, r 10 which lays down that claims for the costs of such repairs 'shall be treated as a liquidated demand'. However, this provision did not help the defendants for the reason that Parker LJ explained as follows (ibid at 250–51):

> 'In the first place the rule ends with the words "shall, unless the court otherwise orders, be treated as a liquidated demand for the purposes of these rules". The defence of tender is a common law substantive defence... The rules cannot in any event amend the substantive law. Moreover, the rule itself gives the court a discretion and a discretion to allow or disallow a substantive law defence available to the defendant is not, even if intra vires, within the contemplation of the rule. If a tender... is bad at common law it cannot in my view thereafter be made good by a provision which states merely that, for the purpose of the rules and unless the court otherwise orders, the claim shall be treated as a liquidated demand.'

CCR Ord 1, r 10 was also considered in *Smith v Springer* [1987] 3 All ER 252 where the facts were similar and where the Court of Appeal followed the decision in the *John Laing Construction* case. However, Sir John Donaldson MR expressed misgivings about his result. He explained that its effect would be to induce insurance companies to pay claimants the legal costs they have incurred in obtaining their compensation and observed (ibid at 256):

> '... I have some sympathy with insurance companies who are prepared to settle in full, but who do not wish also to have to meet legal expenses as the price of avoiding litigation.'

His Lordship concluded with the hope that the rules of the county court would be changed to render claims of this kind liable to tender under Ord 1, r 10. This would be unfortunate. A person who has suffered damage resulting from a road accident does not go to his solicitor in order to spite his insurers. He does so because he has received no co-operation from the insurance company or because he does not know what his rights are. In either case there is no justification for, in effect, deducting his expenses from his damages. There is some authority for the proposition that when a writ for a liquidated claim has been issued, the defendant is liable to the costs of it and cannot tender the sum of the claim less costs (see *The Supreme Court Practice*, 1988, 13/6/3). By analogy, where a plaintiff has had to have recourse to solicitors to obtain an offer from the defendant, the latter should pay the costs.

'Without prejudice' documents

The doctrine whereby communication conducted 'without prejudice' may not be used in evidence, has one aim: to facilitate compromise. This is achieved by enabling the parties to negotiate without fear that what they say will be held against them. To benefit from the immunity it is not enough that a document should bear the 'without prejudice' words. The court, as Parker LJ explained in *South Shropshire DC v Amos* [1987] 1 All ER 340, will look at the document and consider whether it forms part of negotiations between parties to a dispute before accepting a claim of immunity. However, to be covered by immunity a document does not have to contain an offer, it is sufficient that it constitutes an opening shot in an attempt to get negotiations going.

In *Simaan General Contracting Co v Pilkington Glass Ltd* [1987] 1 All ER 345 the plaintiff, a foreign company, brought an action against the defendant company. There had been 'without prejudice' negotiations between the parties, in which the defendants made a substantial offer of settlement, but they came to nothing. When the defendants applied for security for costs, the plaintiffs wished to rely on the 'without prejudice' communications in order to make out that they had a good chance of success and that it was not just to require them to provide security. Judge John Newey QC accepted that the parties' negotiations 'could assist the court in forming views as to a plaintiff's prospects of success and whether a defendant is endeavouring to stifle an action' but he held that such use would be inconsistent with the underlying purpose of the rule and concluded that 'without prejudice' communications were inadmissible even on a summons for security for costs.

The assumption that 'without prejudice' communications may be useful in the determination of a factual dispute between the parties was also at the basis of the Court of Appeal's decision in *Rush & Tompkins Ltd v GLC* (1988) NLJR 22. In a dispute arising out of a construction agreement the plaintiffs sued the first and second defendants. After 'without prejudice' negotiations, the plaintiffs and the first defendants reached a compromise. The action against the second defendants continued. The second defendants applied for discovery of the 'without prejudice' correspondence that passed between the plaintiffs and the first defendants. The Court of Appeal decided that the documents ought to be disclosed. Balcombe LJ said:

'. . . Unless the parties have chosen to give the phrase ["without prejudice"] a different meaning, once the "without prejudice" correspondence has resulted in their reaching a concluded agreement, the protection has served the purpose for which it must be treated as having been intended, and this particular head of public policy has no futher application. The more general head of public policy which lies behind the rules requiring discovery of documents in civil proceedings . . . which is to provide the parties with the relevant documentary material before the trial, so as to assist them in appraising the strength and weakness of their respective cases, and thus provide for the fair disposal of the proceedings before or at the trial . . . can then take effect.'

The Court of Appeal was entirely right to give prominence to the need to secure all relevant documents in order to achieve the ends of justice. However, for a number of reasons it is not clear that the court's judgment advances this end.

First, as the above dictum indicates, the Court of Appeal allowed for the possibility that by using special words the parties could, at least between themselves, preclude disclosure even after settlement has been reached. The practical consequence of this is going to be that the familiar formula 'without prejudice' will give way to a new formula, say 'without prejudice de luxe', and all use in evidence will thereafter be prevented. Thus whatever the present decision had gained for the 'general head of public policy' will have been lost by a new incantation.

Secondly, the present ruling is inconsistent with the basic aim of encouraging compromise because the fear of use in evidence by other parties to the litigation may be as debilitating to the prospects of a compromise as the threat of using the communications between the parties to the settlement.

Thirdly, and most importantly, it is difficult to see how it can automatically be assumed that 'without prejudice' statements are relevant to the matters in dispute, even when the relevance required is the wide relevance of discovery.

Parties who conduct 'without prejudice' communications do so for the purpose of reaching an accommodation. Hence their statements are dictated by a desire to obtain as great an advantage as possible without recourse to litigation. Suppose that the plaintiff offers to settle for 50 per cent of his claim to damages. In common sense this offer does not amount to an indication that the plaintiff realises that he has no right to his full claim. The offer merely reflects the plaintiff's economic judgment as to what it is worth his while to settle for. Of course, to some extent this judgment will be based on what the plaintiff believes his damage actually is, but we cannot calculate from his offer what this belief is because his offer is tempered by his assessment of his chance of success, by the inconvenience value of the litigation and by his ability to pursue it. These calculations denude our plaintiff's offer of any probative value to the issue of the quantum of damages.

Suppose, for the sake of argument, that in the case decided by the Court of Appeal the second defendants were interested in the settlement between the plaintiffs and the first defendants in order to find out what proportion of the claim the plaintiffs set down to the second defendants. For the reasons just set out, the plaintiffs' assessment of the second defendants' liability in the context of their settlement with the first defendants would have proved nothing but the value that plaintiffs placed on the compromise and this is hardly probative of any of the actual facts disputed by the second defendants.

Suppose now that parties to 'without prejudice' communications make statements about the disputed facts. In *Simaan General Contracting Co v Pilkington Glass Ltd* [1987] 1 All ER 345 the dispute concerned the adequacy of tinted glass for the purpose for which it was supplied. Suppose that the supplier, the defendants, had said during the negotiations that they were prepared to proceed on the assumption that the glass was unsuitable for its purpose. Such a statement cannot be proof of the quality of the glass for the simple reason that the defendants did not intend to make a statement about the suitability of the glass. They merely set out a hypothesis upon which they are prepared to conduct the discussion. Logically, a hypothetical statement is neutral as to the existence or non-existence of the facts stated. Even if the defendants did not expressly indicate that their concession was hypothetical, the context of the negotiations will usually render it so. We may therefore conclude that in most compromise negotiations the concept of 'without prejudice' has the effect of hypothesising the statements made by the parties and rendering them useless as evidence.

Of course communications between the parties to negotiations may include third party statements, such as expert opinion, but these are not covered by the 'without prejudice' rule; otherwise parties would be able to render almost all documentary evidence inadmissible by sending it to the opponent under cover of 'without prejudice'.

It is imaginable that in some instances of 'without prejudice' negotiations parties make straightforward factual assertions, but this is likely to be rare. In the run of the mill search for a compromise, especially when conducted by solicitors, the 'without prejudice' cover produces irrelevance. Irrelevance, being a matter of logic and not of law, it remains unaffected by whether or not the negotiations are over and by whether or not they are successful or unsuccessful.

It is possible that the Court of Appeal's theory that once the original purpose is over immunity from discovery must end, has a greater part to play in relation to legal professional privilege when it attaches to communications made in relation to pending litigation.

Execution

Garnishee orders

The decision in *SCF Finance Co v Masri (No 3)* [1987] 1 All ER 194 goes back to an action brought by the plaintiffs against Mr Masri (hereinafter the 'husband') in 1984 when they obtained a Mareva injunction in respect of an account which stood in his wife's name, on the grounds that the husband was the beneficial owner of that account. The wife applied to have the order discharged, arguing that she, and not her husband, was the beneficial owner of the account. Hirst J refused to discharge the injunction and ordered the trial of the issue regarding the beneficial ownership; see *SCF Finance Ltd v Masri* [1985] 2 All ER 747. Although not conceding that the ownership was her husband's, the wife did not pursue her application to discharge the injunction. On obtaining judgment against the husband in the main action the plaintiffs then applied for a garnishee order against the wife on the grounds that the money in the account was owed by her to her husband.

Further, the plaintiffs contended that the wife was bound by issue estoppel on the point of the ownership of the account.

The Court of Appeal held that the wife's application was a summons in the action brought by the plaintiffs and as such could not be withdrawn without the court's leave: Ord 21, r 6. No application for leave was made, and had one been made, it would have been refused. Hence the consequence of the wife's failure to proceed with her application was that it was dismissed. Furthermore, by analogy to judgments by consent, an application dismissed for failure to proceed was binding on all the issues that were open to the wife to litigate in the proceedings.

A party, in the wife's position, who would rather await the outcome of the main trial before undertaking the expensive course of challenging the finding of ownership should therefore apply for leave to withdraw the application to discharge a Mareva injunction.

On the point of jurisdiction to make a garnishee order the wife contended that she was not 'a person within the jurisdiction' for the purpose of Ord 49, r 1(1) because she was not in the country when the order was served. The Court of Appeal decided that temporary presence in this country was sufficient; though this fact may be taken into account in exercising the discretion whether to make the order. It was further decided that presence in this country at the time at which the order nisi was made was sufficient. Here, although the wife was not in the country at the time of the order, she had agreed to accept service of the garnishee proceedings on her solicitors and that was sufficient to make her 'a person within the jurisdiction'.

Lastly, the wife contended that her indebtedness, if it existed at all, existed outside the jurisdiction and could not therefore be subject to a garnishee order. Ralph Gibson LJ dismissed this contention holding that 'Ord 49, r 1 contains no express requirement that the garnishee be indebted within the jurisdiction and we see no reason to read in words to that effect' (ibid at 205). This is a very problematic decision. If a foreign court has jurisdiction over the debt, the danger is that the debtor may be subject to conflicting judgments in different countries. For this reason Balcombe LJ emphasised in *Interpool Ltd v Galani* [1987] 2 All ER 981 that where there is a risk that the garnishee may be made to pay the debt twice the court ought to exercise its discretion against making a garnishee order. See also *DST v Raknoc* [1987] 2 All ER 769 discussed above.

It was held in the last-mentioned case that in conducting an examination of a judgment debtor under Ord 48, r 1, the debtor may be examined about his foreign assets as well as about his assets within the jurisdiction. This is not to say that an English court has jurisdiction to enforce judgments, whether local or foreign, against assets outside the jurisdiction. But the existence of such assets could well influence the steps taken within the jurisdiction.

Disclosure in aid of execution

Ord 48, r 1 empowers the court to order a judgment debtor to be examined about the nature and location of his assets. In *Maclaine Watson & Co Ltd v International Tin Council (No 2)* [1987] 3 All ER 886 the question arose whether such an order could be made against an unincorporated association. Ord 48, r 1 provides:

> 'Where a person has obtained a judgment or order for the payment by some other person (hereinafter referred to as "the judgment creditor") of money, the Court may . . . order the judgment debtor or, if the judgment debtor is a body corporate, an officer thereof, to attend . . . and be orally examined . . .'

Millett J held that the special reference to a body corporate indicated that the word 'person' referred only to natural persons, otherwise the reference to the corporate body would be rendered redundant. This construction is not free from doubt but since Millett J also held that an order of disclosure could in any event be made against an unincorporated association in the exercise of the inherent to prevent a judgment debtor from frustrating the process of the court, the point loses much of its practical importance.

Stay pending determination of other proceedings

Rules of the Supreme Court, Order 47, r 1(1)(a) empowers the court to order a stay of execution of judgment if 'there are special circumstances which render it inexpedient to enforce the judgment'. The issue in *Burnet v Francis Industries plc* [1987] 2 All ER 323 was whether a stay was justified. The plaintiff had been dismissed by his employers, A Co, and obtained a judgment against them for the enforcement of a compensation agreement. The agreement was incidental to a take-over of A Co by B Co. Both the compensation agreement and the takeover were based in part on a forecast of A Co's profits which the plaintiff helped to prepare. When profits fell short of the forecast, B Co sued the plaintiff for negligence. A Co, now a subsidiary of B Co, applied to stay execution of judgment against it while proceedings by B Co against the plaintiffs were pending.

Ralph Gibson LJ made it clear that only in very special circumstances will the court deny the judgment creditor immediate enjoyment of the fruits of his victory. Bingham LJ set out the considerations that have to be taken into account when deciding whether such order was justified. These include the closeness between the defendant and the third party, the inter-relationship between the claims in the two sets of proceedings, the likely delay in the trial of the other claim, the merits of the other claim and the likely prejudice to the judgment creditor. Here it was decided that there was no justification for stay for the following reasons: there was likely to be a considerable delay in determining the action by B Co against the plaintiff; it was unclear whether the claim would succeed; there was no allegation that the plaintiff intended to mislead; the plaintiff was a reputable businessman with residence in this country; and lastly, a stay would cause him prejudice.

Public International Law

CHRISTOPHER GREENWOOD, MA, LLB
Barrister, Fellow of Magdalene College, Cambridge

Most of the 1987 cases on public international law stemmed from a telephone call made by the Buffer Stock Manager of the International Tin Council ('ITC') on 24 October 1985 in which he informed the Chairman of the London Metal Exchange that the ITC could not meet its commitments. Since these commitments were estimated to be in excess of £700 million, the results of that telephone call were far-reaching. This article will therefore concentrate upon the litigation to which the ITC's default gave rise. Since all the cases stemmed from the same complicated series of events it will be necessary to devote a certain amount of space to explaining the background to the litigation before examining each decision. It should be borne in mind that, at the time of writing, appeals were pending in at least two of the cases concerned.

The legal regime of the ITC

The ITC is an international organisation which has existed since 1956, although its antecedents can be traced back to international agreements designed to stabilise the price of tin which were in operation before the Second World War. At the relevant time the ITC was constituted under the Sixth International Tin Agreement, 1982 (Cmnd 8646) ('the ITA'), a treaty to which 23 States, including the United Kingdom, and the European Economic Community were parties, representing a majority (although a much smaller one than in the past) of the principal tin producers and consumers. The ITC's chief object was to promote an orderly market in tin for the benefit of both the producer and consumer members by attempting to ensure that production and consumption were reasonably well matched and that there were no excessive fluctuations in price. This object was achieved by the operation of a system of floor and ceiling prices, maintained by the operation of a buffer stock of tin which was financed by contributions and loans from the member States. If the price of tin rose too high, the Buffer Stock Manager would sell part of his reserves to depress the price. If the price dropped too low, he bought into the buffer stock to remove the surplus from the market.

Article 16 of the ITA provided that the ITC should have legal personality, including 'the capacity to contract, to acquire and dispose of movable and immovable property and to institute legal proceedings'. The management of the buffer stock was governed by articles 21 and 22, which provided, inter alia, that the buffer stock should be financed by contributions from the member States in proportion to their share of worldwide tin production or consumption, government guarantees or undertakings from the member States and borrowing. Under article 2 the member States were to be liable to the ITC up to the extent of their guarantees or undertakings.

The headquarters of the ITC were set up in London under the terms of a Headquarters Agreement concluded in 1972 between the ITC and the United Kingdom (Cmnd 4398). That agreement was given effect in English law by the International Tin Council (Immunities and Privileges) Order 1972 ('the 1972 Order'), a statutory instrument made under the International Organisations Act 1968. Article 5 of the 1972 Order provides that the ITC shall have 'the legal capacities of a body corporate'. Article 6(1) provides for the immunity of the organisation in the following terms (which are substantially the same as those of Article 8 of the Headquarters Agreement):

> 'The Council shall have immunity from suit and legal process except:
> (a) to the extent that the Council shall have expressly waived such immunity in a particular case;
> (b) in respect of a civil action by a third party for damage arising from an accident caused by a motor vehicle belonging to or operated on behalf of the Council, or in respect of a motor offence involving such a vehicle; and
> (c) in respect of the enforcement of an arbitration award made under article 23 or 24 [of the Headquarters Agreement].'

Article 23 of the Headquarters Agreement stipulated that contracts made by the ITC with a person resident in the United Kingdom or any body incorporated, or having its principal place of business in the United Kingdom should include an arbitration clause. Article 7 provided that the ITC should have the same inviolability in respect of official archives as was conferred by the Vienna Convention on Diplomatic Relations 1961, upon the archives of a diplomatic mission. Provision was also made for the immunities and privileges of the Executive Chairman and the officers and employees of the ITC.

The operation of the ITC

In the months immediately prior to October 1985 the ITC's Buffer Stock Manager bought large quantities of tin in an attempt to support the price of tin, which had probably been fixed at an unrealistically high level. Eventually the Buffer Stock Manager found that the ITC could no longer meet the extensive commitments into which it had entered and was obliged to cease trading on 24 October 1985. The Committee of the London Metal Exchange, on which the largest volume of international trading in tin took place, immediately suspended trading in tin. The Committee subsequently ruled ('Rule M') that all contracts for the sale of tin which provided for delivery after 24 October 1985 were to be closed by repurchase contracts at a price fixed by the Committee. Attempts to negotiate a settlement under which the members of the ITC would provide funds to enable the ITC to meet its obligations broke down in March 1986.

Outline of the litigation

In view of the scale of the ITC's liabilities at the date of its financial collapse, it is scarcely surprising that there has been a substantial volume of litigation arising from that event. The actions which have been reported so far have fallen into three broad categories: (1) actions against the ITC itself; (2) actions designed to obtain redress from the members of the ITC (even though the defendant is, in some cases, the ITC itself); and (3) actions between private parties in which the ITC has intervened. The first category has raised problems concerning the scope of the ITC's immunity from legal suit and process. The second category has been dominated by questions regarding the nature of the ITC's 'legal personality' and the justiciability of the rights and duties of the members under the ITA. The third category has involved consideration of the inviolability of the ITC's archives. However, some of these issues arise in more than one type of case and many of the cases involve questions of considerable complexity which have never come before an English court prior to the present litigation, a fact which may explain the presence of some 30 counsel in one of the cases.

Actions against the ITC

The first reported case in the ITC saga was *Standard Chartered Bank v ITC* [1986] 3 All ER 257. This case concerned a loan of £10 million made by the bank to the ITC in 1982 and renewed in August 1985 under a facility letter, clause 7 of which provided that:

> 'This facility letter shall be governed by and interpreted in accordance with English law and you hereby irrevocably submit to the non-exclusive jurisdiction of the High Court of Justice in England and consent to the giving of any relief and/or the issue of any process for enforcement or otherwise against you.'

Following the announcement of 24 October 1985, the bank treated the ITC as being in default and sued to recover the loan and the outstanding interest, not surprisingly taking the view that clause 7 of the facility letter amounted to a waiver of immunity by the ITC within the meaning of article 6(1)(a) of the 1972 Order.

The ITC applied to set aside the writ, arguing on three grounds that it was immune from suit. First, it maintained that article 6(1)(a) did not apply to contractual claims since article 23 of the Headquarters Agreement, which had to be taken into account in interpreting the order, envisaged that all such claims against the ITC would be settled by arbitration so that the question of waiver would not arise in a contractual context. Bingham J rejected this interpretation, which was difficult to sustain given the clear wording of article 6(1)(a). The Headquarters Agreement required the insertion of an arbitration clause only in contracts between the ITC and United Kingdom residents or bodies incorporated, or having their principal place of business, in the United Kingdom. Article 23 did not, therefore, apply to all contractual claims. Although the failure to insert an arbitration provision in the facility letter meant that the ITC was in breach of its obligations to the United Kingdom under article 23 of the Headquarters Agreement, that breach did not preclude the bank from suing on the letter in the English courts.

Secondly, the ITC maintained that article 6(1)(a) of the 1972 Order applied only to a specific waiver made after proceedings had begun and not to a general anticipatory waiver, ie that the ITC was subject to the same rules on waiver as used to apply to States, following decisions like *Kahan v Pakistan Federation* [1951] 2 KB 1003, prior to the enactment of s 2 of the State Immunity Act 1978. The ITC relied in part on a United Nations study of the General Convention on Privileges and Immunities of the United Nations 1946. This argument was also rejected as a matter of interpretation, the judge holding that there was nothing in the text of article 6(1)(a) to suggest that waiver had to occur after proceedings had begun and that the UN study was of little assistance since it did not form part of the *travaux preparatoires* of the Headquarters Agreement and was in any event inconclusive.

Finally, the ITC argued that the 1972 Order had to be interpreted in the light of the law of sovereign immunity as it had stood in 1972. At that date, England still adhered to the doctrine of absolute immunity. Although that doctrine had been superseded, so far as States were concerned, by the State Immunity Act 1978 and a series of well known judicial decisions, it had never been repealed for international organisations. Bingham J emphatically rejected this argument. International organisations like the ITC were not to be equated with sovereign States. They had no common law immunity and possessed only such immunity as was granted to them by legislation. Moreover, in matters of immunity he held that it was important that the English courts should keep in step with the courts of other countries. By 1972 the doctrine of absolute immunity had been discarded in most States: the English courts had then been out of line with most of the world and there was no need to perpetuate the error.

It is understood that, following this decision, the bank and the ITC negotiated a settlement under which the bank received most of the money which it was claiming. Most plaintiffs have, however, been confronted with serious problems in seeking to enforce any judgment or arbitral award against the ITC. Since the total amount owed by the ITC far exceeds the property and funds in its possession, attempts at enforcement have concentrated upon various schemes for proceeding against the Member States of the ITC. These are discussed in the next section. In one case, however, an attempt was made to levy execution against the property of the ITC itself.

In *Maclaine Watson & Co v ITC (No 2)* [1987] 3 All ER 886 the applicants were members of the London Metal Exchange who had obtained an arbitration award against the ITC for approximately £6 million for breach of a number of contracts for the sale and purchase of tin. When this award was not satisfied, the applicants obtained judgment against the ITC for that sum but still received no payment. After an unsuccessful attempt to enforce the judgment by a form of proceeding against the Member States (a case which is discussed in the next section), they sought to levy execution upon the property of the ITC itself. However, since they received no reply to their enquiries as to the extent and whereabouts of that property, they applied to the court under RSC Ord 48, for an order that an officer of the ITC attend before a master to be orally examined regarding the extent and location of the ITC's assets.

Millett J held that the court had no jurisdiction to make the order requested under Ord 48, because Ord 48 applied only to individuals and bodies corporate and the ITC was neither. It was a creation of treaty and, although the 1972 Order conferred upon it the *capacities* of a body corporate, the ITC did not possess the *status* of a body corporate in English law. That did not mean that the ITC could not be subjected to an order of the kind sought—its capacities included a capacity to be subjected to legal process—but since it did not fall into either of the categories to which Ord 48 applied the court lacked the jurisdication to so subject it. However, Millett J was clearly unimpressed with the ITC's attitude to the applicants' request for information, describing the ITC as behaving 'more like a disreputable private debtor concerned only to hinder and delay his creditors than the responsible international organisation that it claims to be' (ibid at 888). He held that the court had an inherent jurisdiction, which was not subject to the limitations of Ord 48, to make the order sought, since it was the policy of the court, within proper limits to prevent a defendant from concealing his assets so as to deny a successful plaintiff the fruits of his judgment.

Millett J recognised that the Executive Chairman of the ITC, on whom the 1972 Order conferred the full immunities of a diplomatic agent, could not be required to attend for examination. He held, however, that the same was not true of the other officers of the ITC who enjoyed immunity only in respect of things done or omitted to be done by them in the performance of their official duties. He rejected an ITC submission that these officers were immune from any legal process to compel them to give evidence about anything known by them by virtue of their official position (ibid at 892):

> 'It is the process itself, that is to say the order of the court, not the evidence which must be in respect of things done or omitted to be done by the officers in question. The order which the appellants seek does not arise from, and is not in respect of anything done or omitted to be done by any of the ITC's officers.'

Attempts to obtain payment from the members of the ITC

The most interesting cases to date in the tin litigation have involved attempts by the ITC's creditors to enforce their claims against the Member States. So far these attempts have taken three different forms: (1) an attempt to have the ITC wound up under s 665 of the Companies Act 1985; (2) an attempt to have a receiver appointed in respect of the 'relevant assets' of the ITC, namely the alleged right of the ITC to require indemnity from its members; and (3) a direct action by creditors against the members.

The winding-up action

In *Re International Tin Council* [1987] 1 All ER 890, Amalgamated Metal Trading Ltd ('AMT'), which had obtained an arbitration award against the ITC for some £5.3 million presented a petition for the compulsory winding up of the ITC under s 665 of the Companies Act 1985. The making of a winding-up order in respect of a company means that the management of the company's affairs is entrusted to a liquidator who is required to apply the assets of the company in satisfaction of the company's liabilities. In the event that those assets are insufficient, the liquidator has the power, under ss 671 and 674, to call upon the members of the company to contribute, in accordance with their obligations under the company's constitution, to make good the shortfall. AMT maintained that the terms of s 665 were wide enough to cover the ITC and that it was just and equitable that the ITC should be wound up, so that the creditors would have available to them the right to enforce against the Member States their liability to contribute to the ITC's debts under s 671. The ITC maintained that as an international organisation established by treaty it was not subject to the winding-up jurisdiction of the English courts and, in the alternative, that it was entitled to immunity in the present action by virtue of article 6 of the 1972 Order.

Millett J found in favour of the ITC on both points. He began by noting that the action raised fundamental questions about the status of the ITC in English and international law. He held that the ITC was an international body corporate created by treaty, the ITA, and possessing legal personality in international law. The judge relied upon the decision of the International Court of Justice in the *Case of Reparations for Injuries suffered in the Service of the United Nations* [1949] ICJ Reports 174 (a case which held that the United Nations had legal personality vis-à-vis a non-member State and that this personality included the capacity to bring an international claim concerning the assassination of Count Bernadotte, the Chief UN Truce Negotiator in the Middle East). The ITA did not, however, confer upon the ITC personality in English law. The status and capacities of the ITC in English law were governed by the International Organisations Act 1968 and the 1972 Order. The 1972 Order gave the ITC the capacities but not the status of a body corporate.

The terms of s 665 were wide enough, the judge held, to be capable of covering an association like the ITC but he took the view that Parliament had not intended that they should apply to an international organisation created by treaty. A winding-up order would be inconsistent with the continued operation of the ITA and the Headquarters Agreement in accordance with their terms. It would compel the Government of the United Kindom either to be in breach of its obligations under those treaties or to attempt to withdraw from them. Moreover, Millett J thought that it was out of the question that an English court would enforce contributions from the Member States under s 671 of the Companies Act. Any obligations on the part of the Member States were derived from the ITA and the extent and nature of those obligations were questions which were not justiciable in an English court. The judge evidently felt that, since the ITC had been created by a treaty between several States, it would be inappropriate for one of those States to assume the power to wind up the organisation. While such considerations could not prevail in the face of legislation which was clearly designed to confer a winding-up power in respect of an international organisation, they were relevant in seeking to determine the intentions of Parliament when a court was asked to interpret a provision as general in its terms as s 665.

The decision on the first argument raised by the ITC rendered a decision on the immunity argument unnecessary. However, Millett J held that, even if he was wrong about the scope of s 665, the action would fail on the ground of the ITC's immunity. He rejected the argument that, in presenting the winding-up petition AMT was merely seeking to enforce the arbitration award in its favour so that the case fell within the exception to immunity in article 6(1)(c) of the 1972 Order (above). A winding-up order would actually preclude the enforcement of the arbitration award and substitute a right for AMT to participate with the ITC's other debtors in a distribution out of such assets as could be realised. Had there been any ambiguity in article 6(1)(c), Millett J announced that he would have felt obliged to construe the order in such a way as to bring it into line with the Headquarters Agreement to which it was intended to give effect and that he would therefore have resolved any ambiguity in favour of immunity.

The receivership action

In *Maclaine Watson & Co v ITC (No 1)* [1987] 3 All ER 787, which also came before Millett J, Maclaine Watson sought to enforce a judgment against the ITC. They applied for the appointment of a receiver under s 37 of the Supreme Court Act 1981 by way of equitable execution over the relevant assets of the ITC, namely the alleged right of the ITC to to be indemnified by, or to demand contributions from, the Member States. The idea behind the action was that the Member States were under an obligation to indemnify the ITC in respect of its liabilities to Maclaine Watson but that the ITC was unwilling to enforce that obligation and had insufficient assets of its own to meet those liabilities. The appointment of a receiver would enable proceedings to be brought against the Member States in the name of the ITC, with any amounts thereby obtained being applied to discharge the ITC's debt to Maclaine Watson. This was a less drastic course of action than the attempt to wind up the ITC since it did not directly threaten the continued existence of the organisation.

Nevertheless, the receivership action failed for much the same reasons as did the winding-up action. Although Millett J held that in principle the court possessed the jurisdiction to appoint a receiver, it would only do so if the applicants could show that the ITC had an arguable cause of action against the Member States; in other words if it was shown that the assets over which the receiver would be appointed actually existed. Millet J considered that any right which the ITC might have to demand an indemnity from its members had to be derived either from the ITA or from an agreement between the Member States in augmentation of the ITA. In either event, it was grounded in international law and therefore was not justiciable in an English court. Millett J was prepared to accept that the relationship between the members might have been that of partnership and that the relationship of the members and the ITC would thus have been one of principal and agent, so that the members would be liable as principals on any contracts concluded by the ITC and governed by English law. A liability of that kind would have been enforceable in the English courts but only by the parties with whom the ITC had contracted and to whom (on this analysis) the obligation of the members would be owed, not by a receiver suing in the name of the ITC to enforce obligations owed by the members to the ITC.

The direct action against the states

Whereas the basis of both *Re The International Tin Council* and *Maclaine Watson (No* were attempts to take over the supposed rights of the ITC against the Member States, in a third action, *J H Rayner (Mincing Lane) Ltd v Department of Trade and Industry* [1987] BCLC 667, another group of creditors brought proceedings directly against the Member States. Staughton J gave a preliminary judgment in this action on 24 June 1987. At the time of writing, this judgment had not been reported and was under appeal. Extensive comment would therefore be inappropriate. Nevertheless, the decision cannot be completely overlooked as it forms an important part of the overall picture of the tin litigation.

The main points of Staughton J's judgment are as follows:

(a) On the question of the legal personality of the ITC and the liability of the members for the actions for the organisation, the judge held that it was unnecessary to decide whether, as a matter of international law, the international legal personality of the ITC necessarily excluded the liability of its members. In English law the ITC was not a corporate person but, by conferring on it the capacities of a body corporte, the 1972 Order in effect provided that for certain purposes it was to be treated as if it were a body corporate. The result was that its members were not laible for the contractual obligations of the ITC merely by virtue of their membership.

(b) While Staughton J thought that there was 'much to be said' for the view that the relationship of the members and the ITC was that of principal and agent, he considered that the terms of the contracts under which the ITC bought and sold tin excluded the possibility that the ITC had contracted as an agent for the members. Moreover, since an agency relationship could be established only by relying upon the terms of the ITA, a claim that the ITC had contracted as agent for its members would be non-justiciable.

Actions in which the ITC has intervened

The measures adopted by the Committee of the London Metal Exchange as a means of damage limitation after the collapse of the ITC (see p 211 above) have also led to litigation. In *Shearson Lehman Bros Inc v Maclaine Watson & Co Ltd* [1988] 1 All ER 116 the plaintiffs, who were not members of the Exchange, sued another tin broker, who was a member, and the Exchange Committee. Both sides intended to make use in the action of numerous documents which had originally come from the ITC. These documents had come into the possession of the parties by various means, including publication in the United States under the Freedom of Information Act and inclusion in a report of the House of Commons Select Committee on Trade and Industry. Most of the documents had originally been disclosed either by a Member State of the ITC (or members of a State's delegation to the ITC) or by officers or employees of the ITC. The ITC intervened in the action to claim that the documents were inadmissible on the ground that they were protected by the inviolability granted to ITC archives by Article 7 of the 1972 Order. The questions of principle which arose in relation to the admissibility of these documents were made the subject of a preliminary judgment by Webster J, which was eventually appealed to the House of Lords.

Lord Bridge, with whom the rest of the House agreed, held that article 7 of the 1972 Order had to be interpreted in the light of article 4 of the Headquarters Agreement, which gave a partial definition of 'archives'. On that basis, he decided that article 7 conferred inviolability upon all documents belonging to, or held by, the ITC and rejected the view, which had appealed to Webster J, that a distinction was to be drawn between documents relating to the transactions between the ITC and its members and those concerning the trading activities of the organisation. Lord Bridge also held that since the purpose of providing that the ITC's archives were to be inviolable was to protect the privacy of diplomatic communications, inviolability was not confined to protection against executive or judicial action, such as seizure of documents in the possession of the ITC or the issuing of an order for their production, but included a right not to have such documents used in court even if they had come lawfully into the hands of the parties to an action.

However once a document emanating from the ITC passed into the possession of a Member State or its representative, Lord Bridge held that it ceased to be held by or to belong to the ITC and thus to form part of the archives of the ITC. Lord Bridge noted that article 14 of the 1972 Order provided that the official papers of representatives of a Member State to the ITC were to be inviolable except in so far as the Member State concerned waived that inviolability. The logical inference to be drawn from that provision was that when the document passed into the hands of the representative of a Member State it was the Member State, not the ITC, which enjoyed protection in respect of that document and which had the authority to waive that protection. Lord Bridge thus drew a sharp distinction, in this context, between the ITC and its members, stating that he 'found it difficult to follow the argument of counsel for the ITC that in the conduct of its internal affairs the ITC could not be treated as distinct from its constituent members' (ibid at 123). Given that the ITC, in the winding up and receivership actions, and the Member States, in the *J H Rayner* action, have consistently argued that in the external matter of contracts concluded by the ITC the ITC must be seen as separate from its members. The theory that this distinction did not exist in relation to the internal affairs of the ITC was, perhaps, a little too subtle.

So far as the documents disclosed by officers or employees of the ITC were concerned, it was unclear whether or not these documents had been disclosed by persons with actual or ostensible authority to do so. Most of them appeared to have been disclosed to various third parties by officers of the ITC either, in the case of those disclosed before 24 October 1985, as part of an attempt to reassure the recipients about the ITC's financial position or, in the case of those disclosed after 24 October 1985, as part of the attempts to arrive at a negotiated settlement. The House of Lords held that a document communicated to a third party by someone with actual or ostensible authority to communicate it belonged, thereafter, to the recipient and thus ceased to be covered by the inviolability of ITC archives. That was not the case if the document was disclosed by someone who had no authority, actual or ostensible, to communicate it. However, this latter ruling was deprived of most of its significance by the decision of the House that the fact that the officer or employee disclosing the document was acting in the course of his employment at the time was strong prima facie evidence that he had at least ostensible authority to disclose the document in question. Lord Bridge regarded it as (ibid at 125-6):

> '... beyond argument that an officer or employee of the ITC authorised to approach a third party to reassure him of the financial stability of the ITC or, when that assurance was falsified, authorised to conduct negotiations for a settlement must thereby have been clothed with ostensible authority to supply any documents to the third party which might assist in promoting the authorised purpose.'

The ITC had sought to rely upon the decision in *Juan Ysmael & Co Inc v Government of the Republic of Indonesia* [1954] 3 All ER 236, in which the Privy Council had held that when a State was indirectly impleaded in proceedings regarding property to which it claimed title, it had only to show that its claim was not manifestly illusory in order to have the case stayed. The ITC argued that, by analogy, it had only to raise a prima facie case that a document formed part of its inviolable archives for the court to be obliged to hold that document to be inadmissible and that the parties to the action before the court were not permitted to controvert or challenge that prima facie evidence. Lord Bridge, however, expressed reluctance to see the rule in *Juan Ysmael* extended any further than was strictly necessary for the purpose of safeguarding the dignity of foreign sovereigns against being impleaded, directly or indirectly. The rule was not to be extended to require a court to decline to consider relevant and admissible evidence merely because a prima facie case had been made out for holding that that evidence constituted part of the inviolable archives of the State or organisation.

Conclusions

Two questions have been of fundamental importance in the litigation concerning the ITC: (1) what is the status of the ITC, or what is meant by saying that it has 'legal personality'? and (2) to what extent are rights and duties derived from international law non-justiciable in the English courts?

To date the English courts have answered the first question by holding that the ITC possesses legal personality in international law but have not attempted to determine the form of that personality or the consequences which flow from it in terms of the liability, if any, of the Member States for the acts of the organisation which they created. The answers to those questions are by no means clear. It is a mistake to assume that there is a single concept of international legal personality for international organisations, applicable alike to the United Nations and the Universal Postal Union as well as the ITC. The differences in the functions of those organisations and in their constitutions suggest that the nature of international legal personality varies from one organisation to another. The fact that contracts concluded by one international organisation do not entail the liability of its members should not, therefore, be treated as conclusive with regard to other organisations.

So far as the status of the ITC in English law is concerned, the courts have held that although it is not a body corporate over which they can exercise jurisdiction in the form of a winding-up order, it does have an existence—or must be treated as though it has an existence—separate from its members. While the status of the ITC in English law has, entirely correctly, been treated as distinct from its personality in international law, that distinction should not be taken too far. In particular, it should not be used as an excuse for imagining that questions of personality in international law are largely irrelevant in proceedings in the English courts. The courts have rightly endeavoured to interpret the 1972 Order, and other United Kingdom legislation, in such a way as to ensure compliance with what are perceived to be the international obligations of the United Kingdom. Yet the international obligations of the United Kingdom with regard to the ITC are bound up with the question: which of the attributes of international legal personality did the parties to the ITA intend to bestow upon the organisation which they created?

On justiciability, the courts have been consistent so far in holding that rights and obligations derived from the ITA or from any supplementary, informal agreement between States cannot be enforced in the English courts. This approach is in keeping with a long line of authorities such as *British Airways Board v Laker Airways Ltd* [1984] 3 All ER 39 (All ER Rev 1984, p 241) and, on a somewhat different point, *Buttes Gas and Oil Co v Hammer* [1981] 3 All ER 616. Nevertheless, it needs to be borne in mind that the tin litigation is very different from anything which has preceded it. If the parties to the ITA had sought to maintain the price of tin by entering into contracts for the purchase or sale of tin themselves, rather than by creating an international organisation to do so, none of them (with the possible exception of the EEC) would have been entitled to immunity in proceedings relating to those contracts. Under s 3 of the State Immunity Act 1978, such contracts would be classified as commercial transactions, as would any loan contracts entered into to provide the funds to sustain tin trading. Instead, however, the States concerned established, by treaty, an international organisation to sustain an orderly market in tin and to maintain the price of tin. While the degree of control exercised by the Member States over the day to day activities of the ITC is apparently a matter of dispute, it is clear that it was the members who determined the objectives of the ITC, the general methods by which it was to achieve them and the floor and ceiling prices which it was to maintain. Moreover, although the ITC was set up under international law, by means of an international instrument, its activities were predominantly commerical and it was central to the achievment of its objectives that it engaged heavily in trade on the London market. In these circumstances it is far from clear why, as a matter of principle, the English courts should refrain from enforcing any liability which might exist for the Member States to meet the ITC's liabilities merely because that liability is derived from a treaty and will thus entail consideration of transactions between States. As Millett J commented in *Re International Tin Council* [1987] 1 All ER 890 at 906: 'there is much to be said for the view that an unprecedented situation calls for an unprecedented solution'. The situation is sufficiently unprecedented for the courts to have scope to provide that solution.

[For a highly critical discussion of the events surrounding the collapse of the ITC, see the reports of the House of Commons Select Committee on Trade and Industry: HC Papers No 305, vols I and II, 1985–6, and No 71, 1986–7. The Government's reply is published as HC Paper No 457, 1985–6.]

Diplomatic immunity

Space permits only a brief comment on one case unconnected with the tin saga. *Fayed v Al-Tajir* [1987] 2 All ER 396 concerned a somewhat bizarre dispute which arose in the London embassy of the United Arab Emirates ('UAE'). In 1982 there was circulated in the embassy a memorandum which was critical of the plaintiff, a businessman who was said to be prominent in the affairs of the UAE. The memorandum was addressed to a member of the embassy staff and censured him for permitting the plaintiff to use the VIP lounge at Heathrow Airport. The defendant, who had been ambassador of the UAE to the United Kingdom until shortly before the circulation of the memorandum and who was still acting, though without any official status, in such a way that the staff of the embassy continued to regard him as possessing the authority of the ambassador, took responsibility for the publication of the memorandum. By the time the action came on for trial the defendant had been reappointed as ambassador but stated that he waived his diplomatic immunity. Nevertheless, he claimed that the memorandum was protected by absolute privilege as an internal embassy document.

After a long review of the legislation and cases relating to diplomatic privilege, Mustill LJ in the Court of Appeal took the view that none of the authorities laid down a rule of law which provided a clear solution to the case. Nevertheless, he decided that considerations of comity required that the plea of privilege be upheld. The background to this conclusion was said to be the twin principles that the law of nations, as relected in the Vienna Convention on Diplomatic Relations 1961 (the relevant parts of which had been incorporated into English law by the Diplomatic Privileges Act 1964), generally regarded embassy documents as sacrosanct and that there were situations in which the English courts would find it inexpedient to investigate the actions of a foreign State, even if they fell within their formal jurisdiction (ibid at 406–7).

Although there were numerous strange twists to this case—the curious status of the defendant at the time the memorandum was published, the fact that the defendant purported to waive diplomatic immunity whereas only the sending State has power to waive immunity in respect of one of its diplomats, and the inconsistency of at one and the same time waiving diplomatic immunity in respect of the person of the defendant yet asserting what was in effect a diplomatic immunity in respect of the document which was at the heart of the case—the decision, it is submitted, is a sensible application of the principle of non-justiciability. Whatever the arguments for setting aside, or at least qualifying, that principle in the tin litigation, *Fayed v Al-Tajir* was a case which cried out for its application.

Shipping Law

R. P. GRIME, BA, BCL
Professor of Law, University of Southampton

Notice of readiness

Disputes about 'arrived ships', 'weather working days' and 'notice of readiness' seem intimately connected with the last decade. The issue can be simply stated: in a voyage charterparty, the charterer is permitted by the terms of the charter so many days for loading or discharging the cargo (lay days) and if the operation is not completed in this time allowed, agreed damages for the overrun, demurrage, must be paid. When time begins to run is as important as which days count and which do not, and the clock is generally set in motion by a notice of readiness given by the owners to the charterers after the vessel has arrived at her destination.

When may such notice be given? Until the great case of *E L Oldendorff & Co Gmbh v Tradax Export SA, The Johanna Oldendorff* [1974] AC 479, the answer used to be given in terms of the so-called 'Parker test' or 'commercial area test', approved by the House of Lords in *Sociedad Financiera de Bienes Raices SA v Agrimpex Hungarian Trading Co for Agricultural Products, The Aello* [1961] AC 135, that in a voyage charterparty which names the port of commencement or destination (a 'port charterparty') the ship is an 'arrived ship' and may give notice of readiness when she reaches that part of a port where a ship can be loaded or unloaded when a berth is available. That test was rejected and replaced, in *The Johanna Oldendorff*, with the 'Reid test' which held a ship to be arrived at a port when she was within it and 'at the immediate and effective disposition of the charterer'.

The important question raised in *Bulk Transport Group Shipping Co Ltd v Seacrystal Shipping Ltd, The Kyzikos* [1987] 3 All ER 222 was whether a fog-bound ship can be an arrived ship. More precisely, whether a ship which had arrived at its port but could not proceed to a berth which was available to it because fog had closed down the pilot station, was in any different position under the Reid test than it would have been under the Parker test. According to the latter, provided the ship had arrived at the commercial area, notice might be given and the clock begin to tick away the hours of lay days notwithstanding weather conditions that inhibited the actual loading or discharge operation. Should the same be so with the Reid test or was it to be that the new language, 'at the charterer's immediate and effective disposition', imported the need for a degree of practically effective control over the vessel's movement by the charterer?

The answer given by the Court of Appeal (Lloyd LJ gave the substantial judgment) was that the Reid test had not introduced such a change. Despite Lord Reid himself having observed that 'geographical position is of secondary importance' the test was not intended to be based upon any substantially different factor. 'It is still a *position* which [Lord Reid] has in mind ([1987] 3 All ER at 228)'. After all, we are seeking a meaning for the phrase 'arrived ship', which must be an answer to the question: 'where must a ship be for a valid notice of readiness to be given'?

This short but important point was not directly addressed either by the arbitrator or by the High Court judge from whose decision the appeal had been taken. The reason was slightly unusual. The charterparty was not a simple port charterparty. It was a berth charterparty: one in which the ship might be thought not have arrived until she had reached the berth defined by the charter. And that might have been the case had not this contract also conferred upon the owners the right to give notice 'whether in berth or not'. The effect of that, said the arbitrator, was to convert the berth charterparty into a port charterparty. He did not address the subsequent question of whether a fog-bound vessel was 'arrived' or not. The judge took a different view, holding that the conferred power could only be exercised when the vessel was in port waiting for a berth to bcome available. In reaching that conclusion he relied upon clear dictum from the speech of Lord Diplock in *Federal Commerce and Naviagation Co Ltd v Export SA, The Maratha Envoy* [1978] AC 1.

Lloyd LJ did not follow that dictum. While he could see the commonsense of it, since the finding of a berth was generally the charterer's responsibility while the getting of the ship to it was the owner's job, he could not limit the generality nor the clarity of the phrase 'whether in berth or not'. It had the effect contended by the arbitrator. The berth charterparty so claused is a port charterparty. We must now await further judicial attention to be paid to the much more difficult companion phrase, not raised for decisions in *The Kyzikos*, 'whether at sea or not'. No doubt aware of this, Lloyd LJ indicated that the only natural limitation of the generality of the words that *were* before him might relate to place. For otherwise notice of readiness might be given when the vessel leaves, which is absurd. It must surely, in *some* sense, have arrived.

Actions in rem

As the business of shipping changes, those who provide services to ships of a new, and often of a less than new, variety regularly seek the advantages of the writ in rem and to that end their advisers scan the further reaches of s 20 of the Supreme Court Act 1981. In *The River Rima* [1987] 3 All ER 1, the plaintiffs, Tiphook Container Rentals Ltd, sought damages for conversion of their containers and for breach of the leasing agreement against Nigerian National Shipping Lines (NNSL). The defendants applied to Sheen J to have the writ in rem struck out. They failed. Their appeal to the Court of Appeal was however successful. Sir John Donaldson who gave the leading judgment presented a masterpiece of strict construction.

The ground most regularly used in cases where the in rem legitimacy of uncertain contractual relationships with ships is tested is that contained in s 20(2)(h) of the 1981 Supreme Court Act: 'Any claim arising out of any agreement relating to the carriage of goods in a ship or to the use or hire of a ship'. Very many agreements can loosely be said to relate to the use of ship. The leading case is *The Jade, The Eschersheim* [1976] 1 All ER 920, HL in which the House of Lords held that an agreement to render salvage services to a ship fell within that paragraph. In *The Sonia S* [1983] 2 Lloyd's Rep 63,

Sheen J had upheld a writ in rem under s 20(2)(h) in respect of a container leasing contract and had relied upon *The Jade*, emphasising that in both cases the function and purpose of the contract related to the commercial use of the ship.

But *The Jade* concerned two ships: the vessel in receipt of the services and the salvage vessel itself hired to render them. Paragraph (h) could be satisfied by regarding the latter as the ship whose 'use or hire' was contemplated. Such a narrow view had commended itself to Lord Keith in the *Gatoil International Inc v Arkwright-Boston Manufacturers Mutual Insurance Co* [1985] 1 All ER 129 (All ER Rev 1985, p 239), in which the House of Lords held that a claim for cargo insurance premiums was not within the admittedly somewhat different Scottish equvalent of s 20(2)(h). Lord Keith had felt that *The Sonia S* 'should be overruled'.

In *The River Rima* therefore the argument in the main kept clear of paragraph (h). Instead the relevance of paragraphs (m) and (n) were tested: '(m) any claim in respect of goods or materials supplied to a ship for her operation or maintenance; (n) any claim in respect of the construction, repair or equipment of a ship . . . '

In the Court of Appeal this was no more successful. The direct connection between the contract and the description in the paragraph insisted on in *The Jade* and *Gatoil*, whose lack had fatally flawed the decision in *The Sonia S*, was as necessary as in s 29(2)(m). It was agreed that paragraph (n) had no application. And such close connection was lacking. Sir John Donaldson MR, while accepting that the container leasing agreement enabled NNSL the better to carry on its business, nevertheless held that it was not 'for the operation of a ship'.

Furthermore the container supplied by the plaintiffs had not been exclusively used on *The River Rima*. The leasing arrangement was wider and the alleged breach more extensive. The ship was the subject matter of the proceedings for the usual practical reason that she was accessible. So apart from the question of whether the generality in such an agreement constituted a further factor which militated against the necessary close connection with the operation of the ship, there also remained the question of *which* ship might be arrestable. Section 21(4) requires that the claim arise 'in connection with a ship' and that the persons liable (in personam) must be the owner, etc, of that ship when the cause of action arises. Since the containers supplied to NNSL were to be used both on their ships and upon other ships, there was in Sir John Donaldson's view, also insufficient precision to satisfy the connection required by s 21(4).

Which brings us finally to the point with which Sir John Donaldson MR opened his judgment. At first instance Sheen J had been 'much influenced' by the outcome of similar proceedings against a sister ship of *The River Rima*, *The River Jimini*, decided by the District Court of Rotterdam in June 1984. That arrest had been upheld: Sheen J had been properly conscious of the need to achieve a common international approach in the application of what was in trust the enactment of an international convention, the Brussels Arrest Convention of 1952.

Sir John Donaldson was much less influenced. While accepting the proposition that international comity was a good thing he pointed out that there is as yet no 'established body of law as to the meaning of

Article 1(1)(b) of the Brussels Convention, which is the equivalent of paragraph (m)'. Further he was able to offer several points of distinction between *The River Rima* and *The River Jimini*. Nonetheless as Europe draws closer, as the consequences of the Civil Jurisdiction and Judgments Act of 1976 become more familiar and as 1992 gets nearer, one may be allowed to regret that a more outward-looking style was not considered appropriate.

Liability and limitation

In the All ER Rev 1986, p 256, we commented on the decision of the Court of Appeal in *McDermid v Nash Dredging & Reclamation Ltd* [1986] 2 All ER 676. It will be recalled that Mr McDermid, a young deckhand, was seriously injured while working aboard the tug Ina, in an accident largely caused by the irresponsible behaviour of the tug master, Captain Sas. McDermid was employed by Nash but was working in Swedish waters on a dredging contract between Stevin, Nash's Dutch parent company, and the Swedish Government. The tug Ina belonged to Stevin who employed Captian Sas. It was being used by Nash who provided an alternate master and members of the crew. At first instance Staughton J had found for McDermid, holding Nash vicariously liable for Captain Sas. The Court of Appeal had not adopted that approach, holding Nash in breach of a general non-delegable duty to care for the safety of their servants, and further held that Nash could not limit liability under the 1957 Limitations Convention (as enacted in the Merchant Shipping (Liability of Ship Owners and Others) Act 1958) since they were not within the extended definition of 'shipowner' nor was Captain Sas their servant.

The House of Lords ([1987] 2 All ER 878) affirmed that decision in both respects. In the course of a typically careful judgment (the major judgment: Lord Hailsham delivered a short concurring speech, the others concurred generally) Lord Brandon commented that 'with great respect to the elaborate judgment of [the Court of Appeal] I think it has treated the case as more difficult than it really is' ([1987] 2 All ER at 887). It may be recalled that, having decided that Captain Sas did not come into the category of persons for whom Nash was vicariously liable, the Court of Appeal saw some difficulty in holding that his behaviour had caused a breach in the, admittedly non-delegable, duty to provide McDermid with a safe system of work. One might regard the system as safe or unsafe (or even as had Staughton J, 'not unsafe') but it was not really the system of giving two knocks on the wheelhouse wall that had accounted for Mr McDermid's legs. Captain Sas had simply not waited for the two knocks at all. Neill LJ in the Court of Appeal had offered a modern synthesis of the old personal non-delegable duties, which included the provision of a safe system of work, and had found general non-delegable duty to take reasonable care of the safety of employees, which might include 'seeing that the safe system was carried out'.

Lord Brandon returned to the tried language of *Wilsons & Clyde Coal Co v English* [1938] AC 57. The non-delegable duty was the old-fashioned one of providing a safe system of work. Provision had 'two aspects: (a) the devising of such a system and (b) the operation of it'. Therefore 'for this failure by Captain Sas to operate the system which he had devised, the defendants as the plaintiff's employers were personally and not vicariously liable to him' ([1987] 2 All ER at 887). Despite Lord Brandon's protestations, it is hard to see this as a simplification of the Court of Appeal's approach.

The limitation point was also affirmed. One further issue was incidentally addressed: ie, whether Nash might have been brought into the primary category of those entitled to limit under the 1957 convention. It was urged before the House that Nash might be considered to be 'interested in' the Ina, since they were using her to carry out work they were engaged on. No, said Lord Brandon, the expression 'means a person having a legal or equitable interest in the ship'. Such argument would also presumably apply to the phrase 'in possession' and exclude Nash, despite their having the right to use the Ina and put crew aboard her. But what of 'operator'? As we pointed out on the last occasion the point will rapidly become academic with the advance of the new 1976 Limitation Convention, now in force.

The Goring in the Court of Appeal

The Goring [1986] 1 All ER 475 (All ER Rev 1986, p 247) gave us both food for thought and entertainment last year. The saviours of The Goring, a Thames passenger launch, five gentlemen members of the Island Bohemian Club at Reading, issued a writ in rem for salvage award and Sheen J refused to strike it out on the application of the owners. The Court of Appeal, [1987] 2 All ER 246, by a majority of two to one, reversed the decision of Sheen J. Thus, well trimmed, The Goring sailed on to the House of Lords.

The question is simple: can salvage be claimed in non-tidal waters? It is, however, susceptible to two quite different answers each of which may inform or even confuse the other. One answer might be: no, for only the Admiralty Court has jurisdiction in salvage claims, and the Admiralty Court has no jurisdiction in non-tidal waters. Second one might say: no, for salvage services can only properly be rendered to maritime property which must be on the high seas or in territorial waters, which does not include the Thames at Reading. Of course in either case a positive conclusion might be reached.

It is one thing to distinguish the jurisdictional from the substantive in this way, but since the jurisdiction of the Admiralty Court is itself partly expressed in terms of a list of substantive maritime claims, the theory and the practice can and do get horribly involved. At first instance Sheen J based himself substantially upon the statutory extention of Admiralty jurisdiction during the nineteenth century to events occurring in 'the body of the county' and perceived good policy reasons for not drawing a substantive definition narrowly along the line of tidal waters so as to defeat the claim.

In the Court of Appeal, Sir John Donaldson MR, who dissented, was also clear that there was no general geographical limitation on Admiralty jurisdiction which would confine the Admiralty Marshall to tidal waters. The questions for him was principally a substantive one: whether salvage rewards were to be payable for services rendered in non-tidal waters.

'The issue is thus whether we can and should further develop and build on those ancient sources so as to extend the English maritime law of salvage to operations taking place on non-tidal waters. If this is too overtly revolutionary to be stomached, it can be approached differently by enquiring whether the various jurisdictional restrictions on the Admiralty Court have obscured the fact that the maritime law of England always did extend to non-tidal waters' ([1987] 2 All ER at 252).

He followed this ringing call for creativity with an analysis of the essential principles of salvage. He distinguished the three elements: the equity of rewarding a volunteer who confers a benefit; the policy of encouraging salvage for the benefit of seafarers; international comity. Relying in respect of the third principle upon Article 1 of the 1910 Brussels Salvage Convention, and in general, as had Sheen J, on the inconvenience of an entitlement to a salvage reward arbitrarily ceasing at Teddington Lock, the Master of the Rolls concluded that the writ should stand.

His brethren disagreed. Bingham LJ gave a substantial judgment. He began with the substantive issue. Salvage was always rendered at sea. The following examples, such as the Great Lakes, were explicable by reference to express statutory extension. As for Article 1 of the Brussels Convention, it had never been enacted in the United Kingdom. There was good reason to confine salvage to the sea: the reward was payable because of exposure to and success over the 'peculiar hazards and exigencies' of the sea. He then moved on to the jurisdictional question. It was not, he allowed, enough that the substantive law of salvage had not yet been developed to cover non-tidal waters. Perhaps it should. But the claim for a salvage reward asserted in rem would seek to activate and utilise a specially extensive jurisdiction, Admiralty jurisdiction, with powers of arrest, maritime lien, etc. The statutory definitions and extensions to the jursidiction of the Court of Admiralty, which Bingham LJ also closely examined, showed only that it had been intended to extend Admiralty jurisdiction to tidal areas of the sea 'within the body of the county'. In his view it was right so to confine Admiralty jurisdiction to the sea. Arrest, liens and other such facilities, more or less conforming to an internationally agreed standard, were developed for the high seas and international waterways where vessels of all nations leave and enter several jurisdictions in the course of their business. There is neither need nor demand for this in the confined waters of the upper Thames.

Ralph Gibson LJ offered, in a short judgment in which he concurred with Bingham LJ, another set of policy condiserations. He would not wish to extend the substantive law of salvage because, inter alia, he perceived a wider and perhaps more significant development on land which would not be assisted by the introduction of the maritime right to reward for meritorious salvage. He referred to the doctrine of 'necessitous intervention' whereby interveners might be compensated: but not, he felt, beyond the recovery of their expenses. Clearly salvage and restitution are distinguishable and should, in the view of Ralph Gibson LJ, remain so.

The appeal in this case has, at the time of writing, been decided by the House of Lords, which unanimously affirmed the majority decision of the Court of Appeal.

Solicitors

BRIAN HARVEY, MA, LLM
Solicitor, Professor of Property Law, University of Birmingham

As in previous years, most of the action concerning the role, duties and liabilities of solicitors took place on the political or legislative stage. But amongst the small crop of apparently innocuous reported cases, one reveals the apparent activities of a poltergeist and another a brutal kidnapping incident. We should not be surprised if behind the dry statement of law there lies a set of facts which can be exceedingly bizarre and the proper performance of a solicitor's duty is not always as apparent at the time as it may subsequently appear on reading the cut and dried verdict in a law report. These reflections apply also to the two cases which stress the ease with which a duty of care, not always to a client, can be broken and the consequences of giving undertakings too lightly, badly phrased or of failing to be assiduous in performing an undertaking.

A solicitor's liability to pay costs personally

The High Court of England and Wales has an ancient jurisdiction to exercise control over its own officers, and these include all who are admitted to the role of solicitors. This principle is reflected in RSC Ord 62, r 8. Rule 8(1) runs as follows:

> 'Subject to the following provisions of this rule, where in any proceedings costs are incurred improperly or without reasonable cause or are wasted by undue delay or by any other misconduct or default, the Court may make against any solicitor whom it considers to be responsible (whether personally or through a servant or agent) an order—(a) disallowing the costs as between the solicitor and his client; and (b) directing the solicitor to repay to his client costs which the client has been ordered to pay to other parties to the proceedings; or (c) directing the solicitor personally to indemnify such other parties against costs payable by them.'

This rule was in issue in *Orchard v SE Electricity Board* [1987] 1 All ER 95 before the Court of Appeal. The facts, which are referred to below, are extraordinary, but the key issue was whether the unsuccessful plaintiff's solicitors in this case should be asked to pay the costs of the case, counsel having applied for such an order on the basis that all who had been involved in the plaintiff's case, including the plaintiff's leading and junior counsel should be condemned and so, presumably, the solicitors if ordered to pay costs, might have claims for indemnity from others.

Sir John Donaldson MR gave a useful clarification of the extent of a solicitor's libility to pay costs in the light of Lord Denning MR's remarks in *Kelly v London Transport Executive* [1982] 2 All ER 842 at 850–51. Sir John Donaldson's view was that it was doubtful whether a solicitor owed a duty to the opposing party where the solicitor was acting with the authority of his client and was not carrying on the litigation on his own account.

However, the duty was undoubtedly owed to the court. The extent of the duty was to conduct the litigation with due propriety and the court could, in the exercise of its traditional jurisdiction over its own officers, order the solicitor to compensate the opposing party where the solicitor is in breach of that duty to the court. Sir John went on to state his doubts whether members of the Bar owed any independent duty to their lay client's opponent, though they did owe a duty to the court as well as to their own client. He went on to point out that the courts had never asserted any jurisdiction over members of the Bar in this way 'and it would seriously undermine the independence of the Bar if they did so'—though this proposition, made obiter, may be doubted. The question here was whether the solicitors had acted in so unreasonable a manner that the jurisdiction as to costs could successfully be invoked. Sir John emphasised that it was a jurisdiction which fell to be exercised with care and discretion and only in clear cases. It was not for solicitors or counsel to impose a pre-trial screen through which a litigant must pass before he could put forward a complaint or a defence to the court. On the other hand, no solicitor or counsel should lend his assistance to a litigant if he is satisfied that the initiation or further prosecution of the claim is mala fide or for an ulterior purpose or in circumstances where an abuse of the process of the court is involved or the proceedings are unjustifiably oppressive.

There is a further complexity. Circumstances can arise in which the impugned solicitor is hampered by his duty of confidentiality to his client from which only his client can release him unless the overriding authority of legislation (eg Legal Aid (General) Regulations 1980, reg 74) can be invoked. Accordingly, there are circumstances where justice required that the solicitor should be given the benefit of any doubt.

The bizarre nature of the facts in this case has already been referred to. It appeared that the plaintiff had been living with his wife and 15-year old son in a semi-detached cottage. The family was troubled by substantial quantities of water appearing in different parts of the cottage, such as the floor, ceilings, and near light sockets. There were other odd phenomena. As Sir John Donaldson put it, these included ([1987] 1 All ER 95 at 100):

> 'the uncovenanted and unexplained movement of physical objects within the rooms and damage to the ceilings and pipework to an extent which caused the cottage to become uninhabitable and the plaintiff and his family to leave for rented accommodation.'

The plaintiff conceived the notion that the phenomena were caused by the escape of electricity through the earth under the cottage. This escaped power heated water, he thought, to a point at which it became steam and caused the water to change into hydrogen and oxygen gases which in turn caused the unexplained movement of physical objects. Somewhat surprisingly expert advice was available to the plaintiff at the trial which supported these theories. The trial judge, who referred to his own findings as 'extraordinary', came to the conclusion that although the plaintiff and his wife were elderly people of excellent previous character and apparently sane, and who furthermore had no motivation to cause these odd events to happen (with the consequence that they had to move out to temporary rented accommodation elsewhere), nevertheless a member of the family must have been responsible for the water appearing. This was despite the independent testimony from the neighbourhood of persons of good character who stated that they believed that they had seen water appearing on the floors and elsewhere in the plaintiff's house.

Although these facts sound barely credible and the plaintiff's conclusion that it was all the fault of the South Eastern Electricity Board might appear ludicrous, nevertheless at *the time* many believed that this was the only explanation for the phenomena.

The plaintiff had succeeded in obtaining legal aid on the basis of a nil contribution. An application by the Electricity Board solicitors at an early stage that the legal aid certificate should be discharged was not accepted. The Board were alleging that the damage in question was self-inflicted and this was clearly quite unacceptable to the plaintiff and something which the legal aid authorities could not be expected to accept lightly. Nor was there any indication by the legal aid authorities that they were dissatisfied with the way in which the solicitors and counsel involved for the plaintiff had discharged their duties to the fund. The position was further complicated by the death of the plaintiff and the absence of any waiver of the plaintiff's privilege with regard to relevant communications by the plaintiff's personal representatives.

In support of their contention that the solicitor should pay the costs in question personally, it was argued that no competent counsel or solicitor and no competent expert could possibly have supported the plaintiff's claim. However, this did not explain how it was that water apparently ran uphill under the plaintiff's cottage, leaving the footing dry, through a layer of bitumen, and in some case also through a damp proof membrane, and then through a layer of thermo-plastic tiles leaving them undisturbed. The other semi-detached cottage was not also similarly affected and the electricity board stated that this experience was unique in the 65-year history of electricity supply. As Sir John Donaldson MR said, (ibid at 102):

> 'whilst I have to agree that all this takes some swallowing, I am far from convinced that it would necessarily have looked like this to the plaintiff's solicitors, counsel and experts preparing for the trial or earlier. The conclusive element . . . is hindsight, knowledge that all these factors were proved at the trial and the plaintiff was quite unable to overcome them.'

The trial judge had found that leading counsel, his junior and solicitors had acted entirely properly. The Court of Appeal unanimously stated that the judge's conclusions were unassailable.

Sir John Donaldson MR added one very important point. He stated that there could be no objection to an application under RSC Ord 62, r 8 at the conclusion of a hearing given appropriate facts. However it would be quite another matter where such an application is threatened *during* or *prior to* the hearing (ibid at 104):

> 'Threats to apply on the basis that the proceedings must fail not only make the solicitor something in the nature of a co-defendant, but they may well, and rightly, make him all the more determined not to abandon his client, thereby losing a measure of objectivity.'

There must be, however, circumstances where it is appropriate to state to one's opponents a properly held view that the opponent's client's case is so wholly lacking in reasonableness that an application under RSC Ord 62, r 8 might be considered in due course. Or has the Court of Appeal now ruled that any such threat would be improper? Whilst one can see the very real danger of abuse, it might be thought that a total ban on drawing the other parties' solicitors' attention to this rule as to personal payment of costs is going rather too far. But however the position is viewed, on the very strange facts in this case the Court of Appeal showed themselves to be sensitive to the sometime acute problems of giving objective advice in complex day-to-day litigation which, with the benefit of hindsight, take on a different perspective. The end result was undoubtedly fair.

Negligence

Negligence in conveyancing has no doubt accounted for a significant proportion of claims on indemnity policies. In most cases whether there has been a breach of a duty of care is fairly obvious. There are additional hazards in leasehold conveyancing and *County Personnel (Employment Agency) Limited v Allan R Pulver & Co* [1987] 1 All ER 289, CA illustrates one rather unusual hurdle.

The plaintiff instructed the defendant firm of solicitors to act in connection with a proposed under-lease. The proposal was for a 15-year under-lease of two ground floor rooms to be used as business premises, negotiations being with the head lessee. The problem in question here concerned the terms of the rent. The proposed under-lease contained an unusual rent review provision. This was that for the term of 15 years the rent was reviewable upwards in the 5th and 10th years by an amount equivalent to the initial rent of £3,500 'increased by the same percentages as the landlord's rent has been increased under the terms of the head lease'.

Although the deceased managing clerk who dealt with the conveyancing at this stage appears to have conscientiously gone over the transaction with his clients, it was clear that the full implications of this very unusual rent review provision were not then fully appreciated. What happened was that the rent under the head lease, originally fixed at £2,250 (found to be the true open market rental) was by agreement under the rent revision clause in the head lease increased to £5,800. The yearly rent payable pursuant to the under-lease, namely £3,500 (a figure at least three times higher than the market rent for the two ground floor rooms in question) rose 'by the same percentages as the landlord's rent has been increased under the terms of the head lease' to £9,022. This compared with the open market value of the two rooms in question of £2,600. The plaintiff understandably refused to pay this rent and the lessor eventually accepted a surrender of the sub-lease on payment of £16,000 plus the sum of £2,761 representing the increased rent payable since the rent review date under the head lease. The plaintiff claimed that sum plus £17,000 lost on the prospective sale of the underlease and goodwill, as damages for negligence against his former solicitors.

In deciding whether or not negligence was present here the Court of Appeal again warned against the dangers of hindsight ([1987] 1 All ER 289 at 295, per Bingham J): 'The correct approach is to view matters as they should have presented themselves to a reasonably careful and competent solicitor' at the material time.

What should have been present in the mind of a 'reasonably careful and competent solicitor' in the circumstances? Apart from the circumstances surrounding the transaction, which might suggest that the head-lessee was out to make a significant commercial profit from the transaction, the main point was the most unusual form of the rent review clause. Bingham J asserted that this should (ibid at 295):

'have caused a reasonably careful and competent solicitor to think about this clause more carefully than would have been appropriate had the clause been in a familiar standard form. It would have been appropriate to consider whether there was anything in the terms of this clause which might prove disadvantageous to the client.'

The obvious problem here was that the under-lessee was required, on both rent reviews, to pay the *same percentage increase* as was made between two other parties to a figure of which the plaintiff and his legal adviser were unaware. Particularly if the head lease rent were below the market level, the percentage uplift to be applied to it at the first rent review would be greater than the percentage uplift experienced in rents generally. The result of this would be that the under-lessee's rent would be increased by more than any general increase in rents warranted. The judge went on to say (ibid at 296) that even assuming that the client was:

'not a naive innocent in the commercial world, I regard this as a classic case in which the professional legal adviser was bound to warn his client of risks which should have been apparent to him but would, on a simple reading of the clause, have been most unlikely to occur to him.'

There was a further issue on the question of the quantum of damages. The case was remitted for the assessment of damages on the basis that the plaintiff appeared to be entitled to what it had cost to surrender the under-lease, and possibly to the value of a saleable lease and goodwill, depending on whether the plaintiff could have negotiated such a lease and if so where, and to what extent that would have affected its goodwill.

A second case involving negligence involved far more bizarre facts. *Al-Kandari v JR Brown & Co* [1987] 2 All ER 302 involved the basic point as to whether the defendant solicitors owed a duty of care to the plaintiff personally pursuant to the terms of an undertaking given by their client to the court in matrimonial proceedings. If there was such a duty, a further problem arose as to whether the defendant solicitors had been in breach of that duty on the facts.

The circumstances of this case were described by French J as 'disgraceful'. In 1981 the plaintiff's then husband had absconded from Bristol to Kuwait with their two small children and the plaintiff had not seen her children since then. The plaintiff and her husband had met whilst being students at Bristol. They were married in Kuwait in 1978 and two children were subsequently born. The matrimonial history involved violence and devious behaviour on behalf of the husband. In 1981 he removed the children to Kuwait. After certain orders had been obtained in the county court the wife flew out to Kuwait and both parties accompanied the children back to

England, the childrens' names being entered on the husband's passport and not the wife's. Shortly afterwards a violent scene ensued after which the wife took the children to Hereford where her parents lived, but to an address unknown to her husband. Custody proceedings ensued. The husband eventually agreed to an order that the custody, care and control of the children should be granted to the wife with access to the husband. The husband undertook, inter alia, to deposit his passport with his solicitors. He subsequently did this.

Later on the husband indicated that he wished to use his passport in order to return to Kuwait and that he wanted the childrens' names removed from it. The defendant solicitors informed the plaintiff's solicitors of this and forwarded the passport to their London agents with instructions to take it to the Kuwaiti Embassy to get the childrens' names removed. In the ensuing correspondence it was agreed specifically in correspondence that the husband's solicitors would not release the passport to their client. The same point was made clear to the defendant's London agents.

As it transpired, the Embassy stated that it needed a copy of the court order before an amendment could be made and that the passport would be retained at the Embassy meanwhile. The husband told the defendants that he would take the necessary documents to the Embassy the next day. The defendants relied on an assurance from the Embassy that the passport would be safe. No-one was present when the husband was at the Embassy and the defendants did not inform the plaintiff's solicitors of what had happened. Due to mischances which were not fully explained, the passport while in the Embassy's possession was inadvertently released to the husband.

There then followed the episodes which the judge understandably dubbed 'disgraceful'. Having obtained his passport, the husband telephoned the plaintiff and prevailed on her to allow him access to the children on the following Sunday. He duly arrived on the Sunday morning and persuaded the wife and the two children to accompany him for a car drive. The husband drove to a place where a large van was waiting. The wife was then snatched out of the car by two large women who forced her into the back of the waiting van. She was then bound and gagged as well as being assaulted by the male driver of the van. She was threatened with execution. The van was then driven off and parked near a railway station. Some time later the wife managed to break herself free and her bangs and cries inside the van were heard. Eventually she was freed. She had severe brusing and rope burns to her wrists. Her hands were swollen and she had a lump on her head. The wife never saw the children again. Her claim for damages was in respect of the costs incurred in attempts made by members of her family and others to recover the children in Kuwait and also for the shock, distress and physical injury she had suffered.

The first question was whether the defendant's solicitors owed the plaintiff wife a duty of care, and if so whether this was in tort or in contract. The judge's answer to this question was that the defendants did owe a duty to the plaintiff in tort. This was a duty to take reasonable care that the passport should not leave the possession of themselves, or, where relevant, their agents. They owed to her a further duty to take all reasonable steps to prevent harm coming to her from any failure to comply with any relaxation of the implied undertaking to retain the husband's passport and not release it to him. (The judge emphasised that the defendant's undertaking in this case was an *implied* one, since the primary undertaking had been given by the husband direct to the court in the custody proceedings, as explained above). The judge, in coming to this conclusion, regarded it as consistent with the decision in *Ross v Caunters* [1979] 3 All ER 580, or possibly an extension of the principles therein. The principle here was that 'a solicitor who has authority from his client to give an undertaking, one of whose objects is to protect and identify the third party, owes a duty of care towards that third party, in that the third party is a person within his direct contemplation'.

The judge then had to approach the question of whether the defendants were actually in breach of this duty. Here again the answer was positive. The defendants were in breach of the duty owed to the plaintiff-wife, in that they failed to foresee or to guard against the obvious possibility that the Kuwaiti Embassy might retain the passport and that the husband might attend the Embassy in connection with the passport in the absence of any representative from the defendant's solicitors or their London agents.

The next question was whether any damage that the plaintiff suffered was a natural and probable consequence of any such breach of duty? As the judge stated, the fact that the appalling events which occurred would not have done so without the defendant's breach of duty did not necessarily mean that any damages were recoverable. The damage must have been reasonably foreseeable, having regard to the defendant's state of knowledge or means of knowledge of the relevant facts. The judge concluded that whilst it was foreseeable that the husband would abduct the children by violent means if necessary, it was not reasonably foreseeable that the Kuwaiti Embassy would part with the passport to the husband in the way that had happened (and despite having assured the defendant's London agents that the passport would be kept safe by the Embassy). Nor was it foreseeable that the plaintiff would suffer damage as a result. The action was accordingly dismissed, with some regret, but the judge went on to assess damages on a putative basis. Having regard to the shock and injury suffered by the plaintiff, the judge assessed general damages in the sum of £20,000, being £5,000 for physical injuries, shock and imprisonment in the van, plus £15,000 for the psychiatric consequences of this episode. In addition, there would, had the plaintiff succeeded, have been the sum of £7,668.14 payable as special damages in relation to the expenses in or about the efforts to recover the children. (In 1988 an appeal was successful on the foreseeability point).

Breaches of undertakings by solicitors

The status of one solicitor's undertaking to another has been the subject matter of debate in various contexts. The importance of these undertakings is impossible to over-estimate. It makes it possible to progress eg conveyancing, commercial and litigation matters which would otherwise come to a dead stop, since one solicitor is entitled to expect exact and complete compliance with any undertaking given to him by another and both parties know that there are powerful sanctions should a breach occur. The need to take care when giving such undertakings and the consequences of breaking them were emphasised in two cases which appeared in the All England Law Reports in 1987.

The decision in *John Fox v Bannister King & Rigbeys* [1987] 1 All ER 737 elucidated the nature of these undertakings. Both Nicholls LJ and Sir John Donaldson MR took the opportunity of further explaining the court's jurisdiction where such undertakings are alleged to be broken. The jurisdiction is 'extraordinary'. It is based on the right of the court to see that a high standard of conduct in maintained by its officers acting as such. It is designed to apply to solicitors, as officers of the court, higher standards than the law applies generally. The jurisdiction is inherent, being the jurisdiction which the Supreme Court has over its officers. Undertaking are, of course, but one aspect of this jurisdiction. In this area, however, as officers of the court solicitors are expected to abide by undertakings given by them professionally. If they do not do so they may be called on summarily, either by an originating summons or by simple application in an action where the conduct complained of occurred in the course of that action, to make good any default. Where a solicitor, directly or indirectly, still has it in his power to do the act which he undertook to do, the court may order him to do that act. Otherwise he may be ordered to make good the loss owing from his failure to perform the undertaking, as loss flowing from a breach of duty committed by a solicitor as an officer of the court (see *Marsh v Joseph* [1897] 1 Ch 213 at 245, [1895–9] All ER Rep 977 at 981 per Lord Russell CJ).

The facts arose out of a dispute between two firms of solicitors, both of whom at various times had acted for a particular client.

The plaintiff firm, referred to as 'John Fox', acted for the client in litigation which was compromised in 1982. John Fox's taxed fees and disbursements plus VAT amounted to over £59,000. The client paid only about £27,000 of this on account. The defendant firm, referred to as 'Bannisters' also acted for the particular client in the sale of two properties. Being concerned about the lack of security for the costs owed to John Fox, that firm obtained from their client a form of authority signed by him and addressed to Bannisters. It read 'I hereby authorise and request you to give an undertaking to account to Messrs John Fox ... for the balance of the retention moneys in connection with the sale of [the property] and also the balance Proceeds of Sale of [the second property].' Some two months later Bannisters handed to John Fox a letter on their headed paper the material part of which referred to a balance of £18,000 belonging to their mutual client 'which is still in my account and which of course I shall retain until you have sorted everthing out'. Bannisters further told John Fox that their mutual client had been told that the £18,000 would not be parted with until John Fox and the client had 'decided what to do about this'.

By this time the solicitors' mutual client had got into serious financial difficulties. The client's company was forced into liquidation. Bannisters considered the matter and decided that they had no alternative but to hand over the money, £18,000, to their client. They did so without reference to John Fox. The client became bankrupt and John Fox was unable to recover the unpaid costs from the client. John Fox therefore issued an originating summons against Bannisters, seeking an order for payment of the sum of £18,000 wrongfully released in breach of an undertaking or, alternatively, damages for breach of the undertaking.

The first question for the court was, obviously, whether any undertaking was specifically given. This was certainly an arguable point. A reference to retaining specific money 'until you have sorted everything out' is hardly precise commercial language. But to the mind of Nicholls LJ, there was no material ambiguity. The judge regarded the sense of the undertaking as being to hold on to the money until John Fox had come to some arrangement regarding it with their mutual client. If this did not occur, in the judge's opinion, Bannisters' obligation could have been terminated on giving reasonable notice to John Fox.

The decision having been taken that the undertaking was broken, Bannisters were required to make good the plaintiff's solicitors' loss. It was not appropriate to order the defendant solicitors to pay the sum into an account to the client's credit or pay the sum into a joint account or into court, since the client was bankrupt. The court was therefore compelled to adopt the course directing an inquiry as to what loss, if any, John Fox had suffered by reason of the breach of the undertaking.

By way of a useful tail note, Nicholls LJ ([1987] 1 All ER 737 at 742) added that a solicitor is not necessarily to be regarded as having misconducted himself by failing to honour an undertaking when, for example, the issue of whether the words amounted to an undertaking, or the further issue of whether there has been a breach, depends on the answer to a final subtle point of construction. In this sense the supervisory jurisdiction over solicitors' undertaking would only be exercised in a clear case. The court can resolve issues of fact with the assistance of cross-examination of deponents or an order of discovery could be made. But, at the same time, the court should be careful to ensure that the solicitor defendant is not prejudiced by the course which is being followed in the circumstances of their particular case.

What morals are to be drawn from this? First, undertakings should not be accepted if they are not clearly worded. Ambiguity of construction will always cause trouble and may cause the court to decline jurisdiction. Secondly, where there is any question of an undertaking having been given, as in this case, the solicitor giving the undertaking should at least inform the other party of his intention to act in a way inconsistent with the alleged undertaking. Had this apparently simply step been taken here the outcome might have been different.

In the second case, the Court of Appeal in *Udall v Capri Lighting Ltd* [1987] 3 All ER 262 drew some assistance from *John Fox v Bannister King & Rigbeys*. In the course of litigation involving summonses for summary judgement under RSC Ord 14, before the summonses were heard the defendant's solicitor gave an oral undertaking to the plaintiff's solicitor that he would procure the execution of charges in favour of the plaintiff by the defendant's directors over their homes or life assurance policies. In return for this, the plaintiff's solicitor agreed to adjourn the summonses. These charges were never executed and judgment was entered against the defendants who, however, subsequently went into liquidation and so the judgment could not be enforced.

Accordingly the plaintiff issued summonses in the two actions asking for orders that the partner in the defendant' firm of solicitors who had given an oral personal undertaking to 'procure second charges on the security of' his clients' relevant properties should procure the second charges pursuant to his undertaking. The trial judge decided (a) that the undertaking in question had been given, (b) that this was a 'clear case' where under the court could exercise its discretionary jurisdiction to control solicitors as its officers, (c) the court could enforce a solicitor's undertaking to secure a third party to do an act to execute a document.

The defendant solicitor appealed on the ground, primarily, that it was impossible for the solicitor to perform the undertaking and therefore it ought not to be enforced.

The Court of Appeal accepted that it was now impossible for the defendant's solicitor to perform his undertaking. This was because the owner of one of the material properties was bankrupt and the owner of the other had died.

On the issue of impossiblity, Balcon LJ pointed out (ibid at 267) the words of Kindersley V–C in *Seawell v Webster* (1859) 29 LJ Ch at 73: 'Put the extreme case of a vendor burning a title deed: the Court could not make a decree that he should deliver it up, and be imprisoned if he does not'. Where, therefore, the court found it impossible to order a solicitor to perform the undertaking, it could instead order the solicitor to pay compensation to any person who had suffered loss because of the solicitor's failure to implement his undertaking, provided it was shown that the failure amounted to professional misconduct or serious dereliction of duty. The defendant solicitor's cross-appeal was therefore allowed and the matter remitted to the court below for consideration as to whether to make an order requiring the solicitor to pay compensation to the plaintiff. This, in turn, would depend on whether the plaintiff could show that he has suffered loss in consequences of his not having had the benefit of the second charges, the subject matter of the undertaking. This would in turn depend on a number of factors, including the value of the properties at the relevant date and the extent of the security afforded by a second charge. Kerr LJ (ibid at 271) added that he found it surprising that the trial judge (Sir Neil Lawson) did not make a prior investigation on the practicalities of enforcing the undertaking when making an order for what was effectively specific performance of that undertaking some time after the event.

This decision, when taken with *John Fox v Bannister King and Rigbeys*, confirms the principle that where a solicitor does not have it in his power to fulfil an undertaking, he may be ordered to make good the loss flowing from his failure to perform the undertaking, as loss flowing from the breach of duty committed by a solicitor as an officer of the court. But, having said this, the difficulties can begin. In this case, for instance, the order that the matter be remitted for decision was framed in terms of what, if any, order should be made against the defendant solicitor in all the circumstances. One of the difficulties may be that the defendant solicitor would be hampered by the legal professional privilege of his client and the general principles of confidentiality in seeking to establish that he was not guilty of professional misconduct in this particular case. That in turn might prevent the solicitor from explaining fully what happened, and why the second charges were not provided. This is a reminder that the essence of this jurisdiction is that professional misconduct or serious dereliction of professional duty must be involved. Here, although it did not appear to be in doubt on appeal that an oral undertaking had been given, it would obviously have been better had the undertaking been framed far more specifically and in writing. The other side of the coin is that the plaintiff's solicitors duty is to ensure that, if he is to rely on an undertaking, it must be clear, unambiguous and capable of being enforced even if the relevant client eg, were to die a few minutes later. Grave difficulties can otherwise ensue, as amply demonstrated by these two decisions.

Sport and the Law

EDWARD GRAYSON, MA
Barrister, South Eastern Circuit

Introduction

'Sport defies definition'. This was the opinion of the late Sir Denis Follows, CBE, given publicly shortly before he died in 1983. At different times he had served it as Chairman of the British Olympic Association, Treasurer of the Central Council of Physical Recreation, and Secretary of the Football association. Two years later it was confirmed by the Director General of the Sports Council, John Wheatley in a written memorandum on *Financing of Sport in the United Kingdom* to a House of Commons Environment Committee. He explained,

> 'A study of the financing of sport produces a problem of definition.
> There is no single list of activities which would meet with universal agreement. Many years ago sport was felt by some to encompass, hunting, shooting and fishing. A much wider view is now taken by many people'.

With the inclusion of ice-dancing in international Olympic Games it is appropriate here to adapt a well-worn formula applied traditionally to easements and negligence: 'the categories are never closed'. My recently published book, *Sport and the Law* (Butterworths 1988) listed 200 reported cases which are merely the tip of a more discoverable iceberg from the last 100 years. Their ripples extend beyond any single boundary. During 1987 four separate judicial areas swam into the sporting world. Police and public order; taxation limits on tennis coaching equipment as plant; an unincorporated association's liability to taxation of land holding; and the impact of rating law on a thoroughbred horse stud farm and farm buildings.

Police and public order

Judicial knowledge is not required for general awareness of crowd control problems at not only professional football grounds. Evidence exists of an increasing concern for those who attend publicly organised boxing, cricket and horse race meeting occasions. *Harris v Sheffield United Football Club Ltd* [1987] 2 All ER 838 now is the guideline for evaluating how the attendance of police at sporting grounds constitutes the provision of special police services for which the appropriate police authority is entitled to claim under the Police Act 1964 s 15(1).

The South Yorkshire Police Authority claimed from the defendant club £51,699 for providing special police services between August 1982 and November 1983. The club denied liability under the heads: one factual and the other of mixed law and fact.

For a period after October 1983 the club challenged that it had 'requested' police attendance at matches, and, more generally, it contended that the overriding duty to enforce the law at the club ground did not constitute special services. Boreham J upheld the claim which the Court of Appeal confirmed. It held, inter alia the no *general* criteria could be formulated for regulating 'special police services': all the circumstances of a particular case demanded examination. Four separate elements required special assessment:

(1) private premises (which qualifies so many sporting areas) provide *prima facie* evidence of special police services;

(2) whether violence or some other emergency had occurred or was imminent (a circumstance which would be unlikely to qualify for special police services);

(3) the nature and timing of the event, eg regularly at weekends when police resources would be strained;

(4) the number of police required to attend the event.

The trial judge and the Court of Appeal paid tribute to the Sheffield United club on the undoubted efforts made by its management and advisers at the famous Bramall Lane ground to become 'one of the safest of soccer grounds'. The evidence caused the Court of Appeal to conclude that 'as a matter of law the judge reached the right conclusion', but recorded, per Neill LJ [1987] 2 All ER at 848:

'One can feel considerable sympathy for the club authorities who are faced with falling gates and a grave escalation of costs to meet violence which they deplore and do their best to prevent. One can only hope that some accommodation can be reached perhaps on a national scale to meet a threat to the finances of the club and other clubs in a similar situation'.

The circumstances of this particular problem were removed in principle, as well as fifteen years in time now, from an earlier judicial necessity to assess a public order issue conerning attendance at a sporting occasion: *Brutus v Cozens* [1972] 2 All ER 1297, [1973] AC 584. The particular sport on that occasion, however, leads to the next important precedent from 1987: tennis.

Taxation limits on tennis coaching equipment

Thomas (Inspector of Taxes) v Reynolds and Broomhead [1987] STC 135 was described by Walton J in the opening words of his judgment as 'a rather unfortunate little case'. He had felt constrained to allow the Revenue's appeal against the General Commissioners' finding in favour of the taxpayers because they had 'not found any *facts* which have entitled them to find that the air dome [ie for tennis coaching purposes] did in fact play a part in the essential running of the business which is carried on', in order to qualify for a first year allowance for 'capital expenditure on the provisions of machinery or plant for the purpose of trade' (s 41(1)(a) Finance Act 1971), [1987] STC at 140). He accepted the Crown's contention that the *facts* found by the General Commissioners comprised merely the ambience or setting within which the taxpayers' business was carried on, and he was thereby bound by the line of cases which included an earlier well-known and oft-cited sporting circumstance: *Brown (Inspector of Taxes) v Burnley Football and Athletic Co Ltd* [1980] STC 424.

More significantly, he also felt bound by the House of Lords equally well-known and oft-cited ruling that any appellate court is bound by the

General Commissioners' findings. When the *taxpayers in person* appeared before him they sought to adduce fresh evidence to support the reality of their situation that the equipment in question *did* meet the criteria of the various judicial guidelines for construing the meaning of 'machinery or plant' (*Cole Brothers Ltd v Phillips (Inspector of Taxes)* [1982] STC 307). This draconian principle is inconsistent with other jurisdictions, such as appeals from magistrates courts to Crown Courts, and the various permutations of civil appeals generally, when in the former always and in the latter by discretion, fresh evidence on appeal is permissible.

This draconian direction also cuts across the dictum of Donaldson LJ (as he then was) in *IRC v Garvin*]1980] STC 295 at 313:

> 'There is a certain fascination in being one of the referees of a match between a well-advised taxpayer and the equally well-advised Commissioners of Inland Revenue, conducted under the rules which govern tax avoidance. These rules are complex, the moves are sophisticated and the stakes are high'.

It was applicable, however, to the next appearance during 1987 of sport in the law courts

An unincorporated association's liability to taxation of land holding

Worthing Rugby Football Club's contests with the Inland Revenue are reported in the books with the name of its own association or those of its trustees as either Worthing Rugby Football Club Trustees or, more accurately and formally *Frampton and Campbell (Trustees of Worthing Rugby Football Club) v IRC* [1987] STC 273; Court of Appeal.

The issues concerned appeals against Revenue assessments for Capital Gains and Development Land Tax Act liabilities following the sale of the club's playing ground premises. Alternative assessments were made upon the club trustees and the unincorporated association comprising the club membership. The Special Commissioners upheld the assessments against the trustees and the club for capital gains purposes, but discharged those against the club under the Development Land Tax Act on the basis that pursuant to the general law and ss 34–36 of the Law of Property Act an unincorporated association is not a legal entity capable of assessment for land tax purposes.

The trustees appealed against both assessments and the Revenue appealed against the discharge of the assessment upon the club as an unincorporated association. Peter Gibson J allowed the Revenue's appeal and dismissed those of the trustees. The Court of Appeal affirmed his decision. For general purposes the verdict sustains the courts construction of Revenue statutes established in *Carlisle and Siloth Golf Club v Smith* [1913] 3 KB 75 that an unincorporated association is assessable for taxation upon profits from its trading or association transactions. Furthermore, although an unincorporated association's landholding generally and traditionally operates through its trustees, the *club* was held to be a 'person' by virtue of the Interpretation Act 1889, s 19 within the meaning of the Development Land Tax Act 1976, s 28(1) even though the disposal of the land was effected in accordance with the usual practice by the trustees on behalf of the general club membership.

The Development Land Tax Act 1976 was abolished by the Finance Act 1985, s 93, Sch 27, Part X, but the principle of taxation liability established here will be of general application for unincorporated associations: a frequent legal framework and structure for many sporting club organisations. The land element also figured extensively throughout the last of the four cases which conerned the world of sport during 1987.

The impact of rating law upon a thoroughbred horse stud farm and farm buildings

In *Hemens (Valuation Officer) v Whitsbury Farm and Stud Ltd* [1987] 1 All ER 430 the Court of Appeal rejected a claim by owners of a stud farm that their stud buildings were exempt from rating as being agricultural buildings or that their valuable thoroughbred horses qualified as bloodstock. On 10 December 1987 the House of Lords affirmed the Court of Appeal, but not reported until [1988] 1 All ER 72. It was a test case on behalf of 400 stud farms in England and Wales.

A local valuation court accepted the owners' claim to exempt four groups of stud buildings and premises at Whitsbury, Fordingbridge, Hampshire, occupied by the farm for breeding thoroughbred horses. The complex includes the area where Rhyme 'n' Reason was trained to win the 1988 Grand National Steeplechase. Two rating statutes were applied:

(1) General Rate Act 1967 s 26(4) on the basis that the properties qualified as 'agricultural holdings... used solely in connection with agricultural operations thereon.

(2) Rating Act 1971 s 2(1)(a) that they were 'used for the keeping or breedings of livestock'.

Consolidated appeals by the Valuation Officer to the Lands Tribunal succeeded. They were confirmed by the Court of Appeal, and ultimately by the House of Lords on comparable grounds.

The key constructions of 'used *solely* in connection with agricultural operations' and 'livestock' which rejected exemptions under both statutes were that:

(1) breeding, rearing and grazing thoroughbred horses in paddocks failed to qualify as 'agricultural operations'; and

(2) thoroughbred horses failed to qualify as 'livestock'.

An earlier well-known Revenue case on comparable circumstances under a different statute, Schedule D of the Income Tax Act 1918, *Lord Glanely v Wightman* [1933] AC 618, HL was distinguished because of different statutory provisions.

Conclusions

All four cases considered here turned on judicial constructions of parliamentary legislation. *The Times* commented after the House of Lords speeches on 10 December 1987 (Saturday, 12 December 1987 p 9):

> 'Breeding and rearing horses to the point of sale is a traditional agricultural operation. It is only after then that they can become a possible luxury. The judiciary has had its say. Next it is for the Government to examine how to clear up an untidy corner of the traditions of rural England'.

Five months earlier on 10 July 1987 *The Times* chief sports correspondent, David Miller, recorded that with '376,000 full-time employees sport is larger than the coal, gas or agriculture industries'.

Its arrival as a new dimension for the Law should surprise no one.

Statute Law

FRANCIS BENNION, MA (OXON)
Barrister, Research Associate of Oxford Centre for Socio-Legal Sudies at Wolfson College, member of the Law Faculty of Oxford University, former UK Parliamentary Counsel

Note

For the convenience of readers this article, like the corresponding articles in previous editions of the All ER Annual Review, is arranged in conformity with the Code set out in the author's book *Statutory Interpretation* (Butterworths 1984), a reference to the relevant section of the Code being given after each heading.

Introductory

As in previous years, attention is drawn at the outset to ignorance of statute law principles displayed in certain cases reported during the year. These are referred to in the notes below respectively related to Code ss 171, 244, 271, 323, 396.

The tort of breach of statutory duty (Code s 14)

Where Act solely creates a criminal offence

Even though an enactment does no more than state that a certain act constitutes a criminal offence it may be taken to indicate that a person injuriously affected by the commission of the offence is intended to have a civil remedy. *Rickless v United Artists Corpn* [1987] 1 All ER 679 concerned the Dramatic and Musical Performers' Protection Act 1958, s 2, which renders it a criminal offence to make a cinematograph film by use of a dramatic performance without the consent of the performer, but does not refer to any civil remedy. The Court of Appeal held that since the Act was stated to be for the protection of performers a civil remedy was to be inferred. It was assisted in reaching this conclusion by the fact that the Performers' Protection Act 1963, which extended the protection given by the 1958 Act to other types of performer, was stated to have the purpose of enabling effect to be given to the 1961 International Convention for the Protection of Performers, Producers of Phonograms, and Broadcasting Organisations (Cmnd 2425), and the Convention requires a civil remedy to be made available.

The court reached this result not withstanding the ruling by Sir Nicolas Browne-Wilkinson V-C (ibid at 685) that 'it is easier to spell out a civil right if Parliament has expressly stated the act is generally unlawful rather than merely classified it as a criminal offence'. It may in any case be doubted whether this ruling is correct. The former practice by which parliamentary draftsmen usually declared proscribed acts to be 'unlawful' has been abandoned in favour of declaring them merely to be 'an offence'. Indeed it is common in modern times for the draftsman to refrain even from this, and merely state that if a person does a specified act he shall be liable to a specified penalty.

Negligence

Under the rule in *Anns v Merton London Borough* [1977] 2 All ER 492 a breach of statutory duty may give rise to a cause of action in negligence. The House of Lords distinguished this in *Curran v Northern Ireland Co-ownership Housing Association Ltd* [1987] 2 All ER 13. The respondent's predecessor in title to a dwelling-house had caused to be built an extension to the house with the aid of an improvement grant made by the appellants under the Housing (Northern Ireland) Order 1976, art 60(5). The construction was defective. The respondent claimed in negligence against the appellants on the ground that they were in breach of a statutory duty under art 60(5), which states that payment of a grant 'shall be conditional upon the works . . . being executed to the satisfaction of the Executive'. *Held* No duty of care was owed because the condition imposed by art 60(5) was to protect public funds, and the appellants had no control over the building operations once approval for a grant was given.

Lord Bridge said (ibid at 19) that for the rule in *Anns* to apply 'the statutory power which the authority is alleged to have negligently failed to exercise or to have exercised in a negligent way must be specifically directed to safeguarding the public, or some section of the public of which the plaintiff asserting the duty of care is a member, from the particular danger which has resulted' (cf Code pp 38–41).

Dynamic processing of legislation (Code s 26)

Decisions arrived at per incuriam

In *Duke v Reliance Systems Ltd* [1987] 2 All ER 858 at 860 Sir John Donaldson MR said:

> 'I have always understood that the doctrince of per incuriam only applies where another division of this court has reached a decision in the absence of knowledge of a decision binding on it or a statute, and that in either case it has to be shown that, had the court had this material, it *must* have reached a contrary decision . . . I do not understand the doctrine to extend to a case where, if different arguments had been placed before it, it *might* have reached a different conclusion.'

It is submitted with respect that this dictum is of doubtful correctness. It is rarely possible to say that, on a certain hypothesis, a court *must* have arrived at a given conclusion. The basis of the per incuriam doctrine is that a decision given in the absence of relevant information cannot safely be relied on. This applies whenever it is at least probable that if the information had been known the decision would have been affected by it. The doctrine of course applies in the Court of Appeal not only in relation to previous decisions of that court but in relation to those of the House of Lords also. It also applies in relation to merely persuasive authority.

Drafting of enactment presumed competent (Code s 77)

The corollary of the presumption that the draftsman of an enactment exercised due competence is that a less formal document such as the rules of a trades union will not be interpreted according to the principles applicable to statutory interpretation because its draftsman is unlikely to have possessed the skill and knowledge of a legislative draftsman. This was held in *Jacques v Amalgamated Union of Engineering Workers* [1987] 1 All ER 621, applying the following dictum of Lord Diplock in *Porter v National Union of Journalists* [1980] IRLR 404 at 407:

> 'I turn to the interpretation of the relevant rules bearing in mind that their purpose is to inform the members of the NUJ of what rights they acquire and obligations they assume vis-a-vis the union and their fellow members, by becoming and remaining members of it. The readership to which the rules are addressed consists of ordinary working journalists, not judges or lawyers versed in the semantic technicalities of statutory draftsmanship.'

Warner J said ([1987] 1 All ER at 628):

> 'The effect of the authorities may I think be summarised by saying that the rules of a trade union are not to be construed literally or like a statute, but so as to give them a reasonable interpretation which accords with what in the court's view they must have been intended to mean, bearing in mind their authorship, their purpose and the readership to which they are addressed.'

Role of counsel in statutory interpretation (Code s 84)

When deciding on the sources to be consulted to arrive at the legal meaning of an enactment the court, at least in civil cases, still tends to be constrained by the submissions of counsel. See the note concerning *Aswan Engineering Establishment Co v Lupdine Ltd (Thurgar Bolle Ltd, third party)* [1987] 1 All ER 135 on p 250 below, related to Code s 244.

Finding of implications: interstitial articulation by the court (Code s 114)

An example of interstitial articulation to supply an ellipsis is furnished by the Court of Appeal decision in *R v Immigration Appeal Tribunal, ex p Swaran Singh* [1987] 3 All ER 690. The court was called on to construe the phrase 'without other close relatives in their own country to turn to' in the Statement of Changes in Immigration Rules (HC Paper (1982–83) (no 169) para 52). Dillion LJ (ibid at 692) articulated the missing words at the end by saying he read the phrase 'as importing "to turn to in case of need", ie any sort of need which may afflict elderly parents...' He went on to give a lengthy description of the needs in question.

Rules of interpretation laid down by statute (Code s 125)

Potency of the term defined

An example of the way the comprehensive statutory definition of a pre-existing legal term may be held to be cut down in meaning by the potency of the term defined (see Code p 276) is given by *Claydon v Bradley* [1987] 1 All ER 522. Here the Court of Appeal held that the definition of 'promissory note' in s 83 of the Bills of Exchange Act 1882, a codifying Act, could not be given its wide literal meaning so as to extend it to a document which was meant as a receipt and was never intended to be negotiable. Neill LJ cited the dictum of Lord Atkin in *Akbar Khan v Attar Singh* [1936] 2 All ER 545 at 550 that receipts 'are not intended to be negotiable, and serious embarrassment would be caused in commerce if the negotiable net were cast too wide'.

Land

The term 'land' as defined by the Interpretation Act 1978, Sch 1 includes a restrictive covenant. See the note on *R v Hammersmith and Fulham LBC, ex p Beddowes* [1987] 1 All ER 369 at p 254 below, related to Code s 333.

Service by post

In *R v Secretary of State for the Home Department, ex p Yeboah* [1987] 3 All ER 999 notice of a deportation decision was sent by recorded delivery but not in fact delivered. It was held by the Court of Appeal that where the Interpretation Act 1978, s 7 (service of document deemed to be effected by posting it and, unless the contrary is proved, to be effected at normal time of delivery) applies to the giving of notice under an enactment its effect must depend on the wording of the enactment. Here the decision in *R v Appeal Committee of County of London Quarter Sessions, ex p Rossi* [1956] 1 QB 682 (where date of receipt crucial, s 7 does not deem notice to have been received when in fact it was not received) was inapplicable because of the wording of the relevant regulations.

Principle that law should be predictable (Code s 130)

For authority supporting the proposition that a lay person cannot be expected to understand statutes and that their intended audience is the skilled lawyer see the note on p 246 above related to Code s 77.

Principle that municipal law should conform to public international law (Code s 134)

For an application of this doctrine see the note on p 249 below concerning *Re International Tin Council* [1987] 1 All ER 890 related to Code s 222.

Presumptions as to legislative intention: that errors to be rectified (Code s 142)

Casus ommissus

In *R v Corby Juvenile Court, ex p M* [1987] 1 All ER 992 the Divisional Court was faced with an error by the draftsman of the Health and Social Services and Social Security Adjudications Act 1983 in so far as it amends the Child Care Act 1980, s 3 (which reproduces the provisions of the Children and Young Persons Act 1948, s 2). The amendment gives parents an opportunity of a court hearing before they can be deprived of access to a child in care. It thus, as Waite J held (ibid 995), has constitutional significance 'establishing as it does the right not to be deprived of access to a child without a hearing as one of the ordinary liberties enjoyed by every subject'.

In listing the types of care order to which the new right applies, the transitional provisions in the 1983 Act inadvertently omit the case of children who are in care as a result of a resolution passed before the commencement of the 1980 Act. They contain however a saving for the Interpretation Act 1978, s 17(2), which states that where an Act repeals and re-enacts a previous enactment then, unless the contrary intention appears, in so far as any subordinate legislation made or other thing done under the repealed enactment could have been made or done under the provision re-enacted it shall have effect as if so made or done.

Waite J began by saying (ibid at 993) that there is a particular harshness in requiring people whose lives are most closely affected by the law of child care, in addition to their other difficulties, 'to undergo the ordeal of taking part as bewildered amateurs in a game whose rules are understood only by those who play it professionally'.

The respondent pointed out that the transitional provisions, construed literally, denied the applicant the benefit of the amendment. He argued that s 17(2) of the 1978 Act did not affect the position because a resolution taking a child into care was not within its wording, not being of the same genus as 'subordinate legislation'.

Waite J found for the applicant. He said (ibid at 997–98):

> 'Parliament cannot have intended . . . to have allowed a whole section of the child population to vanish from legislative view as though they had gone off at the heels of the Pied Piper. It may well be that the draftsman did indeed stumble . . . The deliberate reference in the transitional provisions . . . to s 17 of the [Interpretation Act 1978] . . . seems to me, however, to show Parliament contemplating expressly that such an oversight might occur, and making appropriate provision for it. The legislative intention is plain. Parliament intended the parents of all children in compulsory care, with the exception of those specifically excluded, to benefit from the important and valuable rights introduced . . . The fact that the draftsman had made an unsuccessful attempt to enumerate exhaustively all the prior enactments thought to be affected by new or amending legislation cannot be enough . . . to amount to a "contrary intention" for the purposes of s 17(2) of the 1978 Act.'

He further held that the words 'or other thing done' in the 1978 Act are not to be construed ejusdem generis with 'subordinate legislation'.

Textual amendment (Code s 171)

Rule in A-G v Lamplough

The rule in *A-G v Lamplough* (1878) 3 Ex D 214 requires that where some only of the words of an enactment have been repealed the remaining unaltered words must be given the same meaning they had before the repeal, unless the contrary intention appears from the amending Act (see Code p 420 and All ER Rev 1986, p 276). Although not referred to as such the rule was followed in *R v Greater Manchester North District Coroner, ex p Worch* [1987] 3 All ER 661 at 668 where Slade LJ said:

> 'The original s 21(2) of the [Coroners (Amendment) Act 1926] is no longer law, since it has been replaced by s 23(3) of the Births and Deaths Registration Act 1953. Nevertheless, the original subsection is admissible in construing the section as a whole and, in our judgment, throws light on its construction. It demonstrates that the section as a whole contemplates a two-stage process.'

Retrospective operation: general presumption against (Code s 190)

Nature of retrospectivity

Where an enactment clearly sets out to modify accrued rights there can be no room for the presumption against doubtful penalisation. In *Chebaro v Chebaro* [1987] 1 All ER 999 the Court of Appeal upheld the decision in the court below to the effect that the right conferred by the Matrimonial and Family Proceedings Act 1984, s 12(1) to apply for financial relief where a marriage 'has been' dissolved by a foreign decree applies to a decree pronounced before the commencement of that Act. The judgments, particularly that of Balcombe LJ, confirm the analysis of that decision in All ER Rev 1986, pp. 279–280.

Application of Act: foreigners and foreign matters within the territory (Code s 222)

International organisations

In accordance with the principle of exterritoriality (Code p 494), the power conferred by the Companies Act 1985, ss 665 to 674 to order the winding up of an unregistered company was held in *Re International Tin Council* [1987] 1 All ER 890 not to apply to the international organisation known as the International Tin Council even though that body fell within the literal meaning of 'unregistered company' set out in s 665 and its headquarters were within the United Kingdom. The Council was set up under treaty, and Millet J said (ibid at 902):

> 'Parliament cannot be taken to have intended to confer, by general words alone, the jurisdiction to interpret the terms of an international treaty and to enforce the obligations arising thereunder between independent sovereign states, a jurisdiction at once unprecedented and incompatible with basic principles of English law.'

The decision complies with the doctrine that enactments should be presumed to be intended to conform to public international law (Code s 134).

Pre-enacting history: the earlier law (Code s 231)

Use of processed term

Where an Act uses a term which appeared in an earlier repealed Act dealing with the same subject-matter and, as it appeared in that earlier Act had been processed (that is defined by the court) before the passing of the later Act, it is likely that the draftsman of the later Act intended it to bear the processed meaning.

In *R v Thorpe* [1987] 2 All ER 108 the Court of Appeal considered the meaning of the term *lethal* in the Firearms Act 1968, s 57(1), which defines a firearm as 'a lethal barrelled weapon'. Two pre-1968 cases were cited which ruled on the meaning of that term as used in similar provisions of the (repealed) Firearms Act 1937. *Held* Those rulings should be applied to the 1968 Act definition. Kenneth Jones J referred (ibid at 112) to 'the obvious inference that the draftsman of the 1968 Act had well in mind the decisions in those two cases'.

Enacting history: international treaties (Code s 242)

For a case where the interpretation of an enactment was influenced by a treaty see the note on p 244 above related to Code s 14 and describing *Rickless v United Artists Corpn* [1987] 1 All ER 679.

Enacting history: inspection by court (Code s 244)

Although the court has power to inspect whatever enacting history it thinks fit it will, at least in civil cases, be governed by the submissions of the counsel on either side, at least where they are in agreement. In *Aswam Engineering Establishment Co v Lupdine Ltd (Thurgar Bolle Ltd, third party)* [1987] 1 All ER 135 at 146 Lloyd LJ said:

> 'We invited counsel for Thurgar Bolle to refer us to the Law Commission Report on Exemption Clauses in Contracts (Law Com no 24 (1969)), which preceded the enactment of [the Supply of Goods (Implied Terms) Act 1973], and also to the Law Commission working paper on the Sale and Supply of Goods (no 85 (1983)). But counsel for the appellants objected. I can see no conceivable reason why we should not have been referred to the Law Commission papers, and good reason why we should... In my judgment it is not only legitimate but highy desirable to refer to Law Commission reports on which legislation has been based. But since counsel for Thurgar Bolle concurred in counsel for the appellants' objection, I say no more about it.'

This dictum reflects the still-lingering idea that civil litigation is a kind of joust between the parties, where the Court does little more than hold the ring. It is surely wrong that any court, as an emanation of the Crown, should apply what is not truly the law. To find out what the law is, the court is not merely entitled but under a duty to have recourse to all legitimate sources.

If it hands down a judgment based on anything but what is truly the law, a court denies it function. Moreover the judge or judges involved contravene the judicial oath or affirmation requiring them to apply in their judgments 'the law and usages of this realm' (Promissory Oaths Act 1868, s 4).

Post-enacting history: later Acts (Code s 255)

The court will not only be guided by later Acts, but by later delegated legislation which is in pari materia with the enactment being construed. In *R v Newcastle upon Tyne City Justices, ex p Skinner* [1987] 1 All ER 349 the Divisional Court was called on to construe the Magistrates' Court Act 1980, s 114. This says that magistrates shall not be required to state a case until the applicant for this has entered into a recognizance to prosecute the appeal by case stated. The section says nothing about how the amount of the recognizance is to be fixed, or the means of the applicant. *Held* Guidance is to be sought from the Crown Court Rules 1982, r 26. This rule, governing appeals by case stated from the Crown Court, a higher court than the magistrates' court, says that a recognizance shall be fixed 'in such sum as the Crown Court thinks proper, *having regard to the means of the applicant*'. Glidewell LJ said (ibid at 351):

> 'One finds there the requirement that the Crown Court shall have regard to the means of the applicant. In our view, although the same phrase is not to be found in s 114 of the 1980 Act, the same principle must necessarily apply to magistrates as it does to the stating of a case by the Crown Court.'

The proviso (Code s 268)

It is for the defendant in a criminal case, whether tried on indictment or summarily, to raise and prove an *exception*, whether or not it is expressed in the form of a proviso. See the note on p 255 below (related to Code s 341) concerning the House of Lords decision in *R v Hunt* [1987] 1 All ER 1.

Long title of Act (Code s 271)

In *R v Galvin* [1987] 2 All ER 851 the Court of Appeal rejected the argument that the wide words of the Official Secrets Act 1911, s 2 are to be treated as narrowed by the long title to the Act. Lord Lane CJ said (ibid at 855):

> 'One can have regard to the title of a statute to help resolve an ambiguity in the body of it, but it is not, we consider, open to a court to use the title to restrict what is otherwise the plain meaning of the words of the statute simply because they seem to be unduly wide.'

However this dictum must be regarded as erroneous and given per incuriam. It is contrary to the decision of the Court of Appeal in *Watkinson v Hollington* [1943] 2 All ER 573 (see Code pp 577 and 676), which was not cited to the court.

Principle against doubtful penalisation: danger to human life or health (Code s 289)

In *Bugdaycay v Secretary of State for the Home Department* [1987] 1 All ER 940 the House of Lords allowed the appeal of an applicant for refugee status, and quashed the Secretary of State's refusal of such status, on the ground that the latter had not taken into account or adequately resolved whether the applicant would, if returned to Kenya, be sent back to Uganda (where he would be in danger). Lord Templeman said in relation to judicial review (ibid at 956) that 'where the result of a flawed decision may imperil life . . . a special responsibility lies on the court in the examination of the decision-making process'.

Principle against doubtful penalisation: physical restraint of the person (Code s 290)

In *Bugdaycay v Secretary of State for the Home Department* [1987] 1 All ER 940 the House of Lords allowed the appeal of an applicant for refugee status, and quashed the Secretary of State's refusal of such status, on the ground that the latter had not taken into account or adequately resolved whether the applicant would, if returned to Kenya, be sent back to Uganda (where he would be in danger). Lord Templeman said in relation to judicial review (ibid at 956) that 'where the result of a flawed decision may imperil . . . liberty a special responsibility lies on the court in the examination of the decision-making process'.

Principle against doubtful penalisation: protection of property rights (Code s 295)

The propensity of the law to protect property rights is illustrated by two 1987 decisions.

In *Rickless v United Artists Corpn* [1987] 1 All ER 679 the Court of Appeal ruled that the civil right it held to be conferred on performers by the Dramatic and Musical Performers' Protection Act, s 2 survived the death of the performer. Sir Nicolas Brown-Wilkinson V-C said (ibid at 688):

> 'It has been held that prima facie a right conferred on a man by statute survives his death and that clear words are required if it is to be held that the right dies with the person given that right: see *Dean v Wiesengrund* [1955] 2 QB 120.'

(As to *Rickless v United Artists Corpn* see further the note on p 244 above related to Code s 14.)

In *Chilton v Telford Development Corpn* [1987] 3 All ER 992 the Court of Appeal held that, having regard to the fact that the New Towns Act 1965, s 7 confers statutory power to deprive a citizen of his title and right of occupation of his land and to the fact that Sch 6, para 4(2) of the Act provides protection for an owner or occupier who is subjected to that draconian power, the Act is to be construed in favour of the owner or occupier rather than the acquiring authority.

Principle against doubtful penalisation: impairment of legal rights (Code s 298)

In *R v Corby Juvenile Court, ex p M* [1987] 1 All ER 992 the Divisional Court held that the amendment of the Child Care Act 1980, s 3 effected by the Health and Social Services and Social Security Adjudications Act 1983, by giving parents an opportunity of a court hearing before they can be deprived of access to a child without a hearing as one of the ordinary liberties enjoyed by every subject. The court regarded this as a powerful reason for giving a strained construction to the defective transitional provisions of the latter Act. (For details of the case see note on p 247 above related to Code s 142.)

Nature of purposive construction (Code s 313)

Retrospective alteration of an Act's purpose

A later Act *in pari materia* may have the effect of retrospectively altering an Act's purpose. In *R v Hammersmith and Fulham LBC, ex p Beddowes* [1987] 1 All ER 369 at 379–80 Fox LJ said:

> 'Historically, local authority housing has been rented. But a substantial inroad on that was made by Pt I of the Housing Act 1980, which gave municipal tenants the right to purchase their dwellings. In the circumstances it does not seem to me that a policy which is designed to produce good accommodation for owner–occupiers is now any less within the purposes of [the Housing Acts 1957 and 1985], than the provision of rented housing . . . '

For further details of this case see the note on p 254 below related to Code s 333.

Purposive-and-strained construction (Code s 315)

An example of purposive-and-strained construction effected by the court's artificially prolonging the critical time posited by the relevant enactment is furnished by the decision of the House of Lords in *D (a minor) v Berkshire CC* [1987] 1 All ER 20.

The Children and Young Persons Act 1969, s 1 empowers a court to make a care order in respect of a child if of opinion that 'his proper development *is* being avoidably prevented or neglected or his health *is* being avoidably impaired or neglected or he *is* being ill-treated'. In this case a care order had been made in respect of a baby which had suffered withdrawal symptoms during the period following its birth because of drug-taking by the mother during pregnancy. Since the baby had never returned to the mother it could not be said of any period during its lifetime that the condition was literally met that its health 'is' being impaired etc.

Held To achieve the purpose of the enactment it was necessary to postulate a continuous period beginning before birth and continuing at the time of the order. The word 'is' in the enactment had then to be applied to that period *taken as a whole*. The care order was therefore valid.

Construction against 'absurdity': avoiding an inconvenient result (Code s 322)

For an example of a construction designed to avoid commercial inconvenience see the note on *Claydon v Bradley* [1987] 1 All ER 522 on p 247 above related to Code s 125.

Construction against 'absurdity': avoiding an anomalous or illogical result (Code s 323)

Remedy not available in like cases

The decision of Sheen J in *Coltman v Bibby Tankers Ltd* [1986] 2 All ER 65 (All ER Rev 1986, p 282) (to hold for the purpose of determining an employer's liability for defects that a ship is not 'equipment' when an aircraft or vehicle clearly is 'leads to absurd distinctions and anomalies'), having been reversed by the Court of Appeal (Lloyd LJ dissenting) in *Coltman v Bibby Tankers Ltd* [1987] 1 All ER 932, was restored by the House of Lords in *Coltman v Bibby Tankers Ltd* [1987] 3 All ER 1068. Despite the comments at All ER Rev 1986, p 283 drawing attention to them in this connection, the House of Lords, like the courts below, failed to refer either to the rank principle (Code s 386) or the expressio unius principle (Code ss 388–394).

The decision in *Sherdley v Sherdley* [1986] 2 All ER 202 (All ER Rev 1986, p 283) was reversed by the House of Lords in *Sherdley v Sherdley* [1987] 2 All ER 54 on the ground that in the case of divorce it would be anomalous for a tax advantage to be obtainable in respect of the school fees of children of the marriage where they lived with the mother (who could obtain a maintenance order under the Matrimonial Causes Act 1973, s 23(1)(d) against the father) but not where they lived with the father. Although it was artificial (see Code s 325) to allow the father to obtain a maintenance order against himself (described by Donaldson MR in *Sherdley v Sherdley* [1986] 2 All ER 202 at 209 as 'curial antics') this was outweighed by other interpretative factors, namely that just mentioned and also the need for the court to safeguard the interests of minors (see Code p 772).

Construction which defeats legislative purpose (Code s 333)

Construction enabling persons to truncate statutory functions

A construction will not be allowed which would enable persons charged with a statutory power or function to act in such a way as to truncate or otherwise modify what the legislature intended. On the other hand the exercise of a statutory power, for example to enter into a restrictive covenant, may be held legitimate notwithstanding that its future consequence will be to narrow the operation of some other statutory power in relation to the subject-matter affected.

In *R v Hammersmith and Fulham LBC, ex p Beddowes* [1987] 1 All ER 369 a local authority, on the sale to a developer of part of a block of rented housing owned by it, entered into restrictive covenants as to the use of the part it retained. *Held* In view of the definition of 'land' in the Interpretation Act 1978, Sch 1, the power to dispose of land conferred on the authority by the Housing Act 1957, s 104 (see now the Housing Act 1985, s 32) included entering into a restrictive covenant. Although the covenants encroached on the authority's statutory powers under the 1957 Act regarding the use of the retained land for housing purposes this did not prevent the entering into of the covenants from being a legitimate exercise of the statutory power of disposal. Fox LJ said (ibid at 379–80):

'What we are concerned wth in the present case are overlapping or conflicting powers. There is a power to create covenants restrictive of the use of the retained land and there are powers in relation to the user of the retained land for housing purposes... The policy, it is true, is designed to produce owner-occupancy and not rented accommodation. Historically, local authority housing has been rented. But a substantial inroad on that was made by Pt I of the Housing Act 1980, which gave municipal tenants the right to purchase their dwellings. In the circumstances it does not seem to me that a policy which is designed to produce good accommodation for owner-occupiers is now any less within the purposes of the 1957 and 1985 Acts, than the provision of rented housing... we were referred to the decision in *Ayr Harbour Trustees v Oswald* (1883) 8 App Cas 623. But that was a case where the trustees simply "renounced part of their statutory birthright".'

Implied application of rules of constitutional law (Code s 334)

Human rights provisions

There is an implication that statutory powers and duties are intended by the legislature to be exercised in conformity with constitutional provisions laying down human rights.

In *R v Secretary of State for the Home Department, ex p Herbage (No 2)* [1987] 1 All ER 324 a prisoner sought judicial review on the ground that there had been illegality in the performance of the statutory powers and duties of the Home Secretary and the prison governor. This was founded on the allegation that there had been a breach of the requirement of the Bill of Rights (1688) against the infliction of cruel and unusual punishments.

The Court of Appeal held that this would be a ground for granting judicial review. Purchas LJ said (ibid at 337):

'The argument is... that if in a notorious case, as the applicant's is, it were to be established that serious breaches of the Bill of Rights were occurring then there is a foundation of an allegation that the Secretary of State had failed to perform his duties of supervision imposed generally on him by [the Prison Act 1952, s 4(2)]... counsel for the applicant emphasized that the case against the governor... was not based merely on breaches of [the Prison Rules 1964] but on an alleged breach of the provision of the Bill of Rights, namely that the applicant was entitled not to be inflicted with "cruell and unusuall punishments". This is a fundamental right which, in my judgment, goes far beyond the ambit of the 1964 rules. For my part, if it were established that a prison governor was guilty of such conduct, it would be an affront to common sense that the court should not be able to afford relief [by way of judicial review] under Ord 53.'

Implied application of rules of evidence (Code s 341)

The exceptions rule

In *R v Hunt* [1987] 1 All ER 1 the House of Lords clarified what may be called the exceptions rule, which Lord Wilberforce referred to in *Nimmo v Alexander Cowan & Sons Ltd* [1968] AC 107 at 130 as 'the orthodox principle (common to both the criminal and the civil law) that exceptions, etc, are to be set up by those who rely on them'. *R v Hunt* was concerned only with the criminal law aspect of this rule of evidence and pleading (as to its application to civil pleading cf RSC Ord 18, r 8).

The House of Lords was faced with an argument by the appellant that the burden of proof in the case of statutory exceptions varies according to whether the offence is triable on indictment or summarily. Whereas r 6(c) of the Indictment Rules 1971 states merely that it is not necessary for the statement of offence and particulars in an indictment 'to specify or negative an exception, exemption, proviso, excuse or qualification' the corresponding provision enacted in relation to summary trials by the Magistrates' Courts Act 1980, s 101 goes further. It says:

> 'Where the defendant to an information or complaint relies on his defence on any exception, exemption, proviso, excuse or qualification, whether or not it accompanies the description of the offence or matter of complaint in the enactment creating the offence or on which the complaint is founded, the burden of proving the exception, exemption, proviso, excuse or qualification shall be on him; and this notwithstanding that the information or complaint contains an allegation negativing the exception, exemption, proviso, excuse or qualification.'

The House of Lords, rejecting the appellant's argument, held that the common law and r 6(c) combined apply precisely the same exceptions rule to indictments as s 101 does to summary trials, thus confirming *R v Edwards* [1975] QB 27.

In the light of *R v Hunt*, the exceptions rule as it now applies both to trials on indictment and summary trials may be stated in the following propositions.

1. It is not necessary for the indictment or information to specify or negative an exception (as defined in paras 4 to 8 below).

2. Where the defendant relies on such an exception, the burden of proving that it applies is on him.

3. This burden of proof is a 'persuasive' burden, not an 'evidential' burden, and the civil standard of proof, namely that on the balance of probabilities, applies.

4. For the purpose of the exceptions rule, an 'exception' is a statutory exception, exemption, proviso, excuse or qualification, whether or not accompanying the description of the offence in the enactment creating the offence. Here 'excuse' includes the case where a necessary licence, permission or authority has been obtained.

5. A provision which linguistically forms part of the formulation of the offence is less likely to be an exception than one which stands apart from that formulation.

6. A provision which is prefaced or terminated by such terms of separation as *except* or *provided that* is likely to be an exception.

7. In case of doubt whether a provision is or is not an exception regard must be had to the comparative ease or difficulty that the respective parties would encounter in discharging the burden of proving the fact in question. It is against the public interest either that the prosecution should be required to prove a fact peculiarly within the knowledge of the defendant or that the defendant should be placed under an onerous duty to prove his innocence.

8. It may also be relevant to consider the mischief at which the enactment creating the offence is directed. The more grave the offence the more important it is that the prosecution should be required to prove its entire case beyond reasonable doubt.

Finally it may be pointed out that in deciding whether a provision is an exception the basic rule of statutory interpretation must always be borne in mind, namely that it is taken to be the legislator's intention that an enactment shall be construed in accordance with the general guides to legislative intention laid down by law; and that where these conflict the problem is to be resolved by weighing and balancing the factors concerned (see Code s 117).

(For a fuller account see Bennion, 'Statutory Exceptions: A Third Knot in the Golden Thread?' [1988] Crim LR 31.)

Reliance on illegality (allegans suam turpitudinem non est audiendus) (Code s 345)

The decision in *Phoenix General Insurance Co of Greece SA v Halvanon Insurance Co Ltd* [1986] 1 All ER 908 (All ER Rev 1986, p 286) was reversed by the Court of Appeal in *Phoenix General Insurance Co of Greece SA v Administratia Asigurarilor de Stat* [1987] 2 All ER 152. Since the Court of Appeal gave leave to appeal to the House f Lords, and it is understood that an appeal is pending, the somewhat complex reasons for the Court of Appeal's decision are not discussed here.

Hearing both sides (audi alteram partem) (Code s 346)

Oral representations

Though it will usually be a breach of fairness to refuse the opportunity of making oral representations, the like principle does not apply where no request for this was made. In *Lloyd v McMahon* [1987] 1 All ER 1118 the House of Lords held that the decision of the District Auditor surcharging certain Liverpool councillors for failing to set a rate could not be impugned on judicial review where he had not volunteered an opportunity to make oral representations and the councillors had not asked for one, but had instead made voluminous written submissions.

Term with both ordinary and technical meaning (Code s 368)

Where a term is used which has both an ordinary and a technical meaning it is permissible, in order to determine which meaning was intended, to seek guidance from the pre-enacting history. *R v Nanayakkara* [1987] 1 All ER 650 concerned the question whether 'acceptance' of a valuable security in the Theft Act 1968, s 20(2) meant acceptance in its ordinary meaning or in its technical meaning under the law relating to bills of exchange. In holding that the latter was the case the court was guided by the fact that the technical meaning had clearly been intended in earlier similar enactments such as the Larceny Act 1861, s 90 and the Larceny Act 1916, s 32(2). The court also referred to the Criminal Law Revision Committee's Eighth Report, Theft

and Related Offences (Cmnd 2977 (1966)) para 107 in support of the view
that Parliament intended no alteration in the 1968 Act.

Archaisms (Code s 370)

The Civil Evidence Act 1968, s 8(2)(b) provides for enabling a party to
require a person to be called as a witness unless he is 'beyond the seas', a
phrase which also occurs in the Criminal Evidence Act 1965, s 1(1)(b). In
Rover International Ltd v Cannon Film Sales Ltd (No 2) [1987] 3 All ER 986,
Harman J said of this phrase:

> 'It is a phrase which seems to me to be entirely archaic today. It has splendid
> overtones of Elizabeth I's reign and suchlike matters but is not a matter, I
> would think, of current speech or even lawyers' speech... However
> Parliament in its wisdom has chosen to use that phrase and I have to wrestle
> with it.'

Harman J went on to cite *Lane v Bennet* (1836) 1 M & W 70, 150 ER 350 as
authority for saying that the phrase meant beyond the four seas surrounding
the British Isles, namely the English Channel, the North Sea, the Irish Sea
and the Arctic Ocean. He upheld this meaning on the ground, based on the
purpose of the 1968 Act, that the phrase should be applied in the light of 'the
powers of the court to make people come and give evidence here'. He added
(ibid at 990) 'in my view the phrase means "beyond the seas" in the old
sense and not "abroad" or "beyond the British Islands".'

Ejusdem generis principle: single genus-describing term (Code s 380)

In *R v Corby Juvenile Court, ex p M* [1987] 1 All ER 992 the Divisional Court
held that the words 'or other thing done' in the Interpretation Act 1978,
s 17(2) are not to be construed ejusdem generis with 'subordinate
legislation'. For details of the case see the note on p 247 above related to
Code s 142.

Implication where statutory description only partly met (Code s 396)

Cases where on the facts a relevant statutory description is partly but not
entirely met continue to give trouble (for previous instances see All ER Rev
1985, pp 268–269, All ER Rev 1986, p 289).

This is largely because the courts fail to recognize this as a distinct type of
problem and do not apply the correct principle, which is to base the decision
on whether or not there is *substantial* conformity with the statutory
description.

In *Debenhams plc v Westminster CC* [1987] 1 All ER 51 the House of Lords
was faced with a difficulty which arose, as Lord Keith said (ibid at 56),
'owing to the draftsman, as it would appear, not having kept in view the
distinction between a hereditament and a building'. The General Rate Act
1967, Sch 1 para 2(c), as amended by the Town and Country Planning Act
1971, s 291 and Sch 23, exempts from rates 'a *hereditament*... [listed] as a
building of architectural or historic interest'. The statutory power to list is
however in terms of buildings not hereditaments.

In the instant case a hereditament consisted of two buildings, only one of which was listed. *Held* The exemption from rates did not apply to the hereditament. Instead of applying the correct test of whether or not the listed building formed the *predominant* part of the hereditament, Lord Keith based himself (ibid at 57) on the inadequate ground that 'if Parliament had intended to afford the exemption to such a hereditament it would have done so in express terms'.

The ground is inadequate because, as mentioned above, Lord Keith had already found the draftsman had erred in failing to distinguish between buildings and hereditaments. It thus could not plausibly be assumed that this particular draftsman (already found to be deficient) had in mind the more abstruse possibility that a hereditament might be partly but not wholly listed. Failure to foresee such possibilities is a frequent error of draftsmen. The courts need to recognise this and use an adequate interpretative technique to deal with it.

Succession

C H SHERRIN LLM, PHD
Barrister, Senior Lecturer in Law, University of Bristol

Validity of condition of defeasance

Re Tepper's Will Trusts [1987] 1 All ER 970 is the most interesting of the will
cases decided in 1987 particularly with regard to the admissibility of
extrinsic evidence to assist in resolving an uncertainty. The testator was a
devout Jew and left a share of income on trust for the children of one of his
children. 'Provided that they shall remain within the Jewish faith and shall
not marry outside the Jewish faith'. The residuary estate was left amongst
all of his grandchildren living at the date of his death and to be paid to them
on their attaining 25 years of age, 'Provided however that they shall not
marry outside the Jewish faith'. Clearly the gifts were conditional, but the
crucial question regarding the validity of the clauses on the test of certainty
was, did the clauses create conditions precedent or subsequent? The
distinction is perhaps unfortunate but clearly established by the authorities.
If the clauses create conditions precedent then it is sufficient if the condition
is couched in language that permits a particular individual to come with
evidence before the court and show that he satisfies or does not satisfy, as
the case may be, that condition (ibid at 976–77, per Scott J citing *Re Allen,
Faith v Allen* [1953] 2 All ER 898, *Re Selby's Will Trusts, Donn v Selby* [1965]
3 All ER 386 and *Re Tuck's Settlement Trusts* [1978] 1 All ER 1047). On this
basis the gifts in *Re Tepper* could be valid. But if the clauses operated as
conditions of defeasance, ie as conditions subsequent, then the principle of
Clayton v Ramsden [1943] 1 All ER 16 applied.

> 'The courts have always insisted that conditions of defeasance, in order to be
> valid, should be so framed that the persons affected (or the court if they seek
> its guidance) can from the outset know with certainty the exact event on the
> happening of which their interests are to be divested' (per Lord Russell at 18,
> citing *Clavering v Ellison* (1859) 7 HL Cas 707).

On this test a provision against marrying a person, 'not of Jewish parentage
and of the Jewish faith' was held to be void for uncertainty (ibid). Scott J in
Re Tepper considered the status and character of the provisos in question
with reference to their language and to the context in which they appeared
in the will, and concluded, despite argument in favour of the alternative
construction, that in substance both clauses operated as conditions of
defeasance. On that basis, applying the principles of certainty expressed in
Clayton v Ramsden, both clauses would be void for uncertainty. But the
judge being clearly reluctant to come to that conclusion without more,
decided to adjourn the summons and invited the parties to file further
evidence as to the meaning in this will of the expression 'the Jewish faith'.
   This willingness to have regard to extrinsic evidence to resolve an
uncertainty is unusual but is not without precedent. The common law rules
governing the admissibility of such evidence (the provisions of s 21 of the
Administration of Justice Act 1982 not being applicable) have always

permitted a will to be construed 'from the testator's armchair'. Scott J thought it permissible to ask the question 'what did the testator, sitting in his armchair mean by "the Jewish faith"?' Direct evidence of his intention was not admissible but objective evidence of what was the Jewish faith as practised by the testator and his family was admissible. In so far as this might resolve the matter the judge was prepared to consider such evidence. He derived support for this approach from *Re Tuck's Settlement Trusts* which indicated both a willingness to uphold the testator's testamentary provisions if possible, and established the admissibility of extrinsic evidence to elucidate the meaning in the settlement of such phrases as 'the Jewish faith'. However there are obvious differences between the cases. *Re Tuck* was concerned with the construction of an inter vivos settlement not with a will. Further it will be recalled that in *Re Tuck* the evidence admitted, namely the opinion of the Chief Rabbi, was expressly provided for by the settlement as the formula for resolving dispute or uncertainty, and as such it could be argued was intrinsic, rather than extrinsic evidence.

It is submitted that Scott J's approach in *Re Tepper* should be viewed cautiously. The 'armchair principle' of permitting regard to surrounding circumstances to establish fact and context can surely not be applied to a patent uncertainty, the resolution of which depends on proof of the testator's intention. The evidence admitted can establish as a fact the nature of the Jewish religion as practised by the testator but it is strictly incorrect to infer from that the meaning which the testator itended to be given to the phrase 'Jewish faith' when applied to others.

Construction

The decision in *Re Poulton's Will Trusts, Smail v Litchfield* [1987] 1 All ER 1068 is to be welcomed on two grounds. First, Warner J refused to apply an artificial rule of construction to a will where the natural meaning of the words did not result in any uncertainty. Secondly, the case has finally laid to rest the somewhat perverse decision in *Re Deakin, Starkey v Eyres* [1984] 3 Ch 568 which if not formally overruled can now be regarded as discredited. The case concerned the meaning to be given to the word 'relatives' which, for convenience in order to prevent failure through uncertainty, is normally construed as next of kin. This admittedly artificial construction is beneficial in cases such as gifts by will or gifts in trust where a definitive enumeration of the beneficiaries is required. But no such considerations apply to a simple power of appointment (ie one not coupled with any trust in favour of the class of objects of the power) since such a power will be valid even though the class of objects is incapable of being exhaustively enumerated, provided the qualification for membership of the class is one which makes it possible to decide whether any given person is or is not within the class (*Hawkins and Ryder on the Construction of Wills* (3rd edition) pp 174–178 cited with approval by Warner J in *Re Poulton* at 1070). Accordingly, in such a case 'relatives' is construed in its ordinary meaning as extending to all persons related to the propositus, however remotely. Such was the conclusion in *Poulton* where the testatrix bequeathed to P, her only daughter, the whole of her estate for life and on P's death 'whatever remains to be divided amongst her own relatives according to her own discretion'. P appointed in favour of her cousin's children who, though strictly not her next of kin, were held entitled. *Re Deakin* which had decided, despite the provisions of the Powers of Appointment Act 1874, that relations meant next of kin in powers of appointment, was not followed.

Class gift

There have been a number of modern cases considering the somewhat vexed question of the exclusion of the class closing rules, which are equally relevant to inter vivos settlements or will trusts. Three of the best known of these cases, namely *Re Edmondson's Will Trusts, Baron Sandford of Banbury v Edmondson* [1972] 1 All ER 444; *Re Chapman's Settlement Trusts, Jones v Chapman* [1978] 1 All ER 1122 and *Re Clifford's Settlement Trusts, Heaton v Westwater* [1980] 1 All ER 1013 were applied in *Re Tom's Settlement, Rose v Evans* [1987] 1 All ER 1081. In that case the rules were held to have been excluded by express language in the deed showing an unequivocal intention that the class was to remain open until a defined date. The established analysis of the rules as resolving the inconsistent intentions inherent in most class gifts (ie that all the members of the class should take but that each member should take his share as soon as he was entitled to do so) was restated by the Vice-Chancellor.

Administration of estates

It is trite law that trustees are bound to hold an even hand among their beneficiaries and not favour one as against another, a rule which finds expression in the trust for sale imposed by the rule in *Howe v Earl of Dartmouth, Howe v Countess of Aylesbury* (1802) 7 Ves 137. The general principle was applied in *Lloyds Bank plc v Duker* [1987] 3 All ER 193 to justify an exception to the general rule that a person entitled to an aliquot share of an estate was entitled to insist on a corresponding part of the estate property being distributed to him intact if it was readily divisible, rather than the whole property being sold and the proceeds distributed. A testator owned 999 of the 1000 shares in a company, the remaining share being owned by his wife. The shares formed part of his residuary estate which was bequeathed to his wife and other beneficiaries in specified proportions, the wife's share being 46/80ths. This resulted in the wife being entitled to 574 shares. The wife died before the shares could be transferred to her and she left her whole estate to Duker who thus claimed the 574 shares. The other beneficiaries of the husband's will objected to the transfer of these shares since, because they constituted a majority shareholding in the company, were worth more than 46/80ths of the total value of the estate. The court, whilst accepting the principle of aliquot distribution established in *Re Marshall, Marshall v Marshall* [1914] 1 Ch 192, *Re Sandeman's Will Trusts, Sandeman v Hayne* [1937] 1 All ER 368 and *Re Weiner's Will Trusts, Wyner v Braithwaite* [1956] 2 All ER 482, recognised that the rule could be displaced by special circumstances and decided that such circumstances existed in this case. The majority shareholding was worth markedly more per share than any minority shareholding and whereas the minority shareholders were unlikely to receive any income by way of dividend in the foreseeable future, Mr Duker as controlling shareholder and managing director could take an income by way of salary without declaring any dividends. Accordingly the bank as trustee was directed to sell all 999 shares on the open market and divide the proceeds in the specified proportions.

It seems obvious that the aliquot distribution rule would have no application to land, as to allow one of the beneficiaries to take an individual share of the land would be detrimental to the others because it would leave them with undivided shares, which would be worth less than their proper proportion of the proceeds of sale of the entire estate ([1987] 3 All ER 193 at 198, per John Mowbray QC citing Cozens-Hardy MR in *Re Marshall* [1914] 1 Ch 192 at 199).

The Pink Panther case

In *Rickless v United Artists Corporation* [1987] 1 All ER 679 Sir Nicolas Browne-Wilkinson V-C reiterated the principle that personal representatives are not the agents of the deceased; their powers rest not on the authority given to them by the deceased but on the authority given to them by law to stand in the place of the deceased (ibid at 689). The action was brought by the personal representatives of the actor Peter Sellers and concerned the well known Pink Panther series of films. After Sellers' death the defendant's film company made a new film using clips and discarded material from the previous films without securing the consent of the actor's personal representatives and without paying them for the use of the material. It was successfully alleged that this constituted a breach of s 2 of the Dramatic and Musical Performers' Protection Act 1958. The Vice-Chancellor rejected an argument that the giving of the requisite consent was personal to the actor and could not vest as a right in his personal representatives. Whether rights were personal and died with that person (such as the right to consent to the exercise of a power of appointment) or could vest in his personal representatives, depended in each case on the nature of the right. It has been held that prima facie a right conferred on a man by statute survives his death and that clear words are required if it is to be held that the right dies with the person given that right (Sir Nicolas Browne-Wilkinson V-C at 689, citing *Dean v Wiesengrund* [1955] 2 All ER 432). In the absence of such words in s 2 of the 1958 Act, it was held that the right to consent to the use of the filmed material in the case vested in the personal representatives of Peter Sellers and that since such consent had not been obtained damages were awarded. The judge accepted that this conclusion in effect meant that performers' rights under the statute were (unlike copyright), both of indefinite duration and unregulated by statute.

Intestacy

Re Basham (deceased) [1987] 1 All ER 405 is in many ways the most remarkable of the cases reported on succession in 1987. A step-daughter was held to be entitled to her step-father's intestate estate, against the legally entitled relatives, by virtue of proprietary estoppel. The facts which were considered to justify this novel conclusion were as follows. The deceased married the plaintiff's mother when the plaintiff was 15 and from that time she helped her step-father in his various businesses until his death 30 years later. When she married she was discouraged by the deceased from moving away, and she continued to assist him in his various enterprises. The deceased owned a cottage and had on numerous occasions indicated to the plaintiff that she would get the cottage when he died in return for what she had done for him. He reiterated that intention on his deathbed. The deceased died intestate leaving an estate of some £43,000, comprising the cottage valued at £21,000 and cash of £23,000. Two nieces were his next of kin and prima facie they were entitled to the whole estate under the intestacy rules. Edward Nugee QC (sitting as a Deputy Judge of the High Court) decided that the facts raised a proprietary estoppel in the plaintiff's favour, giving rise to a trust, entitling her to the whole estate. There is, of course, no doubt that principles of estoppel can given rise to proprietary interests in land and other property and this has been forcefully illustrated by recent cases such as *Grant v Edwards* [1986] 2 All ER 426 and *Greasley v Cooke* [1980] 3 All ER 710. But the difficulties of applying such principles to the facts of this case are surely formidable. First, it can be said that the representation relied on to found the estoppel should be related to an existing right or interest, it cannot surely be sufficient if it refers only to a future expectation of inheritance. Secondly, proprietary estoppel is invariably related to a particular identifiable property and seems inappropriate to the whole, or the residue, of a previous estate, which is indefinite, undetermined and fluctuating. In the case there was certainly evidence of representations in favour of the step-daughter as far as the cottage was concerned but the evidence seems less clear in relation to the rest of the estate.

Constructive trusts also have an established role in the law of succession and have been imposed on personal representatives to prevent a fraudulent disposition by property, but these have hitherto been confined to established doctrines such as mutual wills, as in *Re Cleaver (deceased), Cleaver v Insley* [1981] 2 All ER 1018 or secret trusts, as in *Ottaway v Norman* [1971] 3 All ER 1325. The judge justified the imposition of the trust in this case on general equitable principles ([1987] 1 All ER at 415, citing *Griffiths v Williams* (1977) 248 EG 947):

> 'The question then arises in what manner effect should be given to the equity which has arisen in the plaintiff's favour. The extent of the equity is to have made good, so far as may fairly be done between the parties the expectations which the deceased encouraged'.

Such a proposition seems to go beyond existing authorities and could open the door to all manner of claims and disputes against intestate estates.

It is interesting to speculate why the desired result was not sought by invoking other well established jurisdictions of the law of succession. The plaintiff could have pleaded a contract to leave the property to her by will (see *Schaefer v Schuhmann* [1972] 1 All ER 621) or alternatively the case of *Re Leach, Leach v Linderman* [1985] 2 All ER 754 provides some encouragement to a claim as a step-daughter under the Inheritance (Provision for Family and Dependants) Act 1975.

Taxation

JOHN TILEY, MA, BCL
Reader in the Law of Taxation, University of Cambridge
Fellow of Queen's College, Cambridge

1987 has been an interesting year with the usual crop of cases on familiar problems. There have been few cases of outstanding importance.

General

Four matters stand out as being of general importance. The first is the perennial battle about the nature of the task facing the courts when dealing with tax legislation. There are times, particularly when dealing with matters in the areas of capital gains or corporations, when the process of statutory interpretation becomes a very arid exercise. This is all the more likely if the courts are not presented with any arguments based on policy and if, as seems of be the case, counsel involved give the judges such a narrow view of the area of law involved that it is tantamount to studying a work of art by looking at it through the keyhole of a door on the other side of the room.

A strong antidote to a part of this habit is provided by the decision of the House of Lords in *IRC v Mobil North Sea Ltd* [1987] STC 458 where a unanimous House of Lords decided in favour of the taxpayer and reversed a unanimous Court of Appeal which had in turn upheld the decision of the Chancery Division in favour of the Revenue; the Special Commissioners had decided in favour of the taxpayer.

The issue was the meaning to be given to the expression 'in pursuance of' in the FA 1981, s 111 which provided that the section was not to disqualify any expenditure incurred before 1 January 1981 or which is incurred before 1 January 1983 'in pursuance of' a contract entered into before 1 January 1981. The taxpayer (M) was a company with a licence to prospect for oil in the North Sea. In 1979 M made a contract with Bechtel (B) whereby B would arrange for the construction of all necessary installations in return for a fixed fee and reimbursement of expenditure. In 1981 B made such contracts. There were two ways in which B could have made such contracts. One was to use the constructing firm as a sub-contractor for its own liability to M; the other was to make contracts as agent for M. The only difference would be that M could sue and be sued on the agency contract but not on the sub-contract; however as B had to warrant the work of any agent this was not a matter of great import. The Revenue agreed that if the work had been done by a sub-contractor the expenditure would have been allowable as it would have been 'in pursuance of' the contract made with B; however it argued that an agency contract was quite different.

Lord Templeman would have none of this. A literal interpretation of the statute was quite hopeless. The statute was ambiguous and therefore regard should be had to the intention of Parliament as it appeared from the statute.

That purpose was to preserve the right to deduct expenditure to which M was contractually committed—for a period. The period might be arbitrary but the purpose was not. Here M was contractually liable to pay for the work and therefore the expense was deductible.

The Revenue put up a counter-anomaly. What if the M had done the work itself in the course of 1981? Clearly that would not have been deductible so why should it make any difference? Lord Templeman's answer was that s 111 only applied to contracts.

One may contrast the approach of Lord Templeman with that of Lloyd LJ in the Court of Appeal ([1987] STC 1) who found the search for a purpose behind the legislation unhelpful. The purposive approach, he said, was legitimate, and often very helpful, where the statutory purpose was simple and clear. But where it was not clear it was at best a waste of effort and at worst thoroughly misleading. Here the matter was not clear as one could not tell whether the purpose was in s 111(1) which prohibited the deduction or in s 111(7) which allowed an exemption for expenditure to which taxpayers were already committed.

The second case of general importance is *R v IRC, ex p Fulford-Dobson* [1987] STC 344 which states that extra statutory concessions carry their own general anti-avoidance provision. Inside the cover of the booklet of concessions is the statement 'A concession will not be given in any case where an attempt is made to use it for tax avoidance.' This enabled the Revenue to resist judicial review of their decision to withhold the concession.

In this case the taxpayer was attempting to use Conc D2 to avoid CGT. This states that where a person establishes non-residence he is not subject to CGT on gains accruing after the date of his departure from the UK. The taxpayer's wife has inherited property which had subsequently increased in value. He accepted an offer of employment in Germany. Eleven days later she transferred the property to him by deed of gift, a disposal which had to be treated as being at her base cost (CGTA 1979, s 44); he left for Germany and, four days after the gift, he sold the property.

McNeill J held that concessions were lawful and were properly made subject to the condition at the front of the booklet. Moreover there was no procedural impropriety in the Revenue's failure to issue guidelines relating to the operation of the concessions. He rejected the taxpayer's argument that the Revenue was not entitled to discriminate between taxpayers who brought themselves within the terms of the relief and that every taxpayer was entitled to minimise the terms of their liability to tax. As a tail piece one may note that if the taxpayer had been able to time his gift so that the four days period straddled the end of the year of assessment he would not have had to rely on Conc D2 at all. Whether the Revenue would have used *Furniss v Dawson* against him in such circumstances is a fascinating question; if they would not have done one wonders where the justice lies in the decision to withhold the concessionary relief here.

The third case is *R v HM Treasury, ex p Daily Mail and General Trust plc* [1987] STC 157, the Treasury had refused its consent to a change of corporate residence to the Netherlands under TA 1970, s 482(1). The taxpayer sought to challenge that decision on the basis that art 52 of the EEC treaty allowed it to move. McPherson J referred the matter to the European Court—a potent reminder of the effect of the Treaty of Rome.

Lastly there is *R v IRC, ex p Woolwich Equitable Building Society* [1987] STC 654 which is a reminder of the basic principle that income tax is an annual tax charged on the income of one year. Nolan J granted the taxpayers a declaration that reg 11 of the Income Tax Building Societies Regulations 1986, SI 1986 No 482 was unlawful. The combined effect of reg 11 and another regulation was that for the year 1986–87 and 1987–88 the Society and its members would be liable to tax on the dividends and interest for a total period of 29 months. This cannot have been what Parliament intended.

Avoidance

There has been some clarification of the decision of the House of Lords in *Furniss v Dawson* [1984] 1 All ER 530. *Sherdley v Sherdley* [1987] 2 All ER 54, [1987] STC 217 concerned the power of the court to make an order for the payment of school fees against, and on the application of, the custodial parent. The House of Lords reversed the decision of the Court of Appeal and held that it can exercise that power even where the only purpose behind the order is to secure a tax advantage. In the House the only substantial speech was that of Lord Brandon. He held that as the court clearly has the power to make an order where the application is by the non-custodial parent, and the Revenue did not seek to argue otherwise, there was no good reason why the court should not make such an order at the suit of the custodial parent. To grant an order where it was desirable for the children to live with the mother but not where they were to live with the father was nonsense.

Three points should be noted. First, Lord Brandon thought it was clearly open to the Revenue to argue that the practice of treating a court order as outside the scope of TA 1970, s 437 could be reviewed. Secondly, if the force behind the decision of the House is in the avoidance of anomaly it is surely just as anomalous that the parties should be able to deduct school fees if the parents are separated but not if they are living harmoniously together. Thirdly one should note the unqualified rejection by Lord Brandon of Sir John Donaldson's description of the scheme as a sham. The doctrine of the sham is now confined once more to situations in which the parties present to the court a legal characterisation of the facts which is not what they intended of achieved.

This case has been taken to show that the new approach will not undo steps taken to avoid tax simply because of that motive. Yet caution is in order since Lord Brandon did not explain why the new approach should not apply to the school fees scheme; he said simply that it was 'not relevant' to the issue of whether the court should exercise its jurisdiction to make the order. This does not even address the problem. The order is made; the payments are made; can the Revenue now use the new approach to undo the scheme? On this Lord Brandon is completely silent. Yet if such an attack would succeed, should the court be making the order in the first place? This was of course precisely what troubled the Court of Appeal. Such a Revenue move is unlikely but that does not mean that the departmental position is correct. There cannot be one approach for the corporate sector and another for the family area.

Meanwhile practioners are left not only to guess what the tax courts may do but also to wonder just how far the courts will go in allowing parties to obtain orders; the parties have to obtain orders from the court for the tax consequences to follow (*Harvey v Sivyer* [1986] Ch 119) and orders cannot be varied simply because the parties want it. Thus the parties cannot rearrange their maintenance obligations each year to obtain the best tax result; but will the parties be allowed to use a constant formula for their obligations, such as paying to each child such sum as is equal to the personal allowance (or a prescribed fraction of it) for that year and the balance to the parent?

The second decision is found in the 43 pages of judgments in the combined appeals by the Crown in *Craven (Inspector of Taxes) v White, IRC v Bowater Property Developments Ltd* and *Baylis (Inspector of Taxes) v Gregory* [1987] 3 All ER 27, [1987] STC 297.

The essential problem is when steps will be taken to be 'preordained' for the purpose of the test enunciated by Lord Brightman in *Furniss v Dawson*— which allows the courts to link up transactions which are preordained steps in a scheme to avoid tax. In these cases the first step was taken but the second step did not follow when it should have done. In *Craven v White* there was a sale to a different party. In *Bowater* the sale fell through because of lack of money but was then revived when the purchaser's affairs improved. In *Baylis v Gregory* there was no firm purchaser in mind at the time of the first step and the sale eventually took place some 22 months later.

The Revenue's position as put to the Court of Appeal was ([1987] 3 All ER at 36, [1987] STC at 305):

> 'It is only necessary [for the Revenue] to prove that at the time of the first transaction it was intended by the taxpayer that the first transaction should be used as conveyancing machinery in order to achieve a final disposal of the asset if a disposal was ultimately made... [P]rovided the machinery by which the commercial end is achieved is preordained, it is irrelevant that there remains a possibility that its execution may be frustrated by a failure to achieve the commercial end itself or that at the time of the first transaction there was no immediate prospect or intention of finally disposing of the asset.'

As was pointed out by Slade LJ ([1987] 3 All ER at 37, [1987] STC at 306):

> 'The essential link required [by this argument]... does not depend on the identification at the first stage of the ultimate purchaser or the proposed terms of his purchase, or indeed upon the likelihood or otherwise of the second transaction following the first. The essential link is the intention of the taxpayer at the time of the first transaction.'

Thus the new approach would apply even if at the time of the first transaction there was no intention of selling and the first disposal was simply a springboard to a possible sale. This argument was rejected by every member of the court. Steps are only to be linked if there is a practical certainty that the next one will be carried out.

The Revenue's argument may be contrasted with the USA where it is accepted that transactions cannot be linked under the step transaction doctrine if the earlier one is 'old and cold.' There are good reasons both of policy and practicality for this limitation. Anti-avoidance doctrines enunciated by courts are not going to stop all avoidance and the courts must decide whether they are going to accept this and be content with a threshold doctrine that will stop only some forms of avoidance or go beyond that and enunciate formulae, like that contended for by the Revenue, which create great uncertainty in the law, which can be used by the taxpayer as much as by the Revenue and which lack any basis of intellectual credibility. 1988 should see this matter resolved by the House of Lords.

The last two cases concern specific anti-avoidance provisions. In *Bird v ICR* [1987] STC 168 the Court of Appeal was faced with one result of applying *Furniss v Dawson* in connection with TA 1970, s 460 and the meaning of the expression 'tax advantage.' A loan had been made to the taxpayers. As a result of the new approach the attempt to escape tax failed; therefore, said the taxpayers, using the new approach meant that no tax advantage had been obtained, if the new approach is one of construction the logic of this is hard to fault. They were encouraged to take this line by the fact that it was now too late for the Revenue to make an assessment under s 286! The court said that the taxpayer had nonetheless obtained a tax advantage; this was the clearer because s 466 referred to avoiding a 'possible assessment' and here it was certain that a possible assessment had been avoided and likely that a real assessment had been avoided.

This left the most troublesome part of the case—what allowance could be made in the s 460 assessment for the tax that would have to be paid by other companies in the group. At first instance Vinelott J had felt able to distinguish the previous decision of the House of Lords in *Williams v IRC* [1980] 3 All ER 321, [1980] STC 535 which had forbidden such offsets. The Court of Appeal felt unable to make the same distinction and therefore left assessments of tax on the various entities which totalled £2.5m on a total payment of £2.18m which was by way of loan. It is not suprising that Sir Nicolas Browne-Wilkinson V-C described the result as grossly inequitable but it was clear that the doctrine of precedent required it. The key question is what the House of Lords will do. The challenge to prevent such a result while maintaining a sensible system of construction of statutes must be met. The matter is all the more urgent because of the powers of reconstructing tax transactions created by *Furniss v Dawson*; that power must be accompanied by a sensible power to adjust other tax consequences.

Sugarwhite v Budd (Inspector of Taxes) [1987] STC 491 involves TA 1970, s 488. The taxpayer had bought land in London; later he agreed to sell the land to M Ltd, a Bahamian company, at an undervalue which gave a small profit; the contract allowed M to subsell or nominate another purchaser. T Ltd was the eventual purchaser. The purchase money was divided between the taxpayer, M Ltd and other Bahamian companies. The taxpayer reported his profit as the difference between his cost and what he received—£5,000 but the inspector applied s 488 and said that the gains accruing to the Bahamian companies were of a capital nature and so liable to be attributed to the taxpayer under s 488. The taxpayer argued that the gains accruing to the Bahamian companies were of a trading nature so that s 488 did not apply. Vinelott J held that the Commissioners were entitled to apply s 488 since the taxpayer had provided no evidence that the Bahamian companies did anything other than act as passive recipients of profits. Gains could thus be assumed to be capital—presumably because the onus is on the taxpayer to disprove the assessment.

Employment income:

Schedule E

First there are two cases on the scope of employment. The law applicable in this area is reasonably clear; the question is whether the contract under which the work is done is one of service or for services, a test well known in various legal contexts. In *Sidey v Phillips (Inspector of Taxes)* [1987] STC 87 Knox J said that while the question whether a contract is one of service or for services is one of law, the evaluation of the various matters relevant to applying the test is a task for the Commissioners.

The taxpayer was a non-practising barrister with three sources of income, one of which was part-time lecturing on legal subjects for two education authorities, the ILEA and a polytechnic. The Commissioners looked at the contracts and determined that they were contracts of service with the result that the taxpayer was correctly assessed under Schedule E. The taxpayer's appeal was dismissed.

The taxpayer had listed various points but none of them would justify the court in reversing the Commissioners' decision. Knox J described payment by the hour as a relevant but not very weighty factor. The point that there might be other duties which fell outside the period for which he had been paid, such as marking papers, was relevant but not conclusive. The old test of control, especially in its current attenuated form, was satisfied. The taxpayer's argument that he could be dismissed without notice was held to rest on an incorrect construction of the contract. The fact that the contract was not always adhered to provided the taxpayer with stronger ground but in the end did not matter as the court was concerned to classify the contract rather than the way in which it was performed or not performed. Finally the fact that the employment was discontinuous did not prevent it from being an employment.

In *Walls v Sinnett (Inspector of Taxes)* [1987] STC 236 the Commissioners had held that the contract was one of service and Vinelott J held simply that there was ample evidence to support that conclusion. As the income in question came from an established post in a technical college with an established grade (Grade II) one would have thought that this case could have been disposed of on the basis that there was an office.

In *Hamblett v Godfrey (Inspector of Taxes)* [1987] 1 All ER 916, [1987] STC 60 the Court of Appeal upheld the decision of Knox J (see All ER Rev 1986, p 296) that payments to workers at GCHQ for giving up various rights, including that of belonging to a trade union, were taxable. Purchas LJ held that as the rights being surrendered by the taxpayer were 'inextricably connected' with her employment at GCHQ, and without such employment there would have been no need for such rights, the payment was taxable. The position might have been different if the right being relinquished was one to carry on some social activity unconnected with her employment or a fundamental freedom such as freedom of speech. The former presumably refers to cases such as *Jarrold v Boustead* (1963) 41 TC 701 which was cited by counsel but not in the judgment while the latter raises some nice questions if for example a member of MI5 gives up a right to publish his memoirs.

Leave to appeal to the House of Lords was refused. This decision on general principles meant that there was no need to consider FA 1976, s 61; this is disappointing since it would have been interesting to learn how a payment in cash could come within legislation designed to catch benefits in kind.

There are two cases of PAYE. *R v IRC, ex p Sims* [1987] STC 211 is a reminder of the Revenue powers to recover tax from an employee where the employer has wilfully failed to deduct tax under the PAYE system and the employee knows of this failure. Schiemann J held that on the evidence the Commissioners were entitled to conclude that the taxpayer, a director of the company, had knowledge of the failure to deduct. In *R v IRC, ex p Cook* [1987] STC 434 the taxpayers were the only directors and shareholders of the employer. Nolan J held that they were liable for the tax which had not been deducted, even though they had used independent accountants to operate the PAYE side of things and there has been no concealment or suggestion of fraud.

Business income:

Schedule D, Cases I and II

This has been an interesting year with cases embroidering established case law and principles. First there are two cases on receipts. *Ryan (Inspector of Taxes) v Crabtree Denims Ltd* [1987] STC 402 concerns subsidies and involved a re-examination of the decision of the House of Lords in *Seaham Harbour Dock Co Ltd v Crook* (1931) 16 TC 333. The taxpayer company was keen to liquidate or dispose of its business but the Department of Trade and Industry was anxious to keep both business and workforce in place and so to encourage a takeover. To this end the Department offered an interest relief grant of some £47,000. The Commissioners applied the *Seaham* case and held that as the purpose was to keep the business alive and thus maintain employment the grant was a capital receipt. Hoffman J held that this was not sufficient to make the payment capital. The *Seaham* case was based on the finding that, even though the payment was calculated on the basis of interest that would have been charged, the purpose of the payment was to add to the capital available to the company to carry out certain works. A payment which is expressly earmarked for a revenue purpose or even one which is undifferentiated as between capital and income will generally be treated as a revenue receipt *(Poulter (Inspector of Taxes) v Gayjon Processes Ltd* [1985] STC 174); one situation in which it might not be revenue is where the payment is large in size in relation to the capital of the company but that was not so here.

The case is of importance since it illustrates both the tendency to regard payments as revenue rather than capital and the importance of the distinction. If the payment had been held to be a capital receipt there would be no liability, not even a capital gains charge since there was no disposal of an asset.

Donald Fisher (Ealing) Ltd v Spencer (Inspector of Taxes) [1987] STC 423 holds that a surrogatum for increased revenue expenditure is a trading receipt. At a rent review the taxpayer's agent failed to serve a counter notice in time and therefore the taxpayer had to pay a higher rent than would otherwise have been due; compensation was paid by the agent. The taxpayer argued that the case was the obverse of *Tucker v Granada Motorway Services* [1977] STC 353, where a payment to secure a variation of a lease was held to be a capital expense. That case, said Walton J, involved a variation of a capital asset of the company (the lease) whereas here there was no variation of the lease. All that had happened was that negligence on the part of the agent had made the rent higher than it would otherwise have been, citing the well known words of Diplock LJ in *London and Thames Haven Oil Wharves Ltd v Attwooll* [1967] 2 All ER 124 at 134. Whether compensation was for loss of profit or for increase in expenditure there was compensation for the fact that the profits were less than they ought to have been. This raises another thought. Suppose that the effect of the rent review was that the tenant had agreed to pay not an increased rent but a premium; and had received compensation from the agent as a result. As the premium would not have been deductible presumably the compensation for extra premium would not have been taxable—but presumably the agent could have deducted the compensation in computing his profits.

One last matter arises. The payment was a trading receipt of one year; there was no spreading of the receipt over the years to which the claim related. If the taxpayer had wished to arrange for spreading he might have been able to arrange this by accepting that the agent should pay the damages in annual instalments although the Revenue might argue that as the right to the payments had accrued to the trader the whole sum, suitably discounted, should be a receipt of the one year.

The other four cases concern deductions. *E Bott Ltd v Price (Inspector of Taxes)* [1987] STC 100 involved a re-examination of *Heather v P-E Consulting Group Ltd* (1972) 48 TC 293. The taxpayer company made a payment to trustees to enable the trustees to acquire shares in the company. The Commissioners held (i) that the expenditure was revenue not capital but (ii) that it was not wholly and exclusively for company's trade. On appeal Hoffman J reversed the Commissioners on (ii); the Commissioners had distinguished the *Heather* case on grounds which he found to be insubstantial.

The distinctions which had appealed to the Commissioners were (a) that in *Heather* there was an obligation to go on making payments whereas here there was none; (b) that here no reference was made in the settlement to the acquisition by trustees of shares in the company (but Hoffman J said that the purchase was clearly the principal object) and (c) that here there was no obligation on the part of existing shareholders to offer their shares to the trustees; in contrast the trusts in *Heather* were clearly designed to retain the goodwill. Hoffman J added that in *Heather* the Revenue were arguing that another advantage of the scheme was to prevent a hostile takeover, which suggested a capital classification, and the detailed evidence was therefore put in by the taxpayers to show that in the peculiar circumstances of that business there was an advantage to the conduct of the business itself in not having control acquired by an outside purchaser.

In *Beauchamp (Inspector of Taxes) v FW Woolworth plc* [1987] STC 279 the taxpayer company raised a loan of 50m Swiss francs for five years, the minimum period allowed under the exchange control rules then in force. The loans were repaid at a loss in sterling terms; was the loss deductible?

The Special Commissioners were invited by the parties to treat the matter as one of fact and degree and concluded that the company was not seeking to add permanently to its capital structure but was dealing with what appeared to be a short term problem of cash shortage; they therefore held that the loss was deductible. It was agreed on all sides that the precise use to which the company put the money was not be be examined.

In reversing this decision Hoffman J distinguished short term banking facilities, 'short in the sense that they were for short or indefinite periods borrowed as occasion required and repaid as opportunity permitted' from 'money borrowed on a permanent footing, as from year to year' where 'the capital of the concern is in a commercial sense enlarged thereby, and the business extended.' This loan was therefore on capital account. He held that the Commissioners had paid too much attention to what the company was seeking to do, ie get over a cash shortage, rather than what they actually did, which was to negotiate a five year loan. He said that the use to which the money was put would be relevant if there was no fixed term for repayment or where the term was of a borderline nature but that was not the case here.

In *RTZ Oil and Gas Ltd v Ellis (Inspector of Taxes)* [1987] STC 512, billions of pounds were at stake. The issue was whether close-down costs on North Sea oil installations are capital or revenue. The costs concerned a drilling rig and tankers, which had been hired and converted to suit the needs of the Argyll field. At the end of those leases the rig and the tankers had to be reconverted to their original state. The taxpayers also claimed the cost of removing the equipment form the sea bed as capital. Vinelott J held that all items were to meet future expenditure on captial account and therefore barred by TA 1970, s 130(f). The sea bed equipment was part of the apparatus required for the winning of the oil—it was also an item to which they were committed as from the start. The rig and the tankers were profit earning apparatus and the contracts of hire were capital assets, the fact that they were non-assignable and had no balance sheet value did not affect the matter. *Tucker v Granada Motorway Services Ltd* [1977] STC 353 dictated this conclusion. The Commissioners had rejected alternative submissions by the Crown, that the payment was not wholly and exclusively for the purposes of trade, that the losses did not relate to the years under appeal and that the quantification of the losses was too uncertain.

Overseas Containers (Finance) Ltd v Stoker (Inspector of Taxes) [1987] STC 547 revives interest in *FA and AB Ltd v Lupton* [1972] AC 634, [1971] 3 All ER 948. P Co had loans from German shipbuilders in deutschmarks. Devaluation of sterling against the deutschmark was anticipated; the taxpayer company (T) was set up to take over the loans so that they became debts of T not P; P and other companies in the group were debited with the then sterling equivalent of the loans. The purpose of the operation was to enable T to argue that the exchange loss on its loans which would, and did occur, were part of its trading transactions and therefore gave rise to a trading loss and so available for group relief. The loss that would have accrued to P would have been a capital loss.

Vinelott J decided in favour of the Revenue, as had the Special Commissioners. These were not trading transactions since they were entered into solely for fiscal purposes; the interposition of the taxpayer company achieved no commercial purpose. The judgment goes on to consider, inconclusively, whether if the company had been trading it would have been borrowing on capital or revenue account. There are important comments on *European Investment Trust Co Ltd v Jackson (Inspector of Taxes)* (1932) 18 TC 1 and an Australian decision—*AVCO Financial Services Ltd v FC of T* [1982] 41 ALR 225 which distinguishes money borrowed for use in its trade from money borrowed in the course of its trade.

Capital allowances

Four cases raise four short points. In *Elliss (Inspector of Taxes) v BP Oil Northern Refinery Ltd* [1987] STC 52 the Court of Appeal upheld the decision of Walton J that a company is not required to take all the capital allowances to which it is entitled but may take only such allowances as it wishes to take. The Revenue argued that since 1965 corporation tax had treated the allowance as a trading expense and so the previous right to deduct had been replaced by a duty to do so. The court held that while the new tax required the allowance to be given effect as a trading expense it did not make it a trading expense.

Thomas (Inspector of Taxes) v Reynolds [1987] STC 135 is a nice case on the distinction between plant used in a business and the setting in which the business was carried on. Walton J, reversing the Commissioners, held that an inflatable dome purchased by professional tennis coaches to enable them to continue coaching through the winter months was a setting rather than plant, to use the conventional terminology; the test was whether the dome could be said to play any direct part in the taxpayer's business. The case stated had set out four matters; that the dome enabled coaching to be carried on right through the winter; that it protected the playing area from the weather; that it created warmer conditions for the players and that it increased revenue. These, said Walton J, were not enough. Moreover it was too late for the taxpayers to raise arguments based on the fact that the dome provided ideal atmospheric conditions and diffused the exterior flood lighting.

Gaspet Ltd v Elliss (Inspector of Taxes) [1987] STC 362 concerns CAA 1968, s 91(1)(a) which allows a deduction where a person carrying on a trade 'incurs expenditure on scientific research related to that trade and directly undertaken by him or on his behalf.' The taxpayer argued that the phrase covered any research undertaken in its interest or for its benefit but the Revenue argued, successfully, for a narrower interpretation. The Court of Appeal upheldd the decision of Peter Gibson J. There had to be a close, but not necessarily contractual, link. Such a link would clearly be shown where the work was undertaken by someone as agent for the taxpayer. The taxpayer had to be responsible for the research itself and not merely for the financing of it. The judges left open the question whether the allowance is available where there is such an agency carrying out the research but the agent then subcontracts the work to another body.

Burman (Inspector of Taxes) v Westminster Press Group [1987] STC 669 concerns the interaction of capital allowances and CGT. The taxpayers had brought a printing press; they had been given a first year capital allowance but this was retrospectively withdrawn because the press was not used. The press was then disposed of. They claimed exemption from capital gains liability as the press was tangible movable property which was a wasting asset and so exempt under what is now CGTA 1979, s 127(1) but the Revenue argued that while the asset fulfilled all these conditions it was taken out of the exempt category by s 127(2) because the asset had 'otherwise qualified in full for any captial allowance.' Knox J found in favour of the taxpayer. An asset from which the allowance was withdrawn did not qualify in full for the allowance. The disturbing thing about this judgment is the absence of any discussion of the reasons for any of these rules.

Schedule D Case III

IRC v Crawley [1987] STC 147 raises a question about covenanted payments made to a charity more than six years in arrears. When the charity sought repayment of the tax the Revenue said the claim had to be made within six years of the year in which the payment fell due and so refused it. The Special Commissioners decided in favour of the charity but Vinelott J allowed the Revenue's appeal; payments under s 52 were income of the payee in the years in which they fell due. There is much to be said for the decision of Vinelott J at a technical level and it is good to see so thorough a discussion of s 52 and the problems of timing; all this part of the judgment seems entirely correct. Yet there is a practical problem; presumably the Revenue will not make a repayment of tax until the payment has been received by the charity.

Trusts

In *Stevenson (Inspector of Taxes) v Wishart* [1987] 2 All ER 428, [1987] STC 266 the Court of Appeal dismissed the Revenue's appeal from the judgment of Knox J (see All ER Rev 1986, p 300). Payments out of capital to a beneficiary who is entitled to capital are capital payments (and not income payments) even though there are several such payments and are for the maintenance of the beneficiary. This does not mean that the payment escaped tax altogether since, as Fox LJ noted, capital transfer tax had been paid in respect of the distribution; one should add that if they were income payments they would not be subject to CTT–IHTA, s 65(5)(b). If the Revenue wish to maintain that any payment out of the trust to a person interested in income and capital will be treated as income regardless of source FA 1973, s 17 will have to be amended.

Capital gains

First there is the decision of the Court of Appeal in *Kirby (Inspector of Taxes) v Thorn EMI plc* [1987] STC 621. Thorn EMI owned a subsidiary, MI, which in turn held all the shares in three subsidiaries. Thorn arranged for the sale by MI of its holdings in the three subsidiaries to GEC. Under the deal GEC paid Thorn nearly £316,000; in return Thorn undertook to ensure that no company in its group would compete with the trades of the three subsidiaries for a period of five years. Was Thorn liable to tax on the payment received?

The assessment to corporation tax was made on the basis that the payment was a capital gain. The Revenue therefore had to show that there was a gain arising from the disposal of an asset. The Revenue argued that, as a matter of general principle, capital gains can arise where an asset is created by the disposal. Here the covenant by Thorn conferred rights on GEC and the asset thus created by Thorn was disposed of to GEC. This could be derived from the definition of asset in CGTA 1979, s 19(1)(c) which includes 'any form of property created by the person disposing of it or otherwise coming to be owned without being acquired.' This argument was rejected. Where an asset is created by the act of disposal it cannot give rise to liability unless it comes within a special rule, eg that which directs that the grant of an option is a disposal. This can give rise to a difference in tax treatment of two situations which are very close. Thus a contract to sell the copyright of a script not yet written or shares not yet owned would not be a disposal whereas the grant of an option would be. This, said Nicholls L J, simply sprang from the structure of the Act as he had interpreted it. This quite fascinating problem will, one hopes, be considered by the House of Lords in due course.

The House may not get the chance to consider the matter in this case as it was sent back to the Commissioners for the appropriate findings of fact to be made on a different argument, raised for the first time in the Court of Appeal. This was that Thorn had disposed of goodwill. Thorn argued that the payment was for a curtailing of its trading freedom and that was not an asset for capital gains purposes. Nicholls LJ agreed that the freedom to trade was not an asset for capital gains purposes. Property means that which is capable of being owned in its normal legal sense. He also accepted that the goodwill of the trades in issue belonged to the three companies rather than to the Thorn parent. However he held that Thorn itself had a reputation in this area which might attract customers to products with its name and it was precisely for this reason that GEC may have wanted the covenant; there was no evidence suggesting any other reason. He held that this could be goodwill and that the receipt of a sum would be the 'deriving' of a sum 'from' the goodwill and so within CGTA 1979, s 20 — there is a disposal of assets where any capital sum is derived from an asset, notwithstanding that no asset is acquired. The case was remitted to the Commissioners for them to hear any arguments from Thorn as to whether Thorn had a reputation in this sense and what sums if any could be deducted.

There are two cases on the scope of the main residence exemption for CGT. CGTA 1979, s 101 exempts a gain accruing on the disposal of or of an interest in (a) a dwelling house or part of a dwelling house which is, or has at any time been in his period of ownership his only or main residence, or (b) land which he has for his own occupation or enjoyment with that residence as its garden and grounds up to the permitted area.

In *Markey (Inspector of Taxes) v Sanders* [1987] STC 256 the taxpayer had an estate of some 12 acres on which there was the house in which he lived. By the entrance gates and some 130 metres stood a bungalow; this had its own garden and was screened from the view of the main house by a belt of trees and a ha-ha. The house and the bungalow had been rated as a single hereditament. Did the exemption extend to the bungalow? Walton J, reversing the General Commissioners, held that it did not. He took the decision of the Court of Appeal in *Batey v Wakefield* [1981] STC 521 as requiring the separate building to be 'very closely adjacent' to the main building and to increase the taxpayer's enjoyment of the main house. Neither of these conditions was sufficient. Walton J's test was — looking at the group of buildings in question as a whole, was it fairly possible to regard them as a single dwelling house used as the taxpayer's main residence?

In *Williams (Inspector of Taxes) v Merrylees* [1987] STC 445 Vinelott J refused to follow this decision. The taxpayer bought a four acre estate which included a house (where he lived) and a lodge (occupied by a married couple who looked after the house and gardens). The issue was whether the lodge could be treated as part of his residence. The judge felt unable to interfere with the Commissioners' decision in favour of the taxpayer — but indicated fairly clearly that he might not have reached that decision. Vinelott J then referred to the two conditions suggested in *Markey v Sanders* and said that they were an unjustified gloss on the earlier, and broader, approach of the Court of Appeal in *Batey v Wakefield* which he summarised as: is it in entity which can sensibly be described as a dwelling house though split into different buildings performing different functions?

The decision of the Court of Appeal in *Welbeck Securities Ltd v Powlson* [1987] STC 468 upholds the decision of Hoffman J. Under a consent order the taxpayer company (T) agreed to abandon and release an option to participate in a property development in return for £2m; the sum was paid. The Revenue said it was a capital sum derived from an asset and so liable under what is now CGTA 1979, s 20(1). T argued that s 137(4) stated that the abandonment of an option of this type was not to constitute the disposal of an asset by that person and this therefore excluded s 20. Hoffman J rejected T's argument. (see JFAJ 1987 BTR 304).

First Slade LJ held that the word disposal does not include the mere release of an option which is not accompanied by the acquisition of the right in question. Secondly he held that the £2m was derived from the option and not from the right under the consent order, otherwise s 20 would only catch the gain attributable to the period between the order and the receipt; that gain would be exempt as the payment of a debt.

This left the principal point, did s 137(4) exclude s 20(1)? Slade LJ held first that s 137(4) did not constitute an exception to s 20(1); all s 137(4) did was to say that the abandonment was not a disposal; that did not determine the issue whether some transaction of which the abandonment was part could be a disposal. This made it unnecessary to decide whether giving up an option for value could be an abandonment (Slade LJ thought it probably could be).

Lastly the court rejected T's argument that the gain was realised on the date of the consent order, and therefore the assessment (which assumed the gain arose on the receipt) was for the wrong accounting period. This was because CGTA 1979, s 27(1) is subject to s 20(2) which clearly applies the time of receipt as the time of the realisation. This seems odd. Section 20(2) says that the time of the disposal shall be the time the capital sum is received but s 20(3) defines capital sums as any money or money's worth and there seems little reason why the rights obtained under the consent order should not be money's worth.

In *Taddale Properties Ltd v IRC* [1987] STC 411 the question arising under the now repealed Development Land Tax was whether a certain sum was expenditure incurred 'in enhancing the value of the relevant interest' (DLTA 1976, Sch 3, para 1(1), words very close to CGTA 1979, s 32(1)(b)).

In 1978 the taxpayer company (T) sought planning permission from the council to develop site 1. The council insisted that in return for T getting permission to develop site 1, W, another company in the group, must give up its right to develop another site, 2, for industrial purposes. T agreed to compensate W. In order to effect this compensation W bought land (site 3) from a stranger and immediately sold it on to T for £280,000; £80,000 more than it had paid for it. In 1981 T sold its interest in 1. Could the £80,000 be said to be money spent by T in enhancing its interest in site 1 or was the £80,000 paid for site 3 simply paid for site 3? Scott J took the former view, the purpose was to persuade W to enter into the agreement and so enhance the value of T's rights in site 1. One assumes that if T sells site 3 the base cost will be £200,000.

Corporations

In *Frampton v IRC* [1987] STC 273 in which the Court of Appeal held that where the assets of an unincorporated association are held by trustees it is the association (rather than the individual members of the club) that is the person absolutely entitled against the trustees and so an assessment can be made on the club rather than on the individual members. This in turn means that the club cannot use the personal exemptions and allowances of the members; here the issue concerned the annual exemption for CGT (and the now-repealed DLT). This affirmed the first instance decision.

Hafton Properties Ltd v McHugh (Inspector of Taxes) [1987] STC 16 concerns the issue whether a bank is carrying on business in the UK, a matter relevant to the payer's duty to deduct income tax under TA 1970, s 54. The lender was a registered Isle of Man bank which made loans to the taxpayer on the security of property in the UK; the interest was paid to a London solicitor for the bank. The bank had gone into liquidation and the Revenue sought income tax from the borrower under s 54. Peter Gibson J decided in favour of the Revenue and held that as the bank did not take deposits it could not be said to be carrying on a banking business; he also held that the bank did not 'carry on business in' the UK.

The next case involves the interaction of the corporate reorganisation provisions in CGTA 1979, ss 78–87 and the rules for groups, particularly TA 1970, s 273. In *Westcott (Inspector of Taxes) v Woolcombers Ltd* [1987] STC 600 H, the parent company acquired three subsidiaries for £1.3m. Some time later H transferred the subsidiaries to another subsidiary, T, in return for shares in T. T then sold the shares to W, the taxpayer, and another subsidiary, for £0.6m, sustaining a loss of £0.7m as compared with the original acquisition cost to H. Later W liquidated the companies and recovered approximately £0.6m. The question was the acquisition cost to W and that depended on the acquisition cost of T. TA 1970, s 273 would make T's acquisition cost £1.3m; but s 273 applied only where there was a disposal and CGTA 1979, s 85 brought in s 78 which provided that a reorganisation is *not* to be treated as a disposal. Thus the Revenue argued that T's acquisition cost was not £1.3m but £0.6m and so no loss. This was in accordance with the general view was that T would take over at market value (thanks to what is now CGTA 1979, s 29A). However this was rejected by the court, as it had by Hoffman J earlier. Section 273 was to apply even in this situation.

The matter is not an obvious one since there is on these facts a risk of double loss relief; the loss accruing to W will be reflected in the value of W which will in turn cause a loss to its holding company. Conversely if the shares had gone up in value W would find itself liable to tax on the gain as from a base cost of £1.3m. What needs to be tackled is the problems of double taxation (and double relief) where an asset is held in corporate form; the solution may lie in some sort of imputation system for capital gains, at least within groups, but this is emphatically something only the legislature can deal with.

The last case in the section raises fascinating issues on the meaning of 'reorganisation', and so whether or not there was an allowable loss. In *Dunstan (Inspector of Taxes) v Young Austen Young Ltd* [1987] STC 709 the taxpayer (YAY) owned most of the shares in J but a share was held by a nominee (T); YAY wanted to sell J to a third party dealing at arms length (R). R insisted that J's debt to YAY (amounting to some £200,000) should be discharged first. J issued shares to YAY in return for £200,000 cash which J used to pay off the debt. YAY then sold its shares (old and new) in J to R for £38,000; T joined in the sale but got no separate payment. It was agreed that the new shares were not issued under a bargain made at arm's length and so the consideration would be the market value of the shares (probably nil) rather than the price paid. If, however, the issue was a 'reorganisation' there would be a loss of some £178,000 (on the basis of agreed calculations.)

If there had been a rights issue it was accepted that the scheme would have worked, subject to the possible application of *Furniss v Dawson*. Warner J therefore had to decide first whether the facts fitted the two situations set out in CGTA 1979, s 77(2); he concluded that they did not since the issue was not in proportion to existing holdings in J (all the shares were issued to YAY and none to T). He then had to determine whether there was a 'reorganisation' even if the facts did no fit those two categories since s 77(2) says only that the term reorganisation shall 'include' the two situations. He held that, as counsel for the Revenue had agreed, this was possible but, accepting the argument from the same source, what was important about a reorganisation was that there should be no change in the shareholders but only a change in the shareholdings. He went on to conclude that s 77(2)(a) was a virtually exhaustive statement of when an allotment of new shares would be a reorganisation.

International

The effect of *Padmore v IRC* [1987] STC 36 has been reversed by F(No 2)A, s 62, a provision which is deemed always to have had effect, save where a determination had been reached. Peter Gibson J held first that a partnership most of whose members were resident in the UK was nonetheless resident in Jersey as that was where the business was actually managed. He then held that under the UK-Jersey Double Tax Agreement a partnership resident in Jersey was not chargeable to UK income tax and so a UK resident partner was not subject to UK tax on his share of the profits of the Jersey enterprise. The last step seems open to argument but the matter is doomed to silence by the legislation.

In *Aspin v Estill (Inspector of Taxes)* [1987] STC 723 the taxpayer had a US pension; the court held that this was subject to tax in this country as a foreign possession within Schedule D case V. The principal issue in the case was that the taxpayer claimed to have been given telephone advice by the Revenue to the effect that the income could not be taxable. This was not relevant to an appeal against assessment although it might be relevant to judicial review.

Plummer v IRC [1987] STC 698 is a nice case on the rules of domicile as they apply to dual residents.

In *Dawson v IRC* [1987] STC 371 the issue was whether income from assets situated outside the UK could be subject to UK tax when it accrued to trustees but only one of the three trustees was resident in the UK.

The facts were that discretionary trusts had been created by a person resident in the UK who in the late 1960s emigrated with his wife and three minor children to Switzerland; the children were the only beneficiaries under the settlement other than those entitled on failure of the trusts for them and any other issue of the settlor. Two Swiss trustees were appointed but one English trustee was retained so that there could be one within the jurisdiction of the English court accountable for the proper conduct of the trusts under English trust law.

The Revenue assessed the one UK resident trustee in respect of basic rate income tax under general principles and in respect of additional rate under FA 1973, s 16. He resisted the assessment stressing first TA 1970, s 108 which charged income 'arising or accruing to' a person and s 114—income under Schedule D is to be charged on and paid by 'the persons receiving or entitled to' the income.

No income was remitted to the UK and none of the income in issue arose in the UK. The trustees held their meetings outside the UK; the UK resident had no power to conduct the trustees' business while he was in the UK and he did not personally receive any of the income. He therefore argued that he was outside TA 1970, ss 108 and 114. However the Revenue argued that as no beneficiary was entitled to any of the income and as none of the income could be paid out without the agreement of each trustee, there was a degree of 'negative' control which each trustee had and therefore tax was due.

Vinelott J held that this 'negative' control was not sufficient. The basis of his decision however was simpler. The Taxes Act charges income accruing to a person; the singular must be taken to include the plural 'persons'; it followed that the tax could only be due from trustees as the legal owners of the property if they were *all* resident in the UK. This is contrary to current Revenue practice.

The final paragraph is worth quoting in full ([1987] STC at 386):

> 'In the instant case the Crown is, in effect, asserting the right to tax a person resident in the UK solely upon the ground of residence on income from

property outside the UK in which he has no beneficial interest and over which he has no control, and to do so notwithstanding that he may have no right of recourse to the income on which he is assessed to tax and no right of contribution or indemnity against the income or from the person beneficially entitled to it. In my judgment the very clearest language would be required to justify a claim as wide as that.'

Inheritance tax and capital transfer tax

The decision of the Inner House of the Court of Session in *Miller v IRC* [1987] STC 108 concerns the distinction between administrative and dispositive powers in determining whether there is an interest in possession. The trustees were empowered before striking the free income for the year to appropriate such portion of the revenue as they might think proper (i) for meeting depreciation of the capital value of any of the assets in the trust and (ii) for any other reason or purpose which they might in their sole discretion deem to be advisabe or necessary. The issue was whether these extensive powers, which could after all deprive the person of all her income, were sufficient to prevent there being an interest in possession and so a charge to CCT on her death in 1982.

The Revenue argued that the power was wholly administrative; as it was only exercisable before the free income was ascertained, it followed that the person was entitled to receive the whole free income of the trust and so had an interest in possession. The Inner House accepted the Revenue's argument. Among the many points considered was that this power was exercisable in relation to gross income rather than net income; Lord Kincraig also said that the mere fact that these powers might be implied by statute if they were simply administrative did not matter, express administrative powers do not cease to be such because the law will imply them.

Macpherson v IRC [1987] STC 73 concerns the way in which the CTT associated operation provision (now IHTA 1984, s 267) apply in connection with the charge on trusts with no interest in possession under the pre 1982 rules—in particular FA 1975, Sch 5, para 6(3). As this matter is now of historical interest it will suffice to note that the Court of Appeal has by a majority reversed the decision of Goulding J.

Administration

There are some old and some new points this year. There is the old but recurring theme that the burden of proof lies on the taxpayer to disprove the asessment, as witness *Neely v Rourke (Inspector of Taxes)* [1987] STC 30 (where a taxpayer sought to argue against decisions of the inspector on CGT deductions that may strike the reader as very sympathetic to the taxpayer) and *Coy v Kime (Inspector of Taxes)* [1987] STC 114 (where the inspector used figures in the Family Expenditure Survey to justify his rejection of the taxpayer's figures on his income).

This principle applies even where the inspector is alleging fraud. In *Brady (Inspector of Taxes) v Group Lotus Car Companies plc* [1987] 3 All ER 1050, [1987] STC 635 the taxpayer company had won its appeal before the

Commissioners; the issue concerned various payments and what they might have been paid for. The Commissioners held that if the payments had been made they would have been fraudulent and the burden of proof lay on the Revenue to prove fraud. Browne-Wilkinson V-C allowed the Revenue's appeal ([1987] 2 All ER 674, [1987] STC 184) and the Court of Appeal confirmed his decision.

A divided Court of Appeal went on to hold that it should be open to the Revenue to adduce new evidence at the rehearing before the Commissioners. Mustill LJ dissented; for him the proper procedure would have been for the Revenue to seek to set aside the judgment of the Commissioners, a procedure in which the burden of proof would have lain on them, and the matter could then be dealt with by them on the basis of the evidence they had heard and with their error as to the burden of proof put right. As a result of the decision of the majority the matter would be sent back for a fresh start, with the burden on the taxpayer, simply on the bais of an affidavit stating grounds for suspicion of fraud.

Pleasants v Atkinson (Inspector of Taxes) [1987] STC 728 is a short but interesting case holding that where an agent is guilty of wilful default the Revenue can reopen an assessment under TMA 1970, s 36 even though the taxpayer himself is completely innocent. The point is not a new one but such facts rarely arise.

The distinction between judicial review and appeal is another old theme. So in *R v Special Commissioner, ex p Napier* [1987] STC 507 the court said that if the taxpayer wished to complain that matters of law that should have been in the case stated were not, she should have sought amendment of the case stated and, if that did not resolve the matter, appeal to the Chancery Division by motion for the matter to be sent back to the Commissioner if needed, and not judicial review. On the other hand in *Aspin v Estill (Inspector of Taxes)* [1987] STC 723 the court said that complaints about misleading advice that might have been given by the Revenue could only be raised in judicial review proceedings. These points are well established but one wonders whether they are not over-subtle for the lay people for whose protection the system is meant to work.

Brodt v Wells General Comrs and IRC [1987] STC 207 might turn out to be a major case on penalties. Scott J decided that, despite the general reluctance of courts to interfere in such matters, he should reduce the penalties from virtually 100% to 80% apparently because penalties should be uniform across the country, so far as practicable. This suggests the need for a general review of penalties practice at the Commissioner level. Who will provide the funds for the research?

In *R v IRC, ex p J Rothschild Holdings plc* [1987] STC 163 the Court of Appeal upheld a lower court decision allowing an order for discovery of internal Revenue documents as to what the department thought was the correct interpretation of FA 1973, Sch 19, para 10 although not of documents to show how the Revenue had treated other taxpayers. This was in proceedings for judicial review, not appeal, and so the court had to satisfy itself that it was not impliedly ruling on whether the Revenue had a discretion to grant relief or whether the practice was correct in law.

Tailpiece

Walsh v Surrey General Comrs and IRC [1987] STC 456 deserves mention for the most tantalising argument of the year. Vinelott J dismissed an appeal by a taxpayer against an award of penalties for negligence in submitting incorrect returns. The taxpayer had, inter alia, argued that income tax is not only an unfair tax but also illogical and theoretically unsound.

Tort

BA HEPPLE, MA, LLB
Barrister, Professor of English Law, University College, University of London

Negligence

Foresight, proximity and policy

The year 1987 marks an important turning point in the approach of the highest courts of the United Kingdom and the Commonwealth to the duty of care. The gradual retreat from the prima facie duty of care principle, stated by Lord Wilberforce in *Anns v Merton London Borough* [1977] 2 All ER 492 at 498–99, HL has been noted in earlier volumes of this *Review*. This year, in an important trilogy of cases, decided between February and June, the House of Lords and Privy Council groped their way—not always with one voice—to a new approach.

In *Smith v Littlewoods Organisation Ltd* [1987] 1 All ER 710, HL (discussed below under 'Duty to control acts of third parties'), Lord Mackay of Clashfern, Lord Brandon of Oakbrook and Lord Griffiths based their answer to the question whether an occupier was liable for a danger (a fire) on its property caused by the act of a trespasser, solely on the concept of reasonable foresight. Lord Mackay, however, found it necessary to qualify that concept in this context so as to mean (ibid at 727): 'a real risk as distinct from a mere possibility of danger'. Lord Goff of Chieveley, on the other hand, emphasised that he did not think (ibid at 735): 'that the problem in these cases can be solved simply through the mechanism of foreseeability.' He resisted the temptation (ibid at 736): 'to solve all problems of negligence by reference to an all-embracing criterion of foreseeability, thereby effectively reducing all decisions in this field to questions of fact.' For him, too general a notion ('reasonable foresight', 'proximity') could not 'accommodate all the untidy complexities of life'. Instead, the courts had to search for narrower yet still identifiable principles, such as the one which he favoured in this case namely that there was no general duty at common law to prevent persons from harming others by their deliberate wrongdoing, however foreseeable such harm might be, in the absence of 'special circumstances'. Lord Keith of Kinkel managed the seemingly impossible feat of agreeing with the reasons given by both Lord Mackay and Lord Goff, a fact of some interest in view of the judgment of the Judicial Board of the Privy Council which he delivered later.

The next relevant decision of the House of Lords was handed down in April in *Curran v Northern Ireland Co-ownership Association Ltd* [1987] 2 All ER 13, (see 'Exercise of Statutory Powers', below). Lord Bridge, delivering the only speech, cited with approval the criticisms of the *Anns* principle by academic writers and by the High Court of Australia, and said that their Lordships were (ibid at 18): 'entitled to be wary of effecting any extension' of that principle. He questioned the tendency of *Anns* to obscure the 'important distinction between misfeasance and non-feasance' (a distinction, incidentally, on which Lord Goff relied heavily in *Smith*). He reiterated Lord Morris' dictum (followed by Lord Keith in *Peabody Donation Fund (Governors) v Sir Lindsay Parkinson* [1984] 3 All ER 529 at 533–34 (All ER Rev 1984, p 293)) that 'policy need not be involved where reason and good sense will at once point the way'.

The high point was to come in June in the judgment of the Judicial Board of the Privy Council, delivered by Lord Keith in *Yuen Kun-yeu v A-G of Hong Kong* [1987] 2 All ER 705 (see 'Exercise of Statutory Powers', below). This developed a more systematic approach to the duty of care. After noting the criticisms of the *Anns* principle and stating that (ibid at 710): 'the two-stage test formulated by Lord Wilberforce for determining the existence of a duty of care in negligence has been elevated to a degree of importance greater than it merits', Lord Keith indicated that the first stage of the Wilberforce test in fact concealed two separate requirements. The first necessary ingredient of a duty of care is foreseeability of harm. The second is that of 'a close and direct relationship of proximity between the parties' (ibid at 710–11). It would only be in rare and novel cases that a policy consideration would negative a duty of care once prima facie liability had been made out on the basis of foreseeability and proximity.

This new threefold criterion for the existence of a duty of care is likely to prove to be as illusory a solution to the duty problem as was its two-stage predecessor. (1) 'Reasonable foreseeability' is capable of meaning (a) a mere possibility of harm, or (b) the probability of harm (more likely than not), or (c) a high degree of probability of harm, or (d) one of the 'economic' tests, such as that the losses could have been avoided at a marginal cost less than marginal expected damages. (2) 'Proximity' suggests that different degrees of 'closeness' will apply to different types of claim (eg nervous shock, economic loss etc), but it is by no means clear how this can be done without resorting to one or more of the 'foreseeability' tests. Some judges (eg Fox LJ in *Hill v Chief Constable of West Yorkshire* [1987] 1 All ER 1173 at 1177) seem to equate 'proximity' with what is 'just and reasonable' which overlaps with 'policy'. (3) 'Policy' will not be an issue where the situation is covered by precedent. In novel situations (said to be 'rare') some judges since *Peabody* (eg Glidewell LJ in *Hill* at 1183) have equated 'policy', which may negate a prima facie duty with the intuitive 'reason and good sense' of the judge. The refinements of language introduced in the recent cases are based on the unstated premise that liability in negligence (especially on the part of public authorities) has gone too far and should be restricted.

Duty to control the conduct of third parties

As already indicated, there were differences of approach in the speeches in *Smith v Littlewoods Organisation Ltd* [1987] 1 All ER 710. The issue was whether the defendant owners of an empty and unattended cinema were liable to the owners of adjoining premises which were seriously damaged by a fire started in the cinema by vandals. The crucial finding of fact was that the defendants were unaware that their premises were regularly visited by vandals. All their Lordships were agreed that there is a general duty of care on an occupier to ensure that his premises are not a source of danger to neighbouring property. However, Lords Mackay, Brandon and Griffiths went on to hold that since the defendants did not know of the vandalism, and could not be expected to keep a 24-hour guard when there was nothing inherently dangerous on the premises, the fire could not be said to be reasonably foreseeable. In Lord Mackay's words, the fire was a mere possibility and neither highly probable nor very likely to happen. The decision was, therefore, made to turn on the absence of any specific warning to the defendants that there was a danger of vandal damage. Lord Goff based the absence of a duty of care on the general principle of non-liability for omissions (in this case, the failure to prevent third persons causing damage). He listed a number of special circumstances in which such a duty could arise, (ibid at 730–31) none of which applied in this case. He too, would have found that there was liability if the defendants had knowledge or the means of knowledge that a third party had created or was creating a risk of fire, or if the defendants had created or continued a source of danger.

Can the police ever be held liable in tort for the criminal activities of suspects whom they negligently fail to apprehend? *Home Office v Dorset Yacht Co* [1970] 2 All ER 294, opened up the prospect of liability of prison authorities for the criminal acts of escaping prisoners. But this was carefully restricted to damage to property, situated near the place of detention, which the detainee was likely to steal or damage in the course of eluding immediate pursuit. In *Hill v Chief Constable of West Yorkshire* [1987] 1 All ER 1173, CA, an attempt was boldly made, on behalf of the estate of one of the victims of the 'Yorkshire Ripper', to extend this duty to police whom, it was alleged, had negligently failed to detect the criminal prior to the murder of the deceased. Not surprisingly, the Court of Appeal held that there was no such duty and upheld a judge's decision to strike out the claim as disclosing no cause of action. *Dorset Yacht* was readily distinguished both because of the absence of control, and the 'undue width' of the class of persons to whom the duty would be owed ('all young or fairly young women in Yorkshire and Lancashire, if not the whole of Great Britain'). What if a suspect escaped from police custody and murdered the key witness who lived in the vicinity? Although the elements of control and identifiability of the victim would be present, it must be surmised that the Court of Appeal would rule out a claim in these circumstances on policy grounds. Fox LJ said that the courts would not be justified in extending the duty of care to victims of crime because there is already a criminal injuries compensation scheme and the new cause of action could lead to 'unfair and unacceptable differences in the remedies available in respect of criminal injuries' (ibid at 1182). Glidewell LJ agreed with this, and also supported the notion of police immunity on grounds similar to those used to justify the advocate's immunity: the threat of actions for damages would inhibit the exercise of judgment by the police; it could lead to the retrial of matters already dealt with in a Crown Court; and it would involve considerable time and work for the police force. Perhaps more convincing than these sweeping and questionable policy grounds, is the argument that the police's duty to enforce the law should be enforced by an order of mandamus, that is in the field of public rather than private law.

Exercise of statutory powers

Curran v Northern Ireland Co-ownership Housing Association Ltd [1987] 2 All ER 13, HL, is an important decision not only because of the general approach to the duty of care (above) but also because of the narrow interpretation which the House of Lords has placed on the ratio decidendi of the *Anns* case. The plaintiffs alleged that they had purchased a house in reliance on their belief that an extension to the house by their predecessor in title had been properly constructed because it had been the object of an improvement grant paid by the Northern Ireland Housing Executive under Part VI of Housing (Northern Ireland) Order 1976. The Order provides that the Executive must be satisfied that a dwelling for which a grant is given meets certain standards of habitation and the work must be completed to the 'satisfaction of the Executive'. It was claimed that following the purchase the plaintiffs had discovered that the extension had been so defectively constructed that it had to be completely rebuilt. The plaintiffs sought damages from the Executive on the grounds that it had been negligent in causing or permitting the extension to be built negligently. The Court of Appeal for Northern Ireland held that the facts, if proved, could give rise to a duty of care. The House of Lords disagreed and allowed an appeal by the Executive.

Lord Bridge, (ibid at 19) with whom all their Lordships agreed, identified three elements fundamental to the ratio of *Anns*: (a) the statutory power which the authority has negligently failed to exercise or has exercised in a negligent way must be specifically directed to safeguarding a section of the public of which the plaintiff is a member from the particular danger that has resulted; (b) the power must be such that its due exercise could have avoided the danger; and (c) the non-exercise or negligent exercise of the power must have created a hidden defect which cannot subsequently be discovered and remedied before damage results. Applying this interpretation, Lord Bridge found that the object of the Order was to see that public money was properly spent rather than to protect the recipient of the grant and his successors. Moreover, the exercise of the power could not have avoided the danger because the Order conferred no powers of control of building operations analogous to those on which the decision in *Anns* depended. The significance of this reinterpretation of *Anns* is that (a) it limits the class of potential plaintiffs and (b) it all but abandons Lord Wilberforce's much-criticised and 'difficult dichotomy' between an exercise of statutory powers which is a matter of policy or discretion and an exercise of powers which is 'operational', in favour of the critical test whether the exercise of the powers enables the authority to control the acts of third parties (eg builders). This in effect revives the test suggested by Lord Denning in *Dutton v Bognor Regis UDC* [1972] 1 All ER 462.

The Privy Council's judgment in *Yuen Kun-yeu v A-G of Hong Kong* [1987] 2 All ER 705, also puts a nail in the coffin of *Anns*, and indicates that there are strict limits on the range of regulatory agencies which may be liable for negligently failing to exercise their powers or exercising them in a negligent way. It was decided that the Commissioner of Deposit-Taking Companies in Hong Kong did not owe a duty to members of the public who might be minded to deposit their money in companies registered by the Commissioner to exercise reasonable care to see that they did not suffer loss through the companies being carried on by their managers in a fraudulent or improvident fashion. The Judicial Board decided the case on a 'no proximity' basis (see p 285 above). The decisive factors in this connection appear to have been that (a) the Commission had no power to control the day-to-day activities of those who caused the loss; and (b) the Commissioner had not voluntarily assumed any responsibility to investors, and reliance by them on the fact of registration as a guarantee of the soundness of a particular company would be neither reasonable nor justifiable, nor should the Commissioner reasonably be expected to know of such reliance if it existed. The Board saw much force in the public policy arguments against liability (similar to those in the *Hill* case, above) but preferred to rest their decision on this absence of proximity. Nevertheless, the decision once again reveals judicial reluctance to add common law liabilities onto a statutory framework designed to protect the general public interest rather than individual members of the public.

Psychiatric damage

The heading 'nervous shock' is well-established in the authorities and literature, but in deference to Bingham LJ's comment in *Attia v British Gas plc* [1987] 3 All ER 455 at 462, that it is 'misleading and inaccurate' we note that case under the preferred rubric of 'psychiatric damage'. Since *McLoughlin v O'Brian* [1982] 2 All ER 298 (All ER Rev 1982, p 297), this has not been regarded as qualitatively different from any other injury to the person. The novelty of the Court of Appeal's decision in *Attia* is that it recognises in principle that damages for psychiatric damage may be recovered where these result from witnessing not a personal injury to a third person but rather the destruction of property. The judgments do not consider the limits of this extension of liability, preferring to treat the question of reasonable foreseeability purely as a question of fact for the trial judge. There were special features in this case, such as the pre-existing relationship between the plaintiff householder and the defendants who had contracted to install central heating and admitted that they were negligent in causing the fire which destroyed the house. Moreover, the plaintiff actually witnessed the fire. To extend one of Bingham LJ's examples: would there be liability to a scholar who suffered psychiatric damage as a result of coming in the immediate aftermath of a fire, caused by a stranger's negligence, which had destroyed his life's work? There seems to be no reason in principle to exclude such a claim, provided that there is, on the facts, sufficient emotional, spatial and temporal proximity.

Solicitors

When does a solicitor owe a duty of care to the other party in litigation? In *Al-Kandari v JR Brown and Co* [1987] 2 All ER 302 at 308 French J reformulated Megarry V-C's judgment in *Ross v Caunters* [1979] 3 All ER 580 at 699–700 (the disappointed beneficiary case) to hold that 'a solicitor who has authority from his client to give an undertaking, one of whose objects is to protect an identified third party, owes a duty of care to that third party'. On the facts of the case, which belong in a tragic novel rather than the law reports, he found that there had been a breach of this duty, but he denied the hapless litigant a remedy on the ground that the damage she suffered was too remote. The undertaking, embodied in a consent order given by the husband in matrimonial proceedings, was to deposit his passport with his solicitors as a condition of being granted access to his children. By an agreed relaxation of this undertaking his solicitors sent the passport to the Kuwaiti embassy to have the children's names removed and with strict instructions that the passport should on no account be returned to the husband. Somehow the passport got into his hands, he had his wife kidnapped and then abducted the children to Kuwait, using the passport to do so. The children were never recovered. The wife claimed damages, inter alia for physical injuries and psychiatric illness, from her husband's solicitors. Had she been successful the judge would have awarded £20,000 general damages. Professor Markesinis in an interesting note on this decision in (1987) 103 LQR 346 at 358 argues that it 'could prove a very persuasive authority that in principle third parties could always sue whenever affected by the negligent breach of duty imposed by a court order on another person', and he suggests that this goes too far in making solicitors responsible for foreseeable mishaps to third parties. He also points out the confusion which arises from the finding that it was negligent to leave the passport with the embassy (breach of duty) but that it was not reasonably foreseeable that the embassy would part with the passport (damage too remote). The Court of Appeal has reversed the decision [1988] NLJR 62.

In *Business Computers International Ltd v Registrar of Companies* [1987] 3 All ER 465, Scott J held that a person who institutes legal process does not owe a duty of care to the respondent or defendant in regard to the service of the proceedings. It was alleged that a petition for winding up of the plaintiff company had negligently been served at the wrong address, causing the company damages in having the winding-up order set aside and in making up for loss of goodwill. Scott J decided that this did not disclose a cause of action. The authorities show that a civil action can never be based on falsity of evidence given in judicial proceedings, nor on the conduct of the trial. Counsel for the plaintiff argued that this did not prevent a duty of care in regard to proper service of proceedings. The learned judge considered that it would not be 'just and reasonable' (the *Peabody* approach above) to impose such a duty, on the ground that the safeguard against impropriety lies in the rules and procedures governing litigation and not in a superimposed tortious duty of care. This case is, of course, different from *Al-Kandari* because of the undertaking given in that case and the handing over of the passport was not a 'step in the litigation' of a kind which would attract immunity from suit.

County Personnel (Employment Agency) Ltd v Alan R Pulver & Co (a firm) [1987] 1 All ER 289, CA, provides an illustration of the standard of care expected of a solicitor when faced with an unusual clause in a lease. (See also under 'Damages' below).

See further on these cases, the chapter on Solicitors, above p 231.

Insurers

The case of *Banque Keyser Ullmann SA v Skandia (UK) Insurance Co Ltd* [1987] 2 All ER 923, is discussed in the chapter on Commercial Law above, p 20. Here it is worth noting that Steyn J's judgment (ibid at 947–54) contains a number of interesting observations on the criteria for establishing a duty of care in a novel situation, but these now have to be read subject to more recent developments. The judge, in finding that there was a duty of care on the part of underwriters to disclose dishonest conduct on the part of a broker, was not deterred either by the fact that the duty required positive action on the part of the underwriters, or by the fact that the duty arose in a precontractual setting.

Negligent statements causing economic loss

In *Lawton v BOC Transhield Ltd* [1987] 2 All ER 608, Tudor Evans J held that in principle an employer owes a duty of care to his erstwhile employee when he gives a character reference to the new employer of that employee. The implications of this are discussed in the chapter on Employment Law above, p 98. The judgment raises an issue of general interest in the law of tort. This is whether the duty is based on *Hedley Byrne* (reliance) or on *Donoghue v Stevenson* (proximity) principles. The situation was one in which D (the ex-employer) made a statement to X (the new employer), on which X relied but suffered no loss. The claim was brought by P (the ex-employee) whom D knew or ought to have contemplated would suffer economic loss as a result of X's reliance on the statement. Tudor Evans J saw the difficulties in applying *Hedley Byrne* to this situation, but found that *Ministry of Housing and Local Government v Sharp* [1970] 1 All ER 1009, was 'conclusively' in favour of the plaintiff in the present action. Alternatively, Lord Roskill's speech in *Junior Books Ltd v Veitchi Ltd* [1982] 3 All ER 201 at 210, 213, could be used to support a finding of sufficient proximity or neighbourhood.

There are several difficulties with this approach. The first of these, which was not argued because the defendants did not take the point, is whether given *The Aliakmon* [1986] 2 All ER 145, either *Sharp* or *Junior Books* can still be used to admit a claim for economic loss in the absence of a *Hedley Byrne* type reliance or a reliance in a situation 'equivalent to contract'. If *Sharp*, *Ross v Caunters* and *Junior Books* have been affected by *The Aliakmon* then their authority to support the decision is *Lawton* is correspondingly reduced. Secondly, the judge was willing to overcome the need for reliance, if that were necessary in all cases, by a finding that P was relying on D to give a reference based on accurate facts to X. What is missing from this formulation is that the statement was not sought or passed on to P. The 'reliance' found by Tudor Evans J was no more specific than that of Mrs Donoghue on the quality of the ginger beer, and that, as we now know, is not sufficient to give rise to liability for economic loss. Thirdly, it is suggested by Tudor Evans J that an employer could protect himself with a disclaimer of responsibility as the respondents did in *Hedley Byrne*. However, the notion of disclaimer is inappropriate in cases not resting on an assumption of responsibility. What is presumably meant is that the duty could be discharged by an adequate warning that, although the statement was honestly made, the facts on which it was based had not been checked. Unlike a claim in defamation, there is no defence of qualified privilege to a claim based on negligence. But those asked for references can make it clear that the information or advice they are giving is 'off the cuff'. Even where this is not done it may be difficult for the subject of the reference to establish carelessness by the maker. Significantly, the plaintiff in the present case failed for this very reason.

For further comment see BW Napier (1987) NLJ 824; R Townsend-Smith (1987) 3 PN 73; AM Tettenborn [1987] CLJ 391.

Proof of medical negligence

In *Gold v Haringey Health Authority* [1987] 2 All ER 888, CA, the well-known standard in *Bolam v Friern Hospital Management Committee* [1957] 2 All ER 118 at 122, was applied to the question whether the doctors ought to have warned the plaintiff that a sterilization operation might not succeed: see the chapter on Medical Law, above, p 179. The decision of the Court of Appeal that disclosure of medical experts' reports on liability should be the norm, in *Naylor v Preston Area Health Authority* [1987] 2 All ER 353, is discussed in the chapter on Practice and Procedure, above, p 200.

Products liability

The decision in *Aswan Engineering Establishment Co v Lupdine Ltd* [1987] 1 All ER 135, CA, is discussed in the chapter on Commercial Law, above pp 34 et seq. The facts raised again the difficult borderline between 'pure' economic loss and loss resulting from physical damage to other property of the plaintiff. However, it was conceded that economic loss was not recoverable (the point being reserved for the House of Lords). Although the judgments contain some interesting comments on when there is damage to other property of the plaintiff so as to cross the threshold of liability, the decision ultimately turned on the question of fact as to whether there was a sufficient degree of proximity between the purchaser and the producers.

Occupiers' liability

The plaintiff in *Ferguson v Welsh* [1987] 3 All ER 777, HL, was left paralysed from the waist downwards as the result of an accident while he was engaged on demolition work on a building site. The trial judge found that the accident occurred because his employers had adopted an unsafe system of work, and they were held liable. But they had no liability insurance, to pay the £150,000 damages, nor did the main contractors against whom the Court of Appeal had ordered a new trial. So the plaintiff's only hope of getting compensation was by a finding that the owners of the site, Sedgefield District Council, were liable under the Occupiers' Liability Act 1957. He appealed to the House of Lords seeking a new trial against the council. He failed. The council accepted that they were joint occupiers of the site with the main contractor. They had prohibited sub-contracting, but Lord Keith (ibid at 782) held that the ostensible authority of the main contractor to invite the plaintiff and his employers onto the site was enough to make him a lawful visitor (cf Lord Goff ibid at 785). However, his injury had arisen out of the unsafe system of work adopted by his employers rather than the 'use' of the premises by him which would give rise to a common duty of care under s 2(2) of the 1957 Act. The House recognised that there could be circumstances in which an occupier could be liable where an independent contractor used an unsafe system of work, as when a brick falls from a building under repair onto the head of a postman. In deciding whether the occupier is liable in such circumstances, consideration would need to be given to s 2(4)(b) of the 1957 Act. Lord Keith was willing to give a 'broad and purposive' interpretation to this sub-section so as to read 'any work of construction' to embrace demolition. Moreover, he interpreted the requirement that the occupier must satisfy himself that 'the work had been properly done' to cover the situation not only where the work has been completed but also that where the harm occurs as a result of the act of an independent contractor in the course of the work. There is, however an important difference between Lord Keith, with whom Lords Brandon and Griffiths agreed, on the one hand, and Lords Goff and Oliver on the other, as to whether the mere fact that an occupier may know or have reason to suspect that the contractor is using an unsafe system can of itself be enough to impose on him liability under the 1957 Act, or in negligence at common law, unless the occupier had in some way made himself a joint tortfeasor with the employer. In any event, there was no evidence in this case that the council knew or ought to have known of the unauthorised sub-contracting to persons who would use an unsafe system of work.

Ogwo v Taylor [1987] 3 All ER 961, HL, affirming [1987] 1 All ER 668, CA, may come to be known as the 'firemen's charter'. The House of Lords, has adopted and indorsed the judgment of Woolf J in the earlier case of *Salmon v Seafarer Restaurants Ltd* [1983] 3 All ER 729 at 736, that:

> 'where it can be foreseen that the fire which is negligently started is of the type which could, first of all, require firemen to attend to extinguish the fire, and where, because of the very nature of the fire, when they attend they will be at risk even though they exercise all the skill of their calling, there seems no reason why a fireman should be at any disadvantage when the question of compensation for his injuries arises.'

This, said Lord Bridge (ibid at 966) still leaves open the possiblity that there may be some fires which, although calling for the services of the fire brigade, pose no foreseeable risk to firemen acting with due skill and care. However, the House emphatically rejected the attempt, made by counsel for the defendant, to draw a distinction between the 'ordinary' risks inherent in fire fighting and the 'exceptional' risks created by some unusual feature of the fire which arises from the nature and condition of the premises. 'Fire out of control is inherently dangerous' and firemen, it was said, should be treated in the same way as lay rescuers. They are not to be met by the doctrine of volenti 'which would be utterly repugnant to our contemporary notions of justice' (ibid at 965). It might be, however, that the chain of causation between negligence and injury could be broken, for example where the fireman's injuries were sustained by his foolhardy exposure to an unnecessary risk 'either of his own volition or acting under the orders of a senior fire officer,' (ibid at 965). If this is a 'charter' for firemen it is, of course, limited to those firemen who are able to establish negligence and not for their colleagues who suffer similar injuries in fighting a fire the cause of which is unknown. A number of courts in the United States have preferred a 'firemen's rule' which leaves the cost of fighting fires on public funds, considering it too burdensome to charge all those who carelessly cause or fail to prevent fires. This 'rule' now has no place in English Law, but as Lord Bridge said (ibid at 965), the anomalous treatment of some firemen, is a common feature in a system which requires proof of fault as the basis of liability, and 'is the strongest argument advanced by those who support the introduction of a 'no fault' system of compensation.'

Causation

In *Hotson v East Berkshire Area Health Authority* [1984] 1 All ER 210, CA at 215–16, Sir John Donaldson MR remarked that 'it is unjust that there should be no liability for failure to treat a patient, simply because the chances of a successful cure by that treatment are less than 50%'. Yet that is the state of the law, according to the unanimous decision of the House of Lords in this case ([1987] 2 All ER 909), reversing a unanimous Court of Appeal, which had affirmed the judgment of Simon Brown J sub nom *Hotson v Fitzgerald* [1985] 3 All ER 167 (noted All ER Rev 1985, p. 310). A 13 year old boy injured his hip in a fall. Due to the admitted negligence of the health authority the injury was not correctly diagnosed for five days. Its was not in dispute that he was entitled to £150 damages for the avoidable pain and suffering in those five days. The issue was whether he could also recover damages from the health authority for the severe medical condition causing permanent disability of the hip joint which had developed. Simon Brown J found that even if the medical staff had correctly diagnosed and treated the boy there was still a 75% risk of the disability developing, but that their negligence had turned that risk into an inevitability thereby denying him a 25% chance of a good recovery. He awarded an amount representing 25% of the full damages awardable for the disability. The Court of Appeal affirmed this decision on the ground that the damage which the plaintiff had suffered was the loss of a chance of avoiding the permanent disability, and that such damages were not limited to cases in which the action was founded on contract. The House of Lords in effect decided that the lower courts had wrongly classified the issue which, in their view, was not one of quantification but of causation. Since the judge had held on the balance of probabilities that even correct diagnosis and treatment would not have prevented the disability from occurring, it followed that the plaintiff had failed on the issue of causation. The question concerning loss of a chance could not arise where there had been a finding that the damage had already been sustained or become inevitable. Although Lord Bridge (ibid at 913–14) left open the question whether damages could ever be awarded for the lost chance of avoiding personal injury, the speeches of Lord Mackay and Lord Ackner contain strong statements of principle which appear to be against any discounting of damages by the extent to which the plaintiff has failed to prove his case with 100% certainty. Anything that is more probable than not is treated as certain. The decision shows clearly the difficulty in a fault-based system, of proving a causal connection which depends on several hypothetical contingencies. English law has now firmly set itself against the 'lottery ticket' theory that the creation of a risk of harm which in fact occurs should result in limited responsibility.

Another, more straightforward case of two competing causes of damage came before the House of Lords in *Kay v Ayrshire and Arran Health Board* [1987] 2 All ER 417. A 2 year old boy was admitted to hospital suffering from pneumococcal meningitis. During treatment he was negligently given an overdose of penicillin. After recovering from the meningitis he was found to be suffering from deafness. The pursuer was unable to prove that the overdose was capable of causing or aggravating neurological damage since the expert evidence was that there was no recorded case in which an overdose of penicillin had caused deafness, while deafness was a common consequence of meningitis. Accordingly, the House of Lords held that the claim for damages against the health authority must fail.

In neither of these cases was the difficult decision in *McGhee v National Coal Board* [1972] 3 All ER 1008, HL, subjected to close analysis (see Lord Mackay in *Hotson* at 916; and the speeches in *Kay* at 422, 424, 425, 427). It therefore remains to be seen whether the House of Lords will agree with the expansive interpretation of *McGhee* by the Court of Appeal in *Fitzgerald v Lane* [1987] 2 All ER 455, decided before *Hotson* and *Kay* but not referred to by the House of Lords. Mr Fitzgerald (F) was walking briskly onto a pelican crossing when the lights were showing green for traffic and red for pedestrians. When he reached the centre of the road he was struck by Mr Lane's (L) car and a few seconds later by a car being driven in the opposite direction by Mr Patel (P). He sustained multiple injuries resulting in partial tetraplegia. The medical evidence was that there were four possible causes of the tetraplegia: (1) a whiplash effect due to the initial impact of L's car; (2) the impact between F and the windscreen of L's car; (3) F's head hitting the ground at some time between the impact of L's car and the impact of P's car; (4) the impact between F and P's car. The trial judge found that it was probable that the first impact did not cause the injury. However he found that there was an equal probability of the three subsequent impacts being the cause. Therefore he held that both L and P were responsible. The objection to this conclusion on orthodox causation principles is that if at the moment of impact with the second car, F had already been rendered tetraplegic by impact with the first car, then L was the sole cause and P was not liable. Alternatively, if he had already been rendered partly tetraplegic at the moment of impact with the second car then P should have been liable only to the extent that he made the tetraplegia worse. However, the Court of Appeal was not willing to interfere with the judge's conclusions on the basis of *McGhee* as interpreted by a majority of the Court of Appeal in *Wilsher v Essex Area Health Authority* [1986] 3 All ER 801. This is that, where there are two or more separate possible causes of a plaintiff's injuries, a defendant is liable if his breach of duty created a risk that injury would be caused or had increased an existing risk that injury would ensue, notwithstanding that the existence and extent of the contribution made by the defendant's conduct in causing the injury could not be ascertained. While the result certainly accords with considerations of justice (see Slade LJ at [1987] 2 All ER 455 at 472), the reasoning is not easy to reconcile with the strict adherence to causation principles in the more recent House of Lords decisions.

Contributory negligence

The Court of Appeal in *Fitzgerald v Lane* did, however, allow the appeal by both L and P against the judge's apportionment of liability under s 1(1) of the Law Reform (Contributory Negligence) Act 1945. He had apportioned liability equally between all three parties and entered judgment for the plaintiff against both defendants for two-thirds of his damages. The Court of Appeal held that the judge should have considered the position between the plaintiff and each defendant separately. This meant that the plaintiff was entitled to recover from the defendants half, not two-thirds of the damages awarded.

Illegality as a defence in tort

The decision of the Court of Appeal in *Saunders v Edwards* [1987] 2 All ER 651, provides an example of the pragmatic approach of the courts to the defence of *ex tupri causa* in tort actions. The plaintiff's claim was for damages for the fraudulent misrepresentation of the detendant that the flat which he sold them included a roof terrace. The defendant did not appeal against the judge's finding of deceit but contended that the plaintiffs were not entitled to damages because they had suggested, and the defendant had agreed to, a false apportionment of the price for the flat and certain chattels in the contract of sale in order to reduce stamp duty. The Court of Appeal rejected this contention on the grounds that (a) the defendant's own moral culpability outweighed that of the plaintiffs and he ought not to be allowed to keep the fruits of his fraud, and (b) the illegal apportionment in the contract was wholly unconnected with the plaintiff's cause of action in tort. The Court approved the test of public policy suggested by Hutchinson J in *Thackwell v Barclays Bank plc* [1986] 1 All ER 676 at 678 (noted All ER Rev 1986, pp 25, 28, 96)(with an addition by Nicholls LJ at [1987] 2 All ER 651 at 664). The essence of this seems to be that torts should be remedied so long as the court does not thereby promote or countenance a nefarious object.

Nuisance and trespass to land

The main interest of *Home Brewery plc v William Davis and Co (Loughborough) Ltd* [1987] 1 All ER 637, QBD, is that it is, surprisingly, the only English decision on the question whether the owner or occupier of higher land has a right to discharge water percolating through or over his land onto lower lying land, and whether the lower occupier is bound to receive that water. Piers Ashworth QC, sitting as a deputy High Court judge, held that (1) the lower occupier has no cause of action against the higher occupier for permitting the natural unconcentrated flow of water to pass from the higher onto the lower land, but (2) the lower occupier is under no obligation to receive it and may put up barriers, or otherwise pen it back, even though this may cause damage to a higher occupier. However, the lower occupier's proprietary right is limited by the tort of nuisance, of which 'unreasonable user' is an essential ingredient. The steps taken to prevent the water entering onto his land must not be unreasonable. In the present case, the action of the lower occupier in filling in clay pits on his land, so impeding the flow of water from the higher land was done for the respectable commercial motive of developing the lower land as a residential estate and the operations were not unreasonable. However, the defendants had also filled in an osier-bed, which had the effect of squeezing out over a period of five years the water that was present in that bed, thereby causing additional flooding on the higher land. This damage was held to be reasonably foreseeable and constituted either a nuisance or trespass. For comment see JR Spencer [1987] CLJ 205.

The principles on which an interlocutory injunction will be granted to restrain trespass to land were discussed in *Patel v WH Smith (Eziot) Ltd* [1987] 2 All ER 569, CA.

Economic torts

Interference with contract-statutory torts

Rickless v United Artists Corpn [1987] 1 All ER 679, CA, decides that performers have a right to claim damages where their performance is exploited by others without written consent contrary to s 2 of the Dramatic and Musical Performers' Protection Act 1958. On its face, s 2 creates only a criminal offence and the judgment of Sir Nicolas Browne-Wilkinson V-C, analyses, with his usual clarity, the arguments for and against construing the Act so as to create private rights of action. The Vice-Chancellor skilfully found a path through the confusing authorities, in particular *RCA Corpn v Pollard* [1982] 3 All ER 771, CA, (discussed All ER Rev 1982, pp 308–10) so as to give effect to his own views and to the dictum of Lord Diplock in *Lonrho Ltd v Shell Petroleum Co Ltd* [1981] 2 All ER 456 at 462–63, that performers do have a civil right of action under the statute. This right was held to rest in the performer's representatives when he died. The decision leaves standing the unfortunate ratio of *RCA Corp v Pollard* that the record companies have no remedies for bootlegging. Leave to appeal to the House of Lords has been granted on this point.

A second issue in this case was whether the tort of unlawful interference with contract could be committed by interfering with a purely negative contractual obligation, the contract being otherwise fully performed. The Court found that under 'loan-out' agreements between (in one case) the actor, Peter Sellers, or (in other cases) companies controlled by him, and the defendant film production companies and a film director, there were express or implied undertakings that the actor's performance would be used only for the purpose for which a particular contract related. This meant that out-takes and clips from earlier films could not be used without the specific consent of either the actor or his representatives. The defendants argued that they could not be liable (if the other ingredients of the tort were present) for inducing a breach of negative covenants in otherwise wholly performed contracts. Bingham LJ brusquely rejected this submission, for which no authority could be found, adding that in any event the loan-out agreements in question had not been fully performed. If this were not the law there would be no remedy against a third party who, knowing of a lawful covenant against competition for say, 12 months after termination of a contract of employment, induced the former employee of his competitor to work for him during the period of the covenant and in obvious breach of it.

Defamation

Injunctions

Gulf Oil (GB) Ltd v Page [1987] 3 All ER 14, CA is interesting not least because one of the alleged libels was in the form of an aerial display of a sign which could be clearly seen from the plaintiff company's head offices and from a racecourse where the company was entertaining a number of customers. The point in issue was whether the company should be granted an interim injunction to restrain further display of the sign. Warner J refused relief on the ground that the truth of the words was not in issue and that, in a libel action, if a defendant seeks to justify, an interim injunction is, as a matter of principle, never granted. The Court of Appeal, however, allowed an appeal and granted an injunction on the ground that there was a strong prima facie case that the material was being published in pursuance of a conspiracy to injure the plaintiff without any just cause. Unfortunately, time considerations meant that this important point was not fully argued. The only safeguard against abuse of this novel exception to the long-standing principle in libel actions will be the vigilance of the judge. Parker LJ thought (ibid at 19) that it would only be in the 'rarest case that sufficient evidence of dishonest purpose to injure could be made out to warrant the grant of interlocutory relief.'

Fair comment

The actress, Charlotte Cornwell, complained of an article about her written by Nina Myskow and published in The Sunday People. The defendants put in issue the meanings alleged and set up a defence of fair comment. By her reply, the plaintiff denied that the words were either fair or correct and alleged express malice. The jury found for the plaintiff and awarded her £10,000 damages. On appeal, in *Cornwell v Myskow* [1987] 2 All ER 504, the defendants succeeded in having the judgment set aside on the ground of serious misdirections by the judge and of the admission of evidence of the plaintiff's reputation at the time of trial. Parker LJ, delivering the judgment of the court, explained that where the defence is fair comment, not coupled as it often is with justification, the defendant is not asserting the truth, but simply that the comment could at the date of publication have been honestly made by a fair-minded person. Accordingly, the plaintiff's reputation at the date of trial is irrelevant.

Absolute privilege

The decision in *Fayed v Al-Tajir* [1987] 2 All ER 396, CA, that an internal memorandum of a foreign embassy is protected by absolute privilege in libel proceedings, was based on public policy and the international law of diplomatic relations.

Procedural matters

Three of the reported decisions relate to procedural matters of interest to libel specialists. In *Barnet v Crozier* [1987] 1 All ER 1041, the Court of Appeal emphasised that where parties make a bona fide settlement of a defamation action and ask leave to make a statement in open court, leave ought to be granted unless there is a real risk of prejudice to the fair trial of any outstanding issue. In *Atkinson v Fitzwalter* [1987] 1 All ER 483, the Court of Appeal considered the principles to be applied in dealing with an application to amend in order to plead justification at a late stage in the proceedings. In *Ricci v Chow* [1987] 3 All ER 534, the Court of Appeal held that a defendant who had nothing to do with the printing and publication of an allegedly defamatory article and had in no way facilitated its publication, was in the position of a mere witness or observer and so could not be sued and was not in the category of admissible defendants to an action for discovery at common law. Moreover, the Court held, the common law rule that a mere witness cannot be sued in an action for discovery was not abrogated by Sch 2 of the Newspapers Printers and Reading Rooms Act 1869.

Vicarious liability

Employer's liability for negligence of third party

In *Coltman v Bibby Tankers Ltd, The Derbyshire* [1987] 3 All ER 1068, the House of Lords agreed with Sheen J ([1986] 2 All ER 65, noted All ER Rev 1986, p 317), that a ship provided by its owner for purposes of his business is 'equipment' for the purpose of s 1(1) of the Employer's Liability (Defective Equipment) Act 1969. Accordingly, where a seaman suffered personal injury or loss of life in consequence of defects in the ship attributable to fault on the part of the manufacturers, its owner was liable under the Act. This interpretation accords both with the natural and ordinary meaning of 'equipment', and with the purpose of the legislation which, in Lord Oliver's words (ibid at 1074) 'was manifestly to saddle the employer with liability for defective plant of every sort with which the employee is compelled to work in the course of his employment'. This applies to chattels of all sizes. The House overturned the decision of a majority of the Court of Appeal [1987] 1 All ER 932, which had held that 'equipment' denoted something ancillary to something else and could not apply to the workplace (including a movable chattel like a ship) provided by the employer.

In *McDermid v Nash Dredging and Reclamation Co Ltd* [1987] 2 All ER 878, the House of Lords dismissed an appeal from the decision of the Court of Appeal ([1986] 2 All ER 676, discussed All ER Rev 1986, pp 317-18). Lord

Brandon remarked that the Court of Appeal had treated the case as more difficult than it really was. The House's decision is based on the reasoning that the duty owed by the employers was a personal and non-delegable one, rather than vicarious. The House has still, however, to give explicit recognition to the contractual approach favoured by Lord Wright in *Wilsons and Clyde Co Ltd v English* [1938] AC 57. This is that the duty is in effect a warranty by the employer to ensure that reasonable care is taken.

Damages

Personal injuries

The award of £679,264 to the plaintiff in *Thomas v Wignall* [1987] 1 All ER 1185, CA, was the largest ever made in England at the time of Hutchison J's decision in December 1985. A 16 year-old married woman had suffered severe permanent brain damage as a result of admitted medical negligence. The judge had arrived at the sum in respect of the cost of the plaintiff's future care by applying a multiplier of 15. At the date of trial she was aged 27 and she was not expected to live to be older than 55. The judge considered the appropriate multiplier would ordinarily be 14, but to make some allowance for the high incidence of taxation on the damages awarded he increasd the multiplier to 15. The Court of Appeal were divided on the question whether the judge had been entitled to take account of the effect of high taxation on the award. The majority (Sir John Donaldson MR and Nicholls LJ) held that he was, while Lloyd LJ said that he was not. Their Lordships could not agree as to effect of House of Lords decisions dealing with the incidence of inflation, in none of which had the issue of high rates of taxation been directly considered. As a matter of principle, Nicholls LJ thought that it would be unrealistic and Sir John Donaldson MR said that it would be a denial of justice, to ignore the incidence of higher rates of tax where the fund would have an annual income of over £30,000. Lloyd LJ's dissent is based on a concession by plaintiff's counsel that the present case was one in which tax would fall to be paid at ordinary rates and was therefore covered by the ordinary discount of 4 or 5%. This meant the case did not fall within the exceptional category in which a higher multiplier would be appropriate. The size and complexity of the award and all the future uncertainties about tax rates illustrated by this case, surely justify Lloyd LJ's reiteration of the plea for a radical reform of this branch of the law by the legislature. For general comment, see W Bishop and J Kay (1987) 104 LQR 211.

It is customary in personal injuries cases to calculate a multiplier at the date of trial. This practice has been criticised on grounds that it is inconsistent with the practice in fatal accidents cases where the assessment is made at the date of death, and that it leads to excessive awards as well as putting a premium on delay. In *Pritchard v JH Cobden Ltd* [1987] 1 All ER 300, the Court of Appeal rejected a valiant attempt to reverse the practice. The more interesting point in this case was on remoteness of damage. As a result of negligence for which the defendants were liable the plaintiff, then aged 30, had suffered serious and permanent brain damage. His marriage broke up as a result of his injuries and he claimed as a head of damages the financial provision made for his wife in matrimonial proceedings which were heard together with his claim against the defendants. The Court of Appeal held that these damages were not recoverable, despite the concession by the defendant that divorce was a reasonably foreseeable consequence of the plaintiff's injuries. None of the judges thought it was particularly important to decide the label under which such damages were excluded, although 'remoteness', 'novus actus interveniens' or 'indirect economic loss' were mentioned as possibilities. Three principal reasons were advanced: (1) in matrimonial proceedings the court redistributes family assets but does not quantify losses; (2) in those proceedings financial provision depends upon imponderables; and (3) there are evidentiary difficulties and the risk of conflict between the Queens' Bench and family proceedings when these do not take place together. In reaching their decision the Court had to distinguish *Jones v Jones* [1984] 3 All ER 1003, CA (noted All ER Rev 1984, pp 120–21, 176–77), on the unconvincing ground that the present case involved only quantification because the defendant had accepted that the particular loss was foreseeable. The decision must throw further doubt on *Meah v McCreamer* [1985] 1 All ER 367 (criticized All ER Rev 1985, pp 309–10), which relied upon *Jones*. For comment see S Juss [1987] CLJ 210.

The decision of the Court of Appeal in *Dews v National Coal Board* [1986] 2 All ER 769 (noted All ER Rev 1986, p 320), has been approved by the House of Lords ([1987] 2 All ER 545). The House decided that in calculating damages for loss of earnings, the amount of contributions to a compulsory pension scheme should not be included. The fact that it was a compulsory scheme was not regarded as critical, Lord Griffiths indicating that the same principle would apply where a plaintiff had been regularly making contributions to a voluntary scheme. The crux of Lord Griffiths' opinion, with which all their Lordships agreed, is a distinction between income intended for current expenditure, and income intended to provide a pension on retirement. As regards the former, expenditure saved as a result of the injury is irrelevant, apart from sums which would have been spent to earn the income. As regards the latter, the plaintiff would be entitled to compensation if he had lost pension rights, but he could not recover both the contributions and the pension which those contributions would have purchased. On the facts, the plaintiff's pensions rights had not been affected and so he suffered no loss. Lord Mackay, with whom three of their Lordships agreed, formulated a general principle that ([1987] 2 All ER 545 at 551): 'the tortfeasor is concerned with the disposal of any part of the plaintiff's renumeration which is applied to obtain benefits which may be affected by the plaintiff's injury and, if affected, would be a proper subject for a claim against the tortfeasor.' This principle may not, however, always lead to the same results as Lord Griffiths' reasoning: see the examples given by Lesley J Anderson (1987) 50 MLR 963 at 966–67.

In *Hussain v New Taplow Paper Mills Ltd* [1987] 1 All ER 417, the Court of Appeal decided that sickness benefit payments received by an injured plaintiff under an insurance scheme entered into by his employers were deductible from the award of damages for pre-trial and future loss of earnings. The plaintiff's contract of employment made it clear that the benefits were a continuation or earnings and were taxable. It is, therefore, not surprising that the court refused to treat them as the non-deductible proceeds of an insurance policy falling within the principle in *Bradburn v Great Western Rly Co* (1874) LR 10 Exch 1. For comment see Lesley J Anderson (1987) 50 MLR 963 at 967–70. The decision has been affirmed by the House of Lords: [1988] 1 All ER 541.

In *Jackman v Corbett* [1987] 2 All ER 699, the Court of Appeal approved earlier first instance decisions which construed s 2(1) of the Law Reform (Personal Injuries) Act 1948 as giving an exhaustive definition of the extent to which the specified social security benefits can be set off against loss of earnings. Accordingly, no deductions of these benefits fall to be made in respect of benefits after the period of five years from the time when the cause of action accrues.

Economic loss

In *County Personnel (Employment Agency) Ltd v Alan R Pulver and Co* [1987] 1 All ER 289 at 297–98, CA Bingham LJ provided a useful restatement of the principles to be applied in assessing damages for negligent advice (whether in contract or in tort).

Town and Country Planning

PAUL B FAIREST, MA, LLM
Professor of Law, Univesity of Hull

Much of the reported litigation during the year has been concerned with buildings of architectural or historic interest, so-called 'listed buildings'. A number of such cases involve the Faculty jurisdiction of the ecclesiastical courts; another decision divided the House of Lords concerning the meaning of the expression 'a structure fixed to a [listed] building' within the meaning of s 54(9) of the Town and Country Planning Act 1971.

The ecclesiastical cases

Early in the year, in *Re St Mary's, Banbury* [1987] 1 All ER 247 the Dean of the Arches, Sir John Owen, suggested that the status of a church as a listed building might impose an important limitation on the Faculty jurisdiction. Later, the Court of Ecclesiastical Causes Reserved, in its lengthy judgment in *Re St Stephen Walbrook* [1987] 2 All ER 578, disapproved of the remarks of the Dean of the Arches, and held that the same standard should apply to ecclesiastical buildings as to secular buildings.

In the *Banbury* case, the crucial issue was the removal of pews from the nave of St Mary's Church and their proposed replacement by chairs placed on a carpeted area. The existing pews were placed in the church after its rebuilding at the end of the eighteenth century. The church was listed in 1952 as a building of special architectural or historic interest. The diocesan advisory committee had supported the change, although erroneously describing the church as a 'baroque' church. Noting that the pews were a necessary and integral part of the original Cockerell design, the Dean upheld the Chancellor's refusal ([1985] 2 All ER 611) to grant the Faculty. The Chancellor's decision was based mainly on the property rights of the pewholders, and the listed status of the building played only a small part in his reasoning. In dismissing the petitioners' appeal, however, the Dean of the Arches placed considerable stress on the status of the building.

Having agreed with the Chancellor that the right to use the pews was a property right, the Dean of the Arches went on to say that a faculty which might affect the special nature of the architectural or historic nature of a listed church 'should only be allowed in cases of clearly proved necessity' ([1987] 1 All ER 247 at 250).

Later in his judgment, he added a 'few general observations' (ibid at 254):

> '(a) it must never be forgotten that a church is a house of God and a place for worship. It does not belong to conservationists, to the state or to the congregation but to God; (b) in deciding whether to allow a re-ordering the court will not only have in mind the matters listed, for example, by Chancellor Spafford in *Re Holy Innocents, Fallowfield* [1982] Fam 135 at 137–8 but also these other matters; (i) the persons most concerned with the worship in a church are those who worship there regularly although other members of

the church may also be concerned; (ii) when a church is listed as a building of special architectural or historic interest a faculty which would affect its character as such should only be granted in wholly exceptional circumstances, those circumstances clearly showing a necessity for such a change. . . . A re-ordering of such a church solely to accommodate liturgical fashion is likely never to justify such a change; (iii) whether a church is so listed or not a chancellor should always have in mind not only the religious interests but also the aesthetic, architectural and communal interests relevant to the church in question; (iv) although the faculty jurisdiction must look to the present as well as to the future needs of the worshipping community a change which is permanent and cannot be reversed is particularly to be avoided.'

It was these remarks of the Dean of the Arches which were criticized in the later case of *St Stephen Walbrook* [1987] 2 All ER 578. In that case, the Chancellor, Mr George Harold Newsom QC, had refused a faculty for the introduction of a stone altar, carved by Mr Henry Moore OM, into the church of St Stephen Walbrook in the City of London (see [1986] 2 All ER 705). The church, also a listed building, is one rebuilt by Sir Christopher Wren following the Great Fire of London, and, in the words of the Chancellor, 'it is, among Sir Christopher's churches *a* masterpiece and perhaps *the* masterpiece' ([1986] 2 All ER 705 at 707).

The Chancellor's decision was primarily based upon the fact that Mr Moore's sculpture was not a 'table' as required by the Holy Table Measure 1964, s 1. He also thought that the sculpture was not congruent with the building.

Because the issues involved were partly questions of doctrine, ritual, or ceremonial, the appeal lay to the Court of Ecclesiastical Causes Reserved, consisting of Lloyd LJ, the Bishop of Rochester, the Bishop of Chichester, Rt Rev Kenneth Woollcombe, and Gibson LJ. The Chancellor's decision was held by the Court of Ecclesiastical Causes Reserved to be wrong on doctrinal grounds; the sculpture was capable of being a Holy Table within the Canons Ecclesiastical. In addition, however, the court went out of its way to disapprove the stringent test laid down by the Dean of the Arches in *Re St Mary's Banbury*. The Dean's test, it was noted, was much stricter than that which applied in the secular field; churches are exempt from the constraints of listed building control by s 56(1)(a) of the Town and Country Planning Act 1971. As Gibson LJ pointed out ([1987] 2 All ER 578 at 599):

'[T]he ecclesiastical exemption contained in s 56(1)(a) of the 1971 Act could have imposed on the courts exercising the faculty jurisdiction a restriction in the form stated by the Dean of the Arches Court of Canterbury, but Parliament did not do so, and I see no reason to impose it by judicial decision . . . Parliament relied on the care and responsibility of the ecclesiastical authorities, including those exercising the faculty jurisdiction, to ensure that churches of special historic or architectural interest are as fully protected in the interest of the general public as are secular buildings in the secular context. The principles applied in the faculty jurisdiction have . . . long recognised the obligation to protect for the whole community and for future generations churches of special architectural or historic interest against irreversible and inappropriate changes at the hands of those having the immediate care of the building. The extent of that obligation, however, is not in my view defined by the concept of "proved necessity".'

Lloyd LJ agreed with the rest of the court, holding that the fact that a church was a listed building was a relevant consideration, but that the test of 'clearly proved necessity' was too stringent by far.

With respect, this must be right. If Parliament had meant to impose a special fetter on changes to historic churches, it could clearly have done so. The views of the Dean of the Arches seem to have been unnecessary for his decision, and the Court for Ecclesiastical Causes Reserved was right to reject them.

The Debenhams case

The other 'listed building' case, reported early in the year, divided the House of Lords. The point at issue concerned the exemption from rates, under para 2(c) of Schedule 1 to the General Rate Act 1967, enjoyed by an unoccupied listed building. There was no dispute that the building in question was, for the relevant period, unoccupied; the issue was as to the *extent* of the listed building, that is to say, whether the premises in question lost their rate exemption because they included a separate building, used in conjunction with the listed building, but separate from it, or, alternatively, whether the separate building would still allow a claim to the exemption because it was a 'structure fixed to a [listed] building', within s 54(9) of the Town and Country Planning Act 1971.

To elucidate this point, a brief description of the layout of the building, as described in the report of the case (*Debenhams plc v Westminster City Council* [1987] 1 All ER 51) will be necessary.

The building in question was formerly Hamleys toy shop. The main building lies between Regent Street, which runs to the west, and Kingly Street, which lies to the east. Another building (hereinafter described as the Kingly Street building) lies on the opposite (or east) side of Kingly Street (and is known as 27–28 Kingly Street). The premises on either side of Kingly Street were linked by a footbridge, at second floor level, and a tunnel passing beneath Kingly Street.

The main building was 'listed' under s 54 of the Town and Country Planning Act 1971, as a building of 'special architectural or historic interest.' The Kingly Street building was not specifically listed in this way. The main building was vacated on 31 October 1981; the local authority, Westminster City Council, sought to levy a rate on Messrs Debenhams in respect of the period from 1 February 1982 to 31 March 1983. Debenhams refused to pay, on the ground that the hereditament in question was a vacant listed building, and thus they were able to claim exemption under para 2(c) of Schedule 1 to the General Rate Act 1967. In essence, their argument was that the whole of the hereditament was to be regarded as included in the 'list', notwithstanding the fact that only part of it was actually mentioned in the 'list', and the unlisted part was a structure fixed to a [listed] building. The Council eventually issued a summons applying for a distress warrant, and the metropolitan stipendiary magistrate issued the warrant; he dismissed Debenhams' claim for exemption on the ground that the exemption only applied if the whole hereditament was listed; here, only the main building was listed, and the Kingly Street annexe was not. The two buildings together comprised one hereditament, and the exemption was not available as only part of the hereditament was listed.

Debenhams appealed by case stated to the High Court, and were successful before Hodgson J (see [1985] RA 265). Hodgson J's decision was confirmed by the Court of Appeal (see [1986] RA 114).

The local authority's appeal to the House of Lords was successful; the House of Lords, by a majority, held that Debenhams were not able to claim the benefit of the listed building exemption. Although the wording of s 54(9) of the Act required the inclusion as 'part of the building' of 'any object or structure fixed to a building, or forming part of the land and comprised within the curtilage of the building', this did not demand the inclusion of a complete building which was in no way subordinate to the main building.

The leading authority which the House of Lords had to consider was the decision of the Court of Appeal in *A-G (ex rel Sutcliffe) v Calderdale BC* (1982) 46 P & CR 399. In that case, which is concerned with part of West Yorkshire's industrial heritage, the issue was as to the legality of the demolition, without the Secretary of State's consent, of a terrace of cottages attached to Nutclough Mill, a listed building. The Court of Appeal held that such consent was necessary. The cottages in question, which were originally occupied by mill-workers, were attached to the mill by a footbridge. The cottages in question could be regarded as structures fixed to the mill, or, alternatively, as being within 'its curtilage'. Pointing out that a building has to be considered in its setting, Stephenson LJ expounded the rationale of s 54(9) in the following terms (ibid at 405):

> 'The setting of a building may consist of much more than man-made objects or structures, but there may be objects or structures which would not naturally or certainly be regarded as a building or features of it, but which nevertheless are so closely related to it that they enhance it aesthetically and their removal would adversely affect it. Such objects or structures may or may not be intrinsically of architectural or historic interest, or worth preserving, but for their effect on a building which is of such interest. But if the building itself is to be preserved unless the Secretary of State consents to its demolition, so also should those objects and structures be. That object is achieved by s 54(9) requiring them to be treated as part of the listed building.'

Holding the reasoning of Stephenson LJ to be unnecessarily wide, the House of Lords nevertheless considered that the decision in the *Calderdale* case might be justified on its facts, since the terrace of cottages could properly be regarded as ancillary to the mill. Lord Keith thought ([1987] 1 All ER 51 at 55) that the word 'structure' in s 54(9) was intended to convey a limitation to such structures as are ancillary to the listed building itself' for example the stable block of a mansion house or the steading of a farmhouse. . . . In my opinion the concept envisaged is that of principal and accessory.' Lord Mackay of Clashfern, agreeing with Lord Keith, explained that the reason for the provision in the Act was to overcome the problem which had been thought to exist in the case of certain fixtures, as in *Corthorn Land and Timber Co Ltd v Minister of Housing and Local Government* (1966) 17 P & CR 210 ([1987] 1 All ER 51 at 59): 'The provision is dealing with the question whether certain things, namely objects or structures, are to be regarded as part of a building, not whether what is undoubtedly a building or part of a building is to be regarded as part of another building.'

Lord Ackner, who had been a party to the *Calderdale* decision, dissented, holding, first, that the word 'structure', in its ordinary, everyday sense, includes a building. He also argued that a purposive approach would lead to the same result, since the purpose of the listing of buildings is to ensure the protection and enhancement of the local heritage of buildings. Like Stephenson LJ in the *Calderdale* case, he thought that any argument from incongruity, eg the multiple store adjacent to the birthplace of the famous statesmen, could be met by the argument that all the legislation required was *consent* to works of demolition, alteration, or extension; there was no outright *prevention* of such activities, and it could readily be inferred that consent would be forthcoming in such cases.

Contract

MICHAEL P F FURMSTON, TD, BCL, MA, LLM
Barrister, Professor of Law, University of Bristol.

1 Formation

There are three cases on formation of which the most interesting is *A-G of Hong Kong v Humphreys Estate (Queen's Gardens) Ltd* [1987] 2 All ER 387. In this case the parties were involved in long and complex negotiations which ran between April 1979 and April 1984. Under these negotiations if they had been brought to fruition the respondents would have exchanged some 83 flats belonging to them for a Crown lease of property belonging to the Hong Kong government and the right to develop the leased land and adjoining land. It was clear that the parties had reached an agreement in principle subject to contract by January 1981. Much of the proposed agreement was in fact carried out. The Hong Kong government took possession of the flats, fitted them out and moved in senior civil servants. They disposed of the accommodation which those civil servants had previously occupied. The respondents took possession of Queen's Gardens and demolished the existing buildings on the site. They also paid to the Hong Kong government some 103 million Hong Kong dollars being the agreed difference between the value of the two premises. By February 1984 all of the documentation for the transactions had been completed and the contracts were ready for execution when the respondents withdrew. It was agreed that no contract had ever been concluded but the appellants argued that the respondents were estopped from withdrawing from the transaction because the appellants had reasonably relied on the belief that the contract would come into existence and had incurred major expenditure in such reliance.

It was clear that the Hong Kong government had relied on the expectation that a contract would come into existence and incurred a major expenditure in such reliance. It was also clear that such reliance was in a sense reasonable since there was nothing between 1979 and 1984 to suggest that it was at all likely that either party would change its mind. On the other hand the Hong Kong government had itself repeatedly emphasised in the early stages of the negotiations that the transaction was not binding and that either party was free to withdraw from the agreement at any time. The Privy Council held that the appeal failed since the Hong Kong government could not show either that the respondents had created or encouraged a belief or expectation that they would not withdraw or that the government had in fact relied on any such belief or expectation. On the basis of the argument the decision looks inevitable but it does illustrate the starkness of the English approach to whether or not a contract exists. There is little room for a finding that 90% of a contract has come into existence. The common law takes very much an all or nothing approach. Nevertheless it is important to remind ourselves that in this type of situation a party will not necessarily be without any hope of relief. In some cases a party who has received benefits under such an abortive near-contract will be liable in restitution. It may well be that such remedies might have been available on the facts of the present case, though the facts are not sufficiently fully reported to make this clear. On the face of it both parties received advantages and disadvantages between 1979 and 1984 and it is unclear where the balance of advantage lay. The critical point is that a restitutionary remedy would be principally concerned with benefits received by the defendant rather than with losses suffered by the plaintiff.

Harris v Sheffield United Football Club Ltd [1987] 2 All ER 838 raises again some classic textbook issues of consideration and performance of existing duties. In this case the plaintiffs the South Yorkshire Police Authority claimed some £50,000 from the defendants for 'special police services' provided at the defendant's football ground between August 1982 and November 1983. This was a claim under the Police Act 1964 but the scope of 'special police services' was treated by the Court of Appeal as being decided by whether the services were such that the police were already bound to perform them under the general law. This was the same test laid down by the House of Lords for consideration purposes in *Glasbrook Brothers Ltd v Glamorgan County Council* [1925] AC 270.

In his judgment in the *Glasbrook* case Viscount Cave LC said:

> 'if in the judgment of the police authorities, formed reasonably and in good faith, the garrison was necessary for the protection of life and property, then they were not entitled to make a charge for it.'

The club argued that in the present conditions of crowd behaviour a major police presence at the ground was necessary to preserve law and order during football league fixtures. The Court of Appeal agreed that if this were the correct test this would be the correct answer. However, the Court of Appeal thought that there was a major factual difference. In the *Glasbrook* case the threat to law and order was external; it consisted of possible violence by striking miners. In the present case the football club had voluntarily chosen to stage matches, knowing that some violent supporters might attend and at a time when a large police presence could only be provided by calling policemen off their rest days and paying large sums of overtime.

Deutsche Schachtbau-und Tiefbohrgesellschaft v Ras al Khaimah National Oil Company [1987] 2 All ER 769 does not at first sight look like a case on formation of contract at all but it contains some useful material on the degree of certainty required for a valid contract. The parties had entered into an Oil Exploration Agreement dated 1 September 1976 which contained an ICC Arbitration Clause. The parties later fell out and in 1979 the plaintiffs in the present case started arbitration proceedings while the defendants started litigation in the courts of Ras al Khaimah. Both parties succeeded but neither party was able to enforce the award or judgment in its favour. Much later the plaintiffs saw an opportunity to enforce their arbitral award in England because they discovered that the defendants had sold oil to Shell and saw the possibility of obtaining a Mareva injunction against the price of the oil. Litigation along these lines raised the question of the validity of the arbitral award. The arbitrators had decided that the proper law governing the substantive obligations of the parties was 'internationally accepted principles of law governing contractual relations'. (Under the ICC Arbitration rules determination of the proper law is left to the arbitrators and the ICC rules did not explicitly confine the arbitrators' choice of proper law to national systems of law). The Court of Appeal was clear that an agreement by the parties that their disputes were to be resolved by a common denominator of principles underlying the laws of the various nations governing contractual relations was adequately certain.

2 Terms of the contract

Cases on the Unfair Contract Terms Act 1977 are now appearing with marked regularity. The pair of cases *Phillips Products Ltd v Hyland* [1987] 2 All ER 620 (decided in 1984) and *Thomson v T Lohan* [1987] 2 All ER 631 illustrate that the same clause may be inside and outside the scope of the Act depending on the purpose of the clause in the particular fact situation.

Both cases were concerned with Condition 8 of the Standard Conditions of the Contractors Plant Association. This clause provides

> 'when a driver or operator is supplied by the owner to work the plant, he shall be under the direction and control of the hirer. Such drivers or operators shall for all purposes in connection with their employment in the working of the plant be regarded as the servants or agents of the hirer who alone shall be responsible for all claims arising in connection with the operation of the plant by the said drivers or operators. The hirer shall not allow any other person to operate such plant without the owners previous consent to be confirmed in writing.'

This clause is of course aimed at the well-known transfer of servant problem on which *Mersey Docks and Harbour Board v Coggins and Griffiths* [1947] AC 1 is the leading authority. The predecessor of Clause 8 was considered by the House of Lords in *Arthur White v Tarmac Civil Engineering Ltd* [1967] 3 All ER 586. In the *Phillips Products* case the defendants hired an excavator together with the driver to the plaintiffs for use in building work consisting of an extension to the plaintiffs' factory. As a result of negligence of the driver an accident occurred which caused considerable damage to the plaintiffs' factory. The defendants argued that the effect of Clause 8 in the contract between the plaintiffs and the defendants was to transfer to the plaintiffs the risk of negligence by the driver. The Court of Appeal held that in the circumstances the effect of Clause 8 was to seek to exclude altogether the liability of the defendant and that it was therefore subject to s 2 of the Unfair Contract Terms Act and that the trial judge's decision that in the circumstances it was not fair and reasonable should be sustained. In the *Thomson* case the first defendants, a plant hire company, hired an excavator together with a driver to the third party for use at the third party's quarry. The plaintiff's husband was killed in an accident involving the excavator while it was being driven by the driver and owing to the negligence of the driver. In this case the Court of Appeal held that Clause 8 was not as between the first and third defendants an exemption clause but a clause by way of indemnity transferring liability from the first defendants to the third defendants. It did not prevent the plaintiff recovering on proof of negligence against either defendant but simply provided, assuming that both parties were adequately solvent or insured, which of the defendants was to pay the damages. Such a clause was not an exclusion clause and was not within the scope of s 2 of the Unfair Contract Terms Act. Both these decisions seem clearly right and the distinction on which they are based well-founded. Nevertheless, the decisions do reveal the importance of a major gap in the scheme of the Unfair Contract Terms Act which does not bite on indemnity clauses at all except in the restricted area of consumer indemnities. This means that there will be situations where the draughtsman can achieve indirectly what he cannot achieve directly because of the Act. So the Act may forbid or subject to a test of reasonableness a clause excluding B's liability to A; it may permit, however, B to accept liability to A but provide that A shall indemnify B against any damages which B has to pay to A because A has a claim against B. Such a clause appears to be outside the scope of the Act and subject only to common law controls requiring adequate clarity and the like. It is difficult to think of any convincing policy reason for this difference in result.

In *Smith v Eric S Bush* [1987] 3 All ER 179 the plaintiff applied to a building society for a mortgage. She paid an inspection fee and signed an application form which stated that a copy of the survey report and mortgage valuation would be given to the plaintiff. The form contained a disclaimer that neither the society nor its surveyor warranted that the report would be accurate and stating that the report and valuation were supplied without any acceptance of responsibility. In due course the plaintiff received a copy of the report, was granted a mortgage and went ahead with the purchase of the house. Later the plaintiff alleged that the defendant valuer had been negligent in failing to notice that the chimney-breasts had been removed. The High Court judge found for the plaintiff and the defendant's appeal was refused by the Court of Appeal. A different division of the Court of Appeal has recently reached the opposite conclusion on similar facts in *Harris v Wyre Forest District Council* [1988] 1 All ER 691. It is understood that an appeal may be taken to the House of Lords. It is important to note that the argument put in the two cases is not the same although the facts are very similar. The liability of the surveyor in cases of this kind, if it exists at all, exists in tort under the decision of the House of Lords in *Hedley Byrne v Heller*. It will be remembered that in that case the House of Lords held that the defendants were not liable, as they otherwise would have been, because their advice as to the creditworthiness of Easipower was given without obligation. The reasoning of the House of Lords suggested strongly that the disclaimer was effective not as an exemption from liability but as preventing liability ever arising. This is because the House of Lords thought that liability for careless words depended on the defendant having voluntarily assumed liability for the words whereas no such principle applied for liability for careless acts. So a careless driver cannot go on to the road carrying a large sign saying 'Careless driver—keep your distance' but a careless advisor may if he chooses proclaim his advice to have been given off the cuff and without careful consideration and therefore not to be relied on. (Of course one might distinguish between the advisor who boldly says this and the advisor who tries to look careful but uses weasel words to exclude his liability). It can therefore be plausibly argued that at least in some cases a disclaimer for careless words will operate to prevent a duty of care ever arising and that therefore the provisions of s 2 of the Unfair Contract Terms Act do not apply since they only apply when a duty of care has been established and broken. This was in effect the argument put in *Harris* and accepted by the Court of Appeal. The argument was not put in this form in *Smith* which was argued on the basis of the reasonableness of the clause excluding liability in such a situation. It will be interesting to see what the House of Lords makes of this complex and subtle point if one of the appeals is pursued.

Perrylease Ltd v Imecar [1987] 2 All ER 373 should be noted as an authority for the proposition that there is no difference between the rules governing the admissibility of evidence in order to construe written contracts in general and those governing the admissibility of evidence to construe written contracts (such as a contract of guarantee) that are subject to the Statute of Frauds.

3 Undue influence

Although not a contract case *Goldsworthy v Brickel* [1987] 1 All ER 853 is of considerable interest to contract lawyers since the Court of Appeal went as far as is decently possible to suggest that Lord Scarman has gone much too far in *National Westminster Bank v Morgan* [1985] 1 All ER 821 (as suggested in All ER Rev 1985 p 90) in stating that it was an essential part of the doctrine of undue influence that the transaction entered into must be disadvantageous to the party influenced and that it must be shown that the party influenced came under the domination of the influencer. In the present case the trial judge had held that

> 'the defendant had acquired an influence over the plaintiff, based on and arising out of a particular association and an advisory capacity, well short, no doubt of domination which nevertheless made it his duty to take care of the plaintiff in any transaction between them.'

The Court of Appeal held that this was an entirely appropriate test to apply and that it was not 'necessary for the party in whom the trust had confidence is reposed to dominate the other party in any sense in which that word is generally understood.' The court thought that the decision of the Privy Council in *Poosathurai v Kannappa Chettiar* (1919) LR 47 Ind App 1 which was much relied on by Lord Scarman in *National Westminster Bank v Morgan* was not an accurate statement of the English Law on undue influence.

4 Non disclosure

Banque Keyser Ullmann v Skandia Insurance Company Ltd [1987] 2 All ER 923 is one of the most interesting cases of 1987. There are of course many cases in the books stating that the insured owes a duty of disclosure to the insurer and many cases exploring exactly what this involves. Some of these cases including *Carter v Boehm* (1766) 3 Burr 1905, the starting point for the doctrine, says that the insurer is also under a duty to disclose material facts to the insured. The present case not only reaffirms this principle but applies it. In the case a Mr Ballestero persuaded syndicates of banks to lend his companies many millions of Swiss francs and these loans were secured, partly, by gemstones (which later turned out to be virtually valueless) and partly by credit insurance policies covering failure by the borrowing companies to repay the loans. These policies were issued by the defendant insurers. The policies contained clauses excluding the insurers liability in the event of fraud. In the event, therefore, the lenders could not recover the money they had lent to Mr Ballestero's companies when he disappeared with it because the gemstones were useless and the credit insurance policies unenforceable. It appeared that the policies had in fact been procured by an employee of the insurance broker falsely representing that the full amount of the loan was insured when he only held a cover note valid for 14 days and that the insurers had discovered this deception which they had not passed on to the lenders. It was accepted that if the lenders had known of the dishonesty of the insurance broker's employee they would not have gone through with the loan transactions.

Steyn J had little difficulty in holding that the duty of disclosure was reciprocal and that the insurers were just as much under a duty to disclose material facts as were the insured. In the case of non disclosure by the insured, it is clear that the test of materiality is what would be regarded as material by a reasonable insurer. It is of course reasonably possible to establish the reaction of a reasonable insurer by giving expert evidence of insurance practice. Reciprocity would suggest that the test in the present case ought to be what would be regarded as material by the reasonable insured but it would of course be difficult to find expert evidence on this question. In the present fact situation it was perhaps not too difficult to hold that the facts not disclosed were material since it was conceded that if they had been disclosed the loan transactions would not have been completed. A test based on the reasonable insured might provoke some interesting differences of opinion in future cases. In the present case Steyn J suggested that the test should be supplemented by a requirement of what good faith and fair dealing required. Obviously, if this is correct there will, in practice, be a need for a number of further cases to work out the implications of this test.

Perhaps the most important point of the case is what remedy was available to the insured. The normal effect of non disclosure is of course to make the policy unenforceable. But of course the lenders in the present case did not want to set aside the policy, which could in any case not be enforced because of its clause about fraud. It would have been a worthless victory to have established that the insurers were under a duty to disclose but that the result of their failure to disclose was that their obligations were not enforceable! In the circumstances it is not surprising that Steyn J held that the insured had a remedy in damages for the failure to disclose. On the merits the arguments for this solution are clear. On the other hand to hold that non disclosure opens the way for an action for damages has potentially very wide consequences. It is difficult to see why the insurer should not also have a remedy in damages for non disclosure by the insured and there would seem to be great potential for wide development along this route if it is held on appeal to be correctly based.

5 Illegality

There have, as usual, in recent years been a number of cases on illegality. The first two of these involve appeals to the Court of Appeal on cases which were discussed in last year's Review (All ER Rev 1986 pp 94 and 95). The first is *Phoenix General Insurance Company of Greece v ADAS* [1987] 2 All ER 152. This is the first case to reach the Court of Appeal as to the effects of carrying on business under the Insurance Companies Act 1974 without authorisation. (Although there have been three decisions at first instance each reaching somewhat different results). In the present case the plaintiffs carried on an insurance business in London and under the 1974 Act they were authorised for 'marine, aviation and transport insurance business'. Under the original categories employed by the 1974 Act the business which they were writing fell within the authorised categories. In 1977 new regulations were issued which altered the categories in a way which is complex and difficult to understand. The trial judge had held that the effect of this change was to make the business which the plaintiffs were writing unauthorised. The Court of Appeal construed the regulations in a different sense and held that the business was in fact authorised under the transitional provisions. This being so it was strictly not necessary to consider what the legal position would have been if the business had not been authorised. The Court of Appeal having obviously heard full argument on this considered it very carefully and the judgment will obviously be of considerable importance. The Court of Appeal had no doubt where the solution ought to lie.

> 'Good public policy and commonsense therefore require that contracts of insurance, even if made by unauthorised insurers, should not be invalidated. To treat the contracts as prohibited would of course prevent the insured from claiming under the contract and would merely leave him with the doubtful remedy of seeking to recover his premium as money had and received. ([1987] 2 All ER at 175)'

However, the Court of Appeal were also clear that it was not possible actually to reach this conclusion because of the wording of the 1974 Act. This was because the Act did not merely prohibit unauthorised insurers from 'effecting contracts of insurance' but also from 'carrying out contracts of insurance'. The Court of Appeal held that this could not be read otherwise than as prohibiting not only the entering into contracts of insurance but also their performance by paying when the risk occurred. This was an express prohibition and left no room for taking into account considerations either of policy or commercial good sense. The result is obviously unsatisfactory but this is the fault of the draughtsman and not of the Court of Appeal.

Rather similar issues about licensing of banking business were raised in *S C F Finance v Masri (No 2)* [1987] 1 All ER 175. In this case the plaintiffs had been handling transactions on behalf of the defendant in commodity and financial futures. During the period between April 1983 and early 1984 the defendant had lost some 1.7 million dollars through these transactions. About half of this sum had been paid by him to the plaintiffs. The plaintiffs claimed the balance of monies which they had expended on behalf of the defendant. The defendant raised a number of defences of which the relevant one was that the plaintiffs were carrying on a deposit taking business within the meaning of s 1(2) of the Banking Act 1975 but the Court of Appeal held that the sums which had been paid by the defendant to the plaintiffs had not been paid by way of deposit but by way of security for payment for the provision of property or services by the plaintiffs and that even if they had been deposits they had not been accepted by the plaintiffs in the course of 'carrying on . . . a deposit taking business'. Finally, and this is the important point for present purposes, the Court of Appeal agreed with the view of the trial judge that even if the transactions had involved forbidden deposit taking the rights of depositor and depositee would have been unaffected since the prohibition on deposit taking did not operate to make individual contracts of deposit invalid. It would of course on general principles be surprising if an unlicenced deposit taker taking deposits could refuse to return the money on the grounds that he was unlicenced. This common sense approach was reinforced by s 1(8) of the Banking Act 1979 which provides that 'the fact that a deposit is taken in contravention of this section shall not affect any civil liability arising in respect of the deposit or the money deposited.'

In *John Michael Design plc v Cooke* [1987] 2 All ER 332 the plaintiffs sought an interlocatory injunction to enforce a covenant in restraint of trade entered into by the defendants who were former senior employees who had left to set up a business of their own. The Court of Appeal held that if court decided that it would be just to grant an interlocatory injunction in such a situation, the plaintiff was prima facie entitled to be protected in respect of all his customers, who fell within the ambit of the covenant and that it was wrong in principle to try to exclude some customers to whom the covenant should not apply. In particular it is not a good reason for excluding a particular customer from the scope of an interlocatory injunction that that customer would in any case not be prepared to do further business with the plaintiff.

Saunders v Edwards [1987] 2 All ER 651 is a case both of considerable theoretical interest and also of undoubted practical importance to conveyancers. The defendant entered into a contract to sell the lease of a flat to the plaintiffs. During the negotiations he fraudulently misrepresented that the flat included a roof terrace (in fact the defendant had improperly created an access on to a flat roof outside the flat over which he had no rights). The plaintiffs agreed to pay £45,000 for the lease and for certain chattels in the flat. The plaintiffs suggested that the purchase price should be apportioned as to £40,000 for the flat and £5,000 for the chattels although both the plaintiff and defendant well knew that the chattels were not worth anything like £5,000. When the plaintiffs discovered the true state of affairs about the roof terrace they brought an action claiming damages for fraudulent misrepresentation. The defendant argued that this claim was barred by the plaintiff's own impropriety. This argument was rejected by the Court of Appeal. The defendant's fraud, in relation to the roof terrace, was wholly distinct from and unconnected in any way with the parties' arrangements designed to evade stamp duty. The plaintiffs should therefore not be prevented from enforcing this claim against the defendant by their own conduct. This decision should not however encourage conveyancers or their clients to think no harm will be done by this kind of deliberate inaccuracy. The court thought that it might be entirely appropriate to refuse to enforce the contract for the sale of the flat by reason of such behaviour and that a solicitor who was so involved in such a false apportionment would be guilty of professional misconduct.

Another case involving consideration of whether undoubted illegality affected the plaintiff's cause of action is *Euro-Dian Ltd v Bathurst* [1987] 2 All ER 113. In this case the plaintiffs sent diamonds worth over $223,000 US to West Germany together with an invoice stating the value of the diamonds to be $131,411 US. The purpose of this deliberate under-valuation was to enable the customer to avoid payment of German customs duty. The diamonds were subsequently stolen in Germany and the plaintiff brought a claim on their insurance policy which insured the diamonds at their standard value plus 10% of tax which value was agreed at $142,173.90 US. The insurers argued that the plaintiff's claim would not succeed because it was tainted with the illegality involved in the avoidance of German customs duty. This argument was rejected by Staughton J on the grounds that the plaintiff's claim did not in any way require them to plead or rely on the illegal undervaluation of the diamonds.

6 Remedies

There are a number of very important cases on remedies for breach of contract. One of the most interesting is *Miles v Wakefield Metropolitan District Council* [1987] 1 All ER 1089. In this case the plaintiff who was the Superintendent Registrar of Births, Deaths and Marriages in the defendant council's area decided as part of a scheme of industrial action and in breach of his obligations to refuse to conduct marriage ceremonies on Saturday mornings although he carried out his other duties on that morning and during the rest of the week. The council told him that he would not be paid for work on Saturday at all unless he was prepared to undertake the full range of his duties. He refused and the council withheld a proportionate part of his salary. The House of Lords held that although there was no contract between the plaintiff and the defendant the nature of the plaintiff's remuneration and the terms of his tenure of office were so closely analogous to a contract of employment that his rights should be governed by the same principles. This led on to a consideration of the general question of the position of an employee who in breach of contract offers partial performance of his services. The House of Lords held that a plaintiff seeking to recover payment under a contract of employment had to show that he was ready and willing to render all the services required of him and that if he did not do this he was not entitled to be paid at all and that the employer was entitled to receive the services which were tendered and to refuse payment for them even though the employee was not dismissed. This line of reasoning would not be applicable if the employer had shown that he was happy to accept partial performance and some members of the House of Lords thought that there could also be circumstances in which an employee would be entitled to sue on a *quantum* merit basis for such work as he had actually done.

Another important decision of the House of Lords is *President of India v Lips Maritime Corps* [1987] 3 All ER 110. In this case in July 1980 the owners chartered their vessel to the charterer for the carriage of a cargo of phosphate from Louisiana to India. Under the charter party freight and demurrage were to be calculated in US dollars but to be paid in London in sterling at the mean exchange rate ruling on the date of the bill of lading. At that date the exchange rate was $2.37 to the pound. In February 1983 an umpire published an award in favour of the owners in respect of a dispute about demurrage and by that date the exchange rate was $1.54 to the pound. The umpire held that the charterer was liable for demurrage amounting to $24,250 and that because the charterer was liable for damages for late payment the owners were entitled to recover the exchange loss suffered by them because of the fall in the sterling exchange rate. The judge allowed the charterer's appeal and the Court of Appeal allowed the owner's appeal. The House of Lords allowed the charterer's appeal. The principal judgment was delivered by Lord Brandon of Oakbrook who said that a claim to demurrage was not a claim in debt but a claim in damages being liquidated damages for delay in the return of the ship beyond stipulated lay days. He further said that English law did not recognise a claim in damages for late payment of damages and that the appropriate relief for late payment of damages was an award of interest. It was therefore concluded that the appropriate award was demurrage payable in sterling converting at $2.37 exchange rate together with interest running from two months after the completion of discharge which would be the period during which demurrage would usually be settled and paid for.

Another very important case is the decision of the Court of Appeal in *Lombard North Central plc v Butterworth* [1987] 1 All ER 267. In this case the plaintiffs had leased a computer to the defendant for a period of five years on payment of an inital sum of £584.05 and nineteen subsequent quarterly instalments of the same amount. The agreement gave the plaintiffs the right to terminate the agreement if the instalments were not punctually paid. After two punctual payments and four slow payments the plaintiffs terminated the agreement, recovered possession of the computer and sold it for £172.88. The plaintiffs were undoubtedly entitled to terminate the contract under its terms but the question arose as to what liability in damages the defendant had incurred. There was a liquidated damages clause which was held by the Court of Appeal to be in fact a penalty clause. The effective question, therefore, was what claim did the plaintiffs have for unliquidated damages. In the decision of the Court of Appeal in *Financings Ltd v Baldock* [1963] 1 All ER 443 it was held that where a finance company terminates a hire purchase or lease agreement because of failure to make punctual payment in circumstances where the failure is not repudiatory in nature the finance company's loss after the date of termination arises not from the defendant's breach but from the finance company's decision to exercise its contractual right to terminate. This decision has been followed in a number of later decisions but the Court of Appeal held that the present contract contained a clause which made a decisive difference. The hiring agreement provided that 'punctual payment of each instalment was of the essence of the agreement'. The Court of Appeal held that even though the failure to pay promptly was not repudiatory, this clause had the effect of making failure to pay on time a breach of condition. Although failure to pay on time did not normally go to the root of the contract the parties were entirely free to make any particular obligation essential to their contract and that is what the parties had done here. Accordingly, the Court of Appeal held that damages were at large and that the plaintiffs could recover the loss which they had suffered from the transaction having been made abortive in this way. On one view this may be thought to give far too much weight to the particular wording of the clause. This criticism, however, seems misconceived. Whether a particular clause is important or not is a matter which lies well within the parties' discretion: even though the court will have its own view if the parties have not expressed a view. Accordingly there is no reason to penalise a party who engages a competent lawyer who adequately drafts a contract so as to produce the desired result. Obviously this decision is of the greatest practical importance to those who aspire to be competent draughtsmen of contracts.

In *County Personnel (Employment Agency) Ltd v Alan R Pulver & Co (a firm)* [1987] 1 All ER 289 the plaintiffs had entered into negotiations for a 15-year under-lease of two ground floor rooms which they intended to use as business premises and had instructed the defendant, a firm of solicitors, to act on their behalf. The defendant allowed the plaintiffs to enter into an under-lease by the terms of which their rent was to be increased every five years by the same percentage as the head lessee's rent was increased. This was clearly a very improvident transaction since it rewarded the head lessee for his success in agreeing to pay the lessor a high rent! The Court of Appeal had little difficulty in finding that the solicitor had been negligent in failing to discover the rent payable under the head lease or to explain the effect of the rent review clause in the under-lease. Much more difficulty was experienced in deciding what was the appropriate measure of damages. The court thought that although the diminution in value rule was usually the correct rule to apply where a property was aquired following negligent advice by surveyors, it should not be mechanically implied in claims against solicitors nor should one necessarily mechanically apply a quantification at the date of breach approach. The diminution in value approach on the facts of the present case would lead to a very speculative calculation since because of the peculiarity of the rent review clause the under-lease actually had a negative value. There was, however, firm evidence of what it had actually cost a plaintiff to escape from the transaction unless this could be shown to be an unreasonable step to take in mitigation this was a more reliable basis for assessment.

In *Sharneyford Supplies Ltd v Edge* [1987] 1 All ER 588 the Court of Appeal reversed the decision of Mervyn Davies J which was noted in the 1985 Review. The Court of Appeal held that a defendant who wishes to take advantage of the rule in *Bain v Fothergill* must show that he has used his best endeavours to remove any defect in his title. Since the defendant failed to use his best endeavours to remove the tenants who were on the land by giving them notice to quit the plaintiff's claim was not limited to his expenses but included damages for loss of profits. The Court of Appeal did not fail to underline the lack of any adequate modern rationale to *Bain v Fothergill* and to urge its early demise.

In *Dean v Ainley* [1987] 3 All ER 748 the defendant had contracted to sell a house to the plaintiff. The contract contained a covenant by the defendant to carry out work to prevent the 'leaking of water from the patio' into a cellar below. It was found after the plaintiff had gone into possession that inadequate work had been done to prevent water leaking into the cellar from the patio. It was also found, however, that the water penetrated to the cellar from the surrounding ground. The evidence was that waterproofing the patio in accordance with the terms of the contract would cost about £7,500 but this would keep out only some 70% of the water, since it would not prevent water penetrating from the surrounding ground. The cellar could only be made completely waterproof by an operation which would cost some £10,000. The trial judge held that even if the defendants had carried out their contract the plaintiff would not have had a completely dry cellar and that accordingly the plaintiff had suffered only nominal damage. The Court of Appeal disagreed, they thought that the plaintiff was entitled to £7,500, either on the grounds that this was the financial cost of what the defendant had agreed to do or alternatively that waterproofing the patio was the least expensive step to remedying the defendant's breach of contract.